Published by Masters Press
A Division of Howard W. Sams & Company
2647 Waterfront Parkway, E. Drive
Suite 100
Indianapolis, IN 46214

97 98 99 00 01 02   10 9 8 7 6 5 4 3 2

Library of Congress Cataloging in Publication Information

Hammel, Bob.
    Hoosiers--classified : Indiana's love affair with one-class basketball / by Bob Hammel.
      p. cm.
    ISBN 1-57028-162-9
    1. Basketball--Indiana--History. 2. School sports--Indiana--History. I. Title.
GV885.72.I6H35   1997
796.323'62'09772--dc21   97-37007
                                       CIP

Hoosiers: Classified

Indiana's Love Affair with One-Class Basketball

by Bob Hammel

MASTERS PRESS

A Division of Howard W. Sams & Company

Dimming the Hoosier Dream

In the beginning, our state was without form and void. And God created *basketball*.

Then there was Crawfordsville, and Wingate, and Thorntown, and Franklin and Martinsville . . . and Muncie, and Anderson . . . and Shelbyville and Jasper and Madison . . .

And then God said, "Let there be *Milan*."

And there was light.

And that light still shines today.

All I can say, all I can plead, to the guardians of our state's high schools, and of this tournament, and of this game . . .

Please, don't dim the light.

Bob Hammel
Indiana Basketball Hall of Fame
Induction Banquet, March 20, 1996

Credits

Cover Photos: Top left, Milan High School team, 1953; bottom right, 1975 Final Four coaches (from left), Bill Stearman, Jim Rosenstihl, Bill Green, Jack Butcher. (Both photos courtesy Indiana High School Athletic Association) Top right, Damon Bailey of Bedford-North Lawrence, 1990; Bottom left, Glenn Robinson of Gary Roosevelt, 1991. (Both photos ©*Bloomington Herald-Times*)

Back Cover Photo: (from left) Jeremy Sinsabaugh, Djibril Kante, Mario Wuysang of Bloomington North after 1997 State Championship Game. (©*Bloomington Herald-Times*)

Cover Design: Christy Pierce

Chapter-Opening Graphics: Stewart Moon

Edited by Kim Heusel

Page Layout and Design: Kim Heusel

Acknowledgments

The clearest lesson from the many forms of research for this book was that all the caring about this wrenching issue is not confined to one side. To either side. In the passion of raging dispute, that is easily overlooked. The first thing to be acknowledged is that help in telling this story came from everyone asked. There is no qualifier in front of everyone -- not virtually everyone, not almost everyone: everyone. Bob Gardner, commissioner of the Indiana High School Athletic Association, opened himself and his organization to full cooperation though he knew that he, the man in charge when Indiana changed from an open high school basketball tournament to one with classes, was cooperating with a person strongly opposed to that change. Equally willing to help were Bruce Whitehead, the Crawfordsville athletic director who headed the IHSAA committee that recommended the change; Walter Vanderbush, the Franklin principal who articulated his reasons for standing in the midst of tournament tradition and supporting a change; Joe Hart, a small-school coach (Union of Dugger) who typified those like him who wanted class play and said it more openly than most. Far greater in numbers were those coaches who opposed the change. Some were bitter; some, frustrated; some, angry; some, wryly funny; some, and not a lot, against it but willing to give it a chance.

Bitterness was as understandable as was resigned acceptance. The high school basketball tournament is why many, perhaps most, in the coaching profession in Indiana chose their high-risk, high-stress career. For or against, coach or principal or player or fan, Hoosiers had an opinion and were eager to share it. Their candor and how very much they cared made a loud argument lucid, a rare achievement and the perfect environment for a writer/reporter.

Jim Russell of the IHSAA and Jason Crowe of the Indiana Basketball Hall of Fame were generous with assistance, in making photographs available, and in general. David Snodgress, chief photographer of my own newspaper-of-allegiance, the *Bloomington Herald-Times*, was the most generous of many in his field who gave help. John Harrell, my associate at *The Herald-Times* for 25 years, is a student and historian who is in this book uncountable times, most noticeably in the volume of information packed into the appendix. Graphics artist Stewart Moon of *The Herald-Times* made a monumental contribution with the maps and charts that open each chapter.

In my 61st year, my familiarity with the state that I thought I knew so well increased manifold. I went to colorful places I somehow had missed. I added friends and acquaintances by the dozens, a very nice thing to do.

I had a book that was a manuscript until Tom Bast of Masters Press checked it out and gave it a maker. Kim Heusel's patience was as supportive as his valuable editing and superb photo cropping. This is a book from research that started more than a half-century ago, when an 8-year-old in Huntington heard broadcaster Hilliard Gates make living, breathing heroes of Broc Jerrel and Max Allen, plus a whole lot of players who had taken my hometown Vikings to the 1945 State Tournament. Then came Eckrich scorecards, and scorebooks, and a life's work. This is to acknowledge the original, the irreplaceable Hilliard and all those who used microphones or typewriters to open the enchantment of Indiana high school basketball to other impressionables. It is to acknowledge the Jumpin' Johnny Wilsons, the Bobby Plumps, the Oscar Robertsons, the Damon Baileys who gave inspiration and excitement to new generations as the Homer Stonebrakers and Fuzzy Vandiviers and Johnny Woodens had done to others. It is to acknowledge the coaches who gave the game a mastery, the officials whose greatest acclaim was anonymity. It is to acknowledge the administration, from principals to commissioners, from Trester to Gardner, including an especially dear, personal friend, the late Phil Eskew. It is to acknowledge the beautiful, special uniqueness of Indiana's love for its favorite game. May that never end.

Table of Contents

The Season

The Tournament

Introduction

A Confederation of Traditionalists

I'm a traditionalist.

I am, but that's not the point here.

"I'm a traditionalist" was the second-most frequently uttered comment around and about Indiana high school basketball during the worst winter that gym-frequenting Hoosiers have endured since the other period of the Great Depression.

OK, so there was a tendency for people to overstate the gravity, the significance, the impact of the Indiana High School Athletic Association's decision to — effective with the 1997-98 season — end 87 years of one-class, everybody's-in basketball tournament play and break the tournament into four enrollment classes.

Basketball goals will not vanish from the Indiana landscape. Basketball teams will not have to place want ads to get players. Basketball gyms will not be empty of fans or players.

But it won't be the same. The sameness that those who administer Indiana high school basketball opted for was with the rest of the land. The sameness preferred by many of those who live and love Indiana high school basketball was with those first 87 years, during which only one annual high school event in all America grew to national stature.

Now the changes won't even be the same as first promised. Faced with a restive state legislature, after a State Tournament at which the theme of "Final Final Four" played over and over again to palpable hostility and anger, the people who drew up the four-class plan sought middle ground by returning to a plan that would crown one State Champion, or one Grand Champion, or one Champion of Champions — whatever the title will be. The altered plan adopted in April calls for the four class champions to play a week later in a one-day tournament. A few jumped up and down and said, "Hooray! We'll have just one champion after all." To most of those who had supported or at least accepted the first change, the move was a puzzling cave-in. Those who had hated the change to classes had new cause to remember that someone once said a camel was a horse designed by a committee. To them, the new plan was this committee's second hump on what once was a basketball Secretariat.

No classes or four classes: this was an unresolvable argument because it was between mind and soul. Both sides were always right. One, only one, had the voting power.

The mind's one incontestable argument was that the 43 years since the state's Miracle of Milan have proved that a small school has little, almost no, chance to get to even the Final Four in an open-class tournament, let alone win the championship.

The soul's unshakable contention was that Indiana high school teams down through those years have not entered tournament play with thoughts of winning the state championship. The sectional is the thing — ruling the neighborhood, the little guy every now and then rising up against the neighborhood big guy, with the hoarse backing of all the other little guys . . . and scoring a victory that puts that team's picture on its high school's walls forever after.

It isn't, after all, that every citizen who runs for a spot on the school board does so with the idea of advancing to President of the United States. Occasionally, things happen. That was precisely the route that a man who has missed just two of the last 30 Indiana Final Fours, Richard G. Lugar, took politically: from successful school board candidacy all the way to so esteemed a role in the U.S. Senate that he did, indeed, run for the presidency.

But every school board candidate isn't Dick Lugar. Nor is every small-town team Milan. One is all it takes to affirm the possibility. In the soul.

It's not that the mind is soulless nor the soul mindless. But those on the soul side of this square-off know that their idea of what is paramount never will be grasped by minds locked onto logic.

To those tuning in from afar, a few definitions are in order — beyond notifying the reader's ear that in Indiana, it is *my*-lun, not the more cosmopolitan muh-*lahn*.

In Indiana's tournament, sectional, regional, semistate and state are the four rounds of eliminations, and have been since 1936 (for boys; the girls' tournament, with identical assignments, began in 1976).

There is no seeding. All assignments are geographical, all pairings by blind draw. The 64 boys' sectional tournaments usually are played the last weekend in February. Each involves six teams, a few rare exceptions five. The champion of each is picked on Saturday night, and all tournament play after that comes on successive Saturdays. The 64 sectional winners advance to 16 four-team, one-day regionals, played the following weekend. The "Sweet Sixteen" survivors move on to four four-team, one-day semistates. The Final Four play in late March in Indianapolis to pick the champion.

The soul does not underappreciate the state championship round. That is where legends are born. By 1925, Indiana already had a couple of all-time heroes. Homer Stonebraker led a dot on the map called Wingate to consecutive championships in 1913 and '14. Robert "Fuzzy" Vandivier, perhaps the only player who reached the National Basketball Hall of Fame primarily on his high school achievements, was the leader of a Franklin team that won three straight championships and eternal Hoosier renown as "The Wonder Five" (1920, '21 and '22). And the Indiana tournament itself took on such quick stature that the fellow who presented the 1925 championship awards was the game's originator, Dr. James Naismith, who was to say 11 years later on a return trip to the state: "Basketball really had its beginning in Indiana, which remains today in the center of the sport."

One year after Naismith's first visit, sophomore Johnny Wooden led Martinsville to the state championship game. He returned to that round as a junior and senior, scoring 10 points as a junior when his team won the 1927 championship.

There were many tournament heroes after those three, none greater than Oscar Robertson of the mid-50s Indianapolis Crispus Attucks teams, none more acclaimed than Damon Bailey of the Bedford North Lawrence team that won the state championship before an astonishing crowd, 41,046, at the Hoosier Dome.

The tournament was always fit for heroics. When newspaper prose was more flowery, writers considered the annual winner to have reached the top of Mt. Ihsaa. Honest to God they did. Surely not I, even in intemperate youth. But I have seen it.

It did paint a pretty good picture of the accomplishment. No slips allowed. The climb could come from east or west or north or south, but each was a slippery slope. And the peak was so high and so tapered that only one could get there.

The soul saw all that clearly.

The mind said the little guy had no chance of getting there. The soul said Milan did.

The mind said the smallest school to win the championship in the 43 years since Milan was Plymouth (four-year enrollment 894, more than five times Milan's 162). The soul said ah, yes, but a few genuinely little guys had a chance.

Meanwhile, the soul reminds, that 43-year trail's wayside includes a lot of giants who didn't win championships, either, because of infernal, forever-darling Davids.

The decision to change to classes was not an issue with an outcome uncertain until the final seconds. In April 1996, the 17-

person IHSAA Board of Control voted 12-5 to make the change. The voting members were responsible for polling their own district's principals to get the prevailing sentiment before making their vote, and apparently they did. When an appeal of the decision forced a vote by all principals in the membership, the vote again was substantial: 220 to 157, supporting the change. Talk began of a different sort of appeal. House Bill 1318 was drafted, calling for a delay in implementation of the change until a statewide referendum could be conducted on the issue — as part of the 1998 general election.

Majority Hoosier opinion seemed to run along two somewhat antagonistic lines. Yes, they in the main wanted their tournament preserved as it has always been. No, perhaps even more strongly, they didn't want government involvement. The principals in the main represented tax-supported public schools, but they weren't perceived as government — *i.e.*, elected. America revolted against taxation without representation. Vexation without representation was revolting to some Hoosiers, too. But not to the point of even legislative revolt. House Bill 1318 never got out of committee.

The issue itself never died. Hence, this book. DeTocqueville in Hoosierland. A one-man odyssey began in late November, the objective a last, long, loving look at the places that the tournament made big at some point over the years. That part was personal, a desire just to see this crown jewel while it was still in full glory. The rest was professional: while there, people, participants had to be talked to, sounded out, given their voice.

Mostly on Friday nights but whenever openings could be found, I headed out to a high school gym — that one loose criterion usually prevailing: a place, a school, a name that had a bright even if brief spot in tournament history. I logged more than 5,000 car miles pursuing an objective that had a delightful bonus. At each stop, there was first and foremost a game to see, there were new players to watch as Indiana's game plays on. Then came the interviews, the listening.

Regardless of the region, regardless of the view, that comment kept coming:

"I'm a traditionalist."

Saying that was not what separated mind and soul in this argument. It was the next word. The most ardent of advocates for a change to classes did not disclaim reverence for the subject. Their entree into declaration was by tiptoe: "I'm a traditionalist, but . . . "

And so are we all, all traditionalists, all those who care about this.

I made an earlier reference to "I'm a traditionalist" as the winter's second-most frequently uttered comment in Indiana gyms.

The runaway No. 1 was:

"If it ain't broke, don't fix it."

No ifs, ands or, especially, buts.

The
Season

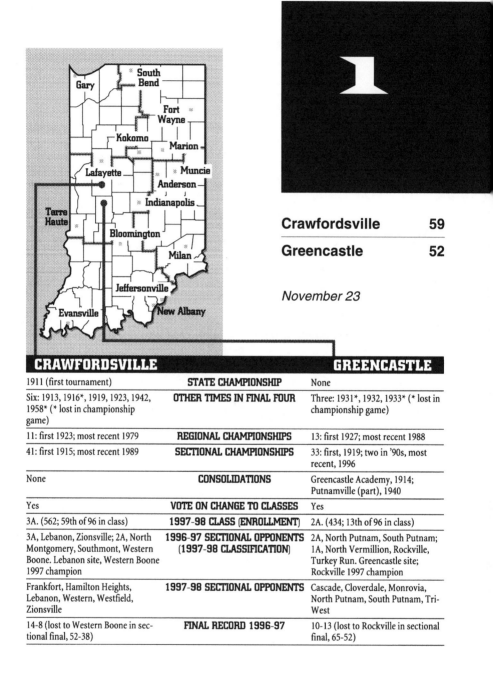

Crawfordsville	59
Greencastle	52

November 23

CRAWFORDSVILLE / GREENCASTLE

CRAWFORDSVILLE		GREENCASTLE
1911 (first tournament)	**STATE CHAMPIONSHIP**	None
Six: 1913, 1916*, 1919, 1923, 1942, 1958* (* lost in championship game)	**OTHER TIMES IN FINAL FOUR**	Three: 1931*, 1932, 1933* (* lost in championship game)
11: first 1923; most recent 1979	**REGIONAL CHAMPIONSHIPS**	13: first 1927; most recent 1988
41: first 1915; most recent 1989	**SECTIONAL CHAMPIONSHIPS**	33: first, 1919; two in '90s, most recent, 1996
None	**CONSOLIDATIONS**	Greencastle Academy, 1914; Putnamville (part), 1940
Yes	**VOTE ON CHANGE TO CLASSES**	Yes
3A. (562; 59th of 96 in class)	**1997-98 CLASS (ENROLLMENT)**	2A. (434; 13th of 96 in class)
3A, Lebanon, Zionsville; 2A, North Montgomery, Southmont, Western Boone. Lebanon site, Western Boone 1997 champion	**1996-97 SECTIONAL OPPONENTS (1997-98 CLASSIFICATION)**	2A, North Putnam, South Putnam; 1A, North Vermillion, Rockville, Turkey Run. Greencastle site; Rockville 1997 champion
Frankfort, Hamilton Heights, Lebanon, Western, Westfield, Zionsville	**1997-98 SECTIONAL OPPONENTS**	Cascade, Cloverdale, Monrovia, North Putnam, South Putnam, Tri-West
14-8 (lost to Western Boone in sectional final, 52-38)	**FINAL RECORD 1996-97**	10-13 (lost to Rockville in sectional final, 65-52)

Crawfordsville — The Root of it All

Let's start at the very beginning,
A very good place to start . . .
Oscar Hammerstein
The Sound of Music

Not the game itself, but the Indiana roots of the game Hoosiers hold so dear began in the small, collegiate town of Crawfordsville, about 50 miles northwest of Indianapolis.

Nicholas C. McKay — like James Naismith an ordained Presbyterian minister, like Naismith a non-U.S. citizen (Naismith from Canada, McKay from England), like Naismith associated with the Young Men's Christian Association (YMCA) — studied under Naismith at Springfield, Mass., after Naismith "invented" basketball in December 1891.

McKay's YMCA career already had taken him to Crawfordsville by then, and in 1893 he introduced Naismith's game there. The new sport was spreading fast, mostly through YMCAs. In March 1894, Crawfordsville and Lafayette YMCA teams played what probably was Indiana's first official basketball game, in the second-floor gym where McKay had first taught the sport.

Bob Whalen is Crawfordsville's basketball historian. No, he didn't see that first game, but he saw that gym. "I took a Scout troop up there in 1964 or '65, just before they tore it down, so the

3

kids could see it," Whalen said. "One of the bankboards was still there." Nothing is there now. The site at 100 Main Street is a parking lot for a heart-of-town bank.

By 1900, Crawfordsville High was playing basketball. Whalen's digging says its first game was a 26-15 loss to crosstown Wabash College in February 1900. In 1900-01, the high school team — the Athenians — played a 12-game schedule, just three of the games against high schools (two with Indianapolis Shortridge, one with Danville, Ill.). They won all three and claimed the state high school championships of Indiana and Illinois.

Before the decade was out, Crawfordsville twice had gone undefeated against high school teams and claimed state championships. Already, without a tournament as a showcase, Crawfordsville High had produced some legends of the sport. Robert "Pete" Vaughan averaged in double figures two straight years, then starred in football and basketball at Notre Dame. A Crawfordsville teammate of his, Ward "Piggy" Lambert, wasn't much of a player but he was an early genius of the game. He coached 11 Big Ten championship teams at Purdue and when in 1962 the Indiana Basketball Hall of Fame was formed, Lambert was one of the five charter members (with Homer Stonebraker, Fuzzy Vandivier, Johnny Wooden and Franklin coach Ernest "Griz" Wagner). Vaughan, who coached basketball at Purdue before Lambert and then coached football and basketball in a long career at Wabash College, was in the Hall of Fame's fifth class of inductees (1966).

Crawfordsville had other stars in that era, maybe the best of all Ernest "Rosie" Herron, who scored 44 points in one game, averaged 19.5 points per game as a senior in 1909-10 and scored 887 points in his three-year career. His senior year, the last before tournament play began in Indiana, Crawfordsville went 19-3 and Herron personally outscored the school's 22 opponents, 419-293.

So, in March 1911 when Indiana was ready to crown a high school champion, Crawfordsville was a 12th-year program with an already-rich history.

That first tournament was unique. Each of the state's 13 congressional districts was invited to send its best team to Bloomington, where an Indiana University Boosters Club was the official tourna-

Crawfordsville's 1911 State Championship team. Front, Hugh Miller; second row (from left) Carroll Stevenson, Orville Taylor, Cleo Shaw, Ben Myers, Newton Hill; back, coach David Glascock, Grady Chadwick. (Photo courtesy Indiana Basketball Hall of Fame)

ment host. Twelve did, and Crawfordsville blew through without a real challenge till the final game. Lebanon was the other finalist. The teams had split two regular-season games. For the first state championship, Crawfordsville won, 24-17.

The next year, the IHSAA took over administration of the tournament. Not until 1957 did the IHSAA formally confirm Crawfordsville as the first state champion. For 45 years, the organization had begun counting titlists with 1912.

And now it was 1996, and a new season — Crawfordsville's 98th, the Indiana tournament's 87th, the purists' last — was starting.

'I Sure Hope They Are Better'

Greencastle was Crawfordsville's opening-night opponent.

This is a rivalry ripened by age and happenstance. The colleges in the two towns — DePauw for Greencastle, Wabash for Crawfordsville — have maintained an athletic rivalry as ancient and as bitter as Indiana-Purdue. The high schools reflect it.

Greencastle can't match that Crawfordsville state championship, but it had its era. Its only three Final Four appearances came consecutively: in 1931,'32 and '33. Twice the Cubs reached the championship game, but Muncie Central in 1931 and Martinsville in '33 denied them a title. One man led all those teams: Jesse McAnally, whose career as a player and a coach landed him in the Indiana Basketball Hall of Fame. Greencastle plays today in McAnally Gymnasium.

The Greencastle-Crawfordsville high school basketball rivalry reached its 80th season with this game. As recently as the '70s, they scheduled two games, home-and-home (one reason Greencastle could be 7-0 against Crawfordsville in the three McAnally years). Frequently over the years, the two have met in the regional, though not recently.

Greencastle coach Terry Ross is at his alma mater. He played there, then stayed in town to go to DePauw. Crawfordsville cannot be among his favorite towns.

But his was a new team, starting a new year, heading into a new era that Terry Ross welcomed. Greencastle was one of the schools voting for the change to classes. "I'm for the change," he said. "It is a different time. It's going to be a great thing for all kids."

For nearly 20 years, this game had come at the end of the schedule, serving as each team's sectional tune-up. This year, a conflict with the NCAA Final Four in Indianapolis had caused the IHSAA to bobtail the boys' schedule by a week, too late for most schools to make an easy adjustment. The one most settled for was moving the last game to the front of the schedule. So this traditional season-closing rivalry game became an opener.

Crawfordsville didn't mind. It was at home. Greencastle didn't mind, either. The last four years, the road team had won this game.

It could have happened again. But Ross saw no evidence of it at the start.

His Tiger Cubs' season opened with a 3-point basket by junior forward Mark Dunn. Then, in 15 possessions the rest of the first quarter, Greencastle made just one shot. At the quarter break, with Crawfordsville leading 8-6, Ross did some talking. Just 18 seconds into the second quarter, before a shot ever was taken, he stood and barked, "Time out!"

"We spent the first quarter standing around," he said. "I told them at the quarter I'd *give* them the first eight minutes of the year, maybe they were a little tight, but it would be a good idea maybe if they would reverse the basketball. The first time down the floor after that they stood there like they were brain-dead. I decided maybe I hadn't said that clear enough."

They missed their next eight shots and the deficit became 16-6. Crawfordsville's lead shrank to 22-19 by halftime, though, and Athenians ball handler Dustan Stevens hadn't scored. "He passed up some shots," Crawfordsville coach Brad Acton said. "The point guard gets that mentality of distributing the ball. He's almost too unselfish. Sometimes he was passing the ball to big guys when he could have pulled up and shot."

In a 65-second stretch of the third quarter, Stevens sank two 3-point baskets, and fellow senior Jathan Rhoads squeezed one in between to open sudden 33-24 daylight.

Keith Miller was Greencastle's version of Stevens. He was one veteran Ross counted on. A senior, he had grown up on basketball. His dad, Doug, was the Greencastle coach before Ross. But, in the first half, Miller had taken just three shots, hitting two.

Down 37-29 with just 10 minutes of opening night left, Miller began to blaze: a 3-point basket, then two straight from closer. It was 39-36, and Crawfordsville was complicit in the rally — two straight turnovers from reckless play. "Fundamentals!" Acton yelled. "Behind the back two times . . . *c'mon*, guys."

The Crawfordsville lead bobbed back to 45-37 with 5½ minutes left. Seemingly hemmed in by two defenders, Miller squeezed through to a basket. When his teammates cleared out a side of the court for him and he drove to one more basket, Greencastle was ahead, 46-45. Rhoads laid in a basket for Crawfordsville; Miller hit again.

Greencastle ran down the last 50 seconds with the ball in Miller's hands, the game tied. "He was so hot we thought he could create a play for us," Ross said. Miller drove, dropped a pass off to T.J. Phillips and — with four seconds left — Stevens leaped in to block Phillips' shot.

In overtime, Stevens gave Crawfordsville the lead with a rebound basket, then hit six straight free throws to open a 59-52 victory, Crawfordsville's 50th in the series. Stevens, the man who hadn't scored the first half, finished with 18 points. For Greencastle, which has beaten Crawfordsville 42 times, Miller led with 22.

"Crawfordsville's pretty good," Ross said. "I think they're a lot better than they were last year (7-14). I sure hope they are." And they were, finishing 14-8; Greencastle, 10-13.

'Father' needed convincing

There was more reason to start at Crawfordsville than that 1911 state championship. Crawfordsville athletic director Bruce Whitehead chaired the IHSAA committee that brought forth the recommended change to classes and the means for implementing it.

Whitehead knows the role popularly assigned to him: father of the change. He smiles at what he considers an irony.

"Most of the people against this think I was always hell-bent for leather on this," he said. "I really wasn't.

"I was on the IHSAA board when this all started. Blake Ress (Martinsville principal at the time, an IHSAA assistant commissioner now) was board chairman. In October of '93, five small-school principals presented documentation that 65 percent of the principals in the state wanted to do a study of this.

"Blake asked me to chair the study committee: I said, 'Blake, at heart, I'm a traditionalist. Are you sure you want an avowed traditionalist chairing this committee? It might not look good to those people who think we ought to move in that direction?' He said, 'I think you'll be OK. You're an athletic director. You played at a small school. You're not at a big school now but you're not at a small school.'

"And I really was (inclined against a change). In fact, if we had taken a straw poll the first day that eight-person committee met, I think it would have been 5-3 for staying the way we were. But as we studied and talked to other states . . . "

The committee picked eight Midwestern states that had class tournaments. "Wisconsin was my state. I talked to people in their state association office first, and I asked them to give me five or six schools in the state, small and big. After I talked to all those people, I came away convinced they were very positive about it. They didn't say all glowing things. It doesn't mean that traditionally losing programs are suddenly going to become winning programs. But they believe it has been a boost to their basketball in the state of Wisconsin, No. 1, and No. 2, they believe it has been better for more kids."

The traditionalists' response is that Wisconsin is not Indiana, especially concerning high school basketball. "It *is* special in Indiana," Whitehead said. "It has always been special to me. As an athletic director, I have to worry about 18 programs, but basketball has been special.

"In my heart, I still like what we've got, but I think the time has come to try something different. It might be a shot in the arm basketball needs. I'm concerned about basketball as we knew it. I think it's dying.

"I think part of it is our society today. Friday and Saturday nights used to be *the* nights to go to the high school game. Now you're there on Tuesday and Thursday (for girls' games). You can't blame the girls' program, but it does split the crowd. And there's boys' and girls' swimming, and volleyball and wrestling, things we didn't have before.

"I did a study at Crawfordsville from 1976 to 1990. The total number of people coming to our athletic events hadn't changed. It was just spread out to different things.

"Another thing that has fueled this is the big differential in our school enrollments now. When Milan won it, I think the biggest school — outside of Indianapolis Tech — was 1,600 or 1,700. Muncie Central was about 1,400.

"I know Bob Plump says it will happen again. My personal opinion is we'll never have another Milan. There are just too many other factors. Those schools are going to have to play more of the bigger schools to win than Milan had to.

"That happened to us in 1979. We got to the semistate, upset Gary Roosevelt that afternoon, and had to come back and play Anderson that night. We knew, as coaches, there wasn't any way we were going to be in the game. We could see it in our kids." Anderson won, 87-55.

9

Whitehead played at a high school with an enrollment of 150 — Madison Township, in St. Joseph County just outside South Bend. "My senior year (1963-64) was kind of a Cinderella story. Everybody knew that Madison was closing up. In the sectional, we drew a first-round bye, then beat a county school, North Liberty, and made it to the semifinals on Saturday afternoon. It was only the second time our school had ever made it that far.

"We had to play Mishawaka. They went 6-5, 6-5, 6-3 across the front; we were 6-1, 5-11, 5-10. I was a power forward at 5-11. We were down 18 at the start of the fourth quarter. We pressed and tied it at the buzzer. We got beat by 2 in overtime. Then Mishawaka got beat by South Bend Central, with (future UCLA star) Mike Warren.

"In the mid-60s, St. Joe County went from 14 high schools to six or seven," he said. Consolidation was happening everywhere. The Indiana tournament field shrank by about 20 schools a year for more than a decade, from 739 in 1957 to 443 in 1970. "I think that's one of the reasons all this came about," Whitehead said. "We're down to 380 high schools.

"We divided into four equal classes, which is what our principals said they wanted, but we still have that large enrollment differential (in the top group: from Lowell's 851 to Ben Davis' 2,798). We may have to take the super 32 schools and make them a class of their own."

Some have questioned whether principals should have had the final say. "Here," Whitehead said, "we talked to our coaches. (Principal Charles Fiedler) talked to me. He cast the vote that the majority of our coaching staff wanted him to.

"I was willing to try it. "I can sit here and give the reasons why, and yet to some people they don't seem sound-enough reasons.

"There are intangible factors. I think the game has changed, to where the skinny little kid in the movie *Hoosiers*, just the pure basketball player, struggles to win. I said last year, 'The best basketball team didn't win the state championship. The best group of athletes did.' Steve (Witty, the coach of champion Ben Davis) did a great job, but the only kid close to a shooter on that team was (final-game hero Jeff) Poisel.

"One thing I discovered across the state was (the class argument) is mainly a generational issue. I'm 50; people my age and older wanted to stay the way we were; people younger predominantly wanted a change.

"I don't know if it's going to be successful. That's why when I made the motion to adopt it last April I put in there that in two years it has to be reevaluated. If it's not working, we need to look at going back the way we were.

"I don't know that we'll ever go back. I think we'll have to do some fine-tuning."

'To Be Honest . . . '

For Crawfordsville coach Brad Acton, first-night victory was sweet, the tournament future uncertain. He went to Brownsburg High, where his dad, Paul, had coached. "I've always been around basketball, because of my dad," Acton said. "He passed away 10 years ago yesterday. It was kind of tough, going into this weekend.

"He saw me coach when I first started. My first coaching job was at Francesville (absorbed into West Central in Pulaski County). I was probably the only guy who wanted the job, but, hey, I'm 24 years old. I'm ready.

"That was a good experience. Then I went to Eastern Hancock and had some good success. I've been here six years."

Crawfordsville's yes vote for the change does not have his endorsement.

"To be honest, I'm a traditionalist. I remember winning my first sectional. In some places, winning a sectional is no big deal, but this is pretty competitive. We have Lebanon, Western Boone, Zionsville, North Montgomery, Southmont — the three schools in Montgomery County and the three in Boone County. It's been a really good sectional for crowds and rivalries.

"Now we'll lose Western Boone and Southmont and get Hamilton Heights and Frankfort.

"I just think the sectional is the big thing. If we can win that, it's like winning the semistate for some others."

2

Harrison	80
Lafayette Jeff	72

November 30

LAFAYETTE JEFFERSON   HARRISON

LAFAYETTE JEFFERSON		HARRISON
Three: 1916, 1948, 1964	**STATE CHAMPIONSHIP**	None
14: 1913, 1919*, 1920*, 1921, 1950*, 1951, 1952, 1956*, 1957, 1963, 1967*, 1974, 1992*, 1996 (* lost in championship game)	**OTHER TIMES IN FINAL FOUR**	None
38: first 1921; four in '90s, most recent 1996	**REGIONAL CHAMPIONSHIPS**	One, 1997
63: first 1916; five in '90s, most recent 1996	**SECTIONAL CHAMPIONSHIPS**	Three as Harrison: 1981, 1983, 1997. Others in corporation 1: Monitor, 1943
None	**CONSOLIDATIONS**	Formed 1970: Battleground, East Tipp (Buck Creek, Monitor, 1958), Klondike
No	**VOTE ON CHANGE TO CLASSES**	Yes
4A. (1,623; 13th of 95 in class)	**1997-98 CLASS (ENROLLMENT)**	4A. (1,086; 66th of 95 in class)
4A, Harrison, McCutcheon; 3A, West Lafayette; 1A, Carroll, Lafayette Central Catholic. Lafayette Jefferson site; Harrison 1997 champion	**1996-97 SECTIONAL OPPONENTS (1997-98 CLASSIFICATION)**	4A, Lafayette Jefferson, McCutcheon; 3A, West Lafayette; 1A, Carroll, Lafayette Central Catholic. Lafayette Jefferson site; Harrison 1997 champion
Harrison, Kokomo, Logansport, McCutcheon	**1997-98 SECTIONAL OPPONENTS**	Kokomo, Lafayette Jefferson, Logansport, McCutcheon
16-7 (lost to Harrison in sectional final, 78-52)	**FINAL RECORD 1996-97**	20-5 (won sectional, regional; lost to LaPorte in semistate semifinal, 76-64)

Patsies No More

The name is Homer Surface. That will surprise some people at Lafayette Jeff. He has always been Dutch. And he has always been there when the Bronchos played basketball. Dutch Surface is a prototypical Indiana high school basketball fan. He already knows he'll be at the State Tournament this year. It will be his 64th straight. He was there in 1934 when Logansport won its only championship, beating Indianapolis Tech in the finals, and he has gone back every year since.

Watching Lafayette Jeff, though, has been his particular passion. "I've missed a few sectionals," he admits. Wife Dorothy has talked him into going to Florida a February or two. Even when he's home, he said, "I've got to the place where I don't run to all the out-of-town games anymore. Used to — wind, rain, ice, whatever."

He remembers that. He remembers well, short- and long-range. He'll never forget something that happened to him just a week earlier. Dutch, a machinist and building supervisor for 48 years at Purdue, has ushered at Boilermaker football games for 45 years. His duty this fall had him working right behind the visitors' bench, and the last 1996 visitor to Ross-Ade Stadium was bitter rival Indiana. You can bet many a Hoosier team got worked over by Dutch's strong lungs during those 45 years, but this one had a senior linebacker who played so very well and so hard that anyone had to notice and admire. The kid was Matt Surface, Dutch's grandson.

"He came up and gave me a big hug with about two minutes to go, when they had the ballgame won," Dutch said. There's no greater rivalry than Indiana-Purdue, no better annual scene than the fight for the Old Oaken Bucket. After all those years around Old Gold and Black, picking a team to root for in that particular game had to be hard . . . right, Dutch? "Not really. Not when you have blood on the other team. The hell with Purdue. He's a really nice kid."

And this night, with this particular opponent in to play the Bronchos, Surface remembered "when we used to have 15 teams come in here from the county for the sectional."

Mr. Crawley's dominion

Dutch Surface did his remembering while sitting in an end of Crawley Center, Lafayette Jeff's basketball home. It is named for the city's basketball legend, a revered man, the late Marion Crawley, who coached back-to-back state champions at Washington in 1941 and '42, then left to take the job at Lafayette Jeff.

Crawley's first year at Jeff, the Bronchos — Bronchos with an H, because . . . because . . . because it has *always* been Bronchos with an H at Lafayette Jeff, that's why — lost in the sectional. Legend says he vowed that would never happen again. It didn't. He coached there 24 more years and won every sectional. He was downright imperious about it, too. He got to the place where he didn't let his teams cut down the nets after a sectional championship, sending a message to the vanquished that beating them wasn't enough of an accomplishment to celebrate.

"He was his own man — nobody told him what he had to do," said Dutch Surface, who already was a veteran Broncho fan when the man he had watched win those championships at Washington arrived in Lafayette.

"He was a good coach."

Clearly, he was one of the greats. His teams won four state championships (with Lafayette Jeff in 1948 and '64, after the two at Washington). He was credited with being the first Indiana high school coach to win 700 games (734 at retirement in 1967, the state record till Howard Sharpe passed him in the '80s on his way to 755, the record now). For 13 years he doubled as the Bronchos'

Marion Crawley, second from right, joins the other Final Four coaches in 1957. With Crawley are Elmer McCall, South Bend Central; Howard Sharpe, Terre Haute Gerstmeyer and Ray Crowe, Indianapolis Crispus Attucks. (Photo courtesy Indiana High School Athletic Association)

football coach, and he went 93-24 in that role, winning five North Central Conference championships.

But basketball was the game that made Marion Crawley as renowned a name in his state, in his time, as the biggest of the state's college coaches. Deservedly, Dutch Surface feels.

"In 1948, when we won the state championship," Surface recalls, "West Lafayette had a kid named Bob Kriebel, and we had Ernie Hall and Bob Masters. Ernie went out on fouls. Crawley put (guard) Bob Masters at center and he took over.

"That was one of the closest games we had. Then we went on and won the State."

Masters was Mr. Basketball that year. The son of Crawley's predecessor as Jeff coach, Arthur "Abie" Masters, Bob went on to

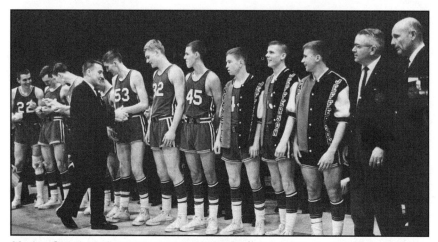

Marion Crawley's final title came in 1964. Members of the Lafayette team were, from left, Denny Brady, Terry Stillabower, Dave Morrison, Jack Walkey, Steve Ricks, Stu Miller, Wally Reeves, John Henk, Jim Aldridge, Dan Walkey, Crawley and assistant coach James "Sam" Lyboult. (Photo courtesy Indiana High School Athletic Association)

Indiana and became an All-Big Ten guard for Branch McCracken. Then he became a doctor. Both he and his father are in the Indiana Basketball Hall of Fame. Crawley was dealing with a pretty good talent when he made that move.

The score of that West Lafayette game was 51-38. It seemed close to Dutch Surface because Jeff's other sectional victories that year were over Battle Ground 67-38, Buck Creek 54-16 and Klondike 78-37.

Those were the Battle Ground Tomahawks, the Buck Creek Cobras, the Klondike Nuggets. That sectional field also included the Clarks Hill Hillers, the Dayton Bulldogs, the Jackson Township Spartans, the Lauramie Rockets, the Monitor Commodores, the Montmorenci Tigers, the Romney Pirates, the Shadeland Peppers, the Stockwell Warriors, the Wea Indians, the West Point Cadets — they were all there in that 1948 Lafayette sectional field. Somewhere along the line, they all felt the Crawley/Lafayette Jeff dominance. Several times.

They found an answer. They ganged up. Consolidated.

What Battleground, Buck Creek, Monitor and Klondike couldn't do as separate entities, they're doing these days as

Harrison High, their modern descendant. Jackson Township, Romney, Shadeland, Wea and West Point all are part of McCutcheon now.

Both Harrison and McCutcheon in the new world will be 4A schools. They're looking the mighty Bronchos — H and all — right in the eye.

And that's what Jeff Van Arsdel and his Harrison Raiders fully intended to do when they came into Crawley Center on this night.

A shooter from Nebraska

Van Arsdel, son of a career football coach, built this team around one of the best football players in Indiana. Football is just one of Josh Whitman's areas of excellence.

Whitman, Harrison's post man, was listed at 6-4, 230 when Illinois signed him as a tight end. He's also valedictorian in a class of 358. "I *really* like Whitman," Jeff coach Jim Hammel said. "He's just a great kid — he's a gentleman, he plays the game the way it's supposed to be played, he's just class. He deserves everything he ever got."

This night, an out-of-bounds play freed Whitman for the game's first basket. He got the second one, too. And the third. Already, Hammel knew he was in trouble, more than the 6-2 score at the time said. He had opened with 6-7, 221-pound senior Matt Preuss on Whitman. "We felt pretty good with Preuss against Whitman, although it didn't pan out," Hammel said. Barely three minutes into the game, he had to go to Plan B: 6-7 sophomore Matt Poynter in for Preuss. Poynter would have been in soon anyway, somewhere, but for his offense, not his defense. Two nights earlier in the Jeff season opener, he scored 28 points against Rossville and hit 14 of the 15 shots he took. He was to start the next Jeff game and stay there, for three years, probably.

But Poynter weighs 181 pounds. "Matt was overmatched by Whitman, physically," Hammel said. "He's so much stronger." That meant, to give Poynter help, the Bronchos "had to get back in on Whitman a lot more than we thought we would," Hammel said.

Whitman didn't score the second quarter. Juniors Adam Tesch and Brent Mason did, a combined 26 points in that quarter as Harrison opened a 42-32 lead. Most of their scoring came over that sagging, Whitman-conscious Broncho defense.

Tesch is 6-1, 190 pounds. He moved in from Nebraska. Doesn't 6-1, 190 pounds form your perfect mental picture of a kid from Nebraska: stocky, tough, a wannabe 'Husker football star? This one came into Indiana, a citadel of shooters, and taught the natives a thing or two about bombing away.

"I don't think anybody that we play is a better shooter than he is," Van Arsdel said. "He is gifted. I am not kidding: he can shoot from 30 feet and it doesn't faze him. I've seen him hit 10 in a row from out of bounds, in the coaches' box.

"He moved in in the spring the year before his sophomore year. We have open gym two days a week. He played a little bit and it was pretty obvious he could play. He's explosive. He can score a lot of points in a hurry."

He can, and this night he did.

Harrison led 18-15 in the first minute of the second quarter when Tesch sank a 3. He hit another, then another, and it was 32-21 with just three minutes of the quarter gone.

Jeff has its own 3-point ace in junior Ryan Sexson, whose grandpa, Joe Sexson, before a great Purdue career and a lifetime in coaching won the Trester Award on the 1952 Indianapolis Tech team that lost to Muncie Central in the state championship game. This night, Ryan missed on his first five tries for 3-point shots. But Poynter was making an impact. He hit four second-quarter field goals in five shots.

So Jeff was back within 34-29 when Tesch hit his fourth 3 of his 15-point quarter. Mason had one 3 in going 5-for-6 from the field and scoring 11 in the quarter. "They really jumped us the second quarter," Hammel said. "Tesch had all those 3s, and they were long-range. Downtowners. At halftime, those three had all their points." It was Tesch 18, Mason 14, Whitman 10, Jeff 32.

Early in the second half, Sexson finally hit his first 3, and Jeff moved within 48-44. Whitman stopped that charge with an old-fashioned three-point play, and Tesch sank another 3.

But Jeff kept battling, behind seniors Kiley Watts (17 points for the game) and Chris Mansfield (13 points, including three third-quarter 3s). When Sexson — by then 1-for-11 on 3s — faked a 3, got his defender in the air and stepped inside him to sink a two-point jump shot, the game was 60-60 with 5:45 left.

Mason hit a 3. Preuss answered with a rebound basket. And Tesch hit a 3. At 66-64, Tesch pulled off Mason's free-throw miss and scored from in close, then hit another 3, his eighth in 11 tries for the night. Now it was 71-64 with 2½ minutes left, and Jeff was out of challenges.

The final was 80-72. Tesch (29), Whitman (23) and Mason (19) just missed matching Jeff's total by themselves.

"What an exciting first game," Van Arsdel said. "Big atmosphere. I was real happy with our effort and our level of play. I thought it was well played by both teams, especially for an opener."

The man in the middle

He didn't mention that it was a win over Lafayette Jeff. Time was that would have ignited bonfires of celebration. "I think in the last three or four years we've kind of stepped over that hurdle," Van Arsdel said. "Our kids get real excited about that game. They look forward to that game. But they don't look at it as a game where they're outmanned anymore.

"It was a real big win when we beat them in 1993-94, the first year they played at our place. The next year we beat them again at Jeff.

"It's a whole different situation. Unfortunately, a lot of those Broncho people don't understand that. We're certainly not the size of Lafayette Jeff and neither is McCutcheon, but we're a lot closer than Klondike, Battle Ground, Wainwright . . . "

He was opening a new season with a team that, with virtually the same personnel, had been pretty good the year before.

The building had begun Whitman's freshman year. Till Christmas that year, Whitman played only on the junior varsity, "so we could play him tons of minutes," Van Arsdel said. "From mid-January on, he was full time with us. I think I started him one time, but generally he was backing up a senior post player."

The next year he was an 11.5 scorer on a 14-8 team. By then, Van Arsdel knew what he had. "He's so solid mentally — he's gifted athletically, but he's the hardest working kid also. He was an eighth-grader the year I took over. He has always been a big kid, especially in the legs — always big and strong. But the physically dominant presence he has now he got between his sophomore and junior years. He has looked that physically imposing since then."

His junior season, he averaged 20.6 points a game, and sopho-mores Tesch and Mason had moved into the lineup, too. The point guard was junior Pat Colletto, son of Purdue's head football coach. The last night of the regular season, the 11-8 Raiders rose up and whipped unbeaten, No. 1-ranked Kokomo. Then in their first sec-tional game, they lost to what Van Arsdel respectfully calls "a really good Carroll team" while admitting that the first-game elimination also was "a product of youth. They didn't understand — especially Mason and Tesch. Tesch had never even seen Hoosier hysteria be-fore.

"Our school hadn't come down from the Kokomo game. That game was here, standing room only, overtime, people storming the floor — it was a neat thing. It was hard to get them back to earth quickly: 'Hey, fellows, you've got the most important thing coming up.' The student body didn't let them come down. They kept talk-ing about last week's game."

Van Arsdel watched how his sophomores dealt with that sec-tional upset.

Tesch and Mason, bitter as the Carroll loss was, went to Crawley Center and watched the Lafayette Jeff struggle but beat that Carroll team and cut down the sectional nets. They were at the Jeff gym, too, when the Bronchos won the regional. They were at Purdue's Mackey Arena when Lafayette Jeff rolled through the semistate to reach the Final Four. And they were at the Hoosier Dome when the Bronchos went down gallantly against eventual state champion Ben Davis.

They didn't enjoy watching their rivals trim all those nets, attract all that attention, gain all that glory. But they watched.

This was their first chance to show the aftereffects of that experience. Van Arsdel liked what he saw, and what he had.

"Last spring," Van Arsdel said, "I sat down with Whitman and I said, 'Josh, four years ago I set out to do some things for this program. We've accomplished everything but the sectional. Let's get it done together.'"

Van Arsdel, Whitman and Harrison had begun.

'It's what we're losing'

Hammel has his own team in the making. Poynter heads a sophomore class that is the foundation for high hopes. Another in the class, guard Abe Honegger, was a contributor to the surprise run to the Final Four the year before, as a freshman. It's a deep class that has had success all the way up the developmental ladder.

Three times, Hammel has taken teams to the Final Four. In 1992, the Bronchos seemed to be delivering him a dream finish. They led, as the seconds ticked down in the championship game. Richmond, the trailing team, had wiggled off the hook in the final seconds against Ben Davis in the semistate championship game, then done the same thing in the morning round at the State to beat Jeffersonville in overtime. One more time, the Red Devils did it, catching up with two late 3-point baskets and winning in overtime. Hammel's son, Richie, had 24 points in the game and won the Trester Award. It's a wonderful award. There's a glum family in the presentation shot.

The tournament has always been big to Jim Hammel, from days as a boy when he sat and watched and days as a player when, under Hall of Fame coach Bob Straight, he played on Huntington teams that won three straight Marion regionals. His senior year the Vikings got within a game of the Final Four, taken out by South Bend Central and Mike Warren. As a Ball State student, Hammel was at Hinkle Fieldhouse the next year when Straight and the Vikings got to the State, shocked unbeaten, No. 1-ranked Columbus, 71-67, but lost in the championship game, 58-55.

To Lafayette Jeff.

It was Crawley's last champion. Twenty-one years later, the job was Hammel's. He had coached Lake Central to victories in the

Lafayette semistate over No. 1-ranked Anderson and Lebanon to reach the 1984 Final Four. Athletic director Joe Heath was impressed. Heath knows coaching. He played for Crawley and took on the monumental job of being his successor. He led the 1974 Bronchos to the Final Four and then became A.D. He's in the Indiana Basketball Hall of Fame.

Coach, athletic director, just about everyone in one of Indiana's most tradition-rich schools is not happy with the coming switch to class basketball. Hammel has been outspoken about it. And unabashed.

"I'm sure when people hear me complaining the first thing they say is 'He's from Lafayette Jeff; they've had a silver spoon for years and years,' " he said.

"I coached at Dunkirk, with 100 kids. I'd have hated it then if you had taken away our chance to play Portland. I coached at Austin; I'd have been totally offended if you had not allowed us to play Seymour or Jennings County. Same thing at Mooresville, if we couldn't have played Martinsville. It's just a sad thing.

"We'll be in great shape in class basketball. We have the sectional on our floor. Then the regional is at Kokomo, and the semistate is back here at home. Kokomo is in our sectional, so if we're playing in the regional, they're not, and vice versa. We will never in the whole tournament have to play anybody on their home floor.

"Obviously we're not going to be as successful, on a yearly basis, in a sectional with Kokomo, Logansport and our two schools here. Sectional championships are going to be spread around, certainly. That's not the problem. It's what we're losing.

"When Central Catholic plays in the sectional, their students — I mean the whole student body, elementary, all of them — meet at Ninth Street and march nine blocks down Teal Road to Crawley Center. They come in before their game, they go up to the balcony and they march around the top of the gym, and they're chanting: 'C.C. . . . C.C. . . . C.C.'

"Their fans just wait on this. They fill their section full. And when those kids walk in that gym and make their appearance, the place is up for grabs.

"I can remember for 11 years grumbling about that, resenting it: 'Who do they think they are?'

"Now, I swear to God, I think about those kids and that intensity and that appearance and that sound, and tears come to my eyes. I think: 'These people voted for class basketball? This will never happen again. They're going to Sheridan and have this emotion?'

"That's just one little example of things like it that happen all over the state.

"The intensity when Central Catholic plays Jeff is unbelievable. The three state finals, the great games we've had against Harrison — I don't think anything matches the first two years when I was here when C.C. was really strong and played us in the sectional. The first year they were undefeated and we beat them. The next year, they had lost one and they beat us.

"I do think there's a good chance we will go back to what we have now. I think people who say it will never happen really underestimate how strong the Hoosier Hysteria sentiment is.

"What really upsets me is when I hear them say, 'We'll just do this two years and go back if it's a mistake. It's no big deal.'

"Hey! I have two kids playing right now, a sophomore (Scott, a guard, part of that deep class) and a freshman (Susie, a starter on the Jeff girls' team).

"You think those two years are no big deal to them?"

Oh, yes. Just for the record: Scott and Susie are related to me. Their dad's my brother.

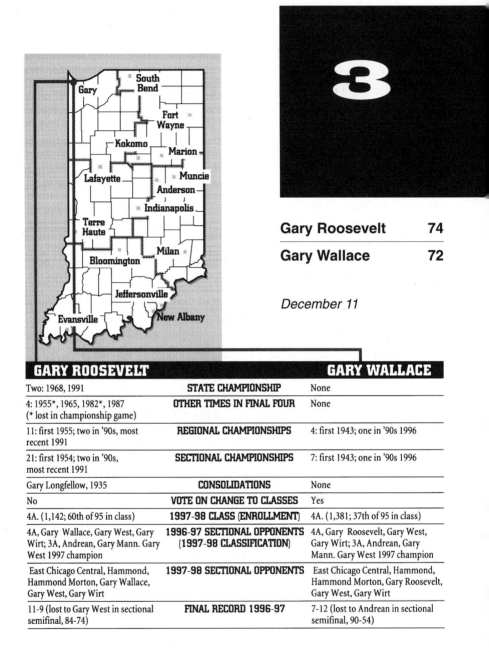

3

Gary Roosevelt	74
Gary Wallace	72

December 11

GARY ROOSEVELT		GARY WALLACE
Two: 1968, 1991	**STATE CHAMPIONSHIP**	None
4: 1955*, 1965, 1982*, 1987 (* lost in championship game)	**OTHER TIMES IN FINAL FOUR**	None
11: first 1955; two in '90s, most recent 1991	**REGIONAL CHAMPIONSHIPS**	4: first 1943; one in '90s 1996
21: first 1954; two in '90s, most recent 1991	**SECTIONAL CHAMPIONSHIPS**	7: first 1943; one in '90s 1996
Gary Longfellow, 1935	**CONSOLIDATIONS**	None
No	**VOTE ON CHANGE TO CLASSES**	Yes
4A. (1,142; 60th of 95 in class)	**1997-98 CLASS (ENROLLMENT)**	4A. (1,381; 37th of 95 in class)
4A, Gary Wallace, Gary West, Gary Wirt; 3A, Andrean, Gary Mann. Gary West 1997 champion	**1996-97 SECTIONAL OPPONENTS (1997-98 CLASSIFICATION)**	4A, Gary Roosevelt, Gary West, Gary Wirt; 3A, Andrean, Gary Mann. Gary West 1997 champion
East Chicago Central, Hammond, Hammond Morton, Gary Wallace, Gary West, Gary Wirt	**1997-98 SECTIONAL OPPONENTS**	East Chicago Central, Hammond, Hammond Morton, Gary Roosevelt, Gary West, Gary Wirt
11-9 (lost to Gary West in sectional semifinal, 84-74)	**FINAL RECORD 1996-97**	7-12 (lost to Andrean in sectional semifinal, 90-54)

The Roosevelt Tradition

The basketball coach, Ron Heflin, grew up just down 25th Avenue from Gary Roosevelt High, so of course that was his high school. He is a nephew of Bo Mallard, a community hero who coached Roosevelt teams to state championships in three sports, his name on the gymnasium where Heflin's teams play. The baseball coach, and freshman basketball coach, and varsity public address announcer, Benny Dorsey, played on "the first sectional championship team in our school's history — that's my class' claim to fame." The principal, William Reese Jr., graduated from Roosevelt, and so did his mother.

"It sounds like keeping it in the family," Dorsey said and smiled. "But Roosevelt has really put out some great products."

Oh, it goes on. The athletic director, John Campbell, coached some state track championship teams and individuals at Roosevelt, among the best his son, Erik, who went on to star in football and track at Michigan. John Campbell has an office just off the playing court at Bo Mallard Gym, and he loves to walk down the hall that links school and gym, loves to identify picture after picture of Roosevelt's state championship teams, loves to mention the significance of a hundred-plus items that chock the trophy cases. Every Hoosier knows Gary Roosevelt won state basketball championships in 1968 and 1991, but the school's athletic teams have won 23 other state championships, too — two in girls' track, one in boys' cross country (1983), and 20 in boys' track, nine in a row (1981-89) under Campbell.

Also in those packed trophy cases are reminders that hurdler Lee Calhoun, *twice* an Olympic gold medalist, and Chuck Adkins, a 1952 Olympic boxing gold medalist, and George Taliaferro, the first African-American drafted in the National Football League, and Dick Barnett of the great Knicks championship teams — all are from Gary Roosevelt.

And that's really not what Campbell or Dorsey or Heflin or Reese is talking about when the subject is The Roosevelt Tradition.

Principals and pride

Black pride is something African-American leaders since the '50s have stressed and encouraged.

It already was firmly in place by then at Gary Roosevelt — "long before it became fashionable," Heflin said. And its origins had nothing to do with athletics. "H. Theo. Tatum and Warren Anderson come to mind," Dorsey said. They weren't coaches. They were principals.

Roosevelt High School was formed in 1930. In 1933, Tatum became principal. That's H. Theo. Tatum — the period always there in the middle name, a reminder that he and the Roosevelt for whom the school was named shared something.

Tatum served for 28 years. When he retired in 1961, his assistant, Anderson, took over for the rest of the decade, then Robert Jones for 19 years.

Pride, Dorsey said, "was always very strong — I think first of all because Roosevelt was the first black school in the city. Everybody of color went to Roosevelt."

Had to go to Roosevelt. Those were shameful days in Gary, in Indiana, in an America that still was a generation away from the 1954 Supreme Court finding "that in the field of public education the doctrine of 'separate but equal' has no place."

Well before that, Dorsey said, the growing Steel City of Gary "opened up a little bit and Froebel (High School), across 15th Avenue, started taking a few blacks.

"But Roosevelt had such a strong foundation. The people who graduated early on — in the '30s, the '40s and the '50s — have come back to keep this thing going. This is what a lot of the high schools in the city are trying to do with alumni associations. With Roosevelt, it was always there."

Oscar night

Dorsey turned 60 during the 1996-97 school year. He turned 17 as a senior in 1954, the year when Roosevelt won the Gary sectional championship for the first time.

"We had strong administrative leadership. Mr. Tatum was my principal. He could walk in a room and I don't care if it was in an uproar, it was immediately silent. He had that much respect. He didn't speak in a loud voice, very quiet, but everybody — teaching staff, student body — respected him. And there was order.

"It was beautiful. Problems were at a very, very minimum."

"H. Theo. Tatum — very bright man," said Heflin, who came along at Roosevelt four years behind Dorsey. "Disciplinarian. Tough. Didn't take any nonsense and believed in educating people. One of the things black kids could be proud of was the heritage at Roosevelt."

The heritage started early for Heflin. "I grew up a block and a half from here. In third grade, I'd come watch all the practices. The football players would help me get there because I wasn't old enough to cross the street."

As a freshman, Heflin sat in the stands at Butler Fieldhouse and watched two black teams — Gary Roosevelt and an Indianapolis Crispus Attucks team with a junior named Oscar Robertson — play for the state championship. Barnett was on that Roosevelt team. So was Wilson "Jake" Eison, who was named the state's "Mr. Basketball" and went on to star at Purdue. It was no contest. "Nobody was going to beat Oscar that night," Dorsey said. The score was 97-74, still the highest-scoring championship game in tournament history. Before that, the most any team had scored in a championship game was 68 — six below Roosevelt's total. That night, Robertson scored 30 points, Eison 31, Barnett 18. "We had those guys and

27

Attucks still beat us by 20," Heflin said. "I think it makes people realize how good Attucks was with Oscar."

That scene might have happened years before, but until 1943, all-black high schools — Roosevelt in Gary, Lincoln in Evansville, Crispus Attucks in Indianapolis — and parochial schools couldn't compete in the state tournament. "We had a team that won the national Negro championship," Heflin said. "They couldn't play teams here, so they'd go to St. Louis, all around. We had a night for that championship team about five years ago. I had a chance to sit down with them."

So did Dorsey. "I talked to 'Shag' Courtney. He's a legend around Gary, one of the best athletes ever to come out of the city. He was on those teams. He said it was a thrill, but it was frustrating to have to go so far to play. He played basketball, football, track — he was truly good. We give an annual Most Valuable overall athlete award which is named for him. He comes every year to the banquet."

'We will . . . be . . . state champs'

Reese came along a decade after Dorsey and Heflin. He was a high school student when Roosevelt finally made its breakthrough and won the 1968 state championship. He was on one of the 16 buses that carried Roosevelt fans to Indianapolis and brought them back very, very late that night — to a tumultuous welcome.

"The players weren't even there — they came back the next day," Reese said. "But 25th Avenue was so packed the buses had to unload about a mile from the school." It wasn't just Roosevelt's first championship. It was the city of Gary's first, after so many great teams from Froebel, Horace Mann, Lew Wallace, Emerson, Tolleston and Roosevelt had fallen short, usually in the semistate at Lafayette.

The breakthrough team hadn't been considered anywhere close to some of those teams that built the "snake-bitten" stigma Gary powers took with them into tournament play. Mallard's '68 Panthers lost five times during the regular season, including their last two regular-season games.

"When the players came back, the reception was awesome," Reese remembers. "It was on the old City Hall steps. They gave gold championship rings. We also had the Trester Award winner (James Nelson). Roosevelt High School was really blessed that day."

Both Dorsey and Heflin had returned to Roosevelt after college and they had served Mallard as advance scouts. So, they weren't around for the sectional, regional or semistate fun. "Everywhere I scouted," Dorsey said, "they'd ask where I was from and I'd say, 'I'm from Gary Roosevelt, the team that is going to be the next state champion.'"

Maybe he even believed it, after all those near misses. But, when he sat in the 40-year-old fieldhouse at Indianapolis and watched Roosevelt rout Vincennes in the semifinals, then Indianapolis Shortridge 68-60 for the championship, "It was a feeling that is hard to put in words, because it was the first time. We had made history." Gary, so rich in athletic history, the home of boxing's Tony Zale and football's Tom Harmon, Alex Karras, Les Bingaman and Hank Stram, finally had its first state high school basketball champion.

Reese recalls Monday of State Tournament week. "Seven players on that team were in my English class, with one of the great teachers at Roosevelt High School — Ida B. King," Reese said.

"Those boys walked in that day and she said, 'Something just came over me, fellows. You guys are going to win the state championship.'

"She asked them to stand and repeat after her: 'We *will* . . . be . . . state champs. We *will* . . . be . . . state champs.'

"Aaron Smith (who scored 28 points in the state championship game), James Nelson (12 points), Cornelius McFerson (eight points), Melvin Robinson (five), LeWayne Henson (eight) — they were all in that class.

"Those guys ate lunch together. They went to the show together with their girlfriends. They went to McDonald's together. They went to church together. The championship was built off the court, not on the court."

Jim Nelson, shown shooting against Vincennes in the afternoon game of the 1968 finals, won the Trester Award and became an Indiana All-Star. (Photo courtesy Indiana High School Athletic Association)

The Big Three

But something bigger had been building a long time before that at Roosevelt High.

"A lot of tradition — a spirit of a true family," Reese said.

"It has been maintained by people still coming who had relatives go here. The first graduating class was in 1934. My mom graduated here in 1936. My dad attended night school here. The tradition just continues over and over, by grandparents telling children about the attitude.

"Mr. Tatum sought the Negro leaders of that time — (singer) Marian Anderson, my mom heard her, right here in school on stage. Count Basie. We had auditoriums where all students were exposed to the black greats. They actually came to Roosevelt High.

"Our teachers were from all over the country. Mr. Tatum had taken it upon himself to travel to the black colleges and get the black teachers who were highly qualified and bring them back to Gary Roosevelt, where the students could be exposed to the best black educators in the country. And when the younger teachers came along, they were aligned with those seasoned teachers, and the tradition for the teaching element passed down."

In the same way that the early principals are revered, the coaches who built Roosevelt's athletic tradition and values aren't forgotten.

A plaque on the wall in the honor hall of pictures and trophies says:

Leonard Douglas: 1938-71. John D. Smith: 1932-66.
Louis Mallard: 1938-75.

In the days when Roosevelt High School first emerged as both an outstanding academic institution and an athletic power, three coaches provided the strong leadership needed to achieve the athletic success. Their effort, struggle and determination helped develop the spirit that has become known as the Roosevelt tradition. They were affectionately known as the Big Three.

In the late '60s and early '70s East Chicago and Gary teams dominated the State Tournament. Beginning with 1968, either a Gary or East Chicago high school was in the championship game five straight years. In 1970, Jim Bradley, left, led unbeaten East Chicago Roosevelt to the title, and in 1971, unbeaten East Chicago Washington won the championship behind (from left) Darnell Adell, Tim Stoddard, James Williams, Junior Bridgeman and Pete Trgovich. (Photo courtesy Indiana High School Athletic Association)

They passed the coaching around and helped each other as assistants. Mallard coached football and track before he took on cross country and basketball. Consider that feat of winning state championships in three sports. Maybe somebody else in Indiana history did that, but no name jumps out. Smith coached the 1955 basketball runner-up team, and Douglas primarily was associated with football. That's why Roosevelt teams play not only in Bo Mallard Gym but also in Leonard Douglas Stadium, in the J.D. Smith athletic complex.

Only, it never comes out Bo Mallard when Dorsey speaks of the gravel-voiced man who lives with his wife in retirement now in Lansing, Mich.

"I still call him Louis Mallard, or Coach Mallard," he said. "I never got to the place of calling him Bo."

A Shot at the Buzzer

It was a Wednesday night, but it was a game night at Bo Mallard Gym. A Big Game night. City rival Wallace was the guest.

Each team in the past had been better. Big, gruff John Hoover had taken Wallace all the way to the final eight the March before, but Lafayette Jefferson punctured that Gary dream. Hoover lost just about everybody from that team and was rebuilding around husky senior forward Michael Bridgeman and a slim, 6-3 sophomore of considerable promise, Herman Ezell.

Wallace — Gary Lew Wallace High, named for the Indiana-born author of *Ben Hur* — came in 0-3. Doesn't matter, Dorsey said. "Everybody wants to beat Roosevelt. That's their claim to fame. No matter what they do the rest of the way or in the tournament, they can say, 'I beat you.'"

Heflin's mostly senior team was 2-2. It included a pretty good shooter named Ronald Heflin Jr.

They do everything they can at Mallard Gym to remind opponents of what they're taking on. All teams that have won state basketball championships flaunt the achievement in some proud way. Roosevelt has life-size cutouts of each of those 1968 players, and coaches, and managers, on the high south wall of the gymnasium

— and just as huge cutouts of each of Heflin's 1991 state champions, including coaches and managers, on the north wall. A Panther head looks up at the center jump, and just in case all else has been missed, a sign notes: "You are now in the Panther den."

Wallace wasn't fazed. Bridgeman hit his team's first shot, then guard Ben Coleman stole the ball and scored and Wallace was up right away, 4-0. Senior guard Damon Bruce and Valparaiso-signed senior forward Monte Gordon scored four baskets each for Roosevelt in the first quarter and the Panthers led 22-18.

With four minutes to go in the game, Heflin sniped a basket that put Roosevelt ahead 68-60, those golden numbers that won the school's first state championship. Wallace showed no reverence. In two minutes, the score was tied 70-70.

Lonnie Jones, Wallace's 6-10 junior center, had tried and tried and tried to contribute, but passes kept slipping through his desperately eager hands, rebounds eluded him, defense was a problem, and Hoover kept pulling him for counsel, then reinserting him, and wincing. In those last two minutes, Jones cleared off two big defensive rebounds. Then, as seconds were running out and Roosevelt — leading 71-70 — was scrambling to cover Bridgeman (18 points), Ezell (16) and shooter Oviere Borom (six 3-point baskets and 22 points), Bridgeman got the ball on the baseline and zipped a hard pass to Jones, who speared it and jammed home the go-ahead basket.

With nine seconds left, Roosevelt took timeout, and Jones — a wide grin where worry had been most of the night — received a sidelines pummeling.

Senior Ardie Jenkins was the most disconsolate of Roosevelt players going to that timeout. Jenkins had scored just one basket all night, but he had fought for a piece of victory. Defending that last-minute 71-70 lead, he had leaped in to block a Bridgeman shot, then pulled off the rebound after another Wallace miss. He was fouled immediately, of course, and 27 seconds away from winning, he had missed both free throws and opened the way to Lonnie Jones' heroics.

Heflin wanted a shot for Bruce (17 points), or Gordon (25 points) or Ron Jr. (10), and nine seconds was plenty of time to get one. But things went wacky, the ball was punched loose, and the man who ran it down was Jenkins, who retrieved it left of the foul circle, turned, jumped and launched a shot that was in the air when the buzzer sounded — and in the nets an instant later, a 3-point basket that gave Roosevelt a 74-72 victory.

Just another Gary game.

'We better win this thing'

Ron Heflin reflected on the job he had, the job he had always wanted, and the one he was to give up a few months later.

"I've been head coach since '75," he said. "I've been offered college jobs, but I love high school basketball, and particularly in Indiana — at the high school in the neighborhood I grew up in. I'm very fond of that."

And no memory is fonder than of that night in 1991 when the team led by the greatest player he or probably even Roosevelt ever had, Glenn Robinson, won the state championship.

It would have been precious under any circumstances, but Heflin had come so agonizingly close in 1982. The championship game that year always is ranked with the greatest finals ever. Roosevelt and Plymouth went back and forth, but Roosevelt had the lead in the final seconds when its best player, Renaldo Thomas, sought to clinch victory with a fast break and threw a behind-the-back pass out of bounds. Gritty Scott Skiles tied the game with a 23-foot bomb at the buzzer and kept firing bull's-eyes till he had 39 points and Plymouth had a 75-74 double-overtime victory, and the state championship.

"That was a tremendous ballgame," Heflin said. "Any time you lose one that close, that you had in your hand . . .

"But Jack (Edison, the Plymouth coach) could have said the same thing. It just wasn't our time. The kids gave all that they had. We didn't play smart at the end, but you don't hold that against them. It was a privilege to get there.

"In '91, I told the kids, 'We better win this thing. We might not get back here for a while.' "

Glenn Robinson, possibly the best player ever for Gary Roosevelt, powered the Panthers to the 1991 State Championship. (Photo courtesy Indiana High School Athletic Association)

And of course there was a personal side, an unforgettable feeling when that championship came.

"The dream of probably every coach in Indiana is to win a state championship," he said. "A lot of good coaches, great coaches never get a chance to win one — never make it to the Final Four.

"It's one of the most coveted championships in the country. Indiana basketball! This is the state championship.

"It's pretty hard to top that feeling, but you keep working at it. And you realize the kids you had were one special group.

"It's particularly satisfying now because they're going to class basketball. I figured it would pass because a lot of the smaller schools wanted a chance. I don't particularly like it. I'm a traditionalist. To me, it's watered down. Then it was a true state championship."

4

Anderson	85
And. Highland	62

December 18

ANDERSON		ANDERSON HIGHLAND
Three: 1935, 1937, 1946	**STATE CHAMPIONSHIP**	None
11: 1914*, 1918*, 1920, 1921*, 1923, 1936, 1944, 1948, 1973, 1979*, 1981*, 1983*, 1986*, 1990 (* lost in championship game)	**OTHER TIMES IN FINAL FOUR**	None
29: first 1921; four in '90s, most recent 1996	**REGIONAL CHAMPIONSHIPS**	2: first 1976; one in '90s, 1991
48: first 1918; five in '90s, most recent 1997	**SECTIONAL CHAMPIONSHIPS**	3: first 1976; one in '90s, 1991
Anderson St. Mary, 1966; Madison Heights, part, 1997-98	**CONSOLIDATIONS**	Formed 1955; added part of Madison Heights, 1997-1998
No	**VOTE ON CHANGE TO CLASSES**	Yes
4A. (1,313; 43rd of 95 in class)	**1997-98 CLASS (ENROLLMENT)**	4A. (1,384; 36th of 95 in class)
4A: Anderson, Madison Heights; 3A, Elwood; 2A, Alexandria, Frankton. Anderson site and 1997 champion	**1996-97 SECTIONAL OPPONENTS (1997-98 CLASSIFICATION)**	4A: Anderson, Madison Heights; 3A, Elwood; 2A, Alexandria, Frankton. Anderson site and 1997 champion
Anderson Highland, Connersville, Muncie Central, New Castle, Richmond	**1997-98 SECTIONAL OPPONENTS**	Anderson, Connersville, Muncie Central, New Castle, Richmond
22-4 (won sectional; lost to Delta in regional final, 56-48)	**FINAL RECORD 1996-97**	10-11 (lost to Anderson in sectional semifinal, 57-45)

Jumpin' Johnny and The Wigwam

The America that came smiling out of World War II was in a mood for heroes, for sports heroes with catchy nicknames — Joltin' Joe DiMaggio, Bullet Bob Feller, Stan the Man Musial, Ted the Splendid Splinter Williams, Clyde Bulldog Turner, Squirmin' Herman Wedemeyer, Felix Doc Blanchard, Charlie Choo-Choo Justice, Clyde Smackover Scott, Big George Mikan, Harry The Horse Gallatin.

There never was a better time to be an Indiana high school basketball star. A little Evansville Bosse guard named Bryan "Broc" Jerrel captivated the state, leading his team to two straight state championships (1944 and '45). Ralph Beard came along at the very same time across the Ohio River at Louisville Male High. To this day Ralph Beard may be the best guard ever produced in Kentucky, and he was recognized as great in his time. Author Dave Kindred, in a splendid chapter of his superb book, *Basketball — The Dream Game in Kentucky*, wrote that Beard, before he was to play in the Indiana-Kentucky All-Star game, while asleep in his bed "squeezed a pillow to his chest, muttering, 'I've got you, Jerrel, you son of a bitch.' " That's how big an Indiana high school star could be, his fame spreading across state lines.

And then, just before the tournament made names for the ages of Shelbyville's Bill Garrett and Terre Haute Garfield's Clyde Lovellette, along came Jumpin' Johnny Wilson.

John Wilson was born in Anderson and grew up there. Those days boys in Anderson didn't play Cowboys and Indians. They played Indians. Little Johnny Wilson's dream was no different from every Anderson youngster's: to wear the red and green of the Anderson High School Indians. "The opportunity to play on the team — that was the greatest thing a kid could have," he said.

Johnny grew up behind two brothers, one two years older than him, the other four. "We played on outdoor courts — the backyard or an elementary school. I was real skinny and scared to get under the basket. Then they'd beat on me.

"They paved the way for me. They *made* me a ballplayer."

And Anderson coach Charles Cummings made him a center. At 5-11.

"I started the fifth game of my sophomore year," Wilson said. The "Jumpin' Johnny" thing started about then, too. Local sportswriter Red Haven pinned it on him. Johnny could jump. He high jumped 6-2, at a time when 6-7 won the NCAA.

Disappointment, then bliss

Jumpin' Johnny considers that Anderson team of his sophomore season the best he played on. It had a pretty good junior guard named Carl Erskine, who could pitch a baseball, too. Kokomo eliminated the Indians in the semifinal round at the State. "We were picked to win that year," he said. "I got hurt and . . ." The ailing Wilson did manage six points, Erskine just one before fouling out. To this day, says Erskine, who was to pitch two no-hitters and set a World Series strikeout record as one of the Brooklyn Dodgers' "Boys of Summer," he is better remembered in Anderson for his basketball as an Indian than his baseball as a Dodger.

And to this day, they remember the 1946 Indians and Jumpin' Johnny Wilson best of all. "My senior year, we had a bunch of guys who just really liked each other," Wilson said. "Everybody picked each other up. We still do."

Nobody picked that Anderson team to win. The Indians lost seven regular-season games. One of them was humiliating: 49-22 to Fort Wayne Central. But in the tournament, Anderson kept winning, till only two teams were left: Anderson and Fort Wayne Central.

Anderson's 1946 State Championship team, first row (from left), John Cochran, James Vanderbur, Harry Farmer, Robert Spearman, Robert Ritter and Johnny Wilson. Back row, manager R. Denny, Clyde Green, Richard Roberts, coach Charles Cummings, Don Armstrong, Isaac Weatherly and assistant coach Carl Bonge. (Photo courtesy Indiana High School Athletic Association)

"We felt we could do it," Wilson said. "They had beaten us 27 points, but we were just determined this one was ours."

That's when "Jumpin' Johnny" Wilson became a Hoosier legend.

The scoring record for the state championship game was 26, set in the second state tournament (1912) by Dick Porter of Lebanon. After 34 years, it fell. With all of Indiana crammed into one of Butler Fieldhouse's 15,000 prized seats or listening in on radio, "Jumpin' Johnny" scored an amazing 30 points and Fort Wayne Central was beaten, 67-53.

"That was the greatest feeling in the world," Wilson said softly. "I played in Madison Square Garden, Boston Garden, all over the world. Nothing compared to that state finals.

"We still get back together. All of us are living. Coach (Charles Cummings) is, too. I see him at our ballgames. He very seldom misses one.

"James Vanderbur, Isaac Weatherly and myself are still here. Robert Ritter lives down at Noblesville. Harry Farmer is in Georgia. Dick Roberts is in the state of Washington. John Cochran is in Chicago. Bob Spearman is at Syracuse, Ind. Don Armstrong is in Kentucky. Weatherly was on a cruise, but everyone else got back for the 50th-year banquet last year."

They already were talking about another reunion. If this Anderson team makes it to the State — "*every*-body's going to be there," Wilson said.

Because Anderson, which got the flame started with state championships in 1935 and 1937, has been back to the State seven times and advanced to the championship game four times but hasn't won it all again since that night in 1946, 51 years ago.

Good enough to win it all

Coach Ron Hecklinski pondered the question for a while: Just how good is this Anderson team?

"We're not going to win every game, I can promise you that," he said. "We're not *that* good.

"When we come out and we're active, we're pretty good. When we're not active, big teams will cause us a lot of problems.

"But, if you were to ask me: Is this team good enough to win the State? Yes, it is. Because of the havoc they can cause other teams."

Hecklinski had just unleashed that havoc on city rival Anderson Highland, and smiled.

Highland coach Ray Sims tried to exploit whatever size problem Anderson had. The Laddies' starting lineup had no one under 6-4. It's a generous measure that makes Anderson's starting guards 5-10 (Eric Bush) and 5-11 (Tyson Jones). But the game they play is down, not up. They live to punch a basketball loose and go after it.

Highland stayed close through 14-12. Then Jones hit his second 3-point basket of the quarter and 6-6 forward Jeremy Ramsey followed with another. Anderson was up 26-18 at the first quarter.

The Indians' lead was 30-20 when Bush picked off a pass and drove to a layup. Highland steadied and moved within 34-28 just before halftime when Jones stole the ball and scored — then jolted the Laddies by tipping a pass upcourt to Corey Evans for a layup that just beat the buzzer and put Anderson up 38-28.

The thievery didn't stop. Bush stole the ball, missed a shot, Highland rebounded, and Jones stole it again. He hit: 42-31. Then it was 50-37, and 59-41.

Highland had a strong team, graded all year long in the state's top 50 by the Jeff Sagarin computer ratings (another mark of Hoosier singularity: for *USA Today* and other newspaper clients, Sagarin's computer ranks college and professional basketball and football, and major-league hockey and international soccer, and Indiana high school basketball). Jake Pinkerton, Highland's 6-4 junior guard, hit six shots in a row in the second half, four of them 3-pointers, in scoring 22 points, and junior forward Arthur Hyatt, a springy 6-4, scored 18, but it was a forlorn chase. The Anderson lead topped out at 27 points before substitutes played things out to 85-62.

"Those two guards are really good," Hecklinski said. "Bush had nine steals. We set a goal of 25 deflections a half. We had 47. We were short." That's just under 1½ a minute, a shellshock pace for an opposing guard.

Hecklinski expected to be good this year. He's been using the same guys for three years.

And they aren't done. The Indians' starters included four juniors: guards Bush (20 points) and Jones (23 points), plus 6-5 center Duane Miller (14 points) and 5-11 nominal forward Brett Manifold (eight points).

Hecklinski saw what was coming and cleared the way for it when this season's juniors were freshmen. He had watched the whole group of them play together at Anderson North Junior High, and go undefeated as seventh- and eighth-graders. "I can't say I didn't have anything else above them," he said of that 1994-95 season. "I didn't have *great* players above them."

He didn't dismiss his upperclassmen. "I played 10 players. I played the older kids just because I felt they deserved to play some, but I also mixed these kids in (the four current juniors, plus Kenny Chamberlain, who moved to Texas). I actually started one of them once, and he just went crazy, so I brought them off the bench their whole freshman year. They played all the time, I just didn't start them.

"They showed great poise — at times. Other times they played like freshmen. We were 12-8, but you could tell that we were good. We beat Kokomo here; they were rated No. 2. We beat New Castle; they were rated sixth."

Bush is the one highest on big-school recruiting lists. "He's good — he's scoring 20 points a game," Hecklinski said. "Right now he is a point guard without a point guard's mentality. He's trying to be too much of a scorer. He's a very good shooter, but he's trying to carry it on his shoulders all the time and he doesn't need to. Sometimes when Eric is on the floor it's a one-pass offense."

Jones, he said, "has good heritage." His step-brothers, John and Shawn Teague, were all-state players at Anderson. His dad was an Indian.

"Miller has good legs. He's a different type of post man — he's not a banger, he's a runner. I think he's going to be 6-6, a big-time jumper, and he'll be a 3." That's college recruiter talk, which Hecklinski is licensed to use. He was an assistant coach at Ball State before taking the Anderson job. Translated, that means he thinks center Miller's speed and athletic ability will make him a good small forward in some future college offense.

Winning a bigger game

Not so long ago, just a few months, the 40-year-old Hecklinski was gravely ill and almost died.

His problem surfaced eight years earlier when he was coaching at Edgewood High School in Ellettsville, just west of Bloomington. "I had a blood test," he said. "They told me I had sclerotic cholangitis, which is a rare liver disease and there's no cure for it. I was put on medication.

"I knew at some point in my life I'd have to have a transplant. I thought I'd be 60."

During the 1995-96 basketball season, the diseased liver "started going bad. I was tired; I fatigued easily; I lost weight. I got through the year but it was difficult. When it deteriorated, it just went real fast."

In July, he went on a donor list for a liver transplant. His wait was relatively short; he had the surgery August 30. "When they took it out, they told me it was almost at the end," he said. "I was very lucky."

He is still battling back. He needs much more rest than before, 14 or 15 hours a day. And he coaches a little bit differently, by choice.

"It has really helped me. I think I'm a much better coach. Before, if something didn't go right I'd scream and go crazy and forget to coach. Now, if a kid misses a shot, it's not the end of the world.

"I really mean that — I think I'm a better coach. I'm still as competitive as I've ever been, but I do feel that I coach more, I instruct more.

"And I can tell you one thing: when I come home at night, seeing my wife and my little girl is big time for me. I almost lost them (wife Pam and daughter Stephanie, 8).

"It puts it all in perspective."

From three to two, then one?

It's an odd school year in the city of Anderson. At the end of it, the old red-brick Anderson High School building will close and only the present Highland and Madison Heights high schools will remain in operation. But, this is Anderson. Madison Heights, which in a 31-year life sent Indiana University four players including future pros and national-champion starters Bobby Wilkerson and Ray Tolbert, will vanish and its former building becomes the new Anderson High School. All the present Indians are expected to be together there. There are boundary lines for assignment to the two schools, but seniors from the old Anderson High will be given their choice of where to go. It would seem to be an unsettling thing for young basketball players, uncertain about their future. "I don't think that's an issue with them," Hecklinski said. "They know we can all be together, we'll still be playing every game in the Wigwam, it's still the Anderson Indians and the red and green, the whole thing."

The Wigwam is in the center of everything. It's the one place visitors from out of town are steered if they ask a Hoosier who has been around where they should go to get the true flavor of this Indiana high school basketball phenomenon. There's nothing hoary about the downtown building. It's nearing 40 years old but still a modern basketball palace. Its seating capacity, 8,998, is the second-largest in all America among high school gyms, which, of course, makes it second-largest in Indiana (to New Castle's 9,314). There are whole college conferences that can't match Indiana's number of huge high school gyms (six above 8,000; thirteen above 7,000; thirty above 5,000).

None of the others, though, makes an event out of a basketball game as they do at The Wigwam. The national anthem is a seven-minute patriotic production. Then, with all lights out except for the spotlights following them, the two who have won spots almost as prized as those on the basketball team, the Indian warrior and the maiden, come onto the court for a dance that the Anderson throngs have seen dozens of times — some of them hundreds of times, because Wigwam crowds are not young. "Half the crowd are in their 70s," Hecklinski only slightly overstated.

That whole atmosphere, there before little Johnny Wilson learned to play on those outdoor courts, is why Hecklinski moved from a Division I college program to high school — and was thrilled to get the chance.

"I thought of it as a college job with no recruiting," he said. "I have a good teaching schedule, I'm going to have 6,000 people watching every night, and I've got players. Money is not an object; we have a booster club that raises a lot of money. I have Booster Club meetings on Saturday and about 100 people show up. We just talk. They're the best high school fans I've ever seen. They rival college fans."

And they're why this unusual switch of schools and names came about, rather than abandoning the old school name and going on with the survivors. "There was just too much pressure," Hecklinski said. "You can't do away with Anderson High School — the Indian, the whole traditional deal.

"It's a big, big thing to about 95 percent in this town, but unfortunately the other 5 percent are on the school board. The tradition and everything in this city — I got a bumper sticker the other day that says, 'We built this city on Indian basketball.' And that's exactly right.

"We're going to two schools next year, but there's a committee of the big people in town. I think in a year or two it's going to end up with one big school, and they'll build the school. You're only talking 3,000 students."

Certainly, that big a school would offer far greater academic possibilities. Marching bands are big in this part of Indiana; maybe that would benefit, though the bitter corollary of the bigger-is-better idea is that fewer kids would be in marching bands, and on basketball teams. A major faction in Anderson was upset about that, upset about losing a relatively young but impressive basketball tradition at swallowed-up Madison Heights.

The underlying aim of everything involved in the unique Anderson Indians atmosphere is getting that fourth state championship, and first in more than a half-century.

"That would be . . . everything," Hecklinski said.

"One of my assistant coaches was the star of that '46 team. He carries those things over to our players. He has been excellent."

'Jumpin' Johnny! I saw you play'

He is Johnny Wilson.

He still doesn't look like a center, but neither is he 5-11. "In high school and college, I was actually 5-11¾. When I was 42 years old, I grew an inch and a half. I stopped jumping and started growing."

As big a star as he was in Indiana after that 30-point game in the state-championship spotlight, college doors weren't wide open for him. One year later, Jackie Robinson came along in baseball, and Bill Garrett, a center quite similar to Wilson in height and skills, led Shelbyville to the state championship. Indiana's Branch McCracken made Garrett the first African-American player in Big Ten history.

But in 1946, Johnny Wilson stayed at home, playing for Anderson College, a small church school (Church of God) that played far from the major-college limelight. He played three years there, then left the school, the town and the sport for a year as an outfielder with the Chicago American Giants, in the dying days of the Negro League. "I thought I was better in baseball than I was in basketball," Wilson said.

That fall, in 1949, he was picked to play with a College All-Star basketball team against the pro champion Minneapolis Lakers. That brought a contract offer from the Harlem Globetrotters — the highest professional basketball level possible for him then, scant months before Chuck Cooper of Duquesne became the first African-American drafted by the NBA.

Those were different Globetrotters from the entertainment-focused team today. Those Globetrotters pioneered in popular tricks, but they also were a skilled team that played against the very best opposition available, when both were playing to win.

"I played in 16 games that we lost," Wilson said. "Very few Trotters can say that.

"That was the heyday of the Trotters. We played the Lakers, the College All-Americans. Chicago Stadium was our home court. We played the College All-Americans 19 games all over the country."

And they were basketball's ambassadors to the world.

"I went to Australia, all over Europe, Asia, Africa. I turned down South America because I didn't want to fly around the Andes Mountains. Everyplace — there was never an empty seat.

"In Brisbane, Australia, we played six straight nights outdoors on a canvas court over a soccer field. One day it just poured down rain. All day. They moved us inside to an auditorium. One whole corner of the floor was gone, because of the stage. We played four games, one after another. People stood out in that rain, waiting for their turn.

"We played on a bullring in Spain, right on the dirt. I don't know who laid out the court for us, but it just about covered the whole bullring. It was that big."

When it was show time, "I was the place-kicker," he said. From just back of the center line, in the flow of the game, he would drop-kick a shot. "You only got one a night," he said. "The first one I ever made was at Marion, and it was the first game my mother had seen me play with the Trotters.

"The next night we went to Cleveland and Lou Groza (the NFL's preeminent place-kicker of the day for the Browns) was there. Abe Saperstein introduced me to him and told him I was going to take his job. That night I kicked it in again.

"The next night at Sandusky, I was the headlines in the newspaper, before the game. That night my kick landed in the foul circle."

Globetrotting ended for Wilson after five years. "I got married and I went back and finished my last year of school. Then I started teaching and coaching." He coached Indianapolis Wood High School for eight seasons, then moved to Chicago in 1969, for four years as athletic director at Malcolm X High before taking over as basketball coach for 16 seasons.

In 1989, in his 60s, he retired and returned to his hometown. He assisted at Anderson University for a few years. "Then I saw that Heck was going to have a good team so I jumped on the bandwagon," he said.

"I'm really enjoying it. We've got a good staff and real good ballplayers. I try to emphasize the importance of education, and of being a team. You've got to be a team. Players have to get along together. And if you're going to be a winner, you've got to work at it. All the time."

If and when the opportunity comes, Johnny Wilson can tell them — when your team is in the state championship game, even against a team that has chewed you up and spit you out not very long before:

Carpe diem.

Seize the moment. Jump all over it.

Because there's a lifetime afterward for not just you but a whole lot of other Hoosiers to remember what happened that night.

"I was out in Wyoming at a filling station. A guy walked up and said 'Jumpin' Johnny Wilson! I saw you play.' Down in Australia, guys there as missionaries came up to me to tell me they remembered me.

"It has happened a lot of times. Opportunities have come to me because of that.

"That's what basketball has done for me."

South Bend
Gary
Fort Wayne
Kokomo
Marion
Lafayette
Muncie
Anderson
Terre Haute
Indianapolis
Bloomington
Milan
Jeffersonville
Evansville
New Albany

5

| Milan | 59 |
| South Ripley | 52 |

December 20

MILAN		SOUTH RIPLEY
1954	**STATE CHAMPIONSHIP**	None
1953	**OTHER TIMES IN FINAL FOUR**	None
3: 1953, 1954, 1973	**REGIONAL CHAMPIONSHIPS**	None
12: first 1932; most recent 1985	**SECTIONAL CHAMPIONSHIPS**	Five as South Ripley: first 1970; most recent 1982. Others in corporation, 10: Cross Plains, 1942; Holton, 1929, 1962, 1954; New Marion, 1961; Versailles, 1924, 1928, 1957, 1958, 1959
None	**CONSOLIDATIONS**	Formed 1966 (Cross Plains, New Marion, Versailles); Holton (part), 1969
No	**VOTE ON CHANGE TO CLASSES**	No
1A. (266; 13th of 96 in class)	**1997-98 CLASS (ENROLLMENT)**	2A. (316; 70th of 96 in class)
4A, East Central; 3A, South Dearborn; 2A, Lawrenceburg, Switzerland County; 1A, Rising Sun. South Dearborn site; Lawrenceburg 1997 champion	**1996-97 SECTIONAL OPPONENTS (1997-98 CLASSIFICATION)**	3A, Batesville, Greensburg; 2A, Jac-Cen-Del, North Decatur, South Decatur. Greensburg site, Batesville champion
Hauser, Jac-Cen-Del, Madison Shawe, Rising Sun	**1997-98 SECTIONAL OPPONENTS**	Lawrenceburg, North Decatur, South Decatur, Switzerland County
7-13 (lost to Lawrenceburg in sectional quarterfinal, 75-52)	**FINAL RECORD 1996-97**	9-12 (lost to Jac-Cen-Del in sectional quarterfinal, 79-72)

Classy Fadeout for a Miracle

Of course there had to be a visit to Milan.

The town of Milan, object of many a searcher and researcher over the last 43 years, is usually approached via Interstate 74, which links Indianapolis and Cincinnati. Sixteen miles west of the Indiana-Ohio border, exit signs point to Milan: a 12-mile trip south from 74 down state highway 101.

Milan athletic director Tom Mathews prefers the view entering town on highway 350 from the east. "The first time I came here, I drove through that grove of trees out by the Legion," Mathews said. "The way everything was manicured, the flat terrain — I love it every time I drive by it."

Roger Schroder prefers to come in on 350 from the west. That allows passing through Pierceville just a few miles outside Milan. Pierceville — population 45 then, not quite so big now — is a sort of Bethlehem to this whole Miracle of Milan. It is barely even defined as a community anymore, a few houses on the main road, a few more on the road shooting off it. One of those is where young Roger Schroder grew up, near the family grocery and the court where Roger and boyhood pals Bobby Plump, Gene White and Glenn Butte all learned to play.

Marvin and Mary Lou Wood drove into Milan last March. CBS was doing a special and the Woods were to meet a camera crew there. Mary Lou was in her early 20s when she and Marvin, the

coach who in his second year there was to win the state championship, drove into the town for the first time. This time, her eyes saw
the little village in a different way. Quietly, observingly, she said:

"It really *was* a miracle."

Plump, Oscar and symmetry

Milan 32, Muncie Central 30: the most famous score, the most
famous game of the nearly 50,000 that have culled out the 87 Indiana state champions.

This 1954 championship game spawned the movie *Hoosiers*.
It made *Reader's Digest*. It generated books. It made lifetime heroes of Plump, whose basket almost at the buzzer won the game,
and of Wood, the 26-year-old coach who produced and directed
The Miracle.

And this victory by a high school with just 73 boys over the
team that was the New York Yankees of its state and sport stood off
proponents of class basketball for 43 years.

For all those decades, campaigns to get Indiana to split its
tournament into classes as Illinois had done in 1972, as almost
every other state had done forever, were stymied by a one-word
counterargument.

Milan.

Finally, that wasn't enough. Finally, enough generations had
passed that the afterglow in which the entire state basked for days
and weeks and months after Plump's shot no longer was a memory
to enough to carry a vote.

When Indiana's one-class system finally died Sept. 17, 1996,
it took a person 50 or older to remember that shot, that night. Indiana and America are getting older, people are living longer, but there
are a whole lot more Hoosiers and Americans under 50 than over.

So it died with splendid symmetry.

They played 43 state tournaments.

Then they played the one that crowned Milan.

They played 43 more state tournaments.

Then they went to classes.

Milan's 1953 state finalist team included, front row (from left), Gene White, Ronnie Truitt, Ralph Preble, coach Marvin Wood, Jim Wendelman, Bob Engel and Bill Jordan. Back row, Dale Smith, Ray Craft, Bobby Plump, Kenneth Wendelman, Jim Call and Roger Schroder. (Photo courtesy Indiana High School Athletic Association)

A case could be made that the whole, beautiful Indiana basketball story peaked in that very midpoint, in the middle of the 1950s.

After Milan won in 1954, Plump was a candidate for beatification. The very next year, the first champion from Indianapolis, the first all-black champion, came along: Indianapolis Crispus Attucks, with its own star who was to be spoken of eternally ever after with reverence, Oscar Robertson.

Robertson's first varsity season ended with a semistate loss to Milan in 1954. Then, leading teams that went 62-1 over the next two years, he changed everything about the face of the tournament.

Milan was the smallest school, the smallest town, to win the championship since Thorntown in 1915. But the champions that followed Thorntown included several from points not exactly metropolitan: Lebanon, and Vincennes, and Franklin, and Martinsville, and Frankfort, and Washington, and Shelbyville, and Jasper, and Madison.

And then came Oscar, introducing Indiana to The City Game.

Oscar Robertson's number at Crispus Attucks was 43.

'We were not planning to slow it down'

Marvin Wood knew about the sophomore around whom Ray Crowe already was building a club when Milan played Crispus Attucks for a Final Four berth in 1954.

"We knew Oscar was pretty good," Wood said. "I don't think anybody knew how really good he was." He scored 22 points in what was to be his only loss in 28 lifetime Indiana tournament games.

Already by that 1954 semistate championship game, Milan and Wood had a reputation for slowing play when it was advantageous. It didn't happen often, but it was part of the repertoire.

"When we played Crispus Attucks, I know they felt we were going to hold the ball right away," Wood said. No, Wood told his players, "we're going to see what we can do with our regular style. If it doesn't work, then we'll have to shift gears."

Milan 65, Crispus Attucks 52.

"It worked pretty well," Wood said.

The Milan legend says Wood knew he had to slow play to beat Muncie Central in the championship game. The legend is right only in retrospect.

"We were not planning to slow it down," Wood said. "But we were hurting."

Bob Engel, the one Milan player considered big enough and good enough to be a major-college prospect before The Miracle, had developed back problems. He scored just three points when Milan won its way to the championship game by beating Terre Haute Gerstmeyer, 60-48. That was in the second afternoon game, and semifinal-round games then were scheduled at 1 and 2:15 p.m. More commonly, the second game started around 2:45 and ended after 4. Whatever time it finished, the championship game started at 8:15. Wood went into the game knowing one of his biggest players, perhaps his best player, was not going to play much.

"Then early in the (final) game, Plump was run over," Wood said. "He was playing in pain."

That's his *two* best players.

"I felt, hey, we have to do everything we can to conserve what energy we have to give us a chance at the end of the game.

Celebrating their State Championship are Milan cheerleaders (from left) Marjorie Ent, Virginia Voss and Patty Bohlke, and players Bobby Plump, Gene White, Ray Craft, Bob Engel and Ronnie Truitt. (Photo courtesy Indiana Basketball Hall of Fame)

"We slowed it down earlier than we ever had."

Down 28-26 with 7:41 to play, Milan stopped play altogether. Plump's four teammates moved out of the way, and he held the ball, almost motionless, for more than four minutes. Muncie Central coach Jay McCreary, his team leading, motioned for his players to back off, to let the clock run down. Milan was the team going against the norm. No one, ever, had stalled when behind in the fourth quarter of a championship game. Wood coolly let the clock run down to under four minutes, to nearly 3½ minutes, and he signaled for a timeout.

The game went back to a normal pace, but now Muncie Central was edgy. Milan caught up on a Ray Craft basket, went ahead on two Plump free throws. Muncie Central tied the game, 30-30, with a basket by its star, Gene Flowers.

With 18 seconds to go, Milan came out of a timeout, moved the other four to the deep left side, and Plump, just above the foul circle, held the ball. Jimmy Barnes, a superb athlete who just about matched Plump's 5-10 size, was the Bearcat isolated one-on-one with Plump. At 0:05, Plump started a drive to his right, pulled up, and sank the 16-foot shot that formally, noisily handed the game over to history.

A perfect movie script

Jimmy Chitwood did the same thing — replicated the drama, the stall, the shot — in *Hoosiers*, and a whole nation exulted.

No sports film has touched Americans so profoundly, so lastingly as the 1986 work of two former Indiana University buddies, writer Angelo Pizzo and director David Anspaugh. New York Yankees owner George Steinbrenner says he has watched it more than 100 times. Teams throughout America, not just in basketball, use it on the brink of competition to absorb its inspiring message: underdogs can win!

Pizzo grew up in Bloomington, Anspaugh in Decatur. Neither was old enough to remember the Milan experience. They were from the legions who came later, two who grew up like Young Tom from Camelot who heard tales from their own King Arthurs and had their own charge:

Don't let it be forgot, that once there was a shot . . .

Pizzo and Anspaugh did their part.

A freshman to build around

So on this night a new season's Milan Indians took on a county rival, South Ripley.

There was no South Ripley in Milan's glory years — and the plural "years" is correct; not everyone knows or remembers that the '54 Milan Miracle started with a stunning trip to the Final Four in 1953, the real introduction of Milan, Wood, Plump, Craft, etc., into Hoosier familiarity.

The Cross Plains Bobcats, New Marion Panthers and Versailles (remember this is Indiana: that's ver-*sails*) Lions didn't come together to form South Ripley High's Raiders until 1966. Some of Holton's Warhorses joined three years later. The four of them together — Cross Plains, New Marion, Versailles and Holton — went 0-6 against Milan in 1954. Versailles, a good team that shared its home gym with Milan that year, lost four of those games.

Today, the merged school is still not huge, its four-year enrollment 414, just enough more than Milan's 349 to put South Ripley in the bottom third of Class 2A and leave Milan among the bigger Class 1A schools a year hence.

Milan's 6-foot senior guard, Brad Callen, started a 19-point night with two baskets that opened an early 10-2 lead. Center Jason Henry, 6-5, pulled South Ripley even at 16 with two baskets opening the second quarter.

Ryan Hixson, a 6-3 freshman, came off the Milan bench in the first quarter and made an impact in the second. He delivered two free throws to put his team up 19-18, and Callen kept contributing. The Indians' lead reached 25-18 on its way to 30-26 at halftime.

Only at Milan would it be noticeable. The scoreboard at one point was flashing those Miracle numbers: 32-30. It was 90 seconds into the second half this night, and for a time it seemed a harbinger of bad things. From there, South Ripley guard Doug Meyer's three-point play started a six-point run to a 36-32 Raiders lead.

Milan led 43-42 early in the fourth quarter when Hixson turned a rebound into a basket, then a free throw. The lead was just 49-47 when the freshman hit two more free throws. When Milan led late and South Ripley pressed, coach Randy Combs put Hixson in the backcourt and his daring with football-type bullet passes helped make the press ineffective. Hixson closed a 10-point night with two more free throws, Milan's last points in a 59-52 victory.

In the stands, Schroder — Milan to the core but a highly successful career coach himself, particularly at Indianapolis Marshall — nodded a silent approval of Hixson. "He's definitely a prospect," said Schroder, who was introduced before the game, *pro forma* for a returning Miracle player.

By the next game, Hixson was starting. He ended the season as the Indians' scoring leader, 13 a game with a high of 32. "He's going to be a special player," Combs said. "He's something to build around. We've got some other good young kids and a couple of big kids in the class ahead of him. He's not going to have to be a post player. I'm going to be able to play him wherever we need to play him. He handles the ball, he's a real good passer, he plays in the post well, he sees the floor real well against a press — he's just versatile.

"We're going to be better next year than we were this year, and the next year a little better, on down the road. When you're building a program, that's what you want."

'This place is unbelievable'

Combs is a name with some history in Milan, too. Just three days before this game, Wood and seven of the 1954 players had returned to Milan to be pallbearers at the funeral of 81-year-old Marc Combs. The Pierceville four (Plump, Schroder, Butte and White) were there, plus Craft, Ken Wendelman and Rollin Cutter.

Combs, a junior high coach when the future champions came along, was credited with teaching the zone defense that Wood later called on him to install with the high school team. That happened two games into Wood's first season at Milan. "From that day forward, that's all we played," Plump said. White, another of the pallbearers, called it "Marc Combs' zone defense with Marvin Wood's adaptations."

Only by name are there any ties between Marc and Randy Combs.

Randy grew up on the opposite side of the state. He also has a state championship ring. He was a senior on the Vincennes Lincoln team that beat Anderson to win the 1981 tournament.

"I was on the team," he said. "They would have won with or without me. I knew that. I was a role player."

And he couldn't have been more thrilled to win a tournament he knew a lot about.

"My dad (Dan, a Vincennes physician who was the '81 champions' team doctor) was a basketball nut. He made sure I went to all the state tournaments and I was caught up on all the history of Indiana high school basketball. So I was fully aware of the Milan history.

"When I was an eighth-grader, I met Bobby Plump. His son, Jonathan, was on an AAU team we played."

Combs was an assistant coach at Greenfield Central when the Milan job opened three years ago. "I was under Larry Angle, just an outstanding coach," Combs said. "I could have stayed there forever.

"I thought (the championship trophy) was something that the kids would think was really neat. I got the opposite view real quick. Everything was based around '54, and kids were tired of hearing about it.

"So I tried to kill two birds with one stone: have the kids build a trophy case for the current trophies, and take all the old trophies out." The new display case directly ahead at the gym's front entrance has only trophies "won during the cycle of the kids who are in school now," Parks said. "I was trying to bring some pride into it — the kids see *their* trophies now.

"But the rumor got out that Parks was going to take the '54 trophy out and stash it up in the attic with the rest of the old trophies. Gosh almighty. Did I ever hear about it! I almost lost my job.

"Their objection? That the trophy was even being touched. There are a couple of things you don't mess with: Mother Nature and Milanites."

But he went ahead. On a side wall, to the left of the main gymnasium entrance, Parks commissioned a second display case for the '54 trophy.

The case is well lighted. Below the trophy is an account of the championship season. "I had a couple of faculty members write it," Parks said. "They tell a little bit of history and list every game. Most people never knew that a lot of those games were pretty high scoring.

"The backdrop is the center circle from the old gym," he said. It was ancient and small, capacity about 600, Schroder recalls. The '53 team played most of its games there. After the trip to the State and the return of most of the team, the '54 team played its home games about 12 miles away, in Versailles' 2,000-seat gym. Then the present Milan gym was built. "They cut up the floor of the old place and sold it," Schroder said. "I've seen a lot of it."

The pieces were there

Marvin Wood remembers the first time he stepped onto that old Milan High basketball court to do business.

It was Oct. 1, 1952, the first day of basketball practice. "I walked out on the floor," Wood said. "In this small school, we had

58 boys come out for basketball, and 50 of them were pretty good. I thought, 'What a dilemma for a small-school coach to be in. I'm going to have to cut good people. And we're still going to be a pretty young team.'

"We had more size than I ever dreamed we would have. They had experience, because most of them played at the varsity level. And we had good quickness. We had all the pieces. The problem was, could I put them together?"

The clear answer after his first season in Milan was yes, which created the second problem. The fact that his 1954 Indians had been to the Final Four once before "was a big factor" in their being cool enough and poised enough to win the championship on their revisit, Wood feels. But in the months between the 1953 Final Four, where Milan lost in the semifinals to eventual state champion South Bend Central, and the start of the next season, that wonderful rookie season for him at Milan became "a big worry for me, as a coach," Wood said.

Prior to 1953, Milan never had won even a regional tournament game. One trip to the Final Four revised all the norms.

"The people in our community were saying, 'We're going to go back and win.' I knew a lot of good things had to happen for that to take place.

"I knew our team was going to have more finesse, and more quickness. I knew we were going to be smaller. If that was going to bother, I didn't know."

He also knew he had extraordinarily sharp kids. "You have to have the people who can execute the game plan to make it work," Wood said. "They could do it. They could play fast, or they could play slow, or they could do it intermediate. Not many teams can make that adjustment."

Then came the third dilemma of the Marvin Wood career. Olympic gold medalists talk of a post-Olympics depression: I'm young, I've won a gold medal, now what? There's still a long life to lead.

What does a 26-year-old coach do for the rest of his career, after a Miracle?

"For a couple of years, it *was* tough," said Wood, who moved on from Milan after the championship to bigger schools: North Central, New Castle, Mishawaka.

"The biggest problem you have is critiquing yourself. 'Here I am at a bigger school, with more talent. Why can't I get this job done on this level?'

"Now I'm an old-timer. I look back and realize you have to have all the pieces to make it work. I never had all the pieces like I had in that little school."

The favorite of 80 percent

A matter of curiosity, Coach.

How did you — not exactly a Norman Dale, or a Gene Hackman — like *Hoosiers*?

"I had to watch it two or three times before I really got into it," Wood admitted.

"They captured something — I'm not exactly certain what it is. It wasn't the Milan story, but there were so many parallels and it was so close. And they were parallels that could happen in any small town or rural school, and people relate to it.

"I love the values that they have in there. I've used them in making a lot of talks. They're values that were good when I was a kid, and they're values that are good for the game."

The present Milan coach is familiar with the film, too.

"I've used it before," Randy Combs said.

"Eighty percent of our kids still say it's their favorite movie. We'll watch it before the tournament starts, for two reasons: to get a tournament feeling, and because it's the last year of one class."

'Never, in my wildest dreams'

After so spirited a reaction to moving a trophy, principal Parks wasn't about to misread his electorate when it came time to cast Milan's vote on the class basketball issue.

"In Milan, you're *going* to vote against it," Parks said.

He would have, anyway.

"I just don't think it's going to accomplish what they really think it will. I don't think it's going to be as much fun. And you're messing around with heritage.

"I hope they really do reevaluate in two years, as they say they're going to. I think it's going to be a financial disaster."

So why did the other school in this game, South Ripley, also vote against it?

"The tradition in Ripley County makes a difference to us," South Ripley principal Ted Ahaus said.

"The four schools in this county (Batesville and Jac-Cen-Del, plus Milan and South Ripley) have all had success. The rest of us haven't been to the Final Four like Milan but we've been up to Hinkle Fieldhouse and in the Sweet 16.

"Year in and year out there seems to be one or two good ballclubs here. Everybody knows how good Batesville has been. People across the state would not realize the only three games Jac-Cen-Del lost (in 1996-97) were to Batesville. South Ripley had outstanding teams the two years before that, but nobody knows it because they couldn't get by Batesville.

"Milan, needless to say, has had its success."

Not a lot lately. In the 43 years since the championship, Milan has been back to Hinkle Fieldhouse just once. The 1973 Indians won the sectional and regional but lost to Richmond in the semistate, 48-43.

Don't minimize that team's feat, Ahaus warns.

Ahaus. coached South Ripley to sectional and regional titles in 1981. "Heck fire, we went up there to the semistate in Hinkle Fieldhouse — that was the thrill of a lifetime for people down here," he said.

"Winning a sectional and winning a regional has been as exciting to these communities as probably anything that could happen. We know realistically at South Ripley we'll probably never win a state championship, but we'd sure like to roll into the New Castle regional and meet up with New Castle, Richmond and Connersville. We'd take our chances.

"And the one time we'd beat even one of them — that's what people talk about forever.

"Personally, I hate to see the class structure. But I felt as a school principal I should vote to reflect my school and my community. You'd be hard-pressed to find a dozen people who support it.

"I realize if we had to go into the Richmond sectional every year, we'd probably feel a little different. But the history of Ripley County basketball doesn't lead to class basketball."

Randy Combs said he has "not been in agreement with the change from the start, and I'd feel that way if I was here or anywhere else. My brother is an assistant at Vincennes. He and I argue about this back and forth. Just a couple of weeks ago he threw at me Union (Dugger) — 'if we had class basketball they'd have won a state championship.'

"I came back at him with 'I suppose because they lost the final game of the regional to the state champion, their season was a complete waste.'

"I never thought in my wildest dreams that they would change. I just never thought anybody would let it happen."

Neither did Marvin Wood, though the push for it wasn't a surprise. "They were talking about (dividing into classes) even when we won it," Wood said.

The 1950s talk that Wood mentions suggests that even though the Miracle of Milan's impact finally faded into vulnerability, it may have bought Indiana as many as 40 years of traditional tournament play.

Wood has heard that, but he would have preferred to pass the torch. "For a long time, I was almost afraid that another small school would win it," he said.

"But we've enjoyed this for 43 years now. I think the boys feel the same way I feel: it's time for someone else to come along and have the same joy that we've had.

"We had a tradition that was so rich. I cannot believe it was broken. It was thriving.

"I just can't see why they wanted to change."

6

DeKalb	72
FW Snider	54

December 21

DEKALB		FORT WAYNE SNIDER
None	**STATE CHAMPIONSHIP**	None
None as DeKalb (Auburn, 1949)	**TIMES IN FINAL FOUR**	None
2 as DeKalb: 1983, 1997. Others in corporation: Auburn 6: 1938, 1945, 1949, 1950, 1951, 1952	**REGIONAL CHAMPIONSHIPS**	None
17 as DeKalb: first, 1968; 5 in '90s, most recent, 1997. Others in corporation, 21: Ashley 2, 1946, 1965; Auburn 18 (first 1925; last 1955); Waterloo, 1960.	**SECTIONAL CHAMPIONSHIPS**	3: 1967, 1972, 1982
Formed 1967 (Ashley, Auburn, Waterloo)	**CONSOLIDATIONS**	Formed 1965; none
No	**VOTE ON CHANGE TO CLASSES**	No
4A. (972; 75th of 95 in class)	**1997-98 CLASS (ENROLLMENT)**	4A. (1,477; 27th of 95 in class)
3A: Angola; 2A, Eastside, Garrett; 1A, Fremont, Hamilton. DeKalb site and 1997 champion	**1996-97 SECTIONAL OPPONENTS (1997-98 CLASSIFICATION)**	4A: Fort Wayne North, Fort Wayne Northrop; 3A: Carroll, Fort Wayne Concordia, Fort Wayne Dwenger
Columbia City, East Noble, Fort Wayne North, Fort Wayne Snider	**1997-98 SECTIONAL OPPONENTS**	Columbia City, DeKalb, East Noble, Fort Wayne North, Fort Wayne Northrop
26-4 (won sectional, regional; lost to Kokomo in semistate final, 69-46)	**FINAL RECORD 1996-97**	5-16 (lost to Fort Wayne Dwenger in sectional semifinal, 70-62)

Recker and Schooley: 49 and '49

In bold red letters 17 cement blocks high, 19 counting the black shading, one end of the handsome DeKalb High School basketball arena shouts DEKALB, and the other answers back BARONS. Now, factually, the fellow for whom this northeastern Indiana county was named — and thus this consolidated school in the county's center — was Johann Kalb, a German. The De part surely stems from the 20 years he fought in a German regiment of the French Army, or from his traveling to the American colonies with the French volunteers headed by Marquis de Lafayette. There's also some question whether he was a baron.

But he was an American hero. As a major general, he at one time commanded the American Army in the South during the Revolutionary War. After an American general took over his command, the 59-year-old Kalb died courageously, wounded 11 times in a terrible defeat in South Carolina.

DeKalb, as a high school basketball team, had a much better time in 1996-97.

Cliff Hawkins had been aiming at this season for five years. This was the year when DeKalb, in its 30-year history never a major factor in the state tournament, truly had a shot.

And, yes, Hawkins said, the possibility that a first DeKalb state championship could come in the last open tournament did sweeten the situation.

"Oh, yes it does," Hawkins said. "To have the best player in Indiana on our team right now — you can believe there has been a thought about that.

"It will be a special, special finish. I've talked to a lot of coaches who have won one. Steve Witty (coach of the Ben Davis teams that won state championships in 1995 and '96) is a friend of mine.

"But we just want to keep this team improving, a step at a time."

"Mr. Basketball" votes were three months away from even being cast, let alone counted, when Hawkins pronounced his man, 6-foot-5 senior guard Luke Recker, No. 1. Not many doubters left DeKalb's gym after the Saturday night in December when Fort Wayne Snider tried to handle Recker and the Barons.

Snider, named for a revered Fort Wayne high school principal, had answered the city's overcrowded schools problem when it was built and opened in 1965, two years before neighbors Auburn, Waterloo and Ashley went together to form DeKalb.

Snider's all-time best athlete was Indiana's best of at least the '80s. Rod Woodson was a solid basketball player for Snider. He was so good a state hurdles champion that he was a legitimate Olympic prospect. And his best sport of all was football. When the National Football League named its 75-year all-time team in 1996, cornerback Rod Woodson of the Pittsburgh Steelers — and the Fort Wayne Snider Panthers, not to mention the Purdue Boilermakers, a three-team progression in which he never had to change from black-and-gold — was one of the few still-active NFL players on it.

Snider won a state track co-championship before Woodson, won the big-school football championship after him, when its leader was a running back named Vaughn Dunbar who went on to be a consensus All-American at Indiana and an NFL player.

But R. Nelson Snider High School on this December night at DeKalb had nobody who could guard Luke Recker. The job went first to 5-9 junior Tim Mustapha. The other starting guard, senior Vince McKinley, was 5-8.

"I knew they weren't going to be very big, as they defended him," Hawkins said later. "In the back of my mind, I had already thought of this. I was hoping that if it progressed this way, we'd take care of it. Get it out of the way."

For the record

He spoke on the night when Recker scored 49 points, setting a school record.

Probably more high school players have scored 49 points (in a 32-minute game, remember) than have done what Recker did in this game. He scored in double figures each quarter: 14 the first (his team actually trailed after it, 16-15), 12 the second (game over: 40-22 at halftime), 10 the third (now it was 57-43, Snider on a game comeback try that was to get no closer), and 13 in the fourth.

Yes, Hawkins admitted, he did let Recker stay in longer than he normally would have — than he had on several previous nights when the record of 47 set a few years earlier by Shannon Carey might have been threatened.

This night, Hawkins took a timeout with 4:10 to go, the Barons' lead 65-48, and brought his team in on the night's only unsettled issue. "I told them Luke had 42," Hawkins said. "(Senior forward Luke) Barnett said: 'How many does he need for the record?' I told them, and Barnett said, 'We'll do it.' "

"Coach left it up to the team," Recker said. "They all said, 'We want you to have it.' That says a lot for my team."

DeKalb ran a play that posted Recker inside against one of those smaller guards. Lob, easy basket, 44 points.

The Barons freed Recker for a 3-point shot on a night when he hit seven of them. This one missed, and when the rebound was deflected out of bounds by Snider, Recker got another 3-point crack and missed again.

Next time downcourt, he hit that seventh 3. Now, 47 points, record tied, three minutes left.

"I kept hoping people were aware of what was happening," Hawkins said. He knew they weren't; with the game decided, the crowd had stilled into a play-it-out ennui. "I could have stood up and talked in my normal voice, and they could have heard me," Hawkins said. "I'd have said: 'This is what we're doing.' "

He didn't, but with just under 50 seconds to go, Recker went to work, one-on-one, against 6-foot Terry Collins. Terry will be the worker, not the defender, on a whole lot of these situations over the next few years. He's a freshman with the looks of a player around whom Snider coach Steve Riley can do the same kind of building Hawkins did 'round Recker.

This time, Recker beat him for the basket that gave him the record and a free-throw chance that could have rounded things out neatly at 50.

It didn't come close. "I was mentally exhausted," Recker said later, laughing and just a touch embarrassed at how inept that last free throw, on this night of peaked excellence, had been.

With 39 seconds left, Hawkins brought Recker out of the game while the now-apprised crowd roared its appreciation.

The chemistry was right

Another year, wearing another uniform, Jim Schooley heard cheers like those.

Auburn was by far the biggest of the three schools brought together to form DeKalb — also by far the best-known in Indiana high school basketball, in part because of Jim Schooley.

The only time a school from DeKalb County had made the Final Four — the *only* time, counting the three schools merged into DeKalb High, the three in the county who have spurned merger (Garrett, Eastside and Hamilton), and six other schools swallowed up in some consolidation through the years — was in 1949, when Auburn did it. Keith Showalter was the coach, and his star was the school's valedictorian and first Indiana All-Star, 6-5 senior center Jim Schooley.

"When I was a kid in Auburn, basically all we thought about was the basketball tournament," Schooley said. "We'd pretend we were playing in the state finals. Every year Auburn would maybe win the sectional and get beat in the regional. We'd weep a little bit about that and think about how, boy, we'd do it when we had our chances.

"Showalter took us to see the state finals when I was a junior. Little did we dream . . . "

A year later, Auburn won 26 games. In regular-season games, the Red Devils beat all three usual Fort Wayne powers — North,

Jim Schooley outlines some scientific formulas for his teammates. Schooley led Auburn to the 1949 State Finals, won an NCAA title at Indiana University and went on to become a distinguished scientist at the National Bureau of Standards. (Photo courtesy Indiana Basketball Hall of Fame)

South and Central. "We considered ourselves 'city champs,' " Schooley said. In the Fort Wayne regional, Auburn did it again, beating Central in the championship game to reach the Sweet 16. There, at storied Muncie Fieldhouse, Auburn thumped tourney-wise Kokomo, 54-43, then New Castle, 45-43, and the unimaginable had happened.

Auburn was going to the State.

Schooley hasn't forgotten, never will forget, that trip.

"In the movie *Hoosiers*, when those kids go into Butler Fieldhouse and look around, and their jaws drop open — there's nobody there, it just looks like a big old barn — that's exactly the way I felt," Schooley said.

"I was watching the movie with my wife, and when they did that, I just started giggling. Mary Alice said, 'What's going on?' I said, 'That's *it*. That's exactly it.'

"We were scared to death."

In the fourth quarter against Jasper, Auburn led 42-36. Jasper, with a closing burst, pulled around the Red Devils to win, 53-48. Hours later Jasper upset Madison, 62-61, and entered history as the team with the worst regular-season record ever to win the championship — up to then, or in the 48 years since. Jasper had been 11-9.

Schooley sat in the stands and watched that championship game. "I was a sad apple that night," he said. "My world had stopped one or two victories short.

"But Showalter said, 'You stay with me tonight. I want you right beside me.' "

Showalter had a pretty good idea what was going to happen. After Jasper was done celebrating and the championship and runner-up awards were handed out, Jim Schooley of Auburn was announced as winner of the Arthur L. Trester Award for Mental Attitude. It's an award of enormous prestige, given annually since 1917 in recognition of academics, and sportsmanship, and basketball excellence. The winner the year before Schooley, Lee Hamilton of Evansville Central, was to become a longtime Congressman, at one time House Foreign Relations committee chairman.

Schooley did his own part to distinguish the Trester Award. He went on to Indiana University and earned two prized rings: one as a member of Indiana's 1953 NCAA champions, another from Phi Beta Kappa.

And he continued to move right along. "I had decided when I was in the seventh grade that I wanted to be a research chemist," he said. "I had no idea what it was, but my dad was a high school science teacher — chemistry, physics and the higher mathematics."

Robert True Schooley fought in World War I with the Army's Rainbow Division. "He was in all the major battles, as were most of the Rainbow Division," Jim said. "He went through a chlorine gas attack. His health wasn't great. He died at 51 of a coronary. I was a sophomore in high school then. I always regretted that I didn't get to take his science classes."

Jim Schooley took that passion to IU. "I was a mediocre basketball player," he said. "As it turned out, my size was almost my only asset." He twinkles over a truism. "About the only thing I can say is in '54 when they had everybody back but me, they didn't win the NCAA championship."

By then he was on his way to a master's degree at California-Berkeley, where he earned a doctorate in nuclear studies. For 30 years, Dr. James Schooley was a scientist at the National Bureau of Standards in the Washington area. By retirement in 1990, he had become America's ranking authority on thermometry.

"People wouldn't imagine that there would be any scientific research to do in measurement of temperature, but there is," he said. NASA, hospitals, oil companies, chemistry companies all depended on the findings of Schooley and colleagues. They measured temperature "in unusual circumstances: in space, or ball bearings, or gyroscopes, or pigs, whatever," he said, "on an international scale for temperature — in length, mass, time and frequency, probably two dozen areas." At meetings in Paris to write a new temperature scale, the United States representative was Dr. James Schooley, Auburn High '49.

"Basketball, both at the high school and college level, has been a cornerstone for who I am," he said. "It really is true — I think back and remember things that were told to me by both Branch McCracken (at IU) and Keith Showalter. Showalter said, 'You may get beat, but you don't have to quit.' 'You fear none, but you respect them all.' Later on, that applies to a lot of things.

"For me, both at the high school and the college level, basketball was a dream that came true."

In May, Schooley went back to Auburn to say thank you. McIntosh High School, where Schooley went and 59 other high school classes also did, was scheduled for demolition. Schooley, who had one B in four years of study in that building, came in from Gaithersburg, Md., to join in an Auburn alumni reunion planned as the building's farewell tribute.

It was a happier time than that. The building got a reprieve, given a new assignment. The reunion introduced Luke Recker to Auburn's Final Four starters, all of them back. And from somewhere in the building's final hours as a school, someone found a long-lost treasure house of trophies, pictures and banners from the Schooley-Final Four years. The era lives.

Goal: 'To win it all,' twice

Recker was to become DeKalb's first Indiana All-Star, the whole county's first "Mr. Basketball."

But on that Saturday night in December, his thoughts were of the assignment dead ahead. DeKalb was to play in the Hall of Fame Classic at New Castle, with fellow powers Anderson, Batesville and Madison-Grant.

Hawkins called his team together in the locker room after the Snider victory and pointed to their opportunity at New Castle. "A few years ago, we were 342 out of the 384 Indiana high schools in the Sagarin (computer) ratings," he said. "Now you're fifth. You have come so far. And we're still developing."

That 342 part was true, he said, his inheritance when he arrived in 1992 as the school's new coach. "Our first year, we started preaching excellence. Andy Schmidt got us started. He won the 3-point championship the first year they had it. Then he hit the baseline shot with 42 seconds to go that won us our first sectional.

"Right now, I don't know if we're the fifth-best team in the state. Because we have Luke and we've won 31 out of our last 33, everybody thinks we're pretty good. We're still developing every day. We're not there yet.

"Luke is one of the constants. He can dribble, pass, shoot it, defend. His shot has continued to develop. He hasn't had his 3 going yet this year. Tonight, he got seven of them. That's the most he's ever shot.

"He is an athlete. You can see where he's going to fit right in at IU.

"The summer of his eighth-grade year, he played with our varsity. I knew those guys liked him. He never played JV ball, I brought him off the bench on the varsity right away.

"The sixth game of the year, I talked to one of my seniors, Nate Tatman. I said, 'Nate, you probably know why I brought you in.' He said, 'Yeah, Recker needs to start, Coach. I can come off the bench.'

"I'll never forget Nate for that, as far as understanding your role on a team.

"Luke handled it great. And his teammates were glad to have him. The East Noble game he dunked it on a break. That was our first dunk since I've been here. Boy, I don't know how many he has had since.

"This is Luke's team now. His leadership is just phenomenal. He understands leadership. He knows how to bring out the best in everybody. Our kids genuinely like to be around him, and they're genuinely glad he got the record.

"Luke plays year-round basketball. He played baseball through his eighth-grade year. At one time, he wanted to be a major-league pitcher.

"But this is what he wanted to do. And his boyhood dream was to be able to play at Indiana."

Recker announced for Indiana as a sophomore, Bob Knight's earliest commitment ever.

"Our goal is to win it all," Recker said. "And then I want to go down to IU and win the national championship.

"I'm not worried about going out and scoring 30 every night here. It's the same situation next year. They've got great players there now. It's a perfect situation for me. I'm just going in to contribute any way I can."

And yes, he said, he did have a feeling about a switch to class basketball, even though it would not affect him.

"I just totally disagree with it. Indiana high school basketball, the way it has been forever, is just wonderful. It's a great tradition. I think it's going to spoil it a lot.

"But Indiana basketball is still Indiana basketball. We'll still have the great crowds and great rivalries."

Hawkins admitted, "Deep down inside, if I look at things realistically, I can understand why people want this done. But in Indiana, basketball tradition has been so special.

"I understand the thoughts behind it. I will support it. But, from a personal standpoint, my moves — from Caston to Tri-Central to Greenfield to DeKalb — were because I wanted to get in a position to compete.

"We have something special in Indiana, and I think we have done something to damage it."

Schooley shared their regret.

"I wrote a letter to the IHSAA suggesting they poll the players and give them some kind of weight as opposed to the principals," he said.

"There just has been such a wonderful history of teams from little schools doing well in the tournament."

Auburn, with its 1949 enrollment of 296, would come to mind.

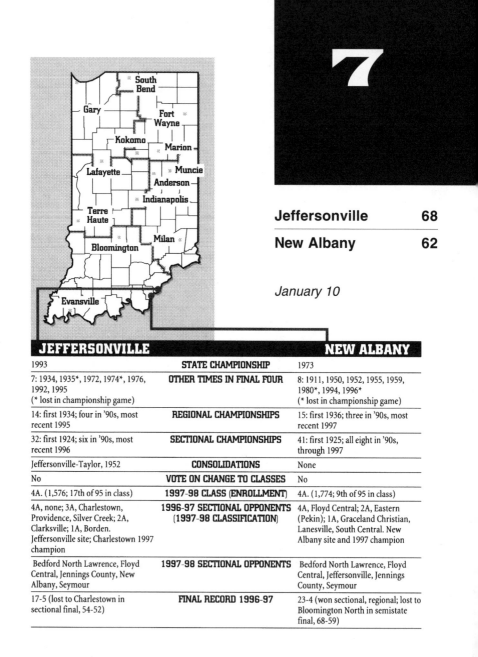

7

Jeffersonville	68
New Albany	62

January 10

JEFFERSONVILLE		NEW ALBANY
1993	**STATE CHAMPIONSHIP**	1973
7: 1934, 1935*, 1972, 1974*, 1976, 1992, 1995 (* lost in championship game)	**OTHER TIMES IN FINAL FOUR**	8: 1911, 1950, 1952, 1955, 1959, 1980*, 1994, 1996* (* lost in championship game)
14: first 1934; four in '90s, most recent 1995	**REGIONAL CHAMPIONSHIPS**	15: first 1936; three in '90s, most recent 1997
32: first 1924; six in '90s, most recent 1996	**SECTIONAL CHAMPIONSHIPS**	41: first 1925; all eight in '90s, through 1997
Jeffersonville-Taylor, 1952	**CONSOLIDATIONS**	None
No	**VOTE ON CHANGE TO CLASSES**	No
4A. (1,576; 17th of 95 in class)	**1997-98 CLASS (ENROLLMENT)**	4A. (1,774; 9th of 95 in class)
4A, none; 3A, Charlestown, Providence, Silver Creek; 2A, Clarksville; 1A, Borden. Jeffersonville site; Charlestown 1997 champion	**1996-97 SECTIONAL OPPONENTS (1997-98 CLASSIFICATION)**	4A, Floyd Central; 2A, Eastern (Pekin); 1A, Graceland Christian, Lanesville, South Central. New Albany site and 1997 champion
Bedford North Lawrence, Floyd Central, Jennings County, New Albany, Seymour	**1997-98 SECTIONAL OPPONENTS**	Bedford North Lawrence, Floyd Central, Jeffersonville, Jennings County, Seymour
17-5 (lost to Charlestown in sectional final, 54-52)	**FINAL RECORD 1996-97**	23-4 (won sectional, regional; lost to Bloomington North in semistate final, 68-59)

River
Rivals

In 1948, when this series was a mere 38 years and 60 games old, Jeffersonville and New Albany were semifinalists in the sectional tournament. In opposite brackets.

Jeff played first. The Jeffersonville coach let the score mount against outmanned Henryville. And then he called a halt. A long halt. Jeffersonville, before closing out the final seconds of a 58-41 victory, took all of its allotted timeouts, then an extra one at the cost of a technical foul. Then another, and another — 17 extra timeouts, 17 technical fouls, 17 delays before New Albany could get onto the court to start the second semifinal game against Silver Creek, let alone get off it after a 51-40 victory and go somewhere to rest before the championship game.

They called coach Ed Denton "Dirty Ed" after that one, and just this winter they inducted him into the Indiana Basketball Hall of Fame — not for that, obviously; he also was an outstanding player for Silver Creek and Jeffersonville and later played at Indiana. His Hall of Fame election was announced just in time for him to be brought onto the Bill Johnson Arena court for an ovation from the 6,000 who, on a bitterly cold January night, packed the place to see these two rivals play for the 127th time.

The Jeffersonville coach took a timeout, then another, in this game, too. Different reason.

Both Mike Broughton of Jeffersonville and Don Unruh of New Albany know this is in many ways their easiest night of the year, and in others, the hardest. Motivation is not a big concern. Exposing passionate supporters to defeat and a guaranteed two months of neighbors' boasts is a big concern — to job security, if repeated often enough.

A year before, Jeffersonville was ranked No. 10 in the state and New Albany was No. 1 when Jeff went to the Bulldogs' arena and won. Here they were again, Jeffersonville No. 10 and New Albany No. 1 — the perfect time to talk about revenge, eh, Coach Unruh?

"The game itself takes care of that," Unruh said. "We don't have to go back to anything that's happened before. We don't even have to say we're playing Jeff.

"Everybody knows it."

Everybody also knew that whatever vengeance was needed came when New Albany advanced to the 1996 state championship game and Jeffersonville had to sit and watch. That's the kind of one-upmanship each has been carrying out on the other the last few Marches, to the enormous benefit of both programs in cities that sit side by side just across the Ohio River from Louisville.

Championships hiked the ante

As hot as it always has been, the series leaped to an all-new level in 1973 when New Albany became the first of the two to win the state championship.

Forever they had been making runs at it. Jeffersonville's 1935 team was on the verge of becoming not just the state champion but, at 31-0, the first to win it unbeaten, till Anderson spoiled everything in the championship game, 23-17. That's going back a long while; 1935 was the last year basketball followed every basket with a center jump. It also was the last year Indiana brought 16 teams to the State and picked a champion in two days. That required three games in one day for the two finalists. The next year, Indiana invented semistates and the Final Four concept that the NCAA didn't come up with for another 17 years.

New Albany coach Don Unruh (Photo courtesy Indiana High School Athletic Association, ©Mark Wick)

New Albany was a semifinalist in the very first tournament, in 1911. The Bulldogs got back to the State four times in the '50s but never won a game there. Jeffersonville waited 37 years to return after that 1935 disappointment but when it did in 1972 it didn't survive the semifinal round.

Then New Albany won in '73. Jeffersonville tried to match that right away, returning to the Final Four in '74 (losing in the final game to Fort Wayne Northrop, 59-56) and in '76 (losing in the semifinals to ultimate champion Marion, 49-47).

In the '90s, the rivalry reached an apex. Five straight years, the five leading up to this one, either Jeffersonville or New Albany was Southern Indiana's representative in the Final Four. In 1993, Jeffersonville won. And in 1996, New Albany came as close as a non-champion can. In Unruh's first season as head coach, the Bulldogs fought reigning champion Ben Davis dead-even through regulation time and two overtimes with thoughts of a third overtime till the Giants' Jeff Poisel put up a 3-pointer that swished at the buzzer.

"When I came here in '90, this was a terrible game," Broughton said. "We won by a couple of points, but neither team played very well. Everyone kinda sat on their hands.

"When we made those runs to State, and they made theirs, it became a bigger deal. Both teams have gotten better. In anything, if one rises up, the other has to catch up."

Butterfly night

Mike Broughton remembers when big game to him meant Hebron against Kouts clear at the other end of the state. Mike played for his dad at Hebron. Now Josh Broughton plays for his dad at Jeffersonville.

And New Albany defines big game.

Tim Gray is a Jeffersonville sophomore with a grand basketball background. His father, Kevin, was a good college basketball player, then an assistant coach under Wimp Sanderson at Alabama. Kevin's job was to recognize good prospects when he saw them. Now he's a father with a chance that he has one.

Tim Gray doesn't start for Jeffersonville. The day before the big game, Broughton suggested to him that he might be better off playing in the junior varsity game, the preliminary. "There's a lot of people out there," Broughton told Gray. "I want you to smile when the game's over, no matter what. You can go down and play JV and be the star.

"He said, 'Coach, I'm not going to be sad when this one's over.'

"He's a game guy."

It was, of course, a coaching ploy. "I was trying to get him fired up a little bit for practice," Broughton said. "He's very proficient on the offensive end. He needs some work on the defensive end."

But the part about the "people out there" he meant. "A kid 15, 16, 17 walks out there with 5,000 people — it's a difficult thing," Broughton said. "You get pumped up. It's a special game.

"In the big scheme of things, it's bragging rights for a couple of months and then you start again, but you walk out there and every seat's sold . . . it makes you a little tight.

"It's one of the neat things about Indiana basketball."

The butterflies Broughton hinted at for sophomore Gray instead attacked like winged piranhas against Broughton's upperclassmen.

Mike Broughton

Darren Ellis slipped inside the big and athletic New Albany team for a Jeffersonville basket in the first minute. The Red Devils didn't get another one for more than five minutes. Twelve times in that stretch Jeffersonville had the basketball; 10 of those times the Red Devils turned it over to New Albany's quick hands and pressuring presence. Broughton watched all that calamity occurring around him and after the seventh turnover, took a timeout. Only 56 seconds later, he took another, the turnover toll at 10 then.

"The first one we talked about how we needed to relax — I just said some things to get them to smile," Broughton said. "Then I wanted to call another timeout and set up our changes.

"I've done that before — two timeouts in a row, because they're so uptight they're not going to listen to you the first time. They glue in the second time: 'Man, what did he call *another* one for? This must be important.' "

It was getting that way. New Albany hadn't even taken on a No. 1 look yet but still led 10-2. "I had to stop the run," Broughton said. "I wasn't going to let them get out 10 or 12 or 14."

A 3-point basket by the best of Broughton's guards, senior Kyle Bixler, cut the New Albany lead to 10-7 by the end of the quarter. But 15 seconds before the quarter ended, Bixler committed his third foul and sat down. Still, Jeffersonville got to halftime even at 23 because young Gray sniped a 3-point basket with 25 seconds left.

It was a half with 28 turnovers worth of ugliness, 17 by Jeffersonville, 11 by the poll-confirmed best team in the state.

The second half was New Albany-Jeffersonville basketball.

New Albany opened with a surge — three baskets by guard Ricky Wright, a 3-pointer by Marcus Frazier, a steal and layup by 6-6 all-state forward Chad Hunter, the most prominent player back from the state runner-up team.

Jeffersonville was playing well enough to stay close, then catch up at 40 when deft passing pulled the New Albany zone to the right and freed Bixler for a 3 from the left side.

Jeffersonville led 43-42 in the last half-minute of the third quarter when sophomore Gray went one-on-one with his man along the baseline and scored. Opening the fourth quarter, Gray was caught in a two-man trap in the deep right corner. "Smart" these days is reacting to such emergencies by burning a timeout. Much, much smarter was Gray's move splitting the two defenders for a surprise drive to the basket and a sudden 47-42 lead.

New Albany got within 57-56 with two minutes left, but Bixler's senior savvy was showing by then. He kept the basketball, drew the fouls and hit five of six free throws that made No. 10 Jeffersonville a winner over No. 1 New Albany one more time, 68-62.

A team of coaches' kids

Nothing against Mike Broughton, you understand, but Kyle Bixler had hoped to be playing for someone else. Dreamed of it, till his dad, Mark, the Jeffersonville coach, developed a brain tumor and died.

"Yeah, I did," Bixler said. "I didn't have that chance, but now I'm playing *for* him.

"I wouldn't be out here if it weren't for him."

His memory of his father "in a basketball context is just his dedication and desire to win. I think they found (the tumor) in '87 or '88. He was coaching up to the day he died."

That was in 1990, and Kyle was 11, "in my fifth-grade year." It wasn't hard for him to stay with basketball, he said. "I'd been playing all my life. I know that's what he would have wanted me to do."

And so senior Kyle Bixler was there when he absolutely had to be in the final minutes, after the early fouls took him out of another crucial stretch. "I probably fouled two out of those first three," he said, a grinning semiconcession, "but I went out and the other guys stepped up."

New Albany-game nerves — "a little bit more than a different game" — may have had something to do with that early sloppiness, Bixler said. "We knew we had to get over that. They didn't get that far ahead of us. We just had to stay calm and take better care of it." He had started working on that the day before, when he followed Broughton's JV psyching with a conversation of his own with Gray. The message: "This would be something he's never been a part of before. I doubt if he believed it, but he really stepped up."

Fouls were more of a plus than a minus for Jeffersonville. "We really attacked their inside," Broughton said. "We had Bixler in foul trouble, but they had Hunter and (Reggie) Wheeler in foul trouble (three fouls each before halftime). We felt we could take it at them and they weren't so prone to smash it down our throats."

Wheeler drew his fourth on a charge early in the third quarter, and his fifth just 39 seconds after he had re-entered to start the fourth quarter. An outstanding player, he didn't score a point in the game, didn't get even a shot in his abbreviated second half.

The effect was to make Hunter all the more cautious, with good reason. "If I'd been on the other side, I've have been saying to him, 'Don't foul,' " Broughton said. "Our inside kids got a lot more action."

A junior reserve, 6-4 Damien McDonald, was one of those benefiting inside players. He had 10 points and Gray nine in a spread-out Jeffersonville scoring attack that Bixler led with 13. Hunter had 20 and Wright 18 for New Albany, and Wheeler that painful zero.

"If Gray and McDonald play well coming off the bench, we're pretty good," Broughton said. "We've struggled getting them to go the speed we want to play." Gray, at 6-3 and 200 pounds, will get speedier as he gets slimmer. "He has lost 10 pounds," Broughton said. "I think he's a lot tougher mentally. I told him after the game, 'Good call, not going to the JVs.' "

Kevin Gray knows his son needs only one coach. A year ago, Kevin had Tim playing at his own alma mater, Louisville Manual. The move across the river to Jeffersonville clearly had Broughton in mind. "His dad has been great," Broughton said. "He just said: 'Here. He's on your team. Teach him.' "

It's a team of coaches' kids. When Bixler was out, Josh Broughton was the most effective player his dad had in making the passes that made the inside game work.

Dad noticed.

"Being a little smaller, Josh has had to be fundamentally sound to play at this level. He can pass the ball as well as any guy I've ever had. He's a survivor. I think that will help him in life.

"The other day after we finished half the season, I told him, 'We've only got a couple of months together. This is the most special time in my life, having you play for me.' It really is. Nobody can ever take away what's in your heart."

'We've voted in mediocrity'

Gray the Elder was thinking of environment as well as coaching when he picked Tim's locale. "The enthusiasm, the spirit, the atmosphere — for high school ball, it's the best," he said of the Indiana-side approach. "Far and away the best. You won't find it anywhere else."

Broughton worries that the change to classes could damage that.

"There was a tournament atmosphere here tonight," he said. "These rivalries are what make it. Now, we'll all be going different directions.

"You've got Jeff-New Albany, but you've also got Clarksville, Providence, Silver Creek — all these kids mingled together. After a couple of years those kids won't even play on the playground together. Maybe Jeff and New Albany will, but the small-school kids will say, 'We don't even play them in grade school anymore.'

"No matter what anybody in the IHSAA office says, I really feel the kids who are competing, the ones it is for, don't want to be separated. It was one of the saddest moments I've had in my education career when they went to this class system. People say, 'That's because you're at Jeffersonville.' I played at a small school and I've coached at small schools and big schools (Hebron, Rushville and Castle before Jeffersonville).

"We won the sectional my senior year, the first one for Hebron in 20 years. That was as big a moment, in my memory, as when I coached and won the state championship. You did something no one else has been able to do.

"There are all kinds of levels for that. It all feels the same. That 1973 team picture is still on the wall at Hebron.

"They say there can't be another Milan. I wish some of those people who voted had been at the semistate the year we won the state championship. The final game we beat White River Valley by two points, and that was our toughest game in the whole tournament." In the 1998 sectional, White River Valley will be playing in Class A.

"We've voted in mediocrity. We've killed rivalries. Kentucky people just laugh — how silly can we be."

It didn't work

It's hard to imagine *this* rivalry dying. "It is a neat game," Broughton said. "In '93, there were 10 Division I players in this game."

Jeffersonville's victory in this one made the series standing 64-63.

You maybe wondered how that 1948 game came out after Ed Denton's 17 technicals.

New Albany was a better team. The Bulldogs had won the regular-season game, 41-31. Denton became "Dirty Ed" working for just enough of an edge to make that up.

New Albany won, 53-31.

That's as good a game as any to pinpoint as the one that, so far, has the balance tilted in New Albany's favor.

8

North Central	74
Ben Davis	62

January 24

NORTH CENTRAL		BEN DAVIS
None	**STATE CHAMPIONSHIP**	Two: 1995, 1996
None	**OTHER TIMES IN FINAL FOUR**	Two: 1993*, 1994 (* lost in championship game)
1979	**REGIONAL CHAMPIONSHIPS**	Six: first 1988; five in '90s, most recent 1996
6: first 1973; three in '90s, most recent 1997	**SECTIONAL CHAMPIONSHIPS**	14: first 1935; six in '90s, consecutively through 1997
Formed 1956	**CONSOLIDATIONS**	Formed 1915
Yes	**VOTE ON CHANGE TO CLASSES**	No
4A. (2,414; 2nd of 95 in class)	**1997-98 CLASS (ENROLLMENT)**	4A. (2,798; highest in state
4A, Indianapolis Broad Ripple; Lawrence Central, Lawrence North; 1A, Indiana Deaf School, Park Tudor. North Central site and 1997 champion	**1996-97 SECTIONAL OPPONENTS (1997-98 CLASSIFICATION)**	4A, Indianapolis Northwest, Pike; 3A, Brebeuf; 2A, Indianapolis Ritter, Speedway. Ben Davis site and 1997 champion
Carmel, Hamilton Southeastern, Indianapolis Broad Ripple, Noblesville, Pike	**1997-98 SECTIONAL OPPONENTS**	Center Grove, Decatur Central, Indianapolis Manual, Indianapolis Northwest, Perry Meridian, Southport
22-4 (won sectional; lost to Indianapolis Cathedral in regional final, 66-62)	**FINAL RECORD 1996-97**	18-5 (won sectional; lost to Indianapolis Cathedral in regional semifinal, 53-45)

Battle
of
Giants

In March 1996, when at least in theory the jury was still assimilating evidence in the class basketball question, the Final Four gathered. From the preservationists' standpoint, it wasn't the most opportune time for the four to be the biggest in combined enrollment in modern times: Ben Davis, New Albany, Lafayette Jefferson and Warsaw. Then the biggest two of the four won semifinal games. Then the biggest of all, Ben Davis, beat New Albany for the championship.

Emerson once wrote: "I think no virtue goes with size." Even Emerson would have winced at the timing of that 1996 State field.

Then a new season began, the class basketball decision made. Halfway through the new year, No. 1 and No. 2 in the statewide polls met. They were North Central and Ben Davis, which happened to be No. 2 and No. 1 in the state in enrollment, too. Emerson was in a very bad slump in Hoosierland.

But basketball boomed. North Central-Ben Davis, before a turnaway crowd at North Central, made the pollsters look good.

This wasn't showy basketball. These kids in large part have been playing each other summers and winters for years now. They had met just a week before on the same court in the Marion County Tournament, and North Central had scraped through, 63-62. These kids knew each other as players and teams, knew what to expect and how to counter it.

For example: when North Central led 17-13 late in the first quarter, its sophomore leader, Jason Gardner, drove to a basket — but the Ben Davis defender whom Gardner drove by had a helper right behind. It became a charging foul, Gardner's basket was wiped out, and Gardner himself left the game seconds later because that already was his second foul.

North Central is not the same without Gardner, so he returned early in the second quarter. He had been on court three minutes when the same thing happened: drive, charging foul. "Our team," Ben Davis coach Steve Witty was to say later, "hasn't consistently done the little things, like making sure you're on the support line so when they drive the ball to the basket you're in position to take the charge." This night, it did, creating a real burden for the Panthers: their leader with three fouls, nearly 20 minutes of play still remaining, and the North Central lead down to 24-23.

"I thought Jason was trying very hard, maybe pressing a little bit," North Central coach Doug Mitchell said. At that point, Gardner hadn't scored.

Ben Davis moved ahead after Gardner's second exit, but North Central used two free throws by 6-5 senior center David DePrez with 6.2 seconds left to get to halftime ahead, 30-29.

Huggy's the name

Ben Davis came out for the second half with Gardner's vulnerability obviously in mind. Guards Derin Graham and Chet Washington attacked. Washington hit a jump shot. Graham sank a 3, his third of what already was a 13-point night. Washington broke out to a layup. The slim halftime lead was gone and Ben Davis was atop a 36-30 lead that hinted a breaking point had been passed. At 39-32, Mitchell took timeout and one more time replaced Gardner, who still had no field goals.

"Graham was killing us," Mitchell said. "Jason had a terrible time focusing on the game. We had a little chat about that." Gardner sat and chatted for just 2½ minutes. That's all it took for his team, operating without him, to score five fast field goals, take a 42-41 lead, and push Witty to the timeout that — certainly it wasn't Witty's intention — let Gardner re-enter the game.

A half-minute into the fourth quarter, Gardner intercepted a Washington pass and drove by him to put North Central ahead, 48-47. Then he hit two free throws. Then he hit three, fouled as he tried to get a 3-point shot away. One more time, Witty took timeout, his team down 53-47. Ben Davis came out of the timeout with a 3-point basket by Washington. Another 3 out of the corner by Don Carlisle tied the game at 55, and it was 57-57, just where No. 1 and No. 2 should be heading toward the three-minute homestretch.

Enter Clinton Dye.

No one knows him by so square a name. As a newborn, little Clinton was swept up by an adoring aunt, who hugged and hugged and gave him a name that stuck evermore. Huggy Dye had played the year before at Danville, Ill., before moving to Indianapolis. He was the piece of frontcourt offense that helped to fill in Mitchell's Panther puzzle. He had 55 points and hit 82 percent of his shots the Saturday before when North Central reached 14-0 by beating Lawrence North and Franklin Central in the semifinals and finals of the Marion County tournament. He was averaging 16.5 as the Panthers' scoring leader when the game began. But through 57-57, he was 3-for-11 with seven points.

Perhaps that's why so established a weapon was left so untended by so renowned a defense, because Dye was by himself out front when he hit the 3 that broke the tie. He came back with another 3 from the corner, then scored on a layup that was the product of Gardner's steal and breakout. One more time the ball was loose, and guard Marcus May tipped it to Gardner for a breakaway dunk. That made nine points for Gardner in the quarter, 12 for the game, 11 for the last nine minutes. "When it was time to go play basketball, he got the job done," Mitchell said.

The three-minute avalanche after 57-57 was 17-2, making the 74-62 final score deceptive accounting for a marvelously competitive game. What happened? "They looked at the scoreboard, that's what happened," Mitchell said. "These kids love to compete. For X's and O's, it was definitely not their best basketball. But when it came down to it, our young men competed. And to me, maybe that's a 10.

"Beautiful.

"Wonderful."

Outside the North Central locker room, Dye came away from a TV interview and gave Mitchell a Huggy hug. "We're No. 1, Coach," he crowed. Mitchell took Dye inside with the rest of the team and said, "Boys, I want to tell you this . . . " And the door closed as he told them whatever that was.

A matter of respect

Witty was directly responsible for Mitchell's elation.

"It's a privilege to be able to say you beat Ben Davis," Mitchell said. "They guard you and they sure know how to compete. Omygod. That's some of the best defense I've seen played in all my born days.

"I think it was a great high school basketball game.

"For me that was a Top 10 personal accomplishment, simply because I got sick of walking out of the gym feeling like a fool every time I had to coach against Steve's team. He and a very few other coaches can make you feel so unprepared — not your game plan, your program. They make you work so much harder during the off-season that to beat them is such a good feeling.

"We didn't play particularly well offensively until about the last minute. But that's them. They make you do that."

Steve Witty, off by himself, left to mull about it, surely must marvel at how fast his personal status has changed. This is not Steve Witty, Golden Boy, success something he saw all along as an absolute inevitability.

Certainly, it had happened. He sat there on this night with a No. 2-ranked team that was trying to give Ben Davis a third straight state championship, a fifth straight Final Four trip — his string of four already beyond anything any other school had accomplished. No other school ever had won four straight semistates. And so easily for Witty and Ben Davis it could have already been five, working toward six.

This has happened at a school that, yes, is big, but always has been big, and never — *never* — had made it to the Final Four till this run began.

Now Steve Witty had Ben Davis doing things that, in the long and rich history of Indianapolis high school basketball, only the Ray Crowe-Oscar Robertson Indianapolis Attucks teams had done.

After winning two straight state championships, Ben Davis was being compared to Indianapolis Attucks. Above is Attucks unbeaten (31-0) 1956 State Championship team. Front row, from left, D. Brown, Stanford Patton, Oscar Robertson, Bill Brown, Albert Maxey, Sam Milton; back row, Glenn Bradley, James Enoch, Odell Donel, John Gipson, Ed Searcy, Henry Robertson and coach Ray Crowe. (Photo courtesy Indiana High School Athletic Association)

Only Attucks (1955-56) and Ben Davis (1995-96) represent Indianapolis among the nine schools that have won two or more consecutive state championships. Ben Davis, playing there only at regional and semistate time, had won 16 straight games at Hinkle Fieldhouse, which was those Attucks teams' private playpen.

Hinkle and its tunnel

Hinkle is the closest thing to heaven that earth yet has shown to 49-year-old Steve Witty. "You could blindfold me, drive me around, not tell me where you're taking me, and walk me into that place blindfolded and I could tell you it's Hinkle. Just the smell, the feel — it's a great place for high school basketball."

At the Indiana Basketball Hall of Fame, they've preserved something only a special few teams ever experienced: the tunnel that leads from downstairs dressing rooms up to the playing area at Hinkle, the tunnel that state champions for years came running up, hair bristling on the back of necks as young basketball players realized where they were.

Ben Davis coach Steve Witty (Photo courtesy Indiana High School Athletic Association, ©Mark Wick)

Teams don't run up that tunnel anymore. The last renovation of the fieldhouse put in brighter, newer, nicer locker rooms at floor level, behind the westside bleachers. "We play a doubleheader there every year with Carmel, Lawrence Central and Pike," Witty said. "Sometimes we get to dress down there."

And run up that tunnel.

"In 1965," Witty mused, "I'm sitting two rows from the top at Hinkle watching Indianapolis Washington win a state championship.

"Thirty years later . . . "

Witty was a senior at Center Grove High then. Center Grove, in Johnson County just south of Indianapolis, is big now, an urban population boom spreading out from Indianapolis making it one of the 25 biggest high schools in Indiana. "We had 622 in the top four grades when I graduated," Witty said. "Where all those $400,000 homes are today is where I used to bale hay."

Franklin won all the sectionals that Center Grove wanted to in Witty's playing years. He played football and baseball, too, and "made up my mind at a very early age I wanted to be a teacher and a coach, because of the teachers and coaches I had.

"Not very many people really have the opportunity to live their dream. I can remember sitting on my back porch one time talking about how some day I was going to be a part of a state championship team . . . if it didn't happen as a player, it was going to happen as a coach. I said that." As a dreaming boy.

He graduated from Franklin College and went into that teaching-coaching career he wanted. For 11 years, he assisted Gayle Towles with the Ben Davis basketball team.

Then Towles resigned in the spring of 1989 and the job was his.

"My first two years as head coach, we won 15 games and 16 games, but we didn't win any tournaments — sectional, county, anything," Witty said. "In 1991, we drew Alan Henderson's Brebeuf team in the first game of the sectional. They beat us in overtime, and they went to the state championship game." Of course watching Brebeuf make that run to the Final Four made Witty think it could have been his team doing that. "We were rated 18th in the state. I remember thinking to myself, 'How many times in a coach's career do you have the opportunity to do that?' "

A challenge met

First, there was that matter of winning a sectional.

In 1992, Witty said, "We specifically challenged our team: 'All it takes is one team to get a tradition of tournament success started.'

"That team won the sectional, won the regional, and got beat on a last-second shot in the semistate." Billy Wright of Richmond did it, and his team kept hitting last-second shots till it was state champion. And today, the Billy Wright who broke Steve Witty's heart in 1992 is an assistant on Witty's staff. "I couldn't ask for anybody better," Witty said.

A few hours before that Richmond game, though, Witty's '92 Giants had knocked out No. 1-ranked Anderson, 96-87. Some people told Witty that was the greatest high school game they had ever seen. Some people have told him that after about half-a-dozen other games since. Greatest-ness has a currency to it. But it was a breakthrough, and Witty always will credit that achievement to Michael Brooks, Scott George, Antuan Harney, Micah Reid and others, including a solid contributor off the bench named Derick Witty.

"A lot of people say, 'That Richmond game must have really been disappointing,' " Witty said. "It was, but I don't dwell on the negatives. I'll always remember how hard we worked, all the great games we had to win to get in that position. Maybe nobody ever remembers the runner-up team, but for the kids who were involved, that was something very special." Kids like Derick Witty, an over-achiever, a role player, a source of terrific pride for his dad. "Very seldom do a father and a son have an opportunity to spend 2½ hours a day doing something they both love," Witty said. "I wouldn't trade anything for the experience. In coaching, the early stages of your career, the game kind of uses your family. We got to the stage where our family used the game — my daughter (Kara, two years younger than Derick) was very much involved, my wife (Jeanie) is very much involved. I've just been blessed."

But when Billy Wright hit that shot that moved Richmond forward and Ben Davis out, Witty realized: "There's another opportunity that got away from us."

'With all that talent . . . '

In '93, Ben Davis went breaking through again: first Final Four, first trip to the championship game, a rocket start to a 27-16 first-quarter lead, a 66-61 loss to Jeffersonville. In '94, Ben Davis went right back. The morning-round 84-69 loss to unbeaten Valparaiso remains the most one-sided defeat of Witty's coaching career.

With future Mr. Basketball Damon Frierson leading the way, Ben Davis finally broke through to win the State Championship in 1995. (Photo courtesy Indiana High School Athletic Association, ©Jill Wick)

And the next year, with Damon Frierson a Mr. Basketball playing in his third Final Four, and with James Patterson and Courtney James, Indiana All-Stars, Ben Davis closed the season once-beaten and No. 1, won a wildly emotional, beautifully played regional duel that was neighbor Washington's last rich basketball moment before closing, then just did outlast No. 2-ranked Merrillville in the state championship game, 58-57.

Steve Witty, the kid who sat on a porch and talked about his dream, was the coach of a state champion.

He laughs now and fills in the blanks of what fans no doubt were saying of him on the climb up. The first two years: "Those are still Gayle's kids." The '92 team that came so close: "He can coach, but he can't win the big ones." The '93 and '94 teams that reached the Final Four: "He can get there, but he can't win it." And the 32-1 championship season in '95: "With all that talent, anybody can win it."

The repeat in '96 was different. "We were 10-6, we had just played a Friday night game against Carmel on TV, and we had played horribly," he said. "I sat them down on Monday and said: 'I don't want you to get the idea that we're mad at you or don't think you can be a good basketball team, but unless you guys wake up, this team may be remembered as the one that in one year destroyed about four years' worth of basketball tradition. Do you want to be remembered that way?' "

With 3½ minutes to go against Franklin Central in the regional, Ben Davis trailed by nine points. In the semifinal round at the State, Lafayette Jeff led the Giants by 14. "Those kids just refused to get beat," Witty said. "We had no business winning the State.

"What won it, I think, was tradition. Our kids expect to win, they've been around winning."

Jeff Poisel helped, too.

Poisel, a kicker, is at Western Kentucky on a football scholarship. He reported late for basketball as a senior because of football, and once out, he hurt an ankle badly. "If my coaching staff had taken a vote, we probably would have cut him, really for what we all thought might be his own best interests," Witty said. "I didn't feel comfortable cutting him. He had lettered for two years.

Jeff Poisel (left) hit a three-point basket in overtime to lift Ben Davis to an unexpected second straight State Championship in 1996. (Photo courtesy Indiana High School Athletic Association, ©Mark Wick)

"At Christmastime I told Jeff: 'You may play two minutes, you may play 10 minutes, you may go three games and not play at all. Can you accept that role? If it gets to the point that you can't, come tell me and I won't cut you, you won't quit, we'll just part company and you can go work on kicking field goals.' He stuck with it and all of a sudden started getting better and better."

In the last second of double overtime in the state championship game, Jeff Poisel launched his game-record sixth 3-point basket and Ben Davis was a repeat champion. "That's Poisel. He wanted the ball in his hands when the game was on the line. He hit some big shots for us down the stretch.

"And he didn't even figure in the mix until January."

This was a new January, and Steve Witty was looking all around for a new Jeff Poisel.

A most fulfilling season

Doug Mitchell was dealing with a new reality: the No. 1 ranking.

The Panthers had played a few games since acquiring it, and Mitchell liked what he had observed.

"We (coaches) don't change and they don't change," he said. "I want them focused on the next possession, not on next week's poll.

"But I do want them to enjoy it. I asked them, 'Are you the same height? Are you eating the same food? Did you believe people a couple of years ago when they told you you were bad? Don't start to believe those same people now.'

"Ratings are great and fine, but when they're really worth something is 20 years down the road when you tell your kids about them.

"I do feel confident these guys will not succumb to pressure. I think they have showed the resilience to be No. 1.

"This is definitely the most fulfilling season I've had as a coach. They're doing it together. They're digging down so deep and competing so hard."

In Gardner, he has the player Witty already calls the best in Indianapolis. It's a heavy load for a sophomore, just as is the other tag given him by some: the new Isiah. It's a common practice in Indiana, pulling out the name of a demigod to describe a budding young talent. It's as silly as it is unfair. There will not be another Isiah Thomas, or an Oscar Robertson, or a George McGinnis, or a Larry Bird, or a Rick Mount-Steve Alford-Jimmy Rayl, or a Damon Bailey, the usual pronouns that become prototypes in this history-minded, future-hopeful state.

In the comparers' eyes, Isiah means a short, compact guard who can lead and score and pass and terrorize on defense. Oscar means a midsize player who is the best who ever was. George means a blacksmith body on a gymnast, an incomparable blend of strength and basketball's finesse-filled skills. Bird means a tall, not outwardly athletic kid who has to be seen again and again to appreciate the degree of his greatness, because at first look it seems to include some luck — the ball just happens to come down where he is on an uncommon number of rebounds, he really couldn't have seen that guy behind him he hit with a pass, you can't tell me he can switch that ball to his left hand and hit that shot on the fly very often — a tall and gangly Minnesota Fats of basketball whose appearance in no way alerts you to what he is about to do. Mount-Alford-Rayl means a level of shooting ability unreached by others even in a state where shooting has always been a collective forte. Bailey means a kid, preferably with a touch of country, charismatic beyond imagination without a hint of courting it, dropped in a position where he is expected to be a Moses, four different times with four different combinations, and he actually does it.

The mind's eye tends to be Xeroxian, replicating as close as possible: the new Bird, Mount-Alford-Rayl, Bailey is apt to be white; the new Isiah, Oscar, George, apt to be black. No reason. So let us all rejoice when we see the next Isiah and he's white, the next Bird and he's black. Something in the way of stereotyping will have been conquered.

Meanwhile, Jason Gardner is the next Jason Gardner.

"I think he has had a really, really good sophomore year," Mitchell said. "By next year, he needs to improve to live up to his press clippings. I think every junior does. If he stays as good as he is now, how good is that? But if he improves each year as much as he has improved the last years, he's right on track to be a big-time Division I college basketball player.

"I'm talking about little things, the fine parts of the game — court awareness, understanding how to read a screen, understanding constant motion on offense, not passing the ball and standing and watching somebody else. He's got to stop watching the NBA. If they're so damned good, how come three of them stand all the time and two of them play?"

'I can compete with them'

Mitchell is not far from home at North Central. He played high school ball just across the county line at Hamilton Heights, then at Butler where he stayed on as an assistant coach for six years. "I wanted to be a head coach and quit traveling so much," he said. "I have four children. I always thought this was a great job. It came open, I knew some people here, and I jumped on it."

Its basketball history is an enigma. The state's biggest or second-biggest school for years, in a school corporation with abundant funding, an end wall in the North Central gymnasium has a neatly rowed display of 41 3x5-foot state championship banners, involving 11 different Panther teams: boys tennis (14), track (3), cross country (1), golf (2), soccer (3), swimming (1) and gymnastics (1); girls tennis (9), track (2), golf (4), gymnastics (1). The program is neither running dry nor short on confidence. There is space for 43 more flags.

Notably absent is basketball, where the North Central boys have not won even a semistate championship. In the school's 40-year history, just one team won a regional — in 1979, when the Panthers reached the semistate championship round, the doorway to the State, but lost 47-46 to eventual state champion Muncie Central.

It is, in short, much the position Ben Davis was in prior to 1993.

Now, even Witty with his solidly entrenched program says, "We're entering an era of uncertainty, going to the new tournament format." Ben Davis — as 32 of the state's 40 biggest high schools did — voted against the change. North Central was by far the biggest school to vote for it. Principal C.E. Quandt did it, though his boys basketball coach had let him know, "I am absolutely, vehemently opposed to class basketball."

Quandt's explanation for his feeling, Mitchell said, was that "he saw the Lawrence North-Deaf School sectional tournament game and just didn't think that was a very even playing field." Lawrence North won that 1996 game, 122-27. It was another example of influential timing. "I tried to tell him the only difference between that game and that Deaf School team playing Sheridan was it would have been 90-27," Mitchell said. Sheridan and the Indiana School for the Deaf will play in Class A, though not in the same sectional.

"I played for a small school," Mitchell said. "We had 94 in our graduating class. That's why this whole class basketball thing irritates me to no end. If you would have taken away the chance for me to win the Carmel sectional, I would have never, ever forgiven you."

Carmel was the big target. "I remember the night we beat them — by about 30 (87-59). Two years later that same bunch, with Mark Herrmann and Bart Burrell, won the State. We beat them in the semifinals, on Friday. I remember going home that night and sitting on my bed thinking, 'God, I can *compete* with them. In anything. Not just basketball. I can be a banker if they can be a banker, I can be a lawyer if they can be a lawyer, I can do anything those people can do at those big places.'

"To take away that opportunity from a kid . . . you're telling him he'll be a second-class citizen forever."

Bloomington N.	60
Bloomington S.	55

January 28

BLOOMINGTON NORTH		BLOOMINGTON SOUTH
One as Bloomington North, 1997. Others in corporation, one: Bloomington High 1919	**STATE CHAMPIONSHIP**	None as Bloomington South. Others in corporation, one: Bloomington High 1919
None as Bloomington North. Others in corporation, three: Bloomington High 1918, 1922, 1960	**OTHER TIMES IN FINAL FOUR**	None as Bloomington South. Others in corporation, four: Bloomington High 1918, 1919, 1922, 1960
Two as Bloomington North: 1982, 1997. Others in corporation: Bloomington High 10 (first 1921, last 1971)	**REGIONAL CHAMPIONSHIPS**	Three as Bloomington South: 1985, 1987, 1988. Others in corporation: Bloomington High 10 (first 1921, last 1971)
10 as Bloomington North: first 1976; two in '90s, most recent 1997. Others in corporation, 28: Bloomington High 25 (first 1915, last 1971), Bloomington University 2: 1946, 1972; Unionville 1966.	**SECTIONAL CHAMPIONSHIPS**	Eight as Bloomington South: first 1973; two in '90s, most recent 1996. Others in corporation, 25: Bloomington High 25 (first 1915, last 1971)
Formed 1972 (Bloomington University, Unionville, part of Bloomington High)	**CONSOLIDATIONS**	Formed 1972 (Smithville, part of Bloomington High)
No	**VOTE ON CHANGE TO CLASSES**	No
4A. (1,026; 70th of 95 in class)	**1997-98 CLASS (ENROLLMENT)**	4A. (1,471; 28th of 95 in class)
4A, Bedford North Lawrence, Bloomington South; 3A, Brown County, Edgewood; 2A, Eastern (Greene County). Bedford-North Lawrence site, Bloomington North 1997 champion	**1996-97 SECTIONAL OPPONENTS (1997-98 CLASSIFICATION)**	4A, Bedford North Lawrence, Bloomington North; 3A, Brown County, Edgewood; 2A, Eastern (Greene County). Bedford-North Lawrence site, Bloomington North 1997 champion
Bloomington South, Columbus East, Columbus North, East Central, Martinsville	**1997-98 SECTIONAL OPPONENTS**	Bloomington North, Columbus East, Columbus North, East Central, Martinsville
28-1 (state champion)	**FINAL RECORD 1996-97**	13-9 (lost to Bloomington North in Bedford North Lawrence sectional final, 48-39, overtime)

Civil
Warriors

Theirs is an unusual rivalry. Officially, they are Bloomington High School North and Bloomington High School South, scholastic twins, each "born" in 1972. That's the truth, and nothing but the truth, but not the whole truth, so help me, God.

Perception altered reality from the outset. Bloomington High School, a charter member of the Indiana High School Athletic Association (1904), operated for years as Bloomington's only high school. In 1939, University High School was formed, with links to the Indiana University School of Education. In Monroe County's small towns outside Bloomington, there were other high schools — at Ellettsville, Smithville, Unionville and Stinesville. In 1964, Ellettsville and Stinesville merged to form Edgewood. Eight years later, Bloomington High, University, Unionville and Smithville went together and divided about evenly between BHS North and BHS South.

Townspeople in Bloomington had in the main identified with old Bloomington High: BHS, the Panthers, the Purple and White. BHS had been one of the most prominent athletic programs in Indiana. The Panthers were Indiana's first state champions, in anything — the track team won the first official IHSAA event in the spring of 1904. BHS reigned in basketball in 1919, won team honors at the state's first wrestling championships in 1933, won in golf in 1938. In its last year of operation, 1971-72, Bloomington High won its fourth straight state wrestling championship, its third straight state swimming championship and its first state baseball championship, and the football team went undefeated — for the fourth straight year.

BHS closed, and Bloomington South opened, in the same building, in the same purple and white, still called the Panthers. The link-up was so firm that state and national record books list as the longest undefeated streak in Indiana high school football history the 60 that Panther teams put together: 41 as BHS, the last 19 as Bloomington South.

That's an example of why there is some justification for the "Second School" complex North has carried around for a quarter-century.

Just three years ago, the city flashed its Panther Pride when South won its first state football championship since the playoff system was inaugurated in 1973. South won the top prize, the big-school championship, with a perfect 14-0 season that included a 47-0 wipeout of a North team that finished that 1993 season 3-6.

Tighter in basketball

Basketball hasn't been nearly so one-sided. When the two rivals met at North's gym in January, they stood 5-5 against each other in the '90s. They split their two meetings the year before, North winning 58-57 at South on a last-second basket by Matt Reed and South retaliating, 52-49, in the sectional tournament, when South freshman Jon Holmes scored 14 of his 16 points in the fourth quarter. "Both games were just alike," North guard David McKinney said. "The team that was behind came back and won."

With those two — Jon Holmes and David McKinney — this matchup gets even more interesting.

Holmes is the primary ball handler and scorer for the South team coached by his dad, J.R.

McKinney has the ballhandling role for the North team coached by his dad, Tom.

Of course the two players looked each other up on-court after each of those tight games the previous year. "Nobody else in the gym knew how both of us felt," McKinney said.

And now they were meeting again.

Jon Holmes of Bloomington South takes a shot, right, while his dad, J.R., coaches, below. (Photos courtesy Bloomington Herald-Times*)*

The first time McKinney touched the basketball, a chant started in South's cheering section: "Daddy's boy, Daddy's boy." Coach's sons in Indiana are used to things like that. "I can only remember once or twice where a crowd really got nasty," McKinney said. "The Martinsville game (a week earlier), they were yelling a bunch of stuff at me in warm-ups. I just laughed it off." But it did sting. And McKinney did answer. "I hit five 3s the first half," he said. So maybe he should have invited more insults like those? "Yeah," he said, "I think so."

But this night the chant from the South stands "didn't bother me at all," McKinney said. "As soon as they started yelling at me, our crowd got on Jon." Tom McKinney didn't care much for that. In postgame remarks, he pointedly objected. He called Jon Holmes "a really fine kid and a fine player . . . there is no place for that kind of chant."

No room for slips

The game was on the court, not in the stands. And it was better than the contrasting pregame records (North 12-1, ranked No. 5 in the state; South 6-6, unranked) suggested it would be.

Holmes' only first-half basket was a layup and North opened a 26-21 lead. North began the second half by working the ball inside to 6-6 Djibril Kante for a basket and to 6-6 Kueth Duany for a dunk. Just 75 seconds into the second half, J.R. Holmes called a timeout, those two close-range baskets the cause. "Our game plan was if they got the ball inside, we were going to foul them on purpose," Holmes said. "We backed off of them. They may not hit those free throws."

The deficit reached 34-23 with pullaway in the air before Jon sniped his first 3-point basket of the game. He hit another from the deep left corner, and in between 6-5 South senior Chris Magdzinski scored twice. It was 37-33, and tense again.

Duany — a junior considered North's one major-college prospect, his older brother already playing in the Big Ten at Wisconsin — slipped into the low post, took a pass, eluded the foul-him-immediately strategy and scored closing out the third quarter for a 40-35 North lead.

Holmes went to a zone defense opening the fourth quarter, and North immediately turned the ball over. After a South miss, North's Mario Wuysang, an ever-willing and eager shooter, found himself unguarded and sank a 3. On the sidelines, his team's hole back to eight points deep, J.R. Holmes steamed. "We were to go to zone one possession," he said. "The second time, four guys went man and the fifth guy was zone — and Mario was his man."

South kept scrapping but never had the basketball with a chance to tie. North won, 60-55, with 22 points from Duany. Holmes' 16 South points included 13 after halftime.

'A lot of pressure'

McKinney was happy. The victory clinched a repeat championship for North in the South Central Conference. "I'm proud of our players for that," he said. He was happier than his fans. At home, with so lofty a state ranking, with South the opponent, Cougar fans wanted a romp.

"I've been through that," J.R. Holmes said, "where if you don't win by 40 — 'What's wrong, Coach?' I told Tom last summer, 'It's going to be the most miserable year you've had, because they're never satisfied. You can be 13-1 and ranked fifth in the state and win a game and people will say, 'You got outplayed' or 'You got outcoached.'

"There's a lot of pressure on the North team. Everybody says they ought to be in the Final Four. And they do have a chance. Not too many coaches can say, 'I have a legitimate chance to win the state championship.' He's one. But that's a lot of pressure.

"I'll tell you why they can beat most teams in the state: when they don't shoot well, *you* can't score against them. In tournament time, in nervous times in the sectional or regional or semistate, offense sometimes is a little shaky for a quarter or so. They can defend the ball."

McKinney, too, remembered Holmes' summertime warning and smiled at its accuracy. Fan expectations didn't bother him, though. "Our players need to understand that South certainly wasn't impressed with our ranking," he said.

He realized that had his team won, rather than lost, in overtime at Anderson in December, its ranking might well be an even more head-inflating No. 1.

But there was another side to all that psychology stuff. McKinney felt he had to convince his team that being best in the state, being the state champion, was not unattainable.

"This particular school, being newer than South, having the diversity we have, and South kinda the old Bloomingtonites — as a coach sometimes it has been a real tough sell for me: 'We're as good (as South) . . . We're as good . . . We're *better*.'

"I've had three or four teams the last 20 years that I thought had better talent than this team — two at North and one at Franklin. But this is the first team I have said to, and meant it: 'We can get beat in the sectional. We can also win the state championship.'

"It takes a lot of commitment and unselfishness to win at that level. We need to convince our players to play together, as a team. Right now, it's a struggle.

"We didn't tonight. We had a couple of places in there that were kinda me, me.

"There is a pretty good coach who has said for years, 'The mental is to the physical as four is to one.' People don't believe that, but he (Bob Knight) is absolutely right."

Diversity High

McKinney mentioned North's diversity. The school with an ancestor that was called University High could well be known as Diversity High.

Within North's 1,245 students, school officials say, there are 70 nationalities. Within the basketball team, there are several. Duany was born in Sudan. Kante was born in Bloomington but spent some early years living in Mali, or its African neighbors, Guinea and Niger. Wuysang was born in Indonesia, junior Jay Robles in the Philippines.

But they are All-American kids, steeped in Hoosier basketball traditions, their language not a bit different from their friends around them because each has spent most of his life in Bloomington. They have run into some redneck resentment, in their travels as Cougars, but they turn ignorance about them into material for good humor.

So does McKinney. "I had a sportswriter ask me, 'Do all your foreign kids speak English?'

"I said, 'They all *speak* English, but sometimes when I'm talking, I'm not sure they understand it.' "

Aiming high in seventh grade

Ranking with the best teams in the state isn't head-turning for North's players because they have looked at 1997 as their year for a long while now.

In elementary school, the Cougars were spread around Bloomington — twins Ryan and Matt Reed with Wuysang in one school, Duany and Kante in another, David McKinney in a third. For a time, Jeremy Sinsabaugh was in California. They came together at Tri-North Junior High, all but Sinsabaugh, who went to a church school in Martinsville as a seventh- and eighth-grader. Still, he knew his future teammates well. They all played basketball together in the summertime.

Duany said he and Kante were close friends with Wuysang, though he was a class ahead of them. Tri-North had separate seventh- and eighth-grade teams. "Mario was always saying, 'We have a good team. We'd kill you guys.' " Duany said. "They did beat us pretty good, but I didn't think they were that much better than us. And I knew in high school we'd be together."

"Our eighth-grade year," Ryan Reed remembers, "we said, 'We'll win the state championship.' "

David McKinney advances it a year: "From the time we were in seventh grade, we talked about winning the State. It was more of a dream back then, a lot of talking. But the farther we got in high school, the more it looked like we really could do it.

"We knew we had a lot of talent. And we all believed in each other. I don't know how that came about. We just never had any doubts about each other. Someone would pull through."

McKinney, who had been going to road games on the bus with his dad and the team from fifth grade on, had developed his own hero during that time. Derek Cross, a standout guard who was a starter and solid contributor at Miami of Ohio after his North years, "played a big part for me. I wanted to be just like him. He would come over to my house and play in the driveway with me. He'd let me come close. I don't think I ever did beat him. Even when he was in college, he'd come back and play one-on-one in the driveway. I benefited a lot."

When Cross wasn't there: "I had a lot of one-on-none games out in the driveway.

"I won the State a lot then."

Always watching

South, which started three other sophomores in addition to team leader Holmes in this game, used nothing but freshmen and sophomores in the junior varsity game, which in its own way was a testimonial to this rivalry.

Most of the crowd already was in place, and in loud form, when the young teams-in-the-making fought to the buzzer. With 17 seconds to go, North sophomore Pat Miller hit two free throws to inch his team in front, 33-32. At 0:05, 5-9 South sophomore Zach Short sank a 3-point basket. The young Panthers — from a program obviously pointing toward big things in the next two years — won, 35-33, over a North team with more immediate plans. North's JVs were to go 17-3 with their roster that included three juniors, who could figure in as seniors when Tom McKinney builds a new team around his big inside returnees, Duany and Kante.

South's younger team was to go 8-11.

It wasn't as if the head coaches weren't watching that preliminary.

After the varsity game Holmes said, "I knew they were going to trap Jon in the corner, off our screens."

You *knew* it?

"Yes," he said. "I saw their reserve team do it."

Whistles and ploys

Neither McKinney nor Holmes has a reputation for baiting officials.

Working officials is a slightly different art, foreign to neither.

The two who worked the North-South game stopped by game host McKinney's office on their way out, for pleasantries.

McKinney mildly apologized for anything that either official might have heard from the two rival coaches at work during the game. "It was one of those crazy games," he said. "I wanted every call, and he wanted every call.

"He was wrong and I was right on most of them, you know."

McKinney asked each if he could send them a tape of the game, for critiquing. "We know people are starting to collapse on us when we throw the ball inside, because we've been pretty strong there," he said. "I want to see if they're holding. I want to see what your thoughts are."

Holmes volunteered the information that there was a lot of holding going on — as part of that game plan that called for a foul before one of North's inside players could put up a close-range shot.

He said he told his players before the game, "We've got all these big guys (four on the roster 6-6 or 6-5) — any time they get the ball in the low post, foul them."

Meaning, Duany and Kante?

"Anybody. I didn't care who.

"I said that for two reasons: one, they haven't been shooting free throws well, and, two, I'm hoping if we get a bunch of fouls, the officials won't let them get as physical with us at the other end. They'll be thinking, 'That's 10 fouls on South' and at the other end tell North, 'Get your hands off them.' I was trying to influence that a little bit, on our offensive end.

"Because they really get after you and play good defense."

In a rivalry game like this, Holmes was asked, because the same two teams likely will meet again for even more meaningful stakes in the sectional tournament, did you tonight — or would you ever — hold back an idea or two, for use later?

"If I'm the favorite, sometimes I will — an offensive thing, maybe, or some little play," he said.

"The two times in the last six years when we were big underdogs to them, we came out and spread them — held the ball. I did not think we could do that tonight because we hadn't worked on it enough.

"But we did it a couple of times in the game, because I thought, 'I've got to give my kids a chance. If we can run a minute or so off the clock, we'll be all right.'

"So, no, I didn't hold anything back. We threw about everything at them that we had.

"I don't think anybody thought we could beat them tonight. We still may not be able to. But coming out of the gym tonight I just wanted our kids to know that in three or four weeks, we've got a chance."

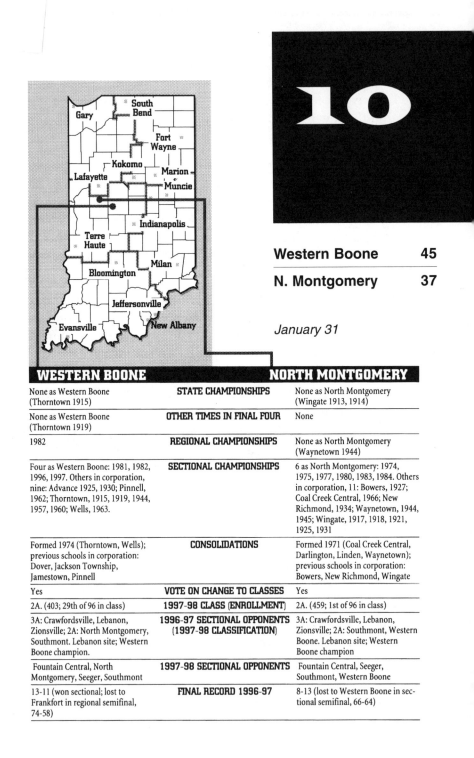

10

Western Boone   **45**

N. Montgomery   **37**

January 31

WESTERN BOONE		NORTH MONTGOMERY
None as Western Boone (Thorntown 1915)	**STATE CHAMPIONSHIPS**	None as North Montgomery (Wingate 1913, 1914)
None as Western Boone (Thorntown 1919)	**OTHER TIMES IN FINAL FOUR**	None
1982	**REGIONAL CHAMPIONSHIPS**	None as North Montgomery (Waynetown 1944)
Four as Western Boone: 1981, 1982, 1996, 1997. Others in corporation, nine: Advance 1925, 1930; Pinnell, 1962; Thorntown, 1915, 1919, 1944, 1957, 1960; Wells, 1963.	**SECTIONAL CHAMPIONSHIPS**	6 as North Montgomery: 1974, 1975, 1977, 1980, 1983, 1984. Others in corporation, 11: Bowers, 1927; Coal Creek Central, 1966; New Richmond, 1934; Waynetown, 1944, 1945; Wingate, 1917, 1918, 1921, 1925, 1931
Formed 1974 (Thorntown, Wells); previous schools in corporation: Dover, Jackson Township, Jamestown, Pinnell	**CONSOLIDATIONS**	Formed 1971 (Coal Creek Central, Darlington, Linden, Waynetown); previous schools in corporation: Bowers, New Richmond, Wingate
Yes	**VOTE ON CHANGE TO CLASSES**	Yes
2A. (403; 29th of 96 in class)	**1997-98 CLASS (ENROLLMENT)**	2A. (459; 1st of 96 in class)
3A: Crawfordsville, Lebanon, Zionsville; 2A: North Montgomery, Southmont. Lebanon site; Western Boone champion.	**1996-97 SECTIONAL OPPONENTS (1997-98 CLASSIFICATION)**	3A: Crawfordsville, Lebanon, Zionsville; 2A: Southmont, Western Boone. Lebanon site; Western Boone champion
Fountain Central, North Montgomery, Seeger, Southmont	**1997-98 SECTIONAL OPPONENTS**	Fountain Central, Seeger, Southmont, Western Boone
13-11 (won sectional; lost to Frankfort in regional semifinal, 74-58)	**FINAL RECORD 1996-97**	8-13 (lost to Western Boone in sectional semifinal, 66-64)

The First Milans, and the Picket Fence

Y_{ou} wonder, perhaps, what North Montgomery and Western Boone are doing in a lineup of schools with distinguished tournament pasts?

Belonging.

And reminding.

There are three state basketball championships in their joint histories, but not by these names. Go back 80 years, and Hoosiers knew all about the northwestern Montgomery County hamlet of Wingate and the northwestern Boone County town of Thorntown.

And they knew most of all about Wingate's favorite son.

Homer Stonebraker was Indiana's first great basketball player — a 6-foot-2, 180-pound athlete who to this day may be the best basketball player ever to come out of Montgomery County. Yes, Crawfordsville's run of outstanding players started even before Stonebraker and included some after. Yes, Howie Williams of New Ross was a 1952 Olympian. Yes, I remember the Alamo star, Charlie Bowerman.

Stonebraker — at a time when Wingate had just 12 boys in high school and seven of them suited up for basketball; when Wingate had no gym and practiced outside whenever winter blasts didn't force a six-mile trip to New Richmond for indoor work — made Wingate Indiana high school basketball's third state champion in 1913.

And he came back in 1914 to make his team the first of what is still a very short list: winners of two or more consecutive state championships. Nine schools are on there, nine that accomplished it 11 times, in 87 years, none of the other eight even close to Wingate in size.

Then Stonebraker went on to Wabash College, where his junior year (1916-17) the Cavemen went 19-2 with a sweep over Big Ten co-champion Illinois (28-26), Purdue (17-9), Indiana (20-17) and Notre Dame (25-18 and 27-17).

Stonebraker served in World War I, then coached for a while. He led Hartford City to its only Final Four finish, in 1920. He coached two years after that at Logansport. Meanwhile, he was still playing. When Indiana's first professional basketball team was formed at Fort Wayne, Stonebraker was the first player signed. When Fort Wayne split a two-game series with the New York Celtics, ostensibly for the 1921 national professional championship, Stonebraker was the team's star. When Fort Wayne became the Hoosiers and played in the first American Basketball League in 1921-22, the team was built around Stonebraker, who played 10 professional years and once — in rare national exposure for a sport struggling for acceptance — had his picture on the cover of popular *Collier's* magazine. After basketball, he served two terms as sheriff of Cass County, then worked for Allison Division of General Motors in Indianapolis for more than 30 years. He was 82 when he died Dec. 9, 1977.

Wingate's first state championship in 1913 came in what is still the longest title game ever played: five overtimes. Wingate finally outlasted South Bend, 15-14. The score was 13-13 at the end of regulation time. Four two-minute overtimes went scoreless. In the fifth, South Bend went ahead with a free throw. Stonebraker had a chance to tie with a free throw, but his miss was recovered by teammate Forest Crane, whose basket won the game. Only Stonebraker (nine points) and Crane (six) scored for Wingate.

There was one other historical note in that 1913 tournament: South Bend got to the finals with a 19-11 semifinal victory over Crawfordsville. That's the only time in 87 years one county — Montgomery, with both Wingate and Crawfordsville — had two Final Four teams.

Crane graduated, but Stonebraker led another seven-man team to the 1914 championship. In his last high school game, Stonebraker scored 18 points. The score was 36-8, Anderson the distant runner-up.

Each of those years, the state tournament was opened to any school that wanted to come to Bloomington's Assembly Hall. It was a workable 38 in 1913. The field jumped to 75 in 1914, 74 games that had to be played off in two days. Four floors were used. Matchups were made as soon as games ended, on almost a "We'll take winners" basis. Wingate played two games on Friday and four on Saturday, and Stonebraker — who legend says ran four miles to school every morning, carrying a shovel during the winter to get through drifts — played every minute of all six games.

The first team to fall to Wingate in that state tournament? Milan, 44-14.

The only reasonably close game came in the quarterfinals, a 17-13 victory over Clinton. Stonebraker scored all 17 points.

Wingate (19-5) played every game on the road and, at a time when Henry Ford's Model T was still newfangled, played at such places as Kokomo, Bloomington, Anderson and Bluffton.

Homer Stonebraker of Wingate High School with 1913 championship trophy. (Photo courtesy Indiana Basketball Hall of Fame)

Lebanon's 1918 state championship team. Front row, from left, Gerald Gardner, Fred Adam, Merrill Gardner; middle, Frank Martin, Clyde Grater, Don White, Henry Stevens, Basil Smith; back, Coach Glenn Curtis, Manager Demaree. (Photo courtesy Indiana Basketball Hall of Fame)

Thorntown had beaten that Wingate team, 16-15, but at the State lost a third-round game to Rushville, 21-15.

The next year, with a 155-team field split up into 14 sectionals, Thorntown won four games in the Lebanon sectional, including a 28-22 revenge victory over Rossville in the finals. Thorntown — the Kewasakees — then went to Indianapolis with the other survivors and hurdled Hartford City, Rochester (17-14, the only close game), Indianapolis Manual and Montmorenci (33-10). Thorntown coach Chet Hill and the team's star, Al Smith (18 championship-game points in almost doubling Montmorenci's total), represent that championship team in the Indiana Basketball Hall of Fame.

In 1953, the year of Milan's emergence in the Final Four, Wingate closed its doors. It hadn't had a winning season in 13 years when it formed Coal Creek Central by merging with New Richmond, the neighbor that had shared its gym for practice in the championship days — and a town used for some of the street scenes in *Hoosiers*. Coal Creek Central lasted only till 1971, when it merged with Linden, Darlington and Waynetown to form North Montgomery. Just three years after that, Thorntown closed down, merging with Granville Wells in 1974 to form Western Boone.

But get out a map. Four schools had won those first five state tournaments (Crawfordsville, 1911; Lebanon, 1912, then Wingate and Thorntown). All were from neighboring counties Montgomery and Boone. None was more than 22 miles (Lebanon) from the Crawfordsville YMCA building where the Rev. Nicholas McKay had introduced basketball to Indiana.

More than 80 years later, Western Boone alumnus and coach Danny Pierce fielded a question: Do you think your players have any idea about that history?

Pierce smiled.

"In all honesty," he said, "they don't.

"I don't think they understand tradition, and probably I wouldn't have, either.

"But as you grow older you do."

37 — not always enough

There were moments when Danny Pierce grew a little bit older on this night.

January was ending, and North Montgomery still was getting its basketball legs. Like Milan, the epitome of Indiana basketball names, Wingate descendant North Montgomery has become a football power. Thanksgiving weekend, the Chargers scored last to win a spectacular Class 2A state championship game from Fort Wayne Luers, 37-34. That was their second state title in a row.

And not until then could they take up basketball. Those players who won the football championship are almost as important to basketball coach Dave Young as they were to football coach Charley German.

Every North Montgomery touchdown in that wild championship game was scored by a basketball player Young started against Western Boone.

Jon Sparks, Young's 6-4 center, threw for 279 yards and three touchdowns and returned an intercepted pass 52 yards for another as German's quarterback. Kevin Templeman, a 6-1, 220-pound basketball forward, as a tailback ran for 253 yards and one touchdown. Shawn Ratliff, a basketball guard at 6-1 and 172 pounds, caught a 71-yard touchdown pass, four receptions in all that game for 119 yards. Jason McCormick, the other basketball guard at 6-0 and 155 pounds, picked up 125 yards on three championship-game catches — 49 yards on one touchdown play and 56 for the final, game-winning TD.

That was one game. And Western Boone was one basketball game.

There was one difference: North Montgomery scored 37 points in this game, too. This time, in this sport, it wasn't enough. Western Boone had 45.

A tough transition

Dave Young has been in this situation before. "If you want to win a state football championship, hire me as basketball coach," Young said. He was at Harrison when that team won the 1992 4A championship. Now, two years in a row at North Montgomery. Still, all that shows through in Young is admiration.

"These kids are a special group," he said, "especially the seniors.

"It's the smallest class we've had at North Montgomery in the four years I've been here — by a great number. They hang together. They work hard in the classroom. They have great parents. They're supportive of each other. They're great role models. They're just a unique group. That's the reason they've been successful in football.

"And we've been successful in basketball. Last year we were 14-8 and we lost the first two." The Western Boone game dropped this team to 5-6, after an 0-2 start.

"I don't think the football team was as talented this year," he said. "They just had to reach down, all the time. They practiced hard and played every game with great intensity. Then when it's over . . .

"They're kids. They had burns all over their arms. It's not a lot of fun to practice basketball and sweat with those things.

"I'd like to see the state really take a look at the seasons, whether it's cutting basketball back to 18 games, whatever."

Shawn Ratliff, who scored nine points in this game, was Young's one starter from Wingate.

Yes, Ratliff said, he is aware of that long-ago title. "Around town, people make up shirts of the championship years and relive it," he said.

"It is kind of funny — a small town like that won the state championship."

Shawn likes basketball and he's giving it a full shot. "I enjoy sports," he said. Late in the football season, peeking ahead as much as he dared, he'd get out the basketball and do some shooting on Sundays. But that was it.

The transition, he said, "was kind of tough. You really don't have the legs that you need at the start of the season. It's tough coming in and running hard.

"We're coming. We'll be ready when the sectionals come along."

Score one for Thorntown

The home team's nickname is symbolized by a big white star that angles into the center of its Tartan court. Flags at one end of the court show that both of these teams are members of the Sagamore Conference. It's not a league of general note, but it's sneaky-fast in state championships. Counting the three in these teams' ancestry, the Sagamore has 11 titles (four for Frankfort, three for Lebanon, one for Crawfordsville). OK, the North Central Conference has 25, but there can't be many others ahead of the Sagamore.

It didn't seem likely a 12th would come from this matchup of a 5-7 team (Western Boone) and a 5-5.

"WeBo," its quickie neighborhood name, opened the game with a 3-point basket by its 6-5 center, Ryan Hanson. Closing out the first quarter, as it did the second and the third, the Stars ran the clock down before taking a final shot. "Any time we've got the ball under a minute, we'll go for one shot," Pierce said. This time, the

Stars ran off 50 seconds before center Hanson beat the first-quarter buzzer with his second 3. "He's one of our top shooters," Pierce said.

The Western Boone lead reached 22-12 in the second quarter, but Kyle Lutes (who didn't score in the state championship game but is a receiver) came off the North Montgomery bench to hit two 3s. Still, the lead was 24-16 at halftime and 33-24 late in the third quarter.

Then McCormick bombed a 3, the start of a nine-point run capped by a rebound basket by Sparks and a turnover cash-in basket by Templeman. The game was tied, 33-33.

Guard Brad Davis is WeBo's only starter from Thorntown. His one basket of the night broke the tie. North Montgomery never caught up again.

'Let's try it'

Both of these schools voted for class basketball.

"I hate to see it," Pierce said, "but times change. You really have to go a long way back before small schools won a state tournament — in fact, if Milan hadn't, you probably had to go way back."

To get that small a winner, *way* back. To 1915 and Thorntown. His team's ancestor.

"Our sectional is very competitive," he said. "And we had alternating sites, Lebanon and North Montgomery. That makes a difference.

"When a school has held the sectional for so many years, and the small school doesn't have a chance, you need to realign and get them into a competitive sectional where they can play and move on a little bit. You think Sheridan really enjoys playing in the Carmel sectional?

"And they also needed to alternate the sites.

"If they had done that, we probably would still have our state tournament the way it is."

Young knows his school represents one of the arguing points that sold class basketball. Football has been operating with classes since the first year of state playoffs, 1973. Football championships were prized items at the North Montgomerys around the state. Western Boone won one, too, in 1988.

"I would agree that football helped sell it," Young said. "People saw situations like ours and thought, 'We could have some success.' But you just can't compare football and basketball.

"Personally, I'm a traditionalist. I'm just not for multiclass basketball. I'm the only one in my school who's against it.

"But it's here. Let it alone. Let's try it. I don't think it ought to be in the legislature. I'm just not for that."

The most famous WeBo Star

The most famous basketball player ever to wear a Western Boone uniform is glad his playing days passed before the change.

Kent Poole was captain of the 1982 Western Boone team that made the greatest tournament run in school history. The Stars won the sectional, for the only time ever won the regional, and in the semistate at Mackey Arena, the slowdown game that captain Kent Poole was a major part of pushed to the buzzer mighty Gary Roosevelt — the Roosevelt team that came within one very late, indiscreet pass of winning the state championship that year.

If a last-second shot had just dropped . . .

Kent Poole's last-second shot.

"They scored to go ahead 38-36 with four seconds left," Poole said, the game a whirring videotape in his mind. "We called a timeout, inbounded it to midcourt, called another timeout with two seconds left, and set up a double screen with me coming off for a baseline shot.

"A guy was coming at me, but I had an open shot. It looked good the whole way. It bounced on the rim four or five times and finally dropped off.

"Teamwise we played well. It was one of the worst shooting days I ever had in my life."

But what an adventure.

"I'll never forget the feeling of walking out of our locker room at Mackey Arena . . . hearing the crowd waiting on us to come out onto the court . . . running up that walkway — that just sends chills down you, an 18-year-old kid in that kind of situation.

"It was really neat."

The low score against Roosevelt was typical of Western Boone's tournament run. "We didn't do that during the season, but when we got to the regional, we were up against bigger teams sizewise and our coach (Howard Leedy) came up with a delay-type offense that relied on backcuts and backdoors.

"In the championship game of the regional, Clinton Prairie just sagged back in and wouldn't let us have a backcut. So the first quarter was scoreless. At halftime, we led 6-4.

"I stood out at midcourt, holding the ball. People say, 'That had to be boring.' But as a player, it was one of the most enjoyable games I ever played in. I'll bet they stopped the game three times because the Clinton Prairie fans were disassembling the bleachers. They were throwing anything from nuts to bolts to quarters out there.

"It takes five guys who can handle the ball and not make mistakes. Every possession can mean the game. It totally rattles the other team. The minute they get the ball back, the only thing they can think about is shooting — they would fly down the floor, take a quick shot, we'd get the ball back and hold it for three minutes. Still today, people here talk about that regional game."

It's reminiscent of another game. That Milan thing. Kent Poole can tell you about that one, too, though he was 10 years short of being born when the game was played.

It's the reason why Kent Poole is the most famous Western Boone basketball player ever. It's the reason why you know him.

You do if you saw *Hoosiers*. And not many real-life Hoosiers didn't.

The kid on the picket fence

Kent Poole played for Hickory in that film.

Kent Poole ran the picket fence to hit the shot that won a game.

Kent Poole, in the locker room at Butler Fieldhouse before Hickory went out to play for the state championship, is the player who said:

"I want to win this for all the small schools that never had a chance to be here."

As Merle Webb, he had other lines, but that one was special. "When I read the script, I thought: This is my situation all over again," he said.

He'll never forget the shiver, the plain raw thrill, he felt the first time he saw himself deliver that line on screen. "Oh, sure, it still happens today," he said. "And I've seen it hundreds of times, because when it first opened we were asked to go around a lot of different theaters and be there when it premiered. I still get chills watching things that mean more to me than other people.

"Just the other night it was on Channel 4 and I happened to be slipping through the channels. I caught the last half."

And there it all was again, that adventure that will be with him the rest of his life. Guaranteed. "I bought five copies," he said. There'll be grandchildren some day, you know.

He'll tell them all about how he was out of basketball and back on his Boone County farm when he heard about tryouts that were going to be conducted in Indianapolis to pick the *Hoosiers* team. He went, almost on a dare the first time, then again and again as the process strung out, eight trips in all, as he remembers it, without any real promise that he'd have any kind of role. He knew there was some pushing and tugging going on. "Orion Pictures wanted actors to be the Hickory players," Poole said. Writer Angelo Pizzo and director David Anspaugh had carried their own dream too far to give in. "They fought hard," Poole said. "They said, 'We're not doing it unless we get basketball players.'"

And he'll tell those grandchildren about the picket fence.

In the movie, coach Gene Hackman intentionally gets himself thrown out late in a tied game, so assistant coach Dennis Hopper can have something to rebuild an alcohol-ruined life around. Hackman puts him in charge and leaves last-second instructions: "Run the picket fence." It was a play to get Merle Webb open for a shot.

The "fence" amounted to a four-man screen. "All the other guys converged down there for me to roll off of them," Poole said. One by one, they were there to cut off Poole's defender. Then he was to hit the shot. Had to. It was in the script. They were going to run that play and run that play and run that play till he got it right.

"The very first time we did it, I made the shot," he said.

"But it wasn't pure net and that's what they wanted. I thought, gee, whiz, you guys are *picky*.

"We ran it the second time through and I drained it — I hit it just the way they wanted it.

"They said, 'Let's take another one, just for good measure.' The director laid a $5 bill on the floor and said, 'I'll bet you can't hit another one.' Sure enough, when I came off the picket fence all I saw was that $5 bill laying on the end line. I didn't even come close."

He was out there, too, when "Jimmy Chitwood" hit the shot that won the State for Hickory.

Jimmy was Maris Valainis. "He's *really* ironic," Poole said. "He didn't even try out. He went to Chatard High School in Indianapolis but didn't play high school ball. He said he was about 5-8 then. He's 6-2 now."

Valainis, who went on to give acting a full try, was found by Don Stratigos and Tom McConnell, friends of Pizzo, each with an Indiana basketball background (Stratigos as a South Bend Central player, McConnell as a southern Indiana high school coach). "They were out looking for extras to put together other players to play against us," Poole said. "They saw him playing somewhere, they just watched him, his style, how he looked, and they said, 'There's our Jimmy.' That's how he got his part."

Jimmy/Maris was the movie's Bobby Plump.

Have no doubts. The Hackman role, the Hopper role, the reluctant star, the whole story line away from the court and in part on it were fiction, by design.

But the shot that won the game and continues to thrill America was Milan. Plump. By design.

"Before we started filming that scene, they brought us in a room and showed us clips of the Milan play," Poole said.

They watched. They studied what their counterparts did. Then they went out onto that storied, lore-filled Hinkle Fieldhouse floor to do it, before a crowd of about 8,000 packed into one side and both ends of the 12,000-capacity arena.

Basically, Poole and the other three "just went to the left and got out of the way," Poole said. Just like Milan.

Still, there was some staging to do.

"We were on the court running through how we were going to set it up and do it," he said. "Maris was down at the other end of the court, working on that shot — to get a feel for the distance, the shot, the whole thing.

"And he could not hit it to save his soul.

"It was so bad the crowd saw it — everybody saw it. He'd shoot and they would groan. I'm sure they thought they were going to be there for a long time. It got to the point where we were giving him a hard time, joking with him. That made it worse because he started thinking about it more.

"Then they started the cameras and he hit the very first one. It couldn't have been any more perfect.

"And the crowd was so shocked they went absolutely nuts — which was just exactly what they wanted for the film."

Since that day, Kent Poole has been in front of cameras several times to film commercials. He has made more *Hoosiers*-connected appearances than he can count, been spotted and recognized often while just being Kent Poole — once in an airport in a small town in Georgia.

But the real Kent Poole is a happy husband (wife Judi's dad played at Thorntown) and father (of Kassi, Trevin and Page, two of them already in school), working his Boone County farm — *Hoosiers* a beautiful memory.

"It's something you dream of," he said, "having an opportunity like that."

Homer Stonebraker and Al Smith, stewards of the same rich soil at the other end of this century, had their own big opportunities and capitalized, too.

Cloverport (Ky)	82
Cannelton	80

February 1

CANNELTON

None	STATE CHAMPIONSHIP
None	TIMES IN FINAL FOUR
None	REGIONAL CHAMPIONSHIPS
Five: 1933, 1936, 1946, 1948, 1952	SECTIONAL CHAMPIONSHIPS
Rome (1935), Tobinsport (1935)	CONSOLIDATIONS
Yes	VOTE ON CHANGE TO CLASSES
1A. (62; 94th of 96 in class)	1997-98 CLASS (ENROLLMENT)
3A, Corydon, North Harrison, Tell City; 2A, Crawford County, Perry Central. Crawford County site, Perry Central 1997 champion	1996-97 SECTIONAL OPPONENTS (1997-98 CLASSIFICATION)
Evansville Day, New Harmony, Northeast Dubois, Tecumseh	1997-98 SECTIONAL OPPONENTS
4-17 (lost to Tell City in sectional quarterfinal, 66-62)	FINAL RECORD 1996-97

Above the
Fire Trucks

Clearly, Jeremy Bennett was not planning to lose . . . was not *going* to lose. No way. Cannelton's 6-foot-4 junior center, listed at 152 pounds though he does not seem slim, scored his team's first basket. He hit his first five shots, missed a 3-point try, then hit three more field goals — eight that came in a variety of ways, none of them easy, except for a quick, lithe jumper whose skills are multiplied by an athlete's timing. Bennett came off screens to hit jump shots, faked and drove to dunks or layups, picked off passes and took them to the hoop, rebounded teammates' misses and went back up to score. "A lot of teams don't like to play us man because of him," Bennett's coach, Mike McClintic, said.

"That Bennett kid," said coach Mike Hensley of Frederick Fraize High School in Cloverport, Ky., "was one of the best kids we've played all year."

Bennett had a career-high 33-point night, but even with 15 fourth-quarter points from 5-11 junior forward Michael Snyder, Cannelton couldn't keep up. My, how the Bulldogs tried, but defeat was an inching-away process. From a last lead of 49-47 with 11 minutes left in the game, then a desperate lunge that cut an eight-point gap to 63-61 as the clock moved inside six minutes, Cannelton fingertips kept sliding. From 65-61 on, the Bulldogs never had the ball with a chance to tie. Three times they scored to be just a 3-point shot away, at 67-64, 75-72 and, with 53 seconds left, 79-76.

Each time the Kentucky team scored before giving the ball back. Then Snyder hit with 20 seconds left to get Cannelton within 80-78, but Jerry Atwell, who hit a monumental 3 for Cloverport two minutes earlier, sank two free throws with 17 seconds to go.

And the game ended 82-80. "We've been doing that all year," McClintic said. "We'll play hard, get a lead, and then for some reason go into a daze where we don't take care of the ball and we take some ill-advised shots. We lost a 10-point lead to Crawford County in the last four minutes. Instead of being 2-12, we should be 8-6 — at the worst.

"It's getting old."

Bennett is the hope. "He can hit 3s, but we have to play him inside," McClintic said. "He can create his own shot. I've never had a kid who could do that as well.

"The other kids know he can play and try to get him the ball — for the most part. But a lot of times we do . . . crazy things."

Defeat is wearying, exasperating for coaches and players at Cannelton. No further down to dig. No solace in a nice try. No thoughts at all of quitting. This 82-80 game was, in one courageous, unrewarded but unrelenting effort, the story of Jeremy Bennett, of Cannelton basketball, of Cannelton itself in 1996-97.

It will fight on.

A new gym rising

Cannelton does not fit the basic operating plan for this book project. Cannelton never has won a state championship, or a semistate, or a regional. Its last sectional championship came 45 years ago.

But in an Indiana basketball season of big-school and little-school concerns, Cannelton was a visit that had to be made.

Cannelton High School plays its games on the second floor of the town fire station. Is that enough for openers?

It's an Ohio River town. It has been there for 160 years. It was a coal-mining community, but a town fire in 1839 burned out everybody but four families, four homes. It rebuilt. It was the proud

Jeremy Bennett, a 6-foot-4 center, was the leading scorer for Cannelton. (Photo ©Bob Hammel)

county seat of Perry County till a year ago, when Tell City, which borders right up to Cannelton, built a new courthouse and took even that away.

But Cannelton has a splendid way of looking ahead, not behind.

There's that ancient, undersized, cramped gym above the fire station, for example.

Cannelton High's enrollment ranks two spots up from the very bottom, 383rd of Indiana's 385 basketball-playing high schools. McClintic had an 18-man squad to stock the varsity and junior

Still under construction, Cannelton's new gym will probably not be ready for the 1997-98 season. (Photo ©Jane Hammel)

varsity. The girls program was bigger news. It played its full season with just five girls — no substitutes at all. But it played every game and won six.

And now, before the first year of class basketball is over, both Cannelton's boys and girls teams can see a brand new gym on the way up. IHSAA Commissioner Bob Gardner, who grew up not far away, was the featured speaker at ribbon-cutting ceremonies August 31. The building likely won't be ready for use this season, but it's going up, across from the high school. It will happen.

There's a statement in there on how long Cannelton plans to keep its high school alive. "Forever," Buddy Bennett said. "I guess the only way we wouldn't is if they legislated us out."

William "Buddy" Bennett retired after 37 years as principal of Cannelton's elementary school. Jeremy Bennett is the step-grand-son of Buddy and his wife, Alice, who taught second grade for 32 years — with him, not under him, he gently corrects the phrasing. "Nobody was 'under' me. The word boss is not in my vocabulary. We were a family."

Buddy Bennett, who served a four-year team as mayor, also is the town's unofficial historian. He still is a volunteer for school reading classes, and once or twice a year he talks to Cannelton kids about local history. He tells them: "A gentleman from Pennsylvania came down the Ohio River and picked this site for settlement." The fellow picked well, Buddy might tell them, because Cannelton's banks go up quickly and sharply, and when the devastating February floods savaged towns all along the Ohio, Cannelton was almost untouched.

Cannelton's boom-town days were not long ago. Two major construction projects in the late 1950s and through the '60s added locks on the Ohio and a new bridge across it. "We had a lot of construction," Bennett said. "Our enrollment was at its greatest." The four-year high school enrollment almost hit 300, topping out between 270 and 280. "That really was a windfall for us," Bennett said. The federal and state projects' impact on the school system brought funds that allowed an addition to the high school.

In those days, Cannelton played football. "We started with six-man football, then moved up to eight," said Bennett, who helped coach. "We had a couple of boys go down to Evansville to play football — Paul Gunn and Charlie Kendall. We thought they'd get lost in the shuffle down there. They started playing right away. Paul was a back, Charlie was an end. Charlie just retired as an elementary school principal."

The eight-man game ("everybody is eligible to receive the football except the center and what you would call the two guards") introduced the sport to all the regional small schools along the river: Poseyville, Boonville, Mount Vernon, Rockport, Dale, and, of course, Tell City. They joined with Cannelton in a league.

Tell City-Cannelton was the rivalry, so intense and so lucrative at the gate for both that when Tell City outgrew the others and began playing regular 11-man football, the contract with Cannelton continued. It took some ingenuity. "When we played at Tell City, we played 11-man football," Bennett said. "And when the game was at Cannelton, they played 8-man."

Then the locks were completed, the bridge was done, the construction workers moved on. "Our last year of football was '71," Bennett said.

The enrollment began to slip. The official freshman-through-junior count this year, for the IHSAA's class-determination procedure, was 62. Only New Harmony (56) and Fort Wayne Christian (55) were smaller.

But Cannelton mayor Mark Gerlach says the community "rallied behind" the $1-million project that will give the Bulldogs a new gym. "If there was opposition, there was very, very little," Gerlach said. Like the present arrangement, the gym will be in a community building, which is why it qualified for matching funds from the Indiana Department of Commerce. "People have fought long and hard for this," Bennett said. "Then this business came along where they were able to get this grant. I don't think anybody doubted that we would be able to come up with the money. It's matching funds, but part of that can be labor — it doesn't have to be just an outlay of $500,000."

Governor Frank O'Bannon, from nearby Corydon, was the lieutenant governor when he helped town officials through the bureaucratic hurdles. Bonds were sold with no problem. Contracts were drawn in the spring, for completion in 270 days. There's still some funding to be completed, but everyone in Cannelton expects to be playing there soon — and so does O'Bannon, who has his own Hoosier basketball roots and wants a chance at making the first basket in the new building.

'You'll know it'

Always pleasantly and always firmly, Bennett denies that this is all a case of a community keeping a high school alive so it can have a basketball team.

"No, not really," he said. "The people here are that proud of having a school. There have been two or three attempts made to consolidate us with the Tell City school system, and (Cannelton people) have fought it each time." When there were votes, the proposals were beaten. "Even a lot of the Tell City people voted in favor of us keeping our school," Bennett said. It seemed the most mellow of ways to say that Tell City didn't want unity with Cannelton any more than Cannelton did.

"I'm sure athletics has something to do with how our people feel," Bennett said. "But it does in every school, especially in Indiana. People just look forward to this Friday night business. It's a happening here. Our baseball team has won four sectionals in the last seven or eight years. We don't go much farther than that because we bump into Evansville Memorial or Jasper in the regional.

"I just know if you went out into the community and said: 'Why don't you consider going to Tell City — the kids are going to get the advantage of this and the advantage of that,' I'm sure you'd hear something you don't want to hear.

"We were one of the first in the state on the buddy system — computers everywhere. I think everybody realizes we don't have advanced math and advanced science, but we have the basics in math and science.

"My wife and I put nine children through the school system here, and seven of them (including Debbie Gerlach, wife of the mayor and assistant coach of the indomitable five-girl varsity team of 1996-97) graduated from a four-year college. We have seven grandchildren in the school now. Our high school graduated 19 kids last year and 17 of them went to either a college or technical school.

"We were the only school system in this part of the state that was operating in the black, until a couple of years ago. We've borrowed like everybody else. Yes, it's a little bit of a financial strain. But we've been operating in the black year in and year out."

He spoke as the varsities were taking the floor.

There is, his visitor reminded him, this matter of playing directly over the fire trucks. What if . . .

"If they go out, you'll know it," he said. "There's a siren on top of the building. If it goes, you'll know that, too."

Just like Boston Garden

Like old Boston Garden, the playing floor of the fire-hall gym is parquet. The court is a few feet short, and regulation width. Nine rows of bleacher seats run the length of the court on both sides. At one end is a brick wall. The other end is wide open, into the concession stand, except for about 10 feet of brick wall jutting out of each corner. Three support poles run along each side, vision blockers to fans, perils to drifting referees. Everything is padded.

The listed seating capacity is 1,099. "I'd hate to see more than 900 in here," elementary principal Stephen Westrick said.

"We have our rivalries — Perry Central, South Central, Forest Park, Hancock County across the river," Bennett said. "We've had games this year where we probably missed filling the gym by maybe 100 people. We've had games where we sold chairs in front of the concession area because the gym was full."

The new gym probably will seat about 1,500. And that's just about the town's population.

Cannelton, the only 1A team in its sectional field this year, did vote for class basketball.

McClintic wouldn't have.

"People think I'm nuts," he said, "but I just like the old way."

In his first sectional as Cannelton coach, the Bulldogs beat Tell City. "They're our biggest rival, and that was the first time Cannelton had beaten them in 22 years," McClintic said. "But I was shocked, the way everybody went wild over it. To me, we had just won one sectional game, and we had to get ready for another one.

"We didn't win a sectional game the next two years. We got beat one year by South Spencer, when they had Parish Casebier. And Heritage Hills beat us when they had Ken Dilger." Casebier went on to star at Evansville, and Dilger, after a playing career at Illinois, is an NFL tight end.

McClintic wasn't opposed to giving small schools a better chance at the spotlight.

"I couldn't understand why they didn't set it up like Kentucky does it — Class A in the middle of the season," he said. "It's fantastic."

Cloverport coach Mike Hensley gives the five-year-old Kentucky plan his full endorsement. "We love it," he said, though his team — 10-7 leaving Cannelton — did lose in its first tournament game this year.

"We got beat by the Whitesville Trinity team that went to the State," Hensley said. "Next year, the regional is at our place."

The Kentucky plan never was forwarded to the Indiana electorate. What was proposed as an alternative to separate end-of-season class tournaments was a plan that had no chance: separate

The Cannelton Fire Department occupies the first floor of the building where Cannelton High School plays its basketball games. (Photo ©Bob Hammel)

in-season tournaments for each of the four classes, to be played over the Christmas break and completed in early January. If the intent had been to find something sure to be rejected, thereby making it possible for the IHSAA committee to say it had tried but now had no alternative but to recommend end-of-season class play, the Christmas tournament plan would have been perfect. Administrators were voting; the last thing administrators want is a clogged Christmas for themselves or their schools. All four classes were to be playing tournaments. Nobody ever asked for a separate 4A tournament.

The biggest support for separation, by far, came in the 1A group. There the vote for class basketball was 79-16, with one school (Union-Modoc) not responding in time. The margin is exactly the 63-vote edge by which the vote from all classes carried (220-157, with eight not voting in time). The top three enrollment classes split exactly evenly, 141-141.

'The best of both worlds'

The unanswered question is how all those votes, particularly the small-school, would have been affected if a Kentucky-style plan had been forwarded: an in-season small-school championship, then everybody back together for the traditional open tournament closing out the year.

Stan Steidel is the man who made it happen in Kentucky. Lexington Catholic's boys and Hazard's girls were champions this year of the eighth Kentucky All-Class A tournament.

"We've got the best of both worlds," Steidel said. "It has worked fine. It has taken care of what we needed to do and it hasn't impacted our big tournament."

Steidel grew up in Dayton, Ky., an Ohio River town where Johnny Wooden got his coaching start during World War II, where future Purdue quarterback great and eventual head coach Bob DeMoss was one of Wooden's players. Steidel came along after Wooden's two years — as a player there, then as Dayton's coach for 30 years. Now he's the athletic director and a member of the Board of Control of the Kentucky High School Athletic Association.

He knows exactly why he pressed for a separate tournament.

"We were not competing any longer," he said. "We were running around with this great dream about David beating Goliath and it was bullcrap. It was the early 1980s and we hadn't had a small school win it since (Carr Creek in) 1955. Every school that only had 900 kids in high school we said, 'That's a small school,' which was crap. We had ceased to compete.

"We started a little tournament up in northern Kentucky with nine teams. We said, 'We're going to run a class tournament. We're going to invite some teams.' Pretty soon we couldn't take care of the demand.

"So we had a meeting one Sunday and said: 'Let's do this (make it a statewide tournament). It will work.' By then we had met enough people from all the other regions to get somebody to take care of each region. That's where it started."

And now?

"This is probably the world's largest invitational tournament, but we're certainly within our (KHSAA) rules. Plus, we run an academic competition and scholarship program. We gave away about $30,000 in scholarships this year. It's all non-profit. We don't have any paid employees. Our schools in it make money. I think our share last year playing in the region was $700."

Teams involved give up, at most, two weeks of their schedule. Under present state laws, Indiana couldn't duplicate it. Games are played during class time on a few days, and the championship games are played on a Sunday. But, Indiana's 96 Class A schools could meet state rules and still play the seven rounds needed to pick a champion in at most three weeks. That could be done with 32 games on a Tuesday, leaving 64 teams for the equivalent of regionals Friday and Saturday of the first week. That would cut the field down to 16 for "semistates" on Friday and Saturday of the second week, and four to play out the semifinals and championships on the next Friday-Saturday. The 92 other schools would be freed to return to their own schedules in the third week, and 80 of them could resume their regular-season schedules after the first week, if they choose.

Kentucky makes it a three-week gala.

"We play the 16 regionals (first-round eliminations) for the girls in one week, the regionals for the boys the next week," Steidel said. "The third week we play statewide — 16 boys and 16 girls in the same week."

All gather at Eastern Kentucky University. "We play eight games a day — start at 9 in the morning, done about midnight," Steidel said. "The girls play eight games on Wednesday, the boys play eight games on Thursday, then there's four girls games and four boys games on Friday, two boys and two girls games on Saturday, and championships on Sunday.

"The boys game is usually on live TV statewide. The girls are televised on a delayed basis on Kentucky education television.

"It's a great tournament — middle of the year, a lot of excitement. It hits about the time when you always go through the doldrums, where you've been playing a while and it's still a while to the big tournament."

139

A boost in March

Actually, Steidel feels the small-school tournament has affected the open season-ending tournament, positively.

"Look at the record: we didn't win any state championships for 30 years, and we've won a couple in the last five years. Last year, Paintsville was the runner-up in ours and won the state — Lexington Catholic won our tournament." Paintsville, an eastern Kentucky mountain town of 3,800, had 296 students. It was the reigning champion in Kentucky when Indiana's first vote to change to class basketball came in.

"A couple of years ago," Steidel said, "University Heights (from Hopkinsville) was runner-up in our tournament and won the state.

"Since we've been doing this, our small schools *have* had a little more success. And I think that's because kids stay in the school. What was starting to happen in Kentucky was if you were a good player in a small school you transferred to a big school so you could go for the glory."

Steidel said he saw *Hoosiers* and fully grasped the underdog theme. "Oh, definitely. I grew up here, I played here, I know what it would be like to accomplish that.

"But the days of sneaking up on people, having three good players and getting in the backdoor — they're all playing big-time now, and half of them are playing illegal. I'm not whistling, I'm telling it the way it is. Maybe it's not that way in Indiana but it is over here. We go to church on Sunday and say what good Christians we are and then we've got to look in the mirror once in a while. 'If I do this, I could kick their butts.' You find out how Christian you are."

He has watched what has happened in Indiana.

"I was surprised, and I very, very much admired the people who made that decision. It's easy to duck out the back door and take the easy way out: 'This isn't what people want.' But it's probably the fairest thing for their kids.

"I serve on our board of control. I know how tough a decision that was. I know what it's like to have people look at you and say, 'You're messin' with the big one.' "

The survey that Indiana's committee members did never reached Steidel, he said.

What he would have told them is that his "invitational" is open to about 130 schools with an enrollment of 425 or below in the upper three grades. Every one of them enters. "They're all eligible to play in it," he said, "and all of them play that are eligible."

Larry Bird country

Even in Indiana's 79-16 small-school support for class basketball, there were pockets of resistance, mainly in the south. In Greene County, all three 1A schools — Bloomfield, Shakamak and White River Valley — voted no. A five-school sectional south of Greene County will include four schools that voted no (Crothersville, Medora, Orleans and Springs Valley).

Medora voted no although it hadn't won a sectional game in 50 years.

And Springs Valley voted the way some thought it wouldn't, because the present system got the 1973-74 Blackhawks beaten in regional play by bigger Bedford, before the rest of the state could hear much about Larry Bird.

It turned out Larry's old school voted the way he preferred all along. On the May day he was introduced as the Indiana Pacers' new coach, Bird was asked his view on what Associated Press called "one of the biggest controversies in Indiana basketball history" — the switch to separate class tournaments.

"I don't like it," he said. "Playing against the big boys and beating them . . . that was my dream and my goal. The only way we could do that was work our way through the tournament.

"Kids should have an opportunity to play for a title and play against the big schools."

An old Bird friend named Mike McClintic couldn't have been surprised.

McClintic and Bird were in the same high school graduating class, and their schools played in the same sectional.

"I didn't know him in junior high — my father is a Methodist minister and I grew up in Columbus," McClintic said. "We moved

Mike McClintic

to Orleans my freshman year. I remember hearing stories about him then. He was 6-2 then, a guard. He shot up in height his senior year and he knew how to handle the ball. And he was a good shooter. That's what made him such a great player when he did grow.

"Our teams had quite a rivalry. We had a good 6-7 player named Curt Gilstrap (who played with Louisville). Those two would go at it. We usually split with Springs Valley during the season, and in the tournament when we faced each other, it was a heck of a ballgame.

"I guarded Larry some, when he would go outside."

That's a 1A level, with two standout 6-7 players in the same graduating class. It went farther; the same small-school sectional that year also had 6-7 Tim Ewbank (a Paoli athlete who was a starting tight end at Purdue) and 6-7 David Smith (another 6-7 Louisville signee, from Milltown).

"My senior year, we played Milltown the first game," McClintic said. "I remember looking up and there sat Bob Knight, Digger Phelps and Joe Hall.

"After college we had an independent team and traveled around playing exhibitions. We had Ewbank, Gilstrap, Smith, all of those guys but Larry (who still had a year of eligibility left at Indiana State). Dennis Jones from Bedford, Danny King from Springs Valley, played at Indiana State — we had a good team. And we had fun.

"Then when Larry left IU and enrolled at Northwood for a while, that's where I was. I knew him well."

New (and long-lasting) Harmony

It's the way things work in small schools. Kinship ties knots. Twice a year, home-and-home, little Cannelton plays slightly littler New Harmony, and it's an all-day family affair.

Cannelton's five-girl basketball team included (from left), Stacy Lawlin, coach Greg Glenn, Brittney Glenn, Christie Alvey, Maria Gerlach, assistant coach Debbie Gerlach and Kristi Hawkins. (Photo courtesy Indiana Basketball Hall of Fame)

"It's probably the longest trip either one of us has," Westrick said. The towns are about 75 miles apart, like Fort Wayne and Logansport, but in southwestern Indiana it's a 90-mile trip, only about half by interstate. Usually, the buses load up with boys and girls teams, JVs, coaches, cheerleaders, and all the teams play. A scheduling mix-up didn't allow that for the games at New Harmony this year (the boys game was played on a Thursday), but the whole thing went on at Cannelton. "Each school's Booster Club feeds the other team — cheerleaders, coaches, everyone," Westrick said. "When they came here, after the games, we took them over for some chili and dessert, and when we went there (in past years), they bought pizzas for our group."

This year, the boys varsities split; New Harmony's girls won both of their games. "We had a whole series of games here — two boys elementary games in the morning, the girls game, the boys JV, then the varsity," Westrick said. That's the way it will be in New Harmony, too, as soon as scheduling gets back to two Saturdays.

All those New Harmony teams probably will be playing in the new Cannelton gym soon. "We're looking forward to getting in there," Westrick said. "It's going to pump a lot of excitement into the community."

They won't be closing the old place. "We're still going to use it for elementary games and maybe some junior high," Westrick said.

There'll be enough basketball in Cannelton to go around.

12

Vincennes	60
Washington	49

February 5

VINCENNES LINCOLN		WASHINGTON
Two: 1923, 1981	**STATE CHAMPIONSHIP**	Three: 1930, 1941, 1942
Five: 1916, 1925, 1968, 1969, 1984* (* lost in championship game)	**OTHER TIMES IN FINAL FOUR**	Two: 1925, 1929
17: first 1921; three in '90s, most recent 1997	**REGIONAL CHAMPIONSHIPS**	16: first 1925; most recent 1983
67: first 1916; seven in '90s, most recent 1997	**SECTIONAL CHAMPIONSHIPS**	39: first 1917; most recent 1983
Vincennes Township 1931, Gibault 1935	**CONSOLIDATIONS**	None
No	**VOTE ON CHANGE TO CLASSES**	No
3A. (799; 13th of 96 in class)	**1997-98 CLASS (ENROLLMENT)**	3A. (627; 49th of 96 in class)
3A, Sullivan; 2A, North Knox, South Knox; 1A, North Central (Farmersburg), Vincennes Rivet. Vincennes Lincoln site and 1997 champion	**1996-97 SECTIONAL OPPONENTS (1997-98 CLASSIFICATION)**	1A, Barr-Reeve, Shoals, Loogootee, North Daviess, Washington Catholic. Washington site, Barr-Reeve 1997 champion
Gibson Southern, Jasper, Pike Central, Princeton, Washington	**1997-98 SECTIONAL OPPONENTS**	Gibson Southern, Jasper, Pike Central, Princeton, Vincennes Lincoln, Washington
18-7 (won sectional, regional; lost to Bloomington North in semistate semifinal, 52-50)	**FINAL RECORD 1996-97**	16-6 (lost to Barr-Reeve in sectional final, 47-37)

Lincoln, Washington and History

It's one thing for Johnny Wilson to grow up in Anderson dreaming of being an Indian. It's another for a boy to grow up in Vincennes praying that some day he'll be . . .

An Alice?

Start by understanding that when the 20th century opened, Indiana's national renown was not for basketball or for auto racing but for writers. Historian James H. Madison noted in his book, *The Indiana Way*, that from 1850 through 1920 more best-selling books came out of Indiana authors than from writers of any other state except New York. "Just why Indianans were a scribbling people has not been and perhaps cannot be satisfactorily explained," Madison wrote. One of a spate of books that Madison described as "sentimental and romantic, often nostalgic in its appeal to traditional rural and small-town values" was *Alice of Old Vincennes*, published in 1900; the author Maurice Thompson.

That was just about the time basketball was catching on as a high school sport in southwestern Indiana. Indeed, the first game of this long, long, long-running Vincennes-Washington basketball rivalry was the first game Washington High ever played, the second for Vincennes. It was December 16, 1905, and home-team Washington won, 18-12 — to great indignation in Vincennes. A newspaper account of the game there called Washington "the roughest boys ever seen" and the team's Jack Lillie a football player who played the "roughest and unfairest" form of basketball. Now, this is not the kind of data handily accessible in most schools 91 years later, but as modern proof that Hoosiers still are scribbling there are basketball histories recently out in both towns: *Hatchets — A comprehensive history of Washington High School basketball (1905-1996)*, by Bob Padgett and Bill Richardson, and *90 Years of Alices — A History of Vincennes Lincoln High School Boys Basketball 1905-1994*, by Vincennes dentist Bill Stedman.

It could well be that Jack Lillie is the real reason Washington is called the Hatchets, though they like to think in Washington the legend of George and his cherry tree is behind it.

There is no question about the name origin of positively the only Alices ever to win a state basketball championship. Maurice Thompson probably had no idea the lasting clout he held when he mulled over names for his story's heroine. *Priscilla of Old Vincennes* — naw, bad rhythm. *Olive of Old Vincennes* — tough on the tongue, teeth and lips; *Mable . . . Clara . . . Hortense?*

There's another matter of names. Since the 1915-16 school year, one which started in the 50th anniversary year of President Abraham Lincoln's assassination, Vincennes officially has been Vincennes Lincoln High School. To the home folks, it's Lincoln period. Outside the city limits, certainly outside Knox County, it's Vincennes period. With malice toward none and clarity the goal, it will be Vincennes here.

Then there is the name of the present Alices coach: Gene Miiller. An umlaut Americanized on his ancestors' arrival from Germany gave the Newton County Miillers their distinguishing extra I. It's still pronounced miller. And as he approaches his mid-40s, it's still a continuing problem for Gene Miiller when it's time to fill out official forms. "I mark it that the extra I is correct, and it still gets changed," he said. "A nephew of mine had a teacher who argued with him — told him *he* was spelling it wrong." In the Goodland area, northwest of Lafayette, there are lots of Miillers. And one now-brighter teacher.

Then there is George Clark — George Rogers Clark, actually. Could the 29-year official scorer for Vincennes' basketball team be better-named?

Unless, of course, he was a she named Alice.

Basketball in Indiana is not a name game. Few Hoosier schools can match the basketball tradition and achievements of either the Alices or the Hatchets.

And they still don't play a very peaceful game.

When old friends meet

A rivalry that has been renewed at least once annually for the last 84 years (ponder that a minute: Army-Navy, Michigan-Ohio State and Indiana-Purdue are among the storied football rivalries that can't match that) was a little bit bigger than usual this time. They were playing for the Big Eight Conference championship.

Technically it wasn't true. Washington (4-0 in the league entering the game) still would have had to win over Jasper in its final conference game to clinch. But Vincennes (5-0) was ending its season with this game and had a chance to close everything out.

And the Alices did, winning 60-49, but not quite so easily as that double-figure margin sounds.

Every rebound was the last hunk of bread dangled before *Les Miserables*. Every loose ball created bruises and floorburns. Game face in this one meant a glare. But there was nothing cheap, just two intense rivals going after one victory.

"We knew it was going to be a physical war," Washington coach Dave Omer said.

"We played hard. They're better than we are. We took it to 'em and I was pleased with that. I told our kids after the game I was just as proud as if we'd won. I hate to lose, but I liked the effort."

This game that was the latest in a series that now includes 94 Vincennes victories and 77 by Washington "was war," Miiller agreed. "It's a real long-standing rivalry, and tonight's game, because it was for the conference championship, made it even more important.

"Our kids took a while to adjust. Early in the ballgame they were really taking it to us. The referees were letting them play, which was fine. It's going to take its toll tomorrow. Both teams are going to be tired."

Someone suggested the rivalry hadn't really been intense of late and this might rekindle some flames. "It won't hurt it any," Miiller agreed.

"It was a very physical game — just a very good basketball game. The fans were in it. This is a great place to play.

"I thought it was a great night."

Free-throw blues

Washington's Morrie Portee really didn't need introduction to the Alices. A strong, lithe 6-2 junior, Portee played some as a freshman and last year his 15.2 average made him the first sophomore in 23 years to lead the Hatchets in scoring — just the fifth in 90 years, a Hatchet legend, Leroy "Hook" Mangin of the 1941 state championship team, among them. Both Portee and 6-3 senior center Ryan Hill repeatedly bounded over the taller Alices early. The sight raised questions — track has all those events where jumping skills come in handy. Turns out both Portee and Hill prefer to spend their springs starring in baseball.

This night, Portee scored Washington's first four field goals. He did it in a variety of ways, one of them rebounding. That keyed Washington's 15-9 breakout. After Portee's fifth basket put the Hatchets up 19-11 early in the second quarter, Vincennes' defense clamped down hard. Washington turned the ball over seven times in going scoreless on eight straight possessions. Vincennes capitalized by scoring 13 straight points to go up 24-19.

In that stretch, Washington ball handler Clay Havill tried for a loose ball and pain flashed across his face. He stayed in the game, came out once and returned. At halftime, his night was over. He had broken the ring finger on his right (shooting) hand. He didn't return till the sectional tournament.

Before halftime, though, Portee one more time hurt the Alices. His 3-point basket with 1:08 left stopped the dry spell and helped Washington get to the break tied 24-24. "We got some things off our defense," Miiller said, "and then we let them back in the game. Portee hit a big 3.

"We've been trying to get to our kids' pride. The second half we shut him down."

Offense director Havill's absence also might have been part of the reason Portee didn't score in the second half, finishing with his first-half 13. Still, the game was tied with 2:30 to go in the third quarter and Vincennes led just 38-36 when sophomore Derek Cardinal closed out the third quarter by hitting a 3-point shot from the deep left corner. Derek was a solid contributor for the Alices, but he hit just three of those all year, in 19 shots.

That one sprang Vincennes out front by five, and when Clint Barnes and Dan Cleveland opened the fourth quarter with baskets, Washington was down 45-36 and — though still driving, still battling, still exhorted hard from the sidelines by Omer — all but out.

All but.

Miiller must have had nights this year when he woke up screaming at thoughts of getting his team into the lead in the final minutes and then watching victory flit away on missed free throws. It happened twice in a week at home, in nine-year-old, 5,600-seat Alice Arena where Miiller is the only man ever to coach Vincennes and where the Alices never have lost twice in a row. The two losses that came in the week wrapped around Christmas did have a home victory squeezed in between, but Miiller agonized over the free-throw problem.

"Both games we lost were against good teams (Lafayette Jefferson and North Central of Indianapolis)," Miiller said, "but it's been a big problem." The Alices were 9-5 going into this game. "Four of the five we could have won by hitting free throws," Miiller said.

Particularly painful was the free-throw slump that had gripped his best player, 6-8 junior center Charles Hedde. Hedde kept his scoring average well over 20, he shot 63 percent from the field, but he struggled all year to stay above .500 on free throws. "He just has to go up to the line confident," Miiller said. Hedde seems to have everything needed, including basketball bloodlines. His father, Charles, played for Indiana assistant coach Ron Felling at nearby Lawrenceville, Ill., High and now is a Vincennes team physician. "Charles is a great kid," Miiller said. "He's going to be a good player for somebody in college because he'll work hard and play hard."

Washington won the State Championship in 1941. Team members were, front row (from left), Ivan Wininger, Calvin Thomas, James Riffey, Arthur Grove, Robert Donaldson and Charles Harmon. Back row, coach Marion Crawley, Leroy Mangin, Forrest Crane, John Dejernett, William Harmon, Garland Raney and manager Boger. (Photo courtesy Indiana High School Athletic Association)

But it became clear after Washington fell in that 45-36 hole and Omer took a timeout, the Hatchets were going to foul Hedde every time they could. Hedde wasn't the only available target; the whole Vincennes starting lineup averaged just .576 on free throws for the year.

Hedde missed a one-and-one, then hit one of two before drawing his fourth foul at 2:56, the lead down to 47-40. Miiller replaced him with 6-5 Justin Lowe (a 78 percent free-throw shooter), and the fouling shifted to others. Cardinal (56 percent) missed the first of two, as here-we-go-again visions danced for not just Miiller but others in the huge Vincennes fan following.

Then the Alices hit nine free throws in a row, five of them by Cardinal. "I like this club," Miiller said, "but that has really been a problem for us. We did hit some big ones tonight."

'A great sectional,' but . . .

Miiller and Omer talked a little more than usual during the evening. They share a mutual distress: next year, when both can expect to have pretty good clubs. The ground rules will be different then, because of the change in the tournament structure.

"I'm a traditionalist, a conservative," Miiller said. "I think we had the greatest tournament in the world. The only tournament that comes close to it is the NCAA tournament, and here we are changing to make ours like the also-rans. I'm really disappointed.

"But there's not much we can do about it now. The sectional is probably going to be over here (at Washington), and it's going to be a great sectional — Jasper, Washington, Princeton, Vincennes, Gibson Southern, Pike Central. It will be one that the fans will really enjoy.

"I just hate to see us tear down the greatest tournament in the United States."

"We *are* going to have a great sectional here next year," Omer said. "But it's just not going to be the same."

Omer counts as one of his biggest annual kicks from the tournament the way Hatchet House splits, loudly and passionately, between Loogootee — whose Hall of Fame coach, Jack Butcher, has won the Washington sectional just about half the time — and whoever is playing the Lions.

That very atmosphere is what *Vincennes Sun-Commercial* sports editor Dave Staver sees as a reason for a change: to reduce neighbors' venom and ease animosity. Where Loogootee has done well at Washington, Vincennes has spread-eagled the field in its sectional. The Alices lead everybody in the state in sectional championships with 67. That includes 19 of the last 20, and 29 of the last 33. Now, Staver feels, the teams the Alices have been squashing — 3A (as of 1997-98) Sullivan, 2A North Knox and South Knox, and 1A North Central (Farmersburg) and Vincennes Rivet — will feel better toward the Alices if they're going for a state championship, and Vincennes people can reciprocate the support for local teams making their own tournament run. Whether he's right or wrong about that, the other five in what has been the Vincennes sectional did vote for the change to class basketball. Unanimously.

Loogootee coach Jack Butcher, far right, joins (from left) Bill Stearman of Columbus North, Jim Rosenstihl of Lebanon and Bill Green of Marion at the 1975 Final Four. (Photo courtesy Indiana High School Athletic Association, ©Bob Doeppers)

Omer had talked earlier in the day with Mark Barnhizer, who coached some outstanding teams at little Eastern High in Greene County, teams never really heard of because they were routed into the Bedford North Lawrence sectional where they disappeared. After the 1995-96 season, Barnhizer became head coach at a big school, Perry Meridian in the southern suburbs of Indianapolis.

"Mark and I are good friends." Omer said. "He said, 'Dave, I don't like class basketball, but if I'd lived in Eastern all my life, I'd probably have wanted it. I'm tired of getting beat by Bedford.'

"So he went to Perry Meridian and he's in there now with Ben Davis. I said, 'What have you gained, Mark?'

"I'm totally against it," Omer went on. "I'm just sick about the whole thing. There isn't any part of it that I like. I'm so ticked off about the whole thing I don't even know if I'll *let* myself like it if it is likable. I think they've just destroyed one of the best things in this state.

"The bottom line is that the small schools in northern Indiana, which control just about everything anyway, have been beaten by the Marions and the Muncies so long and screamed so loud that now they've got these principals who think they're going to make a mark in history by being the principal of a state champion at Norwell, which ain't gonna win a damned tournament if they play the rest of their life.

"Why couldn't we have realigned some of those little schools out of Marion and Muncie? If Blue River is all upset about playing New Castle, find a way to route some of those teams out. They can't say they're worried about travel, because travel's going to be a big-time worry anyway. They're going to run people all over southern Indiana trying to fill out a 2A sectional.

"The sectional for Eastern next year will be Eastern, South Knox, North Knox, Paoli — well, now, who in the hell knows anything about Paoli in Eastern? Or South Knox and Paoli? People in South Knox never heard of Paoli.

"I just don't see that you have to win the state tournament in this state to be successful. That's a myth.

"I can't visualize how we let this happen. If we still had Phil Eskew (commissioner of the IHSAA from 1962 to 1976), we wouldn't have it. Phil Eskew would never have let 'em in the door.

"And we know if it happens, it's never going to un-happen.

"I don't know if the (bill to delay class basketball until after a state referendum in November 1998) has any chance. I don't think so. I think if I had been (commissioner) Bob Gardner and the board, I'd have *wanted* to know how the people in the state really feel about it."

Geography class

Omer is a Kentucky native but he has been coaching Indiana high school basketball for more than 30 years. He arrived just about the time school consolidations were changing not only the makeup but also the sound of the Indiana tournament. In 1923, when Vincennes won its first state championship, 596 schools entered the tournament. By 1930, when Washington won its first state title,

Vincennes coach Gunner Wyman hugs star Doug Crook after the Alices won the 1981 State Championship. Wyman retired after the season. (Photo courtesy Indiana High School Athletic Association)

the total was up to 760. In 1941 and '42, the Hatchets won back-to-back championships under young coach Marion Crawley and then lost him to Lafayette Jefferson, where he won two more state championships. In '41 and '42, the entry lists were 777 and 769 — parochial and black schools still not permitted to enter (the 1943-44 season was the first open to those two groups).

The second Vincennes state championship came in 1981. By then, the figure had dipped below 400, to about where it is today.

Once it seemed that every one of Indiana's small towns had a high school and representation by name in the tournament. The attention paid to the state tournament, starting at the sectional level, was so intense that after Draw Day in February every newspaper ran every pairing throughout the state. Then, from the first night of sectional play on, every newspaper ran every score — 192 of them on the concluding Saturday alone. A highly popular Hoosier game from the '20s through today is attempting to pick champions at each of the 64 sites. Anything over 40 is considered very good. Anything over 50 is considered postdated.

Scrutiny of those sectional draws and the follow-up scores was Indiana Geography 101 for a whole lot of Hoosiers. People knew that Birdseye was somewhere around Jasper because they were in the same sectional, that Klondike was near Lafayette, Bippus near Huntington and Royal Center near Logansport for the very same reason.

The drive to Washington for this game passed through Elnora and Plainville, with signs pointing to Odon and Epsom. All at one time were names on high schools. None is now.

Omer smiled. He has made that drive, seen those town names. "You see that sign, you think of the Epsom Salts," he said. And that, indeed, was what teams were called at the Daviess County high school that closed its doors in 1963.

"Every place that I know in Indiana is associated with basketball," Omer said. "If I drive through a town, I know of it — if it ever had a team.

"Hell, I've applied for a job in most of them."

I cannot tell a lie, Honey

Washington is a town of not quite 11,000 and "Hatchet House," the arena it has been playing in since 1966, seats just over 7,000. They've liked basketball in Washington for a long time.

That 1930 state championship team included center Dave DeJernett, the first black player on a state championship team. If it hadn't been DeJernett, it would have been Muncie center Jack Mann, who battled DeJernett in the 1930 championship game and then led the Bearcats to the 1931 championship.

A star on both the 1941 and '42 Washington championship teams was another great black athlete, Chuck Harmon, like

DeJernett an Indiana Basketball Hall of Fame player. Harmon also made it to baseball's major leagues, with the Cincinnati Reds.

On the day of this 171st Vincennes-Washington game, *Sun-Commercial* sportswriter Bill Richardson told his readers of the Hatchets' 1931 visit to Vincennes. DeJernett still was playing, and he received a threat: death, if he dared to play in the game. He played, scored 11 points and his team won, 34-27. His father approved his playing but went to the game carrying a concealed pistol.

The only horror at the game that night was a fatal heart attack that claimed a fan. DeJernett's father made the 18-mile postgame trip home, and his anxious wife asked if there had been any trouble. It was the question DeJernett obviously had hoped for. He pulled out the gun and as he put it away, answered solemnly:

"Honey, a man died in Vincennes tonight."

Way, way back

Washington hasn't been back to the Final Four since that '42 championship, but the Hatchets had an Indiana "Mr. Basketball" in 1979, Steve Bouchie, who played on three Big Ten championship teams and one NCAA champion at Indiana. As a Washington junior, Bouchie just missed a Final Four trip. The Hatchets led Terre Haute South 53-46 with a minute to go in the semistate championship game. South scored the last nine points and won. A guard on that Terre Haute team, Cam Cameron, started on three straight Final Four teams, went to Indiana as a football quarterback and part-time basketball player, then returned to IU in January as the school's new head football coach.

Another Hatchet was Sam Alford, father and New Castle coach of future "Mr. Basketball," IU star and Olympian Steve Alford. Another was Craig Neal, who played under his dad, Stan, at Washington, in the '80s, starred at Georgia Tech and played some NBA ball.

Vincennes' history starts 160 years before there was such a thing as basketball. The French in 1732 made Vincennes the first permanent settlement in what is now Indiana. Young American hero

George Rogers Clark's victory over the British at Vincennes in 1779 was the major American triumph on the Revolutionary War's western front. In 1800, Vincennes was made the capital of the original Indiana territory, which extended north from the Ohio River to Canada and west to the Mississippi River, including the present states of Illinois and Michigan and part of Wisconsin as well as Indiana. That's the Old Vincennes that Alice came from.

The basketball Alices came to life when coach John Adams came in from Smithville to coach in the fall of 1920. Adams' 1921-22 team won 38 straight games, the state record until the first unbeaten champion, Indianapolis Attucks, 35 years later strung 45 wins. There was no schedule limit in the '20s, so Adams' Alices played everybody they could and beat them all till they ran into Bloomington in the state tournament semifinals. It was an ironic way to die: Vincennes had beaten Bloomington twice, and Adams was a Bloomington High alumnus.

The next year, Vincennes lost once during the season (31-29 to Evansville Central) but swept through to the state championship with a 34-1 record, which meant 72-2 over two years and 107-8 over Adams' first three years. Franklin's "Wonder Five" through its three-year run of championships was 89-9; Marion, during its three straight titles from 1985-87, was 84-4. The first two of those three big Vincennes years overlapped the "Wonder Five" years, but Vincennes and Franklin never met in those seasons.

Vincennes, with future IU player Jerry Memering starring, had two straight Final Four teams closing out the 1960s, getting there unbeaten in 1969 before losing to Gary Tolleston. Not until 1981 did the Alices get to Indianapolis and come back with their second state championship. Veteran coach Gunner Wyman retired after that, and Miiller came in from Kankakee Valley to coach the Alices. In three years, he had them back in the State, losing in the championship game to Warsaw.

"Oh, it was a thrill to play in the State tournament," Miiller said. "I was 30. I think (Warsaw coach) Al Rhodes and I were the youngest two ever to play for the championship.

"It would be nice to get back there this year. The last true champion."

13

Franklin	101
Martinsville	**78**

February 7

FRANKLIN		MARTINSVILLE
Three: 1920, 1921, 1922	**STATE CHAMPIONSHIPS**	Three: 1924, 1927, 1933
Four: 1912*, 1939*, 1973, 1974 (* lost in championship game)	**OTHER TIMES IN FINAL FOUR**	Four: 1916, 1917, 1926*, 1928* (* lost in championship game)
12: first 1921; one in '90s, 1997	**REGIONAL CHAMPIONSHIPS**	16: first 1921; most recent 1990
43: first 1918; four in '90s, most recent 1997. Others in corporation, 2: Union Township 1952, Hopewell 1916	**SECTIONAL CHAMPIONSHIPS**	33: first 1916; two in '90s, most recent 1995
Providence 1907, Needham 1927, Hopewell 1936, Needham Township 1939, Masonic Home 1944, Union Township 1963	**CONSOLIDATIONS**	Brooklyn 1911, Paragon 1956
Yes	**VOTE ON CHANGE TO CLASSES**	No
3A. (838; 5th of 96 in class)	**1997-98 CLASS (ENROLLMENT)**	4A. (1,322; 42nd of 95 in class)
4A, Center Grove; 3A, Greenwood, Roncalli, Whiteland; 1A, Indian Creek. Greenwood site, Franklin 1997 champion	**1996-97 SECTIONAL OPPONENTS (1997-98 CLASSIFICATION)**	4A, Mooresville; 3A, Owen Valley; 2A, Cloverdale, Monrovia; 1A, Eminence. Martinsville site, Mooresville 1997 champion
Beech Grove, Brown County, Greenwood, Roncalli, Whiteland	**1997-98 SECTIONAL OPPONENTS**	Bloomington North, Bloomington South, Columbus East, Columbus North, East Central, Martinsville
24-3 (won sectional, regional; lost to Delta in semistate final, 61-54)	**FINAL RECORD 1996-97**	16-6 (lost to Mooresville in sectional final, 64-59)

Fuzzy, Griz and Johnny

The early legends that convinced America Indiana was its true basketball capital came from communities all around the state and involved a whole lot of players, coaches and teams.

Towering over all were Fuzzy Vandivier, Griz Wagner and the Franklin Wonder Five.

Stories about that team would be Paul Bunyan-esque, except these were true. Franklin really did win three straight state championships, and at the end of that run, gathered players and coach together again for four more big years a block away at Franklin College.

The "Wonder Five" tag that forever since has been the team's identification never did fit the three-time state champions. Only Vandivier started on all three teams, but that's a lot of "only." Vandivier started as a freshman on a Franklin team that made the 16-team state tournament but lost its first game there to Crawfordsville, 28-26. It was the start of a remarkable Franklin run for Vandivier who, in an era when teams usually scored in the 20s, closed his four-year high school career with 1,540 points. It was a major Indiana story in 1990 when Damon Bailey of Bedford North Lawrence became the state's all-time career scoring leader, taking the record that Marion Pierce of Lewisville had held for 29 years. From the moment Vandivier passed whoever held the record before him, in 75 years there have been just four career record holders:

Franklin's 1921 State Championship team included, left-to-right, Carlyle Friddle, Robert "Fuzzy" Vandivier, Harry King, John Grant, Harold Borden, Wendell "Ike" Ballard, James Ross, Hubert Davis, Charlton Williams and coach Ernest B. "Griz" Wagner. (Photo courtesy Indiana High School Athletic Association)

Vandivier, Arley Andrews (who passed Vandivier as a junior and wound up with 2,772 in 1954), Pierce (3,019, finishing in 1961) and Bailey (3,134) — Vandivier's 32-year reign the longest.

As a sophomore, Vandivier outscored runner-up Lafayette in the 1920 state championship game, 17-13, the last of the five times a player did that in the championship game. The score of that game was 31-13. He had 13 when Franklin beat Anderson, 35-22, for the 1921 title and 12 in a 26-15 final-game victory over Terre Haute Garfield in 1922.

Vandivier came back to Franklin High to coach the basketball team for 18 seasons. His 1939 team reached the championship game before losing to Frankfort.

But only in retrospect were the three state championship teams he played on called "The Wonder Five." History (much of it chronicled in Phillip Ellett's 1986 book *The Franklin Wonder Five*), says the name came after Vandivier's and his teammates' high school days were over. Their coach, Ernest "Griz" Wagner, signed at Franklin College a month after his team's third straight state high school championship. Vandivier, Johnny Gant, Carlyle Friddle and Ike Ballard from that last championship team joined 1920 teammate Burl Friddle at Franklin College, and those five started Wagner's first Franklin College game, a 69-7 victory over Indiana Law School.

Four weeks later Franklin went on the road to win at Butler, DePauw and Wabash, in a four-night stretch. These were considered state powers, on a par with Indiana, Purdue and Notre Dame. A team of four freshmen and a sophomore, sweeping the three on the road on almost successive nights, prompted from the most respected Indiana sportswriter of his era, William F. Fox Jr. of *The Indianapolis News*, a story that gave the group its name:

CRAWFORDSVILLE, Ind., January 10 — Well, it's time to drag out the word "wonder." If the Interstate Special of two cars that pulled out of this historic little old village Tuesday night didn't haul a "wonder five," there never was one.

The "Wonder Five" finished that year 18-0 and claimed the state championship. The team's national coverage was such that the best professional team of the era, the New York Celtics, challenged Franklin to a postseason game in Cleveland, the winner to be named world champion. Wagner turned it down. "The team has had enough and we are ready for a rest," he said.

Coach Ernest Wagner played on the first Franklin High School team. As a boy, he had been called "our young grizzly bear" by older brother Charles, and he was "Griz" for the rest of his life. In his honor, Franklin College named its teams the Grizzlies. The high school followed up in 1933-34 by naming its teams the Grizzly Cubs. Before that, including when the "Wonder Five" was winning its championships, apparently there was no team name. The 1934 high school yearbook says before the student election that picked Grizzly Cubs, the team was simply Franklin, or the Blue and the White.

And so it was that in the 75th year after the last high school game of "The Wonder Five," the Franklin Grizzly Cubs came into Martinsville to play the Artesians.

Martinsville High School, known as Artesian City, won the 1927 State Championship. A member of the team who went on to redefine basketball coaching standards was John Wooden, first row, far left. (Photo courtesy Indiana Basketball Hall of Fame)

Legends all around

The game was played in John R. Wooden Gymnasium.

Three times in the late '20s, flashy John Robert Wooden, who was to go on to coach 10 NCAA champions at UCLA and swear that he never topped his high school thrills, led Martinsville teams to the state championship game. The Artesians — their name coming from wells that once were a community staple — had been there before. In Wooden's seventh-grade year, Martinsville won the 1924 state championship.

Wooden's teams finished second in 1926 (30-23 to Marion), first in 1927 (26-23 over Muncie), and second in 1928 (13-12 to Muncie — an epic championship game, decided by a last-minute shot from center court by Charles Secrist, who fielded his own center-jump tip and launched the shot).

Martinsville had its own version of "Griz" Wagner in coach Glenn Curtis, who had coached Lebanon to the 1918 championship before winning with Martinsville in 1924, '27 and '33.

When the Indiana Basketball Hall of Fame was formed in 1962, three of the five charter electees were Vandivier, Wagner and Wooden, and the third five-man group in 1964 included Curtis. In a corner of Wooden Gymnasium is a display of Martinsville's five Hall of Fame electees: Glenn Curtis, Wooden, Claude Curtis — in 1918 the winner of the first Gimbel-now-Trester Award — and Les Reynolds and Arnold "Sally" Suddith, teammates of Wooden's on the 1927 state champions.

And so it was that the two teams meeting on this night each had a glorious basketball history — and, together, six state championship trophies, six that came in just a 14-year stretch from 1920 through 1933. These were the reigning powers when Indiana became basketball's capital.

'A tough place to play'

Franklin coach Dave Clark came into Wooden Gymnasium thinking payback. "We felt like we kinda let the game get away from us last year against Martinsville," he said. "We challenged our kids this week, that this is a tough place to play and we're capable of playing with them or anybody."

The Cubs' 13-2 record had Martinsville coach Tim Wolf convinced. "They just beat a good Jennings County team," Wolf said.

The polls hadn't noticed Franklin's start. Clark didn't mind. He just appreciated it all, in a season when guard Mark Pitcher was his only starter back. Clark began the season worried, and stayed that way at least a few minutes into the season.

"We opened up with Center Grove, which is one of our big rivals," Clark said. "We got down 17 points." Franklin still trailed by 14 at halftime. "I told my assistant, 'If we don't get back in this game in the next couple of minutes, it's going to be a long last half.'"

The Grizzly Cubs had the deficit down to one by the end of the third quarter and nosed ahead for the victory.

"That was a big win for us," Clark said.

Wolf was still smiling from a valued victory three nights earlier at Bloomington South. With 34 points from senior guard Tim Majors, his class' valedictorian, Martinsville won 85-80 over one of its ancient rivals. He pointed across his office to a pleasant reminder of that game. "We play Bloomington South for that shaving mug right there," he said. "It dates back to 1939. I would hope we don't lose a lot of those things."

He still was smarting from an earlier trip to Bloomington. North thumped the Artesians, 87-53. Martinsville athletic director Don Lips was impressed. "We just got drilled," he said. "I don't think there's that much of a discrepancy but there certainly was that night. It wasn't a fluke where they just slopped in a bunch of stuff. Boy, they took it to us."

"They were great — on fire," Wolf said. The Cougars were 10-for-18 on 3-point shots. "They didn't have a player shooting over 33 percent from 3-point range, and they hit nine of them in the first half. We thought we could make them shoot the ball from outside.

"They did. They shot it.

"North's pretty good. They have a chance. A lot of teams don't have that chance, but they can climb a couple of levels. North has a chance."

He didn't have to fill in any blanks. "A chance" in February means winning the whole thing.

Cruisin' past 100

Dave Clark was in the first graduating class at Bloomington North. So maybe he watched that North-Martinsville film extra closely.

His Cubs did a good imitation. In Wooden Gym on this night, they shot it.

Franklin almost screeched with its takeoff. The Cubs hit 10 straight first-quarter shots, three of them 3s. Majors didn't have a Martinsville basket. Of such are long nights made. Franklin led 27-10 and rushed it on up to 40-13 just over two minutes into the second quarter. That's a 125-point pace. Wolf, already assessed with a technical foul by then, had the look of a man who wouldn't have been at all surprised if the pace stood up. Very clearly, very early, this was Franklin's night.

Majors hit his first field goal, a 3, just over a minute before half-time, which came with Franklin's lead at 53-29. The Cubs didn't cool. They zoomed past 75 in the third quarter and cruised in, 101-78.

"We seem to bring out the best from teams," Wolf said.

"I think they're pretty good, too."

Pitcher, a 6-foot senior, scored 26 points, unusual on what Clark considers "a pretty well-balanced team. We have four kids in double figures, and the fifth one is 9.8."

On this night, he had five double-figure scorers, a sixth player with nine, and the Cubs got to 100 with almost nothing from 6-8 senior center Joe Hougland — two early field goals, no more shots or points, one rebound, four fouls.

Certainly, his off-night was affordable. Pitcher alone made up for it. "We've had good leadership throughout the year," Clark said. "Mark has been our floor leader the last two years. I just thought he held his composure against people who really put a lot of pressure on you for 32 minutes.

"Most of these kids came off the bench for us last year. A lot of people counted us out. These kids have kinda made that an emphasis, to show they could play their roles."

Putting tradition to work

Nobody has to tell Dave Clark about Franklin's tradition, or almost anybody else's. He grew up with Indiana basketball tales. His grandfather, Harold "Babe" Wheeler, is in the Indiana Basketball Hall of Fame for the way he played at Terre Haute Garfield (he outscored Vandivier, 13-12, in that 1922 championship game) and Purdue and coached for a long career at Brazil.

Clark works his team every day in 36-year-old Vandivier Gymnasium, the place's name the first reminder of how rich that Franklin tradition is.

"There are big, big team pictures at one end of the floor of all three championship teams," Clark said. "There's a banner, not only for the three state champions but also the four others that went to the Final Four but didn't win." Those trips were in 1912, the second tournament; 1939, when Frankfort beat Vandivier's Cubs for the state championship but Franklin's George Crowe, later a major-league baseball player, was named Indiana's first Mr. Basketball; and 1973 and '74, when the McGlocklin twins, Jon and Don, led the way to back-to-back State trips. That Jon McGlocklin is not to be confused with uncle Jon, who starred at Indiana with another set of twins, Dick and Tom Van Arsdale, and then started with Oscar Robertson in the backcourt of the 1971 NBA-champion Milwaukee Bucks.

It all adds up to a tradition that didn't end with the "Wonder Five," but assuredly took on a life then.

"That was why I was interested in coming to Franklin, because of that tradition," Clark said. "I was leaving White River Valley, where maybe the talent wasn't always going to be there but you have kids who really want to play.

"Basketball is a main focal point in the community at White River Valley. Here, there are a lot of other things going on. But still you have that tradition in the background in the community.

"I think you want to go someplace that has some expectations. We've put some expectations on these kids.

"We use that tradition. Oh, yes."

'We thought we had a chance'

Clark, as a young coach, took little White River Valley to two straight semistates and pushed 1993 champion Jeffersonville to the buzzer in the semistate finals. That experience, more than talks with his grandfather, shaped his views on the class basketball issue.

"There's no doubt our kids and I, we all thought we had a chance to win it all," Clark said. "We played in the Hall of Fame tournament, we played Cincinnati Woodward, which was a top-ranked team; we went to St. Louis and played in the Shootout there against the top-ranked team in Missouri. It comes around just once in a lifetime, maybe, or once in a few years, but — you talk about

'Hoosier Hysteria.' We got to play in places like Terre Haute and Evansville and big gyms across the state. It's true, not every little school gets to go there, but to have that opportunity just once, or twice, and have that atmosphere . . .

"I just thought they could have done so much better.

"I know there are some schools that really have a long shot of winning a sectional. If they want classes, do it at the sectional and regional level. I just don't understand their thinking, when they had a good thing going, to completely wipe it out."

A personal irony for Clark is that his school voted for the change. Magnifying the irony: of 38 schools with direct name and linkage to teams that have won state championships, 36 voted against the change. The two former champions who said yes: Crawfordsville, the first winner, and Franklin, "The Wonder Five" school.

"Our principal (Walter Vanderbush) wants to change," Clark said. "He makes the decisions and he went that way. You have to respect him for that, but that wasn't the consensus. Our community is not for it, our coaches are not for it. A lot of people couldn't understand, with the tradition that we had in the state tournament, how could we vote against it?"

Convictions of a 'foreigner'

Walt Vanderbush chuckles as, one more time, he starts in on an explanation of just why he cast Franklin's vote in favor of class basketball.

Yes, he said, he certainly knew the sentiment out there, though he didn't feel it was nearly so strong against the change as opponents felt. He voted as he did not essentially in Franklin's interest — if there's a reclassification in two years, Franklin likely will be moved to 4A, one of the littlest of the big schools. Rather, it came from a strong personal feeling that the change was best for the entire state, and for its kids.

Even opponents of the switch know that educational times have changed in Indiana. Once, there was an almost automatic advancement, particularly in smaller schools, of basketball coach to principal to superintendent. Now, administration is a field of its own. A significant number of Indiana high school principals come from out of state; another significant number are women. Professionalizing principalships clearly is an educational advancement, but it also altered whatever special feeling coach-turned-principals had for the tournament structure — for the better, toward more objectivity, one argument runs; for the worse, taking heritage and heart out of the issue, the other side contends.

Vanderbush distorts the stereotypes. Yes, he is a "furriner." He grew up in New Jersey and was a principal in Michigan before taking the Franklin job 14 years ago.

But he's also a former player and, for 13 years, a head basketball coach. "Even though the people here sometimes talk about me as a foreigner I do have a pretty good background," he said.

"I played as a high school basketball player in New Jersey where we had four groups. When I was in junior high, our school won the Group 4 (biggest schools) state championship. Then I coached in Pennsylvania and New York, where there were class sports. When I was principal at Buchanan, Mich., we won the Class C (second-smallest enrollment group) state championship twice. One year we were 28-0 and my sons were the starting guards."

Pleasantly, comfortable enough with his convictions to interject laughter at times, he made his points.

"I've been around class sports in four different states, and I've had an emotional tie either as a coach, player, parent or principal, and I've been here for a long period of time. I think I have a better background to judge this than some of the people who are so-called experts.

"I get a kick out of listening to people like George McGinnis, Damon Bailey and Steve Alford who were all very successful winners of this particular tournament and they were considered to be the experts. If they want to talk to people who are experts, they should go to Edinburgh, where the girls have never won a sectional game. Those are the people who are not getting spoken with.

"In 1954 when Milan won the state championship, I wasn't here, obviously, but I've done a lot of reading about it. Gene White is on our faculty. He and I have debated this to the point where we don't bother anymore.

"It was a miracle in 1954. They called them the Miracle Men of Milan. Conditions are much, much, much more against the small schools now than they were in 1954. If it was a miracle then, it's almost an impossibility now.

"The game is much, much more physical. I look at the game now and the brutal wrestling that takes place in the post area — I was a head basketball coach from 1956 until 1969. I could play five guys the whole game and get away with it. Today, you really can't.

"So the small schools have another disadvantage. They obviously don't have the depth that the big schools have.

"Finesse isn't as valuable as it once was. The good shooter who learned to shoot in the driveway or the barnyard isn't quite so important as he was in those days, because of the physical nature of the game. Even a guy like Rick Mount couldn't make it in the NBA. That has shifted down to college and now down to high school. I think that's a shame, but that has made it more difficult."

"The difference in enrollment numbers has always been a huge problem, if you look back at who wins the state tournament. But now the big schools have all kinds of additional advantages, including things like weight programs, full-time trainers who get their athletes back into circulation, and many more coaches than the small schools have. And they still have the home-court advantages which they've had.

"Another thing that has happened in Indiana for a long time is the good athlete at the small school says, 'I don't have a chance.' That athlete's parents frequently decide, 'We'll move somewhere where we do.' That makes the problem worse. The strong get stronger and the weak get weaker.

"It's just not fair. It would be like Franklin College having to play IU in basketball in the NCAA tournament. People would think that's absurd. That's what it's like with Edinburgh having to play Ben Davis. It's absurd.

"The people who are upset now are the people at the schools that had a pretty good lock on winning the sectional and in some cases the regional because they could skate right through against little schools. They're not going to win so many trophies. The smaller schools are going to win some now, playing against schools with equal size and equal resources. There's going to be a different distribution of the trophies.

"I hear people say winning the state tournament won't mean anything anymore. That's silly. If there are 96 schools in a particular class, the average school is going to win about once a century. That's still quite an achievement.

"We're looking at equity, as opposed to watering things down.

"The big schools themselves have had inequities. Some big schools, for example Lawrence North, have had to go against other big schools right away. It has been a devil of a thing to get out of the sectional. Then there are the Marions which have been able to go against little schools and come out. The tournament itself has been completely unequal.

"But now — boy, how exciting it's going to be to have New Castle, Anderson, Muncie Central, Richmond and Connersville in a sectional.

"Schools like Seymour (host to Jeffersonville, New Albany, Bedford North Lawrence, Floyd Central and Jennings County under the new arrangement) are going to sell a whole lot more season tickets, because people are going to have to buy season tickets to get the sectional tickets."

The 36-2 vote of former champions against a change Vanderbush — one of the two — saw as an argument for his stand.

"People voted selfishly," he said. "I don't think they voted on the basis of what's in the best interests of the kids of Indiana, which is what they should have voted. And they were forced to vote that way.

"I've talked to a number of principals who told me, 'Hey, you're right. But, politically, I couldn't vote that way.'

"And the New Castles vote the way they vote because they want to keep on pushing people around.

"I've been a lot of places. I'm a basketball nut. People love basketball in Indiana, just like they love football in Texas. It's not the one-class tournament that has caused Indiana to love basketball. Indiana would love basketball under any kind of structure, I'm convinced of that, and they'll continue to love basketball.

"I think a lot of people in Indiana, big-name people, were afraid to say anything. They were afraid they would be attacked publicly, or ridiculed. There were closet class basketball proponents.

"I don't think the opponents recognized that."

In May, Vanderbush said he was "appalled" by the switch that will bring the four class champions back to play for one overall state championship.

"If we had done it in the beginning and this had been the IHSAA's idea, I would have thought it was probably not a bad move," he said. "The world is made of compromise. We have to try to keep as many people happy as possible and still accomplish things. You just can't change everything overnight.

"But the way it happened with the state legislature threatening that the IHSAA would be disbanded — that was terrible. I wouldn't have picked this as the thing to do, but I'm more upset about the reason for doing it."

The Davids 'always had a chance'

Vanderbush will not soon convince Martinsville coach Tim Wolf about class basketball. "I'm willing to accept the change and give it a chance," Wolf said. "But I grew up with the David and Goliath thing, Lafayette Central Catholic vs. Lafayette Jeff."

Wolf played at Central Catholic. The year parochial schools were admitted to the IHSAA, 1943-44, Lafayette Jeff under Marion Crawley began a string of sectional championships that ran through the rest of Crawley's career and Wolf's whole lifetime — up to 1973 when Central Catholic snapped the Bronchos' record string at 29.

Wolf's senior year at Central Catholic was 1964, when Crawley won his last state championship. "Jeff was 19-1, Central Catholic was 16-4 and I think West Lafayette was 17-3," Wolf said. "People were scalping tickets. It was in the old Jeff gym." Wolf was through college and back at his alma mater as an assistant coach under Al Brown when Central Catholic finally snapped that generation-spanning Jeff sectional streak.

Fuzzy Vandivier, first row, left, joined other Indiana basketball greats on Tony Hinkle's All-Time Dream Team in March 1972. Other members of the team were, front row after Vandivier, Tony Hinkle of Butler University, Bobby Plump of Milan and John Townsend of Indianapolis Tech. Back row, George McGinnis of Indianapolis Washington, Willie Gardner and Oscar Robertson of Crispus Attucks, Homer Stonebraker of Wingate and Bob Ford of Evansville North. Another member of the team, John Wooden of Martinsville, was not present. (Photo courtesy Indiana High School Athletic Association)

Brown moved on and Wolf became head coach. "My first year, we had the second-largest crowd they ever had at Jeff for the sectional finals. They beat us in the fourth quarter.

"Winning a sectional was like winning a state championship. If you did that, you were local heroes forever. Granted, that didn't happen often, but that didn't keep us from working to make it happen. The enthusiasm was there.

"David vs. Goliath. It happens a few times every year.

"You always had a chance. Everyone had a chance.

"We pinpoint the fact that the little guy doesn't win the state. But in the tournament you climb a lot of steps. Each year a lot of small schools make a jump, and it's important to them.

"I think we're losing perspective on what we have.

"People — a number of people — travel here this time of the year just to see the tournament. I used to go work camps and all people wanted to talk about was our tournament: 'Let's have lunch and talk about it.'"

So, a listener asked, how *did* this change happen?

"That's what a lot of people are asking. People got elected to this board or that board and they changed things. That's not always representative of the majority.

"I think if you ask the fans, that's not what they want."

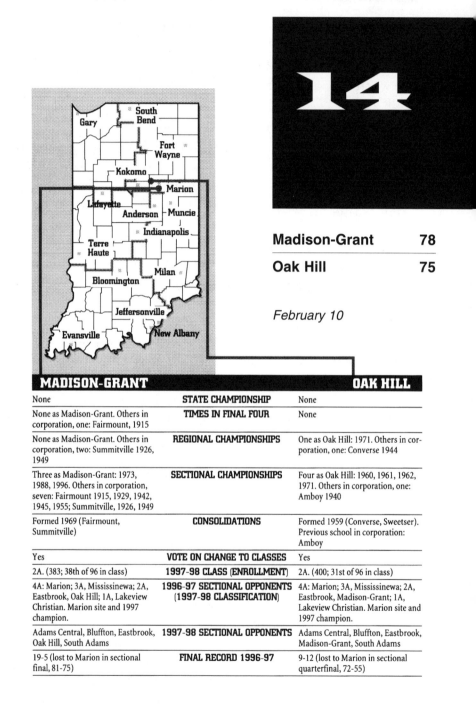

14

Madison-Grant	78
Oak Hill	75

February 10

MADISON-GRANT / OAK HILL

MADISON-GRANT		OAK HILL
None	**STATE CHAMPIONSHIP**	None
None as Madison-Grant. Others in corporation, one: Fairmount, 1915	**TIMES IN FINAL FOUR**	None
None as Madison-Grant. Others in corporation, two: Summitville 1926, 1949	**REGIONAL CHAMPIONSHIPS**	One as Oak Hill: 1971. Others in corporation, one: Converse 1944
Three as Madison-Grant: 1973, 1988, 1996. Others in corporation, seven: Fairmount 1915, 1929, 1942, 1945, 1955; Summitville, 1926, 1949	**SECTIONAL CHAMPIONSHIPS**	Four as Oak Hill: 1960, 1961, 1962, 1971. Others in corporation, one: Amboy 1940
Formed 1969 (Fairmount, Summitville)	**CONSOLIDATIONS**	Formed 1959 (Converse, Sweetser). Previous school in corporation: Amboy
Yes	**VOTE ON CHANGE TO CLASSES**	Yes
2A. (383; 38th of 96 in class)	**1997-98 CLASS (ENROLLMENT)**	2A. (400; 31st of 96 in class)
4A: Marion; 3A, Mississinewa; 2A, Eastbrook, Oak Hill; 1A, Lakeview Christian. Marion site and 1997 champion.	**1996-97 SECTIONAL OPPONENTS (1997-98 CLASSIFICATION)**	4A: Marion; 3A, Mississinewa; 2A, Eastbrook, Madison-Grant; 1A, Lakeview Christian. Marion site and 1997 champion.
Adams Central, Bluffton, Eastbrook, Oak Hill, South Adams	**1997-98 SECTIONAL OPPONENTS**	Adams Central, Bluffton, Eastbrook, Madison-Grant, South Adams
19-5 (lost to Marion in sectional final, 81-75)	**FINAL RECORD 1996-97**	9-12 (lost to Marion in sectional quarterfinal, 72-55)

Shootout II

Kyle Runyan and Jarrad Odle, A-minus students and 25-plus basketball scorers, are just a couple of months apart in age, but the difference separated them into different academic classes — Runyan a 6-foot-5 senior guard for Madison-Grant, Odle a 6-7 junior forward for Oak Hill.

Their athletic relationship goes back to Little League baseball. It grew tighter as they grew older, and as they rose in stature among not just area stars but the best-known players in the state.

They had an early collision in the Grant County Tournament that brought back memories of the state's all-time most legendary shootout: Ray Pavy 51, Jimmy Rayl 49, when New Castle beat Kokomo in 1959.

This time, Odle set an Oak Hill scoring record with 43 points but Runyan delivered a Madison-Grant record of 45 and Runyan's team won, 99-83. "I've never seen anything like that," Madison-Grant coach Terry Martin said. "I've seen occasionally where one kid has a great game. To have two — that was something special. They scored inside, outside — those kids were just on."

Only a few days later, Odle, the state's leading scorer, accepted a 1998-99 scholarship offer from Indiana coach Bob Knight. Runyan longed for one of those.

And so it was that when they met again, Knight was there — set up with a prime viewing area, in a classroom above and beyond one basket, slightly off to the shooter's right.

Players today grow accustomed to playing before college scouts — in games, in practices, in summer AAU play. It's different when the coach watching is the one a prospect hopes to play for. And, certainly, there is no more potential for intimidation than when the viewer is Knight — the only basketball coach not just today's players but in great part their parents as well ever have seen or associated with IU, which is not the only college basketball program in Indiana but the one with the strongest border-to-border following throughout the state.

Intimidation happens. Pat Graham, one of the greatest shooters ever to play for Knight, had an awful night when he knew Knight was there watching and evaluating. Graham missed a jump shot early, then another, and another, and another. The basket, Graham laughed later, "got really small." The best scorer Knight or the Big Ten has ever had, Calbert Cheaney, had a similar experience. He finished 8-for-25, but most of the eight came after Knight had left early in the fourth quarter. In his entire 2,613-point, 1,820-shot, 132-game Indiana career, Cheaney never missed 17 shots in a game. The significant thing is Knight took both players. Evaluations are not made on one game.

Still, Odle and Runyan wanted better starts than they had this night.

Over a 10-minute stretch of the first half, Odle missed six straight shots. Very early, Runyan sank a 3-point basket and was fouled, a 4-point play. Then Runyan encountered the Pat Graham Syndrome. Open for a 3 in the right corner, he missed everything — "Air ball!" is the derisive chant opposing fans use to celebrate shots like that one. Runyan laughed on recalling Graham's terminology. "After I air-balled one, the basket got a *lot* smaller," he said.

He missed four straight 3s through halftime, then another opening the second half. At that point, a gifted 3-point shooter who has hit as many as 10 in a game basically put that shot away. He moved his operations inside, much of the time one-on-one against Odle.

At the other end, Runyan guarded Odle much of the time, too. That hadn't happened often when they scored their 45 and 43. This time, Runyan had 31, Odle 25, and the game came down to a steal and Odle's shot from center court at the buzzer — "right on line," he said later, "but about two feet short." So Madison-Grant won, 78-75. "A pretty good game," Oak Hill coach Bryan Alexander called it. "If you sat in the stands and didn't care who won, it was a great game."

Matchup of friends

Martin is an obvious Runyan fan, but he also likes Odle. "Holding him to 25 I thought was a great job," Martin said. "We worked pretty hard on him when he got his 43.

"He's so big and mobile he presents a lot of problems. He's so darned good and so tall you're not going to stop him, and he's hard to keep from getting the ball because they're always looking for him."

Alexander called Odle "kind of a quiet scorer. So steady. He has scored in the upper 30s or low 40s when I thought he had 25.

"He's shooting 58 percent from the field. He can step out and hit the 3, he can post up, he can drive. If you have to have a basket, you know if you get him the ball there's a good chance he'll get one for you.

"He's a scorer."

Runyan said his biggest defensive intention going against Odle is "not to let him touch the ball. When he does get it, he's tough. His height helps, but he's just a good basketball player. He won't throw it away, and he won't force up a bad shot."

And, when they're paired at the Madison-Grant end: "Being a little bit smaller, I try to get him one-on-one," Runyan said. Odle tries to avoid that. "Basically I just want to stay in his face and not let him penetrate or drive. Just keep him contained, really. He's going to get his points."

The Knight-pressure matter "may have had some effect on Jarrad" at the start, Alexander said. "We tried to tell him before the game there was no pressure on him. Runyan was the one with the pressure. But I'm sure it still affected him."

Kyle Runyon, right, of Madison-Grant eyes Oak Hill's Jarrod Odle and, from high above, Indiana coach Bob Knight watched both in their rematch at Madison-Grant. (Photo ©Jeff Morehead, Marion Chronicle-Tribune*)*

"A little bit, yeah, but it wasn't that bad," Odle said. "Some of it was jitters. I finally started hitting the bucket." He took 17 shots and hit nine (making seven of his last eight shots, two of them 3-pointers); Runyan took 19 shots and hit 12.

The next night, Odle and Runyan were on the telephone together, head-on competitors one night, chatting buddies the next. "We've known each other six or seven years," Odle said. "Last summer we started running around together and playing together a lot."

Odle was glad college selection was behind him. "I'm definitely a little looser than I was," he said. "Now that it is over I can just go out and have fun. That's exactly what I wanted."

Rebel in argylls (almost)

Madison-Grant High School was formed in 1969 by one of the first Indiana consolidations that crossed county lines. Merged were Summitville of Madison County and Fairmount of Grant County. Hence, the school name.

The nickname is different. It's Argylls, as in argyle socks.

"That's a crazy story," said Martin, a 6-7 center who had led Greensburg High in its finest tournament hour (final eight in 1966, beaten for a Final Four berth 79-75 by eventual state runner-up Indianapolis Tech) and was three years into his career at Miami of Ohio when all this happened.

"Summitville and Fairmount had nicknames of Goblins and Quakers," Martin said. "They weren't real sharp on nicknames up here."

Pause right there to consider that Fairmount name: Quakers. Fairmount's all-time best-known basketball player, and a pretty good one for 5-7, was Jim Dean. As a senior in the 1949 Marion sectional, Dean scored 13 and 12 as Fairmount avenged early-season losses, then 15 points in a game attempt to upset Marion (down just 34-32 late, Fairmount lost, 40-34). Six years later, Dean was famous, and dead — a movie star (*East of Eden, Rebel Without a Cause, Giant*) who took on lasting, almost mythical stature because of his talent that had surfaced so quickly and his death so young in an auto accident. Only in Indiana, only in a Fairmount basketball uniform, were James Dean and Quaker linked.

Argylls wouldn't really have fit him, either.

"I've heard the kids voted in something the school officials didn't like," Martin said. So, there was a revote. "A farmer in the area said if they would name them Argylls, which had nothing to do with our school but something with his family crest, he'd buy band uniforms.

Actor James Dean, a Fairmount native, was one of his team's best players. Here he is during his senior year for the Quakers. (Photo courtesy Indiana Basketball Hall of Fame)

"So they did it, and then he didn't buy the band uniforms. But we got stuck with the name."

Argyll County in Western Scotland has as its identifying tartan for kilts and the like the multicolored diamond pattern of the socks that were high teenage fashion in the '50s.

But as a team name: "I'm sure we're the only ones in the world," Martin said.

Kyle, Kyle, Kyle, Kyle and . . .

Runyan has a nickname, too. By necessity.

"We call him T — his middle name starts with T," Martin said. "One of our plays is called T, for him."

The necessity? Martin started Kyle Runyan, Kyle Young and Kyle Elsworth. Usually, the first player off the bench is Kyle Beckley. All are seniors.

"That's been a real problem," Martin said. "We've had to work out what we're going to call each other — one of them goes by the last name, one of them is Kyle, one we use a nickname for. If the other one gets in, we're in a lot of trouble."

Before the coding system, Martin said, "In the heat of a ballgame, I'd say 'Kyle, do something' and have three kids trying to do it."

Stalking the Giants

By late January, everything takes on a tournament context for players and coaches. To Odle, the importance of the near-miss at Madison-Grant was that "it kinda raises our confidence for the tournament. The first time we played them we got killed."

Both Madison-Grant and Oak Hill play in the Marion sectional tournament. Marion's nickname is Giants. For the others in the Marion sectional, the name is perfect.

It's the situation that has been classic for Indiana sectionals through the years: the host team as the dominant power, all the others in the field dreamers that they might be the Jack who fells the beanstalk Giant.

It happened for Madison-Grant just last year. Happened on Friday night, in the sectional semifinals. "After we beat them, we didn't want to act like we just won the sectional because we hadn't won it yet," Runyan said. "But we went in the locker room and celebrated a lot.

"It's a real big goal to go back to Marion and upset them again. It will be very hard.

"But just playing at Marion, in that gym, gets that extra adrenaline popping.

"I always remember being at the sectional, when they were state champions (three times in a row, from 1985 through '87, kindergarten through second grade for Kyle Runyan). Just watching them play gave you chills, sitting in the stands and waiting to get your chance at them."

Then, going out onto the court to play: "We all felt it," Runyan said. "That was something else — just walking in there for warmups and seeing everybody in the stands."

"That's a big experience," Odle agreed, "the atmosphere when you run out there, the way the crowd is, basketball-loving people. There's just not a way to explain the feeling.

"Last year I was just overwhelmed by it. This year I'm looking forward to it."

Alexander grew up in a similar atmosphere, his high school Northwestern in a sectional dominated perennially by Kokomo.

"We didn't win the sectional when I was playing," Alexander said, "but my brother's team in '81 did — and won again in '82. They beat Kokomo both times — the first time in the championship game and the second time in a semifinal game.

"The one in '81 was the first time in 26 years Northwestern won the sectional. I can't imagine that community being any more excited over a 2A state championship than they were over beating Kokomo and winning that sectional."

Martin has been on both ends of that traditional sectional situation.

"At Greensburg, we were the big school," he said. "That was great, too — to come out with everybody hating you. That was exciting.

"A school like ours — just to win the sectional, that's like winning the State. That's a great week afterward. It's a super feeling.

"I never had a problem with the best team winning it, which seems to be a problem for some people. I wanted our best team to be the state champion. If we were the best team, fine. If we weren't, let the best team win. In education today, mediocre is what counts."

Principal R. Larry Martin, not a relative of Terry's, cast Madison-Grant's vote for the change.

"The players in the state didn't want it, the fans didn't want it, the principals are the only group that favored it," Terry Martin said. "Our kids were unanimous in not wanting to change.

"I don't like it at all. I should be liking it."

Madison-Grant obviously will have a better chance to advance in the new tournament.

"That's the whole thing," Martin said.

"That's what made our sectionals unique and great. We're a school of 500 kids and we're going to play in one of the biggest gyms in the world, in front of 6,000 or 7,000 people, for a sectional championship. Next year, my kids will drive to Adams Central or someplace and play in front of 1,500 people for a sectional championship. While we may have a better chance to win that, the experience to me is going to pale by comparison."

Alexander will have Odle as a team leader when the first class tournament is played, and his principal, Jean Shonkwiler, also voted for the change. "We've got to feel like we can be pretty competitive," Alexander said.

"But I don't care for it, really. I'm a traditionalist. I've loved the tournament, the way it has been, and I hate to see it change.

"It's my first year at Oak Hill. They haven't won a sectional since 1971. But, still, you've got a crack at it every year. I just hate to see that change.

"But we've changed it. I'm not going to dwell on that. We'll just readjust our thinking. Right now, as a smaller school, your major goal is to win a sectional. Then our major goal will be to win a state championship."

Odle is trying to keep an open mind. "I like the big atmosphere, but our chances look a lot better in the smaller one," he said. "Maybe things will shape up and we'll get a better chance of getting to the State.

"We're playing a lot of juniors. Our next year's team should be pretty well experienced, and that will help.

"I guess I'm going to have to play in both situations to see what I like best."

Runyan won't have that opportunity, and he's glad.

"I'd rather it be single-class. Luckily I'm out of it and won't have to go through it, but I still wish it had stayed single-class. It's a lot more fun that way."

Martin won't be checking out the next experience, either. At 49, after 16 years as Madison-Grant's coach and nearly 40 years in basketball at some level, he announced his resignation at the end of the year. He'll stay on as a teacher of biology, zoology and microbiology.

Runyan in April signed with former Knight player and assistant Jim Crews' program at Evansville.

15

Richmond	64
Marion	**61**

February 12

MARION		RICHMOND
Six: 1926,1975, 1976, 1985, 1986, 1987	**STATE CHAMPIONSHIPS**	1992
Seven: 1922, 1947, 1950, 1968, 1969, 1980, 1983	**OTHER TIMES IN FINAL FOUR**	Four: 1935, 1953, 1985*, 1987* (* lost in championship game)
33: first 1922; two in '90s, most recent 1994	**REGIONAL CHAMPIONSHIPS**	21: first 1923; three in '90s, most recent 1992
61: first 1921; seven in '90s, most recent 1997.	**SECTIONAL CHAMPIONSHIPS**	62: first 1917; six in '90s, most recent 1996
Marion Bennett 1954	**CONSOLIDATIONS**	Riley 1939, Morton 1942, Boston 1963
No	**VOTE ON CHANGE TO CLASSES**	No
4A. (1,323; 41st of 95 in class)	**1997-98 CLASS (ENROLLMENT)**	4A. (1,453; 30th of 95 in class)
3A, Mississinewa; 2A, Eastbrook, Madison-Grant, Oak Hill; 1A, Lakeview Christian. Marion site and 1997 champion.	**1996-97 SECTIONAL OPPONENTS (1997-98 CLASSIFICATION)**	2A, Centerville, Northeastern, Winchester; 1A, Randolph Southern, Union (Modoc). Richmond site, Winchester 1997 champion
Fort Wayne South, Fort Wayne Wayne, Homestead, Huntington North, Jay County	**1997-98 SECTIONAL OPPONENTS**	Anderson, Anderson Highland, Connersville, Muncie Central, New Castle
16-8 (won sectional; lost to Kokomo in regional semifinal, 63-50)	**FINAL RECORD 1996-97**	10-10 (lost to Winchester in sectional quarterfinal, 48-42)

Pride,
Ghosts
and Pitfalls

This is a matchup that has been played in glorious settings. Twice. In 1985 and again in 1987, these were the teams that won their way to the state championship game at Market Square Arena.

History hardly notices Richmond's role. It was the runner-up when Marion won the first and last of its record-tying three straight championships.

Marion hasn't made a strong run at another state championship since that last one in 1987, but the aura remains. Just the weekend before this Wednesday night makeup of a game previously snowed out, Marion had clouted No. 1-ranked North Central, 82-61, and followed up with a 73-64 victory over Harrison.

Both were home games, tempering the results just a bit, but not in quick-believing Marion. What went into the weekend a rather average 9-5 season took on instant power.

"These kids won those two games," first-year coach Moe Smedley said, "and they weren't out of the gym before I could hear people talking, 'All the way!'

"They don't mean 'all the way through the sectional' here."

Rick Baumgartner, the Richmond coach, knows exactly what they mean. Rick used to ride along to Marion when his dad, Dick, was Richmond's coach. Dick's coaching years included a surprise run all the way to the state championship game with Crawfordsville in 1958. His election to the Indiana Basketball Hall of Fame was announced in January. As a boy, then as a Richmond player, Rick Baumgartner learned some things about tradition by going on the road with his dad.

The long road back

Richmond under Dick Baumgartner, and then under George Griffith, was one of the state's most consistent basketball powers throughout the '70s and the '80s.

Just one thing was missing. Richmond, through all that time, had to live with the reality that it was the only school in the North Central Conference that had never won a state championship.

Football took the blame for a while. It was too good. Through the '50s and '60s, the Richmond Red Devils were as consistently strong in football as any school in the state. Bill Elias coached there, so well that he advanced into major college football. Hub Etchison came along after him, for a long and triumphal tenure — so much so that Richmond High School is on Hub Etchison Parkway.

The best of the Richmond football players also helped the school to its brightest basketball hour in that period. Lamar Lundy, long before his Fearsome Foursome renown with the Los Angeles Rams, was the center and leader of the one Richmond team that made it to the Final Four: in 1953, when the Red Devils ended the two-year reign of bitter rival Muncie Central with a double-overtime regional victory. At the State, Terre Haute Gerstmeyer got 16 points from Arley Andrews, 17 from his twin Harley and four more from their uncle Harold to stop Richmond in the semifinals, 48-40.

That was at Butler Fieldhouse. When the Final Four moved out of there (first to Indiana University's Assembly Hall, then to Market Square Arena in Indianapolis, then to the Hoosier Dome in 1990), picturesque old Hinkle nee Butler Fieldhouse retained the Indianapolis semistate and became the place where Richmond dreams went to die. Eight times in a 12-year period, Richmond teams won regionals and lost in the semistate, one net-cutting short of the State. The '72 Devils epitomized Richmond's agonies. That

George Griffith directed Richmond to its first state championhip in 1992, ending a frustrating series of close calls and unrealized dreams. (Photo courtesy Indiana High School Athletic Association, ©Mark Wick)

team had size, speed, skill, the look of a state champion. It lost 62-61 in its first semistate game to last-shot hero Guy Ogden of unheralded Center Grove. It got worse: Center Grove promptly lost by 18 at night to another heated Richmond rival, Connersville, which didn't just get the Final Four trip but thumbed its nose at the Devils as State champion.

Mike Lopresti, one of America's best deadline writers and columnists for the sports arm of Gannett News Service, was a manager for Baumgartner's 1971 team. Lopresti by then was infatuated with the Hoosier tournament. He covered several for the *Richmond Palladium-Item* before being pulled in by Gannett when it was first birthing *USA Today*. As a national writer, he kept his home in Richmond and returned somehow every March, from wherever he was, to watch the Red Devils die.

When Richmond finally broke through to the State in 1985, Lopresti drove all night through fog, 10 hard hours from Birmingham to Indianapolis, because the Friday-Sunday scheduling of the NCAA Regional gave him Saturday free. That let him see his Red Devils beat future baseball star Kenny Lofton and East Chicago Washington but lose the first of those two championship-game matchups with Marion. But he also was there in 1992 when the Devils delivered a couple of miracle victories, twice hitting late 3-point shots to get into overtime and, there, defeating first Jeffersonville, then conference rival Lafayette Jefferson to win that agonizingly elusive first state championship.

And in April 1996 when the committee vote came in, pointing the way to a change to class play, Lopresti explained the action to Gannett readers across the land, including *USA Today's* millions:

"A state treasure that for more than 80 years withstood war, depression and blizzards could not survive the vote of those who do not understand their own state."

The open, one-class high school basketball tournament, Lopresti wrote, "was something people cared about together. And if that is naive, a state caught up by the boyhood games of teenagers, so what? In a time where caring about anything is nearly erased, naivete was a small price to pay. In a society fractured and classified along innumerable lines of race and age and gender and income and home and birth and job and creed and religion and sexual preference, this was the quaint exception. Everyone with their eyes on the same prize. Indiana gathered around its tournament like a family once gathered around a radio.

"Monday they killed it. . . .

"The principals called the tune. Many of them who have never understood the special feeling Indiana had for this tournament, never felt its pulse. The tournament, with its wonderful quirks and unforgiving nature and unconventional demands, did not fit into their precise modern educational philosophy. It did not fit into their mentality of the 1990s. . . .

"I grew up spellbound by the sounds and smells and colors of the Indiana state tournament. I have wandered into the high-roller district of the Super Bowl and World Series and still not found anything with more drama or emotion. How rare now to see something still so relatively unspoiled, still so played straight from the gut, still so captivating to an entire state.

"On Monday I watched it blown to bits. Behold progress."

A swift descent

George Griffith, the coach who delivered that first state championship to Richmond in 1992, guided the Red Devils through one more successful season before retiring, a genius — either in coaching or in timing, for the long run of strong, talented Richmond teams ran out coincident with his departure. Lopresti was on the search committee that found successor Steve Austin, who had taken South Bend St. Joseph's to the 1989 Final Four. When after two rough winters Austin decided to return to the South Bend area to coach, Lopresti was on the Richmond school board that hired Rick Baumgartner. The rebuilding continues slowly; Richmond hasn't won a regional since its state championship.

Baumgartner knows all about the markings of success. "Look at the banners up there," he said in Marion's arena. There are six of them, hailing the Giants' state championships, five in the last 22 years.

"That's tradition. Call it a mystique or whatever, there is something special about coming in here. The Fieldhouse in Muncie, or the Wigwam in Anderson — there's a tradition that goes back many, many years, because of the number of state championships.

"This is a huge, huge win."

That was the shocking part. Richmond, struggling to stay above the break-even point all year, caught Marion after that weekend crest and beat the Giants on their own Bill Green Athletic Center court, 64-61.

"I don't want to take anything away from Richmond, but, dammit, we just weren't there," Smedley said.

"We have very little offense, but if we play good defense we can beat some teams. Our defensive intensity just wasn't there. And I could sense it in the first minute of the game.

"How do you bench kids who four days earlier beat two great teams?"

The Wright brother's shadow

Marion's 5-7 scooter, junior Andre Betts, has had better games, but his 13 points and his speed up and down the court kept the Giants thinking victory eventually would come. The Red Devils just wouldn't let it happen. They had slim leads after each of the first three quarters. The score was tied five times in the fourth quarter before senior guard Chad Romack broke the last tie with a 3-point basket with 1:50 to go. Marion never caught up again, senior guard Curtis Wright of Richmond closing out his 11-point fourth quarter with a basket and four straight free throws in the final 65 seconds.

Richmond was in that position because Marion, with no true center, couldn't handle 6-7 Richmond junior Andy Brown. He scored 23 points, stepping outside to hit a 3-point basket from the top of the foul circle with 3:55 left, when the game was swinging back and forth.

Brown is slim, just 174 pounds on that 6-7 frame. "If he develops a little more physically, he'll be a big-time player," Baumgartner said. "He can shoot the 3, he's got moves inside, great touch — he can score anywhere on the floor. And the kids are doing a better job of getting the ball into him."

One of those kids who kept Brown well fed was Wright, whose brother Jamar, a sophomore, also started.

The original Wright brothers, Orville and Wilbur, had some roots around Richmond, but these two were connected to another, very special Wright. Older brother Billy was the leader when, after all of those tournament disappointments that were more painful than the two runner-up finishes, Richmond won that first state championship in 1992. Billy was an outstanding player, an Indiana All-Star, a good college player for Bradley.

For the senior he calls "Curty," playing in the long shadow of brother Billy "was a monumental thing to have to deal with," Baumgartner said.

"He's real proud of his brother, and his brother was a heck of a player. But Curty is Curty and Billy is Billy. Curty has to create his own identity. But that's a lot of pressure.

"I told him this was his best game.

"I was real proud of our kids. They made a lot of runs at us. This is one of the toughest places to play in the state."

'That is my dream'

Smedley wants every opponent to think the Giants' 7,682-seat arena is full of ghosts from victories past.

"Definitely," he said. "We use that.

"Every week we give our kids a scouting report, and at the bottom it says: 'This is our house. Don't forget it.'

"But there's that thin line: the house isn't going to win for us. This game was a prime example of what I'm fighting.

"I've got to get these kids to understand, yes, there is a Marion pride, and it is a great pride, but you don't get it by putting on the shirt.

"We want to use it, but we want these kids to understand they have to earn that. I think they think the tradition is going to carry them."

But that tradition, that link with teams that indeed did go all the way, that pressure of high expectations all combined to make the Marion job one that Moe Smedley dreamed about getting. And still loves.

"The pressure of coaching here has never affected me," he said. "Maybe that's because I'm 52. Maybe if I got fired, it would be the best thing. I could go fishing."

The possibility of coaching a state championship team:

"That is my dream. That's why I came back.

"Not that I couldn't have done it at Manchester, but it's more realistic."

Bill Green is the only coach of six state championship teams. He won five of them at Marion, which named its arena for him. (Photo courtesy Indiana Basketball Hall of Fame)

Smedley had built a good program at Manchester, in northern Wabash County. He left it when Marion was offered him. "I wanted the job in 1976," he said. "I felt then I could do the job. I never once felt I couldn't, especially when I went to the (1994) semistate with Manchester, a school of 500."

Smedley was an assistant coach at Marion when Bill Green won consecutive championships in 1975 and '76 and retired, the first of three times Green left the job that twice pulled him back. That first time in the spring of 1976, Smedley said, "I was told I should go out and get some varsity experience. I was 31 — I thought that was old."

He coached two years at East Central, in southeastern Indiana near Cincinnati, then three years at Delta, where he cut seniors, kept sophomores to build a future program, and got dumped before he could coach that third-year team. For a year, he was reeling. "I sold school supplies," he said. "It's tough to get back in (after a firing)."

There's no question about the point in the calendar when he missed coaching most. "Sectional time," he said. "That was really hard on me. I had told those Delta kids in the dressing room they'd win the sectional the next year, and they did."

He got back into coaching at Carroll, a consolidation whose ancestry includes Flora, a surprise 1946 Final Four team. After five years there, he went to Eastbrook, and after four years there went to Manchester for five very good years. Well, four and a half. "Believe me, Manchester has pressure, too," he said. "They had a petition out against me halfway through my first year."

"One thing that really spurred me on to take this job is I was told that I couldn't have discipline here like I've had at other schools. But we are having discipline. I look at Anderson — I think Heck (coach Ron Hecklinski) does a great job of disciplining his kids.

"That's what I'm happy about right now. These kids are coachable.

"If we had a center we'd be a pretty good team."

Draw day, and those brackets

Smedley grew up in a corner of Wabash County, just north of Marion. His 1962 graduating class, the last before LaFontaine High School joined with Lagro, Noble Township and Somerset in forming Southwood, numbered just 24. LaFontaine, the town and school, were named for a renowned Miami chief, whose name usually was pronounced French-ish, *la*-fon-*tayne*, not the way the town and school usually came out in Hoosier-ish: luh-*fount*-en. Why they were called the Cossacks someone else will have to explain.

Young Morris Smedley — Moe forever after a neighbor girl couldn't get any farther than that in trying to pronounce Morris — grew up loving Indiana's tournament.

"I can remember in eighth grade my coach drawing the brackets on the blackboard in math class," he said. That was on draw day. A Wednesday in mid-February. At 7 a.m. they started drawing names out of a hat, sectional by sectional, alphabetically, then regionals, then the semistates, then the State — wire services throughout Indiana shut down to everything else so the draw could be expedited through, announcers at radio stations throughout the state breathlessly carrying the pairings as soon as they came across the wire. It was one of Indiana's greatest days of the year.

"The first time seeing those brackets . . . " Moe Smedley said.

"It *grows* on you.

"I guess I can't explain it to most people.

"I just know I'm in this profession because of my experiences in that high school, one of the smallest in the state. We never won even a sectional, but I still had that desire to win.

"These are the intangibles people seem to ignore."

When there's not a championship to remember, not a gigantic upset to relish, near-misses will do. Wabash was LaFontaine's target. "We never did beat them," Smedley said. "My junior year, we were up six with about two minutes to go and we got beat on a last-second shot." That was in the sectional championship game, and Wabash won, 74-73. "Another starter and I fouled out," Smedley said. Bet on it: Moe Smedley cried in bed that night.

And maybe he did again the night in April 1996 when Indiana's one-class tournament was voted out.

"I just hate it that those who chose to quit and give up are dictating to the rest of us," Smedley said. "The ones who obviously are not competitive are telling us who are competitive that we can't have our tournament."

Baumgartner is just a little bit milder. "I was disappointed," he said. "I've coached at all different levels. I was at Pendleton Heights in 1987. Anderson had made it to the '86 state finals and got beat by Marion, and they had everybody back. They were expected to win the State, and we knocked them off in the sectional. There's no better feeling, and that's not going to be there for the smaller school anymore.

"It was special for the crowd, to watch a game like that. Or to watch an Argos.

"My contention is if you've got a good thing, you don't mess with it. But it's here. Unfortunately, it's probably here to stay."

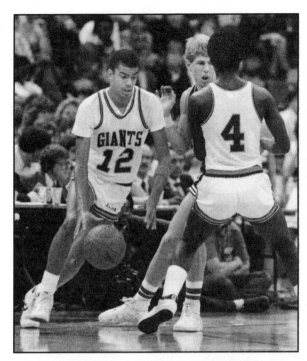

Jay Edwards (12) and Lyndon Jones (4) at left were driving forces in Marion's three straight titles beginning in 1985, while Dave Colescott (below) was a key to Marion's two straight titles in 1975-76. (Both photos courtesy Indiana High School Athletic Association)

16

Batesville 63

Rushville 47

February 14

BATESVILLE   RUSHVILLE

BATESVILLE		RUSHVILLE
None	STATE CHAMPIONSHIP	None
One: 1943	TIMES IN FINAL FOUR	One: 1976 (lost in championship game)
Six: 1934, 1943, 1951, 1952, 1971, 1994	REGIONAL CHAMPIONSHIPS	19: first 1922; most recent 1979
23: first 1927; four in '90s, most recent 1997	SECTIONAL CHAMPIONSHIPS	44 as Rushville: first 1922; one in '90s, 1993. Others in corporation, seven: Arlington 1942, 1947; Milroy 1920, 1946; New Salem 1943, 1944, 1952
None	CONSOLIDATIONS	Webb 1929; Raleigh 1955; Mays 1966; Arlington, Manilla, Milroy, New Salem 1968
No	VOTE ON CHANGE TO CLASSES	No
3A. (464; 93rd of 96 in class)	1997-98 CLASS (ENROLLMENT)	3A. (723; 27th of 96 in class)
3A, Greensburg; 2A, Jac-Cen-Del, North Decatur, South Decatur, South Ripley. Greensburg site, Batesville 1997 champion	1996-97 SECTIONAL OPPONENTS (1997-98 CLASSIFICATION)	4A, Connersville; 3A, Franklin County; 2A, Cambridge City Lincoln, Hagerstown, Union County. Connersville site and 1997 champion
Franklin County, Greensburg, Madison, South Dearborn	1997-98 SECTIONAL OPPONENTS	Greenfield, Mount Vernon (Fortville), New Palestine, Pendleton Heights, Shelbyville
26-2 (won sectional; lost to New Castle in regional final, 61-58, overtime)	FINAL RECORD 1996-97	10-11 (lost to Connersville in sectional quarterfinal, 64-46)

Ripley's Candidate

If they were from a big city or a big school, from any point in Indiana, they would be what they are: a very good basketball team with a chance to win the state championship. But Batesville's Bulldogs are from Ripley County, so the extra baggage they have acquired in their noble quest is inevitable.

They are the people's choice in this emotional high school basketball season which Indiana people have taken more note of than any in — could it be? — than any since that other Ripley County team, Milan, achieved what Batesville oh, so deeply wants to.

There is the risk of a Milan overload in this.

Melvin Siefert, the Bulldogs' bright young coach, knows that, and senses that. Siefert grew up in Batesville, about 10 miles cross-county from Milan. Other coaches across America commonly pull out *Hoosiers* to give their team an eve-of-battle charge. Siefert hasn't for a while, and won't.

"I used it my first year (1993-94)," he said. "We got together the night before the regional.

"That was," he said — the grin creeping across his face bordering on sheepish — "the year we won the regional.

"We've just let it rest for a while. We haven't wanted to beat that horse another year. Part of it is because we're so close to Milan and we hear it all the time. We don't want our kids thinking, 'Here we go again; we can't be ourselves, we have to be another Milan.'

"But that movie *is* good."

Batesville is not Milan. Its enrollment is almost twice the size of the present Milan, four times the one that won the 1954 state championship. It beat Anderson to win the Christmastime Hall of Fame Classic. It is ranked No. 3 in the state.

Siefert's on-court leader, 5-10 guard Michael Menser, doesn't want what he says to come out abrasive. "It's great to know that it happened," he said, "but the Milan of today, to any of our team, doesn't really represent that. It's 10 minutes away, but none of us ever go to Milan.

"When we play at Milan, we always look at all the photographs, and we glamorize the lines of *Hoosiers*. But basically other than that . . . "

Other than that, there is legend, which is quite a lot.

"It gives you hope," Menser said. "You see that the small school can do it. We actually did think we could do it when the season began — we started with a goal of being that last state champion. You see their state championship banner and you see that it's possible.

"But to tell you the truth, the first time I saw *Hoosiers*, I didn't know it was based on Milan. I was probably 8 at the time. One of my friends was talking about the movie and said, 'Milan must have been pretty good.' I said 'What?' I just thought of it as Hickory High. He told me, I said, 'Wow,' and went back and watched it again."

Siefert went right back to Batesville High when he graduated from Butler (hmmm: a coach from Butler, a 5-10 leader at guard — how many parallels does this thing need?). "My athletic director when I first got here was Glenn Butte," he said. Butte was a sophomore on the 1954 Milan team. "I've talked with Glenn an awful lot about the situation. I know times have changed, but that was a special thing."

And now as the last open-class state tournament approaches, it is Batesville's team, Melvin Siefert's team, Michael Menser's team, that is Ripley County's team. "That's true, a little bit," Siefert said.

"I think we've all taken a lot of pride in the fact that Milan came from Ripley County. And that kind of thing has carried over to this year. When we won the Hall of Fame tournament, we heard from people from all over the county — they bought tickets and sat in our section. That was kind of special.

"We knew that the way we played last year and the way the kids worked this summer, we had a legitimate shot at winning the State. You have to be realistic. A lot of years, that isn't true. But realistically we feel like there's an opportunity here."

This game at Rushville, against one more set of regional disbelievers, was Step 21 toward that opportunity.

'Hurts you so many ways'

To imply that Rushville coach Jerry Craig is a Batesville disbeliever is neither fair nor right. "Batesville is a great example, just the epitome of why we should have one-class basketball," Craig said. "They're an excellent basketball team. Melvin has done a great job with them."

Craig's No. 1 concern in preparing for the Bulldogs was "their overall team speed and quickness — and they just play great defense. My starting lineup is not the quickest in the world, but they're so good defensively.

"It's not like it's all Michael Menser. It's all of them. He's a great player, but they all get after it."

Craig set out like most Batesville opponents, trying to keep Menser and the basketball separated. He scored the game's first basket in the first half-minute of play.

With 3:50 left in the quarter, 6-4 Rushville junior Travis Koors scored to tie the game 10-10. In 45 dizzying seconds, senior guard Justin Wagner scored for Batesville; Wagner stole the ball back and got it to Brad Sandifer for a layup, and Menser stole the ball and took it in himself for a layup. Zap, 16-10.

With Menser resting, Batesville opened the second quarter with four straight turnovers and the lead shrank to 16-13. Back he came at 18-13 to assist on center Aaron Ertel's three-point play and score three baskets himself on the way to a 31-15 halftime score, another flurry of four straight Rushville turnovers closing out the half. The margin held up in the 63-47 final score.

"I thought our half-court defense was pretty respectable," Craig said. "Our problem was we didn't take care of the basketball. I told our team it's hard to defend when you're chasing to keep them from shooting layups.

"The end of the first quarter and all of the second quarter, they were just outstanding on defense.

"Menser just hurts you so many ways. You key on him and he gets the ball to the open guy. He plays great defense. He has such great hands. We had a play tonight where I thought we were going to get a layup. He gets a hand on the ball and the next thing I know we're chasing him down the floor.

"I'm impressed with him off the court, too. We've had some guys who really haven't represented us well as Mr. Basketball. I really appreciate the kind of kid Michael Menser is. And I was really impressed to see what kind of grades (DeKalb's Mr. Basketball candidate) Luke Recker has and what all he does."

Nitpicking, at 20-1?

Menser's 22-point night was just above his season average. "I thought Michael played pretty well," Siefert said. "In that little stretch in the second quarter he had two steals in a row.

"I don't think either team ever got into a real flow. A physical game like that is going to be choppy. They were one of the strongest teams we've played all year."

Siefert had spent much of the second half with his team in a zone defense and him up and barking, trying to coax more defense out of it.

"The first half was about as well as we've played on defense," he said. "The second half definitely wasn't. They had 10 points the first four minutes of the game and we held them to five the rest of the way out.

"It's difficult. We're 20-1 and sometimes you feel like you nitpick. We're not yelling to yell. We're trying to get better. We know

Batesville's Michael Menser looks for an opening during the 1996 Hall of Fame Classic championship game in New Castle. (Photo courtesy Batesville High School)

that we're capable of much better than we had tonight, and that's concerning because it's so close to tournament time.

"Maybe sometimes we coaches think too much. We're thinking we ought to have something else to go to if the man-to-man isn't working, or we're in foul trouble. We've been very fortunate this year not to be in that situation.

"The zone we used tonight wasn't really for this team, it was for somebody we're going to face down the road. We hadn't used it in a game situation. That's why I stayed with it longer than I might have.

"We're going to have to go back to what we do best."

In this game, Menser said, "Our pressure got to them and we got some easy layups off that. That helped us open up the game."

But a full-court press is not the Batesville defense. "We started the year doing it, and we struggled the first couple of games," Menser said. "So we went back basically to our half-court defense. Sometimes for two-minute stretches we put traps on, but basically we're just man-to-man."

There is the sound of a coach-to-be when he ponders such things. "Defense comes from the heart. On offense you have to have some skills that not everybody at the high school level has. But anybody can play defense if he just has the heart and the desire to do it."

Menser's steals in this game were typical; he averages more than three a game. "We have rules. We try to force people to one side, and if we get it on that side, keep it there. I try to look for a weakness a team might have and exploit it any way I can, ball pressure or getting in passing lanes, whatever.

"We know we can score points. We try to go out every time and hold our opponents under 50." Mission accomplished.

Learning from winning, and losing

An eight-day period over New Year's solidified Batesville's state championship approach. The Bulldogs went to the Hall of Fame Classic in New Castle for two games on the floor where in March they fully expect to face the strong host team in the regional tournament. Those two had met in a classic game last year, a desperation 3-point shot at the buzzer pulling the Trojans around stunned Batesville, 62-61.

The extra time on the Chrysler Fieldhouse court was an appealing extra benefit of the December 28 trip for Siefert. The Bulldogs were there primarily to test themselves in the most prestigious in-season Hoosier tournament, the one-day, four-team invitational that is the main fund-raiser for the Indiana Basketball Hall of Fame next door to Chrysler. The prestigious Hall of Fame event turned out to be more than a tuneup for Siefert's team. Batesville topped Madison-Grant in a matchup of first-time invitees, then shocked the state by beating Anderson for the tournament championship.

A week later, Batesville played at Kokomo in a game that wasn't even listed on early-printed Batesville schedules. "Basil and I worked something out on the golf course," Siefert said. "We thought we could play with them." Kokomo coach Basil Mawbey didn't need a fill-in on where Batesville is. "When he won the State at Connersville (1983), they were the only team to beat Batesville and they did it twice," Siefert said. Mawbey maintained that hex. The Bulldogs led Kokomo most of the way but lost on another buzzer-beater, 42-41. So far, it's their only loss, and Kokomo is 16-3.

"More than anything, winning the Hall of Fame Classic gave us the mind-set that we can play with the Andersons," Siefert said. "At Kokomo we probably outplayed them except for the last three minutes. That happens.

"But I wouldn't trade that loss for anything right now because I think we learned a lot from it. I think our kids got more hungry."

And tougher, Menser feels.

"Our plan was just to go up there (to New Castle) and have a good showing, see what happens," Menser said. "Winning the championship game over Anderson — the 17th-ranked team in the *country* — that was unexpected. I think our defense basically won us the game.

"I remember sitting down with Coach Siefert up there and talking: 'How are we going to defend against Anderson?' "

The big concern was Anderson guards Eric Bush and Tyson Jones. Menser got Bush, at both ends of the court.

"We usually funnel people to the side," Menser said. "Basically, I just tried to keep in front of him, and on offense I focused on handling the ball and not letting him do what he's the best at: taking it away.

"Winning that game definitely helped us. Our problem in the years past was we didn't know if we could really play with the big schools. Down where we are, we don't play them.

"The Kokomo game brought us back down to earth. We did some very uncharacteristic things. We turned the ball over three or four times in the last three minutes, when we had the lead. And we didn't block out. We didn't do a lot of the things that we always feel are necessary to win.

"I don't think we'd have wanted to go into the tournament undefeated. It was a defeat that helped us, I think."

The best 'team'

Siefert's hours of tape-watching during the year gave him one particular chuckle. Looking at his 1993-94 team in the Indianapolis semistate against Ben Davis, he spotted Michael Menser in action and blinked. "He was a *little* fellow," Siefert said. "I couldn't believe how little he looked out there."

"I was about 5-6," Menser said, "and right around 100 pounds. I remember being really nervous, a freshman playing in front of however many thousand fans."

That day, that experience at Hinkle Fieldhouse still is a Menser memory with a one-word description.

"Awesome.

"You hear the great stories of *Hoosiers*. My uncle (Tom Buck) played there in '71." That team, Batesville's first to win a regional in 19 years and last to win one for 23, was routed through Connersville. Its loss at Indianapolis was to New Castle, 68-63. That was almost a decade before Michael was born, but he had heard about the feeling of coming up the Fieldhouse tunnel and running onto that springy court, playing in front of that crowd. And then he lived it. "Just to be able to play there, especially being a freshman — I was in total awe of the situation."

Playing a what-if game that didn't really appeal to him, Siefert allowed that if class basketball had been in all along, this might not be his best challenger for a 3A championship. The team Menser's freshman year "probably would have had a better shot," Siefert said.

Menser was invited to make his own assessment: which was best of the four Batesville teams he played on?

"Each one had its strong points," he said. "They were different teams. My freshman year, I was just along for the ride. My sophomore year, I was a bigger part of it but other guys still led it. My junior and senior years, I sorta took charge, with a couple of other guys.

"I do think this year we could be classified as a true team. I don't know if our talent was better than other years, but we played so well together. Some teams play together and that's it, but we're all really good friends. We like to hang out. I'd have to say this is the best 'team.' "

'You get that sick feeling'

Both Rushville and Batesville voted against a switch to classes. Neither has won a state championship under the present system, and Rushville came the closest.

At the Final Four in 1976, the Lions trailed No. 1-ranked East Chicago Washington 33-12 before rallying to a 68-59 victory. They lost in the state championship game to Marion, 82-76, despite 19 points and 16 rebounds by center Brad Miley, a starter three years later when Indiana State went 33-0 before losing the NCAA championship game to Michigan State.

Rushville's girls were runners-up, too — in 1981 to Evansville Reitz.

"Cinda (Brown, Rushville's girls coach in 1981 and now) and I were pretty much in agreement," Craig said, "and our principal (Barb Barger) voted the way we wanted her to.

"I've been around the state and most of the coaches I've talked to are against it. I don't know how many former players from little schools have told me, 'We lived for that one game, to try to beat somebody in the tournament.'

"I played at Muncie Burris — on the little Muncie Burris team that upset big Muncie Southside in 1978, when Central went on to win the State. Southside had beaten Central during the season, and we upset Southside in the sectional.

"It was a great feeling. I lived for that one game. Central destroyed us in the final game, but that made the season right there — playing in the Fieldhouse.

"When the decision first came out, I tried to look at the good and the bad. After I did I was completely distraught. I think they hurried up and railroaded it through. That bothers me. There were so many unanswered questions that had not been discussed and thoroughly investigated, but we were told to go ahead and vote.

"It's the old adage: if something's not broke, don't fix it."

Siefert said, "Anybody who's played high school basketball in Indiana, or coached in Indiana — you just get that sick feeling in your gut that something isn't right.

"We're a small school that the past four years would have benefited from a class tournament. When they first talked about it several years ago, I thought that deep down maybe I would be for it. But we've been able to compete with about any level. I realize that isn't going to continue forever and ever, but we're going to be good next year. We'll be able to compete down the road.

"That's not a concern."

Rushville athletic director John D. Wilson gave the principals' vote his own puckish analysis. Those directional schools that came out of consolidations were a factor, Wilson suggested.

"North, South, East, West — if there's one of those in their school name, for the most part they voted for class basketball," he said.

How accurate was he?

Excluding South Bend, East Chicago and West Lafayette, where direction in the name had nothing to do with consolidation, the North-South-East-West count was 41-12 for changing to classes. Central Noble didn't vote.

17

Bloomington N.	75
Seymour	**47**

February 17

BLOOMINGTON NORTH / SEYMOUR

BLOOMINGTON NORTH		SEYMOUR
One as Bloomington North, 1997. Others in corporation, one: Bloomington High 1919	**STATE CHAMPIONSHIP**	None
None as Bloomington North. Others in corporation, three: Bloomington High 1918, 1922, 1960	**OTHER TIMES IN FINAL FOUR**	None
Two as Bloomington North: 1982, 1997. Others in corporation: Bloomington High 10 (first 1921, last 1971)	**REGIONAL CHAMPIONSHIPS**	Eight: first 1932; most recent 1975
10 as Bloomington North: first 1976; two in '90s, most recent 1997. Others in corporation, 28: Bloomington High 25 (first 1915, last 1971), Bloomington University 2: 1946, 1972; Unionville 1966.	**SECTIONAL CHAMPIONSHIPS**	44: first 1916; one in '90s, 1992. Others in corporation, one: Cortland 1927
Formed 1972 (Bloomington University, Unionville, part of Bloomington High)	**CONSOLIDATIONS**	Shields 1922, Cortland 1965
No	**VOTE ON CHANGE TO CLASSES**	No
4A. (1,026; 70th of 95 in class)	**1997-98 CLASS (ENROLLMENT)**	4A. (961; 76th of 95 in class)
4A, Bedford North Lawrence, Bloomington South; 3A, Brown County, Edgewood; 2A, Eastern (Greene County). Bedford-North Lawrence site, Bloomington North 1997 champion	**1996-97 SECTIONAL OPPONENTS (1997-98 CLASSIFICATION)**	4A, Jennings County; 2A, Austin, Brownstown Central; 1A, Crothersville, Medora. Seymour site, Jennings County 1997 champion
Bloomington South, Columbus East, Columbus North, East Central, Martinsville	**1997-98 SECTIONAL OPPONENTS**	Bedford North Lawrence, Floyd Central, Jeffersonville, Jennings County, New Albany
28-1 (state champion)	**FINAL RECORD 1996-97**	14-8 (lost to Jennings County in sectional semifinal, 60-59)

No. 1, on the Blocks

Caesar said, "The die is cast." Hoosiers say, "The pie's in the oven." They mean the same thing.

Preparation time is over. It's prove-it time.

That's the feeling Indiana high school basketball coaches and players have had forever, once the last regular-season game is played and the next step coming is the sectional tournament.

Tom McKinney of Bloomington North felt almost as good as he could have on that score on this night. Steve Brett of Seymour didn't. "We've got to put this one behind us and get ready for the tournament," Brett said after No. 1-ranked North blew his team apart, 75-47.

Seymour came to play a basketball game and wound up serving, volleyball-style. In the game's third minute, 6-4 Seymour center Jeff Peters shot from close range. Splat! The ball came back at him, slapped down by 6-6 Djibril Kante of North.

Three minutes later, guard Ryan Schrink attacked the basket. Splat! North's Ryan Reed, 6-3, blocked that one.

Guard Brett Roeder drove for Seymour; 6-6 Kueth Duany smashed his shot aside. Peters tried again; Kante blocked it again. Peters picked the ball up, got it to Schrink, and Kante blocked his shot, too.

Five blocks. A 23-15 North lead. It is still the first quarter.

No white flags went up, but this one already had the look and the feel of a game decided. The sound, too. Splat!

On display was an art of debated virtue. "Coach doesn't want us blocking shots unless we know we can get them," Duany said.

"I don't think any coach is a fan of blocked shots," McKinney said. To a coach, blocked shots mean a vulnerability to fakes. *"Don't leave your feet!"* There is an unspoken proviso: ". . . unless you *know* you can block it."

This game, North's 10 blocked shots were not so much showy as functional. McKinney agreed with that ("Their kid had gotten around us and gotten inside, so we went ahead") and it was the most useful that one little-encouraged phase of his team's strong defense had been in a game all year. It was not a bad notice to leave for future tournament opponents. Those North big guys don't want to leave their feet. They don't really want to have to block your shot. But they can. And they will.

And they did so many times on this night that Brett was disgusted.

"You've got to start faking and drawing some fouls — doing *something* different instead of doing the same thing every time," he said.

"Our big guys didn't play like they're capable of playing. They got intimidated, I thought." Peters and 6-5 forward Joel Keinath came into the game with a combined 29-point scoring average. They teamed for 10 in this game.

The Seymour tent folded right after North's sixth block. Duany got it when 5-10 guard Pete Terkhorn moved in a little too close just over two minutes into the second quarter.

The North lead was 25-17 then. Three minutes later it was 37-17, on its way to 43-17 before Roeder — at safe range away from those misdirecting swats — sank a Seymour 3 closing out the half.

North's lead was never under the 23-point halftime spread in the second half, which played out to the 28-point Cougar victory.

"The physicalness got to us," Brett said.

"I thought it was kind of a fiasco that we didn't get to the bonus till 25 seconds to go in the fourth quarter." High school teams start shooting a one-and-one with the opponent's seventh foul each half. North was called for just six fouls in the first half and six in the first 15½ minutes of the second half. "There was a lot more contact than that," Brett said.

"They're a good basketball team. Very good. The difference was on the boards, especially early. They dominated the boards."

That, of course, is where Duany and Kante live.

They're an interesting pair.

Kueth, Djibril and 'Doc'

Kueth Duany was born into a diplomat's family in The Sudan. That's coo-*eth* (but quicker than that, more like *kweth*) doo-*ane-ee*. Djibril (Gabriel in French, juh-*brill* in Hoosier) Kante (*conn-tay*) was born in Bloomington, but he spent much of his childhood in Africa, going back and forth.

Kueth was just 5 when the Wal Duany family moved to Bloomington. His and Djibril's families lived in the same Indiana University adult housing unit, Tulip Tree.

They met right away, on the Duany family's arrival. "We played a lot of soccer and basketball," Duany said. "Then he started moving back and forth, from country to country. He'd come back in the summers, then go back. He finally decided to stay his eighth-grade year."

By then, Kueth's older brother, Duany, was on his way to career scoring records at North. Americans made jokes about the name Duany Duany, continued to make them even after he made the Indiana All-Stars, signed a Big Ten tender with Wisconsin and, after an injury-caused red-shirt year, started frequently as a freshman for the Badgers. It was not a joke. The first-born son carries the family surname as his first name in the Duanys' culture.

There's a three-year difference between Kueth and Duany. Early in the older brother's career, teammates and even classmates called him Doc — after a junior high coach compared him to "Dr. J" Julius Erving. Kueth never uses Doc or any other nickname. His brother to him is Duany.

Though he came to the United States so young, Kueth Duany has memories of Africa. "I remember games we used to play, how

211

the weather was. My brother played a lot of tennis when we were in Africa. I used to follow him and watch. He didn't know I followed him sometimes. He was a big influence on my life.

"Still to this day he is. He still gives me advice — on everything, life in general."

In basketball: "Little things. He's been in the game more than me. He just knows a little bit more. He tries to help me as much as possible. He wants to see me get as far as him. Maybe farther.

"I can't argue with him. He's been through it. I haven't been there yet. He never comes down on me in a negative way. It's always positive."

Their eighth-grade year is when Kante decided to stay year-round in Bloomington.

"By then I was really seriously into basketball," Duany said. "Djibril was like my brother, so we were always together. He just started to pick up on basketball.

"He always had big feet, and I always knew he would be tough. When we were playing together, he'd usually be the center, throwing his body around. He was a lot bigger than he is now. And it wasn't muscle. But he always had good feet, because of soccer. You could see he could be good if he got bigger and lost a little weight. And that's what happened."

Kante agrees that basketball wasn't important to him until his eighth-grade year. "I played soccer until then," he said. "I lived in Africa, in Niger and in Guinea. I was pretty good. I was a midfielder. I was about 5-11. I can't tell you I could play soccer now.

"My eighth-grade year here, I figured, 'I'm taller than everybody else. Soccer's fun and all, but that's a big field to be running up and down.'

"They were all way ahead of me in basketball when I started the summer my eighth-grade year. It wasn't really frustrating. I was just out there to have fun. I didn't think of them being ahead or me being behind."

On the eighth-grade team that year, "I didn't start at all. I barely played." After a summer camp at North, Kante said, "Coach told me I might play JV my freshman year. That's when I got serious about it."

Duany's memory is that Kante "got serious after our freshman year. He didn't play very much that year. I think that's what made him better. He wanted to be good, and people were saying: 'You're so big. Why aren't you good?'

"Now look at him."

Memories of a dunk

Kante was overweight when he first began to work at basketball. "Kueth was always taller than me," he said. "Eighth grade, he had three or four inches on me."

That was the year Duany dunked. It was a milestone event vivid in Kueth's memory.

"My first dunk ever was on the outdoor court at Tulip Tree," he said. "My brother had dunked in seventh grade. I couldn't. I was mad.

"When I finally got it (the summer before his eighth-grade year), it was early in the morning — about 6 o'clock. I was out there by myself and I dunked it.

"We were living on the second floor of Tulip Tree. I threw the ball up and hit our window. I was yelling '*Duany!*' He came to the window, and I went up and dunked it again. He yelled, 'Yeahhhhhh!'

"It was a great day."

As a freshman, Duany said, "I was real thin. I probably weighed 130, maybe 120. I was about 6-2. But I could jump. Coach McKinney put me on the freshman team for the first couple of weeks. Then he moved me up to the reserves." He joined the six seniors of the 1996-97 Cougars, sophomores then. That JV team went 20-0. "That's when a lot of the talk really started, about winning the state championship," Duany said.

"Djibril was on the JVs. He was 6-4 and about 190."

Those are football numbers. "I think he went out for football and tried it for about a week," Duany laughed. "He couldn't handle it. He came back to playing basketball."

At "130, maybe 120" pounds, Duany never even thought about it.

Back to 'rehab'

In the Seymour game, Kante had six of his team's dunks, including a thunderous one closing out the game. He hit all seven shots he took, scoring 15 points. He had nine rebounds (Duany 11, plus 19 points, as North overwhelmed the Owls in rebounds, 39-19).

"Djibril really took the ball to the basket," McKinney said. "He was against a good, strong kid.

"We talked to Duany at the end of the first quarter. I just didn't think he was playing at all. Boy, he really got after it. He can play inside and outside. He'd rather play outside, but he was a man on the boards tonight."

This was a 12-6 Seymour team.

"We played about as well as we could," McKinney said.

"You don't say that very often."

He wasn't without a worry. A minute into the second quarter, starter Ryan Reed drove to the basket and crumpled, his left ankle injured. "I made a cut and drive, and when I jumped my foot was on somebody else's foot and it just rolled over," Reed said. He didn't play the rest of the game, and the countdown was on. The sectional started for North in eight days.

Reed knew what he was in for. Just before Christmas, playing at Dugger, he had hurt his right ankle.

"We've always had a real big threshold for pain," he said of him and twin Matt, the fourth man in the three-position front-court rotation McKinney used. "We've played on real bad ankles. People say, 'You must really enjoy the game.' That *is* a big part of it."

He remembered he spent three weeks playing through the soreness of the first injury. Then came this injury, to the other ankle. He couldn't afford three sore weeks. That would extend past the regional, and North in his years never had won even a sectional tournament.

"The doctor is telling me 'You're not going to be ready.' I say, 'Yeah, but I'm 6-3, I'm not going pro, and so far I haven't had a call for college. If we lose in the sectional, I could be done right then.' "

He knew the hurry-up healing process. "When they put that electric stem on it, your toes curl," he said. "But it gets the swelling out, and the swelling is what slows you down."

McKinney was hopeful about Reed's tournament availability. "I didn't think it was too bad," he said. "Ryan took this last week off to try to mend his knee (tendinitis in the left). We need him. He can play inside and out; he can guard a guard or a forward."

Reed's memory saw good things ahead — for the sore knee. "When I hurt the ankle, I was off it for a while, trying to heal the ankle, and the knee got better," he said.

No. 1 concern

North entered the week ranked No. 1 in a state coaches' poll and No. 2 (to New Castle) in The Associated Press' poll of writers and broadcasters. The votes were close, and this final week of regular-season play they switched: North to No. 1 in AP, New Castle to No. 1 with the coaches.

"It's not a concern of mine," McKinney said. "As a coach, you always think, 'I wouldn't mind being No. 1 sometime during the year, but not at the end of the year.'

"Very honestly, I don't think an awful lot of people who voted us No. 1 have seen us play. I scouted with a friend of mine the other night, and I said, 'Do you really think we're No. 1?' He said, 'God, no.'

"The teams in the sectional obviously don't have a fear of the ranking, because we know each other so well.

"But it's an honor the kids can look back on 10 years from now."

McKinney was a sophomore reserve on the Columbus team that was unbeaten and the overwhelming No. 1 choice in the 1963-64 poll. "We might have been No. 1 from wire to wire," he said. "Then we got beat (by Huntington in the semifinal round at the State, 71-67).

"We need to stay loose; we need to play. But I would not trade that ranking for being 5-15."

215

So, he was asked, how *do* you feel about this team as it heads into the tournament?

"For three years, our seniors have been tough to beat. As sophomores a lot of them played varsity ball and they were tough to beat. We still think we are.

"Sometimes we're a little rough out there, not really smooth. But they attack so well.

"We have not recently had tournament success. That has been our aim all year long. If we can get our kids healthy, it's going to take somebody good to beat us."

Big gym, big hunger

Brett replaced a Hall of Fame coach at Bloomfield, the late Guy Glover. After successful years there, Brett was brought in at Seymour, where another Hall of Fame coach, Barney Scott, once had the basketball program consistently in Indiana's Top 10.

It's a hungry basketball community. The town of 15,000 built the biggest high school gym in southern Indiana — 8,110 capacity, No. 4 on the arena list in a state that has 13 high school gyms above 7,000 capacity. The rest of the United States has one (in Dallas, seating 7,500).

Seymour's is the only one in Indiana's Top 10 from south of Indianapolis. That, in the site selection system through 1997, guaranteed a regional for Seymour, and home gyms usually translate to at least some advantage. But Seymour is one of the oldest big Indiana high schools that never has been to the Final Four. Barney Scott once had the Owls knocking on the door regularly. From 1962 to 1975, Seymour played in the semistate championship game five times. Those five games are the farthest Seymour ever has advanced.

Since 1975, when Loogootee took the Final Four trip away from the Owls as it had done in 1970, Seymour hasn't won a regional. That doesn't necessarily translate to poor play by Seymour. During the Damon Bailey years, Bedford North Lawrence came through the Seymour regional three times. It was there, with 31 points in a 77-57 regional victory over Scottsburg, that Bailey became Indiana's all-time leading scorer. The one year Bailey's team didn't win the Seymour regional and move on to the State, Floyd Central — with Bailey's future Indiana University teammate, Pat Graham — did. The Seymour regional also has been the meeting place for rivals Jeffersonville and New Albany. From 1987 through 1996, nine of the 10 southern semistate champions came out of the Seymour regional (all but Terre Haute South in 1991).

And now, going in to class basketball, Seymour will be the host again, but its sectional will be one of the most loaded in Indiana — Jeffersonville, New Albany, Bedford North Lawrence, Floyd Central and Jennings County the Owls' company.

Hall of Fame coach Barney Scott had Seymour consistently among the top 10. (Photo courtesy Indiana High School Athletic Association)

Brett's team did defend its home court well this year. In regular-season play, its only loss there was to New Albany, in overtime. Before even getting out of North's gym on this night, he was invited to compare the two, Bloomington North and New Albany, as the tournament neared.

"Duany isn't going to get all those dunks against New Albany," he said. "He'll get some of those blocked. They've got some guys who can get up there, too.

"They'll challenge him more defensively, too. They've got some guys with a little more height and more offensive moves than we showed. They'd probably have some foul trouble defensing New Albany the way they defensed us.

"New Albany's guards are probably a little bit better, but North is deeper. North has seven or eight guys and New Albany has five, maybe six. (New Albany's Chad) Hunter is probably a better all-round player than anybody North has. Duany would probably be the next-best player on the floor, if those two teams happen to meet.

"It would be an interesting matchup. Hopefully it will never happen."

There was that matter of a Seymour regional between New Albany and any semistate meeting with North.

18

Union (Dugger)	88
White River Valley	55

February 20

UNION (DUGGER) — WHITE RIVER VALLEY

UNION (DUGGER)		WHITE RIVER VALLEY
None	**STATE CHAMPIONSHIP**	None
None	**TIMES IN FINAL FOUR**	None
One, 1930	**REGIONAL CHAMPIONSHIPS**	Two as White River Valley: 1992, 1993. Schools in corporation, three: Lyons, 1923; Switz City Central, 1955; L&M, 1985.
12: first 1926; one in '90s, 1997	**SECTIONAL CHAMPIONSHIPS**	Four as White River Valley: 1991, 1992, 1993, 1996. Schools in corporation, 16: Lyons, 1923, 1925, 1933, 1935; L&M, 1968, 1969, 1984, 1985; Marco, 1950; Switz City Central, 1931, 1944, 1955, 1956, 1973; Worthington, 1949, 1977
Pleasantville, 1965	**CONSOLIDATIONS**	Formed 1991: L&M (Newberry, Marco, 1947; Lyons, Marco 1958), Switz City Central, Worthington
Yes	**VOTE ON CHANGE TO CLASSES**	No
1A. (106; 81st of 96 in class)	**1997-98 CLASS (ENROLLMENT)**	1A. (268; 12th of 96 in class)
2A, Linton; 1A, Bloomfield, Clay City, Shakamak, White River Valley. White River Valley site, Union (Dugger) 1997 champion	**1996-97 SECTIONAL OPPONENTS (1997-98 CLASSIFICATION)**	2A, Linton; 1A, Bloomfield, Clay City, Shakamak, Union (Dugger). White River Valley site, Union (Dugger) 1997 champion
Bloomfield, Clay City, Eminence, North Central (Farmersburg), Shakamak, White River Valley	**1997-98 SECTIONAL OPPONENTS**	Bloomfield, Clay City, Eminence, North Central (Farmersburg), Shakamak, Union (Dugger)
21-4 (won sectional; lost to Bloomington North in regional final, 62-51)	**FINAL RECORD 1996-97**	9-12 (lost to Union in sectional semifinal, 75-40)

Best
of the
Little Guys

Joe Hart, who may have been coaching the best little basketball team in Indiana this enrollment-conscious year, worked hard to give that team a full shot at the state championship. He believed in that team, and he knew what a state championship for it would mean in this of all years. Union High School of Dugger could prove that a Milan still could win.

And then Hart and Union would enter the era of class basketball. Cheerfully. "I've been in favor of it since the second year I taught," Hart said as he approached the last weekend of competition before the tournament.

Of all the coaches with even a remote chance to get to what was being widely called The Final Final Four, Joe Hart may have been the most open, the most vocal about his eagerness to get on to class play.

Many objected to how swiftly the change came. "I thought it took a long time," Hart said. "I'm excited — definitely. My only regret is that we didn't have it this year (the senior year of his 6-5 star, Jared Chambers).

"I would have voted for it a long time ago. But my experience with it is different from other people's."

Different era

A long time ago, Joe Hart played on the same court where his Union team was finishing its season this night against White River Valley.

The 3,000-seat gym is the reason there was no real question about where White River Valley High School would be when Greene County rivals L&M, Worthington and Switz City Central merged. Switz City had built this place in 1956, an early version of the genre of arenas built down, not up, street-level entry into the place just behind the top rows of seats.

Joe Hart was Switz City Class of '61. WRV athletic director Roger Weaver was a year behind him. They are at opposite poles on this issue. Greene County was an exception in the general, state-wide tendency for big schools to vote no and little ones yes on the proposal to go to a four-class tournament system. Bloomfield, Shakamak and White River Valley were three of the 16 schools in the new 1A class that voted against the change.

"Our situation is a lot different," Hart said. Union plays now in the sectional at White River Valley with most of the Greene County teams. Before being assigned there in 1993, Union frequently went to Terre Haute.

"We had some awful good teams that drew a Terre Haute team the first game of the sectional," Hart said. Three years in a row, Union was taken out by Terre Haute South. There were times, Hart recalls, when if Union had beaten South, "the next night we had to play Terre Haute North. White River Valley or Bloomfield never had to put up with that.

"When I played at Switz City, if you beat Bloomfield, you beat a big school — or a good school anyway. They won sectional after sectional (under Hall of Fame coach Guy Glover). When I graduated in '61, they went to the semistate.

"That kind of rivalry is different. You knew the kids from Bloomfield, and if you were lucky enough to beat them, boy, that was great.

"We're going to be the smallest school in any sectional we play in, probably. But there's a lot of difference between playing a school with an enrollment of 300 and one of 2,000.

"You look at Ben Davis. I saw a team picture. They had a coach for each player.

"The bigger schools have a weight program during school, advanced P.E. classes where they can start practice. Then you get to Indianapolis where they bus in players.

"We've had a few kids boat in here from Finland and Sweden, but we've never had anybody bused in."

Union has one of those "boat-ins" on this team: 6-4 senior Jani Jarvinen of Finland. "In 1989, a real good kid from Sweden named A.J. Johanssen was our sixth man and our best defensive player. Jani is not as good as A.J. was, but he picked a bad year to come. On a regular team, he could be a pretty good player."

Saw them coming

Hart had served a happy and successful tenure as Union's head basketball coach when he resigned as the '90s began, the better to follow son Joey's progress as a college player (at Vincennes University, then at Coastal Carolina).

It was during those three "off" years that Hart filled in some time by coaching the school's fifth- and sixth-graders. "They didn't have anybody to do it," he said. "I said, 'I'll take them, but any time they have a game that interferes with Joey's schedule, I'm going to his game.'

"So I coached them, and I knew they were pretty decent."

It was a group that included the present team's seniors, most notably Jared Chambers. Joey's college graduation coincided just fine with his father's renewed coaching interest. "When Chambers became a freshman, I started coaching again," Hart said.

"I imagine by the time Boyd's a senior, that will probably be my last year."

That's Brody Boyd. He and Clark Golish are starters on this Union team as freshmen. Both Chambers and Hart knew all about the little kid coming along three grades back of the Chambers class.

"Brody practiced against us when we were eighth-graders, and he was in fifth grade," Chambers said. "He was killing our point guard then. I knew something was going on."

Chambers also played as a freshman, averaging 12.8 points and 7.2 rebounds but taking some beatings along with it. That team went 6-15.

By the next year, help began to arrive. His scoring average went up to 23.5 and the team reversed its record, finishing 15-7. Clark's brother, J.T., was a grade back of Chambers and so was Bobby Cox, a 6-footer who was developing as a shooter. A year ago, with junior Chambers averaging 21.7, the Bulldogs were 13-9.

And this year the freshmen arrived. Union, Hart, Chambers *et al* were ready.

Adjusting and learning

"Chambers kinda took the freshmen under his wing," Hart said. "They're real close to him. They run a lot together. There's not that much difference in age between them. Chambers is awfully young for his class (17)."

"He could be a sophomore," Boyd said. "An old sophomore. He definitely could be a junior."

Chambers said the immediate prominence for Boyd and Golish "wasn't any problem at all" for upperclassmen to handle. "Everybody wants to win, and everybody realizes they're two of our top five players, easily."

Adaptation wasn't automatic for the rookies. "Brody didn't shoot the ball real well the first of the season," Hart said. "At one time he was 39 percent from the field and about 25 from 3-point range. Now he's at 49 percent from the field and over 40 percent on 3s.

"I think his biggest problem was adjusting not so much to how we played but to how we were playing him. I think you will find a lot of kids this way; if they've got the ball in their hands a lot, they'll shoot better. In junior high he probably handled the ball 80 percent of the time for his team. Now he's not our primary ball handler. He had to adjust to that."

Union had several adjustments to make. In its second game, it went to North Knox and lost, 71-66. "We were up 10 points in the fourth quarter," Boyd remembers. "We thought, 'It's over.' We got our butts kicked." The teams met six weeks later for the Greene

County Invitational championship and kickee became kicker, 47-15 at halftime, a cruising 80-53 at the finish. "I don't know that I've ever had a team play quite like that," Hart said that night. "That wasn't a bad team we were playing. Our defense in the first half was out of sight."

A freshman was the key — Clark Golish, not Boyd. "I'm not so sure he isn't our best defender," Hart said. "That game he ended up on Ryan Kerns (a 6-5 senior who averaged 19 points a game) and stripped him three times. He made a believer out of me.

"Made a believer out of Kerns, too."

Halftime adjustments

Hart figured to win this game easily, but he was wary. There was one tricky angle: these teams were paired in the first round of the sectional, a week away. There also was last year: White River Valley ended Union's season with a victory in the sectional, and the primary perpetrator of that deed still was around.

"Last year, they beat us by 30 points on our floor (in regular-season play)," Hart said. "We came back and lost by 3 points in the sectional, by holding the ball.

"Ryan Huffine (this WRV team's 6-2 senior guard) made the shot that probably beat us. Just before halftime, he banked in about a 30-footer, after we got a 5-second call that was ridiculous. We were up 3, all of a sudden it was tied." White River Valley won, 27-24.

This Union team doesn't play at that kind of pace, as WRV learned about three beats after the national anthem. Chambers missed a shot but rebounded and scored, and Union's Bobby Cox stole the ball for a layin. It was 4-0, after just 25 seconds.

When Boyd and Chambers hit 3-point shots, WRV coach Kevin Roy took a timeout. Chambers hit another 3, and Roy took his second timeout, down 13-2 with just 2½ minutes gone. The look of a very long evening already was there for the home team.

It was 26-8 at the quarter and then Union got hot. Especially Cox. In the second quarter, he took seven shots and hit six, three of them 3-pointers — a 15-point quarter. "Cox is our most improved player by far," Hart said. "He's had other quarters like that. Some nights I think 'What's he done?' I look in the book and he's got 18 points. It just amazes me. You know Jared's going to score, and Brody will."

Union went to the halftime locker room leading 55-22.

Hart has become expert at handling such situations. He doesn't really change the running, pressuring game. "This is the way we've been successful this year, playing at this pace," he said. "When we slow it down, we're not near as good." But he broke up his team. He let Chambers and J.T. Golish play with reserves the third quarter, then sat them down and let starters Cox, Boyd and Clark Golish play the last quarter with the same backups. Chambers scored 29 points in his 24 minutes and Cox finished with 21. The winning margin (88-55) was the same as halftime.

"We've been doing that," Hart said. "The last six or seven games, we've been up anywhere from 40 to 70 points at the end of the third quarter. Chambers is averaging playing about three quarters, and the other kids are averaging about 20 minutes. It's hard telling what he could score if he was on a team that had to fight every possession. His numbers (23.4 points a game after this one) would be a lot higher."

Boyd came as close to blushing as a player on a team that wins by 33 can. "It wasn't eighth grade out there, I'll tell you that," he said. "Man, I got it stolen from me three times tonight. Everybody's a lot stronger."

The system of holding the score down may have contributed to his uncharacteristically sloppy play. "You get in there, it's your time to play — you force things," he confessed.

Hart knows his generosity toward outmanned opponents risks a loss of game-style conditioning. "We've tried to make up for it in practice, with some extra running," he said. "Like last Saturday, we came in and played a game — everybody played 32 minutes before we played our game that night."

A long line of Boyds

Chambers was Brody Boyd's role model.

"He did a lot for me. He gave me a person to look up to all year, especially in practice — his dedication, how hard he worked, he and Bobby Cox, all year long. Jared's an Indiana All-Star. I just want to follow his tracks."

Brody has been following tracks for as long as he can remember. There has been a long run of Boyds at Union. Brody's father, Benji, was a standout player there, and now he's an assistant coach on Hart's staff. Benji's younger brother Doug and Brody's older brother Ben were also Union stars.

Brody's basketball memories go back "to about 4 years old," he said. "My dad coached a junior high team. I went out with him every night. From the time I was in kindergarten, I scrimmaged with them. My first AAU game, I was probably about 7."

He had his summer planned: AAU ball with an Indianapolis team that included North Central star Jason Gardner. "That's all I want to do, play basketball," he said. "I love it. Deeply." It's truly not *all* he does. His grade average is 3.2.

And yes, he said, thoughts have crossed his mind about what it would be like to be on a big-school team. "My parents asked Ben when he was 14 if he wanted to move to Bloomington to get more exposure," Brody said. "I don't know if I'd like it or not. I like playing at a small school. For exposure, a big school obviously would help.

"Now we have class basketball. I'm ready for it. Our freshman class is real good."

Hart thinks so. "We took these freshmen to Rensselaer last summer and they won 16 games up there without being beat. They beat the Lafayette Jeffs and the Lebanons, Jeffersonville, teams like that. It was kinda funny; we only had six kids. People just couldn't understand how they could do that."

Chambers seemed glad he wouldn't be around for the new era. "I feel lucky. It's a tradition that is going to be gone. We'll be the last class of seniors to play in this, so it will be kind of special. If we could do something in the tournament, it would really mean a lot, especially to the smaller schools around the state.

"We've got a tough regional. If we play well, we can be all right."

Tough understates it. There's that potential regional final against, probably, No. 1 Bloomington North or Terre Haute South, No. 20 in the final rankings.

Union coach Joe Hart, an outspoken supporter of the new four-class system, gets a celebrating hug from Jared Chambers, the school's first all-star. (Photo courtesy Bloomington Herald-Times)

"That's kinda what it's all about," Chambers said, "the small school has to go against the big schools. If we can make some noise up there, it would be something special, that's for sure.

"We've wanted to play Terre Haute South all season. We even tried to get our coach to schedule them. We'd love to play Terre Haute South. Or North. That would really be something good, to play one of those schools."

The only solid defeat for these Bulldogs was 80-62 to No. 1-ranked Bloomington North in December. "We learned we have to play hard all the time," Chambers said. "We kinda rushed some things. I'm confident we can play a lot better the next time."

"North has a really good ballclub," Hart said. "I haven't seen anybody better. They play above the rim some, and against us they shot well from outside — 8-for-12 from the 3-point line, which I don't think is characteristic of the way they play.

"They almost invited us to take the ball to the middle. They overplayed us so much, almost played us parallel where if you wanted to go right to the basket, you could, because they had the feeling: 'If you do, those guys (North's 6-6 inside pair, Djibril Kante and Kueth Duany) are there.'

"I have seen some times where they've had trouble with pressure."

Hart knew his tournament schedule. North was four tournament victories away. An eternity. Clearly, though, the mind was at work.

The Oliphants: Elmer, Tom and Jeff

White River Valley, though still a Class A school, is the ultimate result of the mergers of what once were five high schools with interesting backgrounds.

Among them: Marco reached the 16-team State tournament in 1914, losing to Lebanon; Newberry in 1917, under coach L.V. Phillips who later was commissioner of the IHSAA, beat Worthington, 140-2, and its star, Snowden Hert, scored 90 points; Lyons made it to the 16-team State tournament in 1923, losing to eventual champion Vincennes.

Newberry merged with Lyons in 1947. Eight years later, Lyons and Marco went together to form L&M. The last of the mergers put L&M, Switz City Central (a Sweet 16 team in 1955) and Worthington together.

L&M came very close to giving Indiana a 1980s Milan. The L&M coach was Tom Oliphant, whose roots go to the greatest Greene County athlete ever, future Purdue and West Point all-time football All-American Elmer Oliphant. (Roots is a proper term here; Tom's great-grandfather was a brother of Elmer Oliphant's dad).

Elmer played on a 1908 Washington team that claimed the state football championship, then moved to Linton in January 1909 because, Hatchets lore goes, he wanted to play basketball and Washington had temporarily dropped the sport. In the 1967 book, *The Big Ten*, co-authors Kenneth "Tug" Wilson and Jerry Brondfield called Oliphant "a brilliant halfback from Purdue . . . Only a poor team record kept him off the All-America teams. He sparkled in basketball in 1913-14 and in those same years was a great catcher, outfielder and prodigious hitter in baseball, and a sprinter and hurdler in track. He set a world record for the low hurdles on track." He also was a prodigious drop-kicker. From Purdue he went to West Point and played three more years, scoring almost 500 points as a collegian. Knute Rockne was the source for the "all-time All-America" ranking.

In 1984-85, Tom Oliphant's son, Jeff, and Tony Patterson gave L&M two 6-5 players who were top students (both are lawyers now), Big Ten recruits (Oliphant at Indiana, Patterson at Purdue) and Indiana All-Stars. Oliphant and Patterson had help, including 6-4 forward Chad Grounds, a 15-point scorer with Patterson and Oliphant just under 25 each.

For two years in a row, they had L&M up with the giants in the Top 10 of the state polls. They went unbeaten in regular-season play in 1983-84; they were 22-1 and No. 3 in the rankings when the 1984-85 tournament began. *Esquire* magazine sent David Halberstam to profile the team. *Sports Illustrated* featured L&M in a major story on Indiana basketball.

Their senior year, Oliphant booked them against every major school that would play them, and L&M played in the Hall of Fame Classic. A loss there to South Bend Adams was the Braves' only defeat until they outran Evansville Bosse in the second afternoon game at the Evansville Semistate, 76-71, then had no legs at night as Southridge broke away to an easy win.

Mount a victim

The L&M experience one more time raised an issue that even some tournament purists long had sought to change: two games in one day. Not so very long ago, some teams in 16-team sectionals had to play four games in two days to win. That has been eased. The Saturday schedule for sectionals, regionals, semistates and states has been eased a little. In the sectionals, semifinals were moved to Friday night with the finals on Saturday night in the sectionals. At regional, semistate and state levels, the only concession the IHSAA made was advancement of the semifinal round from 1 and (unrealistically but always listed that way) 2:15 to 10 a.m. and 11:30.

But, despite the strong urging of doctors, the IHSAA has refused to change the schedules enough to build in a day of rest between the two rounds. "It is time to not allow any basketball player to play two games in one day," a doctor wrote to the IHSAA in 1990. "The fact is: a muscle cannot replenish its glycogen supply in less than 24 hours. This prevents the muscle from functioning properly and increases the likelihood of cramping, inefficiency and less than maximal muscle energy."

The most dramatic illustration of the problem probably cost Indiana tournament fans a chance to see Lebanon great Rick Mount, who scored 47 points in a one-point semifinal victory at the 1966 semistate and had his team ahead of East Chicago Washington in the championship round when leg cramps forced him out. Two games in one day, an issue even before that, picked up considerable steam because of the Mount example, but — 30 years later — there has been no change, though there's little argument that the game of today is considerably more taxing than in even Mount's day. That, speaking as a purist who opposed almost any alteration in the basic tournament structure, was the one thing that should have been changed and was a primary reason why small schools with obviously less depth haven't had much breakthrough success of late.

"That second game's a killer," Hart said, aware that if that Bloomington North rematch or Terre Haute South matchup came, it would be after his team played one of those second games.

19

New Castle	49
Kokomo	36

February 21

KOKOMO		NEW CASTLE
1961	**STATE CHAMPIONSHIP**	1932
Seven: 1925*, 1941, 1944*, 1959*, 1962, 1989*, 1997 (* lost in championship game)	**OTHER TIMES IN FINAL FOUR**	Three: 1967, 1971, 1984
32: first 1925; four in '90s, most recent 1997. Also in corporation: Kokomo Haworth 1970	**REGIONAL CHAMPIONSHIPS**	16: first 1926; five in '90s, most recent 1997
66: first 1916; last seven in '90s, through 1997. Also in corporation: Kokomo Haworth two, 1970, 1972	**SECTIONAL CHAMPIONSHIPS**	52: first 1915; all eight in '90s, through 1997
Kokomo Haworth 1984	**CONSOLIDATIONS**	None
No	**VOTE ON CHANGE TO CLASSES**	No
4A. (1,527; 22nd of 95 in class)	**1997-98 CLASS (ENROLLMENT)**	4A. (872; 93rd of 95 in class)
3A, Western; 2A, Eastern (Howard), Maconaquah, Northwestern, Taylor. Kokomo site and 1997 champion.	**1996-97 SECTIONAL OPPONENTS (1997-98 CLASSIFICATION)**	2A, Knightstown, Shenandoah; 1A, Blue River Valley, Morton Memorial, Tri. New Castle site and 1997 champion
Harrison, Lafayette Jefferson, Logansport, McCutcheon	**1997-98 SECTIONAL OPPONENTS**	Anderson, Anderson Highland, Connersville, Muncie Central, Richmond
23-5 (won sectional, regional, semistate; lost to Bloomington North in state semifinal, 50-43)	**FINAL RECORD 1996-97**	24-2 (won sectional, regional; lost to Franklin in semistate semifinal, 71-65)

Memories of a Shootout

Ray Pavy was there, in his usual spot atop the northwest corner of, as a sign at the south end of the building says, The Largest And Finest High School Fieldhouse In The World. Ray Pavy is there every time he can be, just as he is at his other alma mater, Indiana University, every time he can be when the Hoosiers are playing a basketball game.

But this night is special. Kokomo is in town, to play New Castle. That triggers memories, to more than just Ray Pavy.

This is the last night of the regular season for both teams, and a North Central Conference championship is at stake. New Castle (5-1 in the eight-team league) could win it outright if Anderson (also 5-1) were to lose to Richmond. Kokomo (4-2) could get a piece of the championship.

It was about like that on the final night of a regular season 38 years ago . . .

"We had lost one NCC game and Kokomo had lost two," Pavy said. But there was a difference. Muncie Central also had lost just once in the league, in 1959, but the Bearcats were a half-game up on New Castle because Muncie Central had beaten Anderson twice and both games counted. "Believe it or not, Anderson was one of the easy games on their schedule then," Pavy said.

But Kokomo-New Castle was a big game, and it had some extra emotion: it was the last game in New Castle's gymnasium

Ray Pavy (left) and Jimmy Rayl in front of the old fieldhouse in New Castle where their legendary shootout took place in 1959. (Photo courtesy Indiana High School Athletic Association)

before the Trojans would be moving a few blocks away to The Largest And Finest High School Fieldhouse In The World.

"There was standing room only — you didn't go to the bathroom because when you came back you wouldn't have a seat," Pavy said. "We were both in the top five in the state.

"Thousands of people have told me they were there. The place held 1,800, and it was SRO, so it might have been 2,200."

New Castle won the game, 92-81. That's not what Hoosiers remember about the night.

Ray Pavy (23, above) defends a shot by an opponent. At left, Jimmy Rayl (32) takes a shot during his 40-point effort against Fort Wayne South in the Fort Wayne Semistate. Rayl's basket with one second left gave Kokomo a 92-90 victory. (Both photos courtesy Indiana High School Athletic Association)

The item of history is that Ray Pavy of New Castle scored 51 points.

And Jimmy Rayl of Kokomo scored 49.

This was the classic shootout. Pavy hit 23 of 38 shots. Rayl sank 18 of 33. That's each player taking more than one shot a minute, start to finish.

And that's 51-49 without benefit of the 3-point shot.

If today's scoring rules were in, Pavy said, "I might have had a couple of 3s, but Jim — I have no idea how many he would have had. He had such great range. I don't know of anybody who ever played who had the kind of range Jim had.

"In a horse game with anybody, I'd take Jim. He could shoot it from far enough away that other people couldn't even get it up.

"He was such a great basketball player offensively. Truly, when he crossed the line he was ready to shoot. And if you didn't guard him, he would."

Not that Pavy (38 shots) was bashful.

"I probably had the worst first quarter I ever had," Pavy said. "I missed seven layups. I could have really had a game if I had made a few layups.

"I got four points in the first quarter and 21 in the second." By halftime, "Yeah, I had a feeling that something was going right."

What Rayl had was a normal feeling. It was his career high, but barely. He had 48 the game before, 45 when Kokomo won an earlier Big Game from Muncie Central, 72-70. He averaged 40 over his last six regular-season games, and in the Fort Wayne semistate, Rayl outscored Fort Wayne South star Tom Bolyard, 40-34, including the winning last-second basket from a bare stride or two across the center line in the spectacular 92-90 game that dethroned the 1958 state champion. *Truly, when he crossed the line he was ready to shoot. And if you didn't guard him, he would.* Truly.

Rayl, Pavy and Bolyard — all three of them enshrined in the Indiana Basketball Hall of Fame just a long block or so away from the Fieldhouse — were teammates at IU. There, Rayl was to have two 56-point games, still the Indiana record. Bolyard made All-Big

Ten and he was the 19th player taken in the NBA draft, three spots ahead of Rayl. Pavy played one varsity year, then, on Highway 41 in northern Indiana, he was gravely injured in an auto accident. His fiancee died in the accident. Pavy has spent the rest of his life in a wheelchair.

The son of a Methodist minister has lived that life cheerfully. He stayed with basketball, coaching at two New Castle-area high schools before moving into an administrative position in the New Castle schools. Rayl had a brief taste of professional basketball, then returned to Kokomo and made his living in sales.

On this night, Pavy was back to see another big New Castle-Kokomo game. They always seem big, and tight. Going in, the all-time standing between the two was 41-41.

Before this game ever began, the thought occurred:

Could it be that neither team will score as much tonight as its representative in that 51-49 duel?

Basil Ball

They call it Basil Ball.

Kokomo coach Basil Mawbey is not the least bit caught up with scoring points. When his Connersville team won the 1983 state championship, the Spartans' scores from semistate on were 67, 70, 62 and 63 — not racehorse but not bad. Basil coaches a more controlled game now. This Kokomo team scored in the 80s once and the 60s seven other times, every one of them a victorious contribution toward the team's 16-3 record.

But, teams playing Kokomo know if the Wildkats (that's the Kokomo spelling, emphasizing the K as in Kokomo) are leading and you're playing a zone defense, you just may not see the ball again for a while. Could happen if you're in man-to-man, too. With a lead against a strong opponent, Basil Ball milks the clock, sometimes rather early.

Whatever the pace, Basil Ball does include some fierce defense, virtually all of it out of a 2-3 zone.

It's a fluid zone. Mawbey teams do a great deal within that basic 2-3 concept.

"I get asked about defense a lot," Mawbey said. "We try to practice a little offense, too.

"Our concept of a good offense is getting a good shot every time.

"We didn't play very well right around Christmas. We lost to McCutcheon, 28 to 30. There were rumors then that I didn't know *anything* about offense." That was at 6,850-seat Kokomo Coliseum, where Rayl-type gunners were worshipped, pre-Basil, and 30-28 seemed like a whale of a first-quarter score. You can bet Basil Ball was under fire by the natives after that one.

The other Kokomo losses were within the conference, 53-45 at Marion and 59-56 at Anderson. For the year, Kokomo opponents were averaging just over 45 points a game, and it wasn't all due to slow pace.

The name is Skipper

Rayl would have loved the New Castle approach to this game, almost as much as he would have loved playing with the 3-point shot.

Skipper Rowland of New Castle got the evening's scoring started by slipping open on the side for a 3-point basket, and following it with another from the deep left corner. It was kind of neat. Skipper even wore Rayl's old IU number, 22 (he was 32 at Kokomo, Pavy 23 at New Castle).

Kokomo patiently worked its way to two inside baskets, so the score was 6-4 when Rowland's partner at guard, Brandon Miller, fired over the zone for a 3. Then it was 10-9 when Rowland got open at the right wing and hit his third 3-pointer, with more than a minute left in the first quarter.

"I came out and looked up at the crowd — everything was on the line," Rowland said. That was in warm-ups, when every one of the 8,000 permanent seats in The Largest And Finest High School Fieldhouse In The World was sold and filled.

It was a stimulating atmosphere. When the game began, Rowland said, "I was feeling it, and I let it go from there. They were' falling for me.

Kokomo coach Basil Mawbey isn't afraid to slow down the pace of a game when the strategy can work in his favor. (Photo courtesy Indiana High School Athletic Association, ©Mark Wick)

"They started out in a 2-3, just to stop Joe (Gaw, the Trojans' 6-foot, 8-inch senior center who came into the game with a 16.1 average). They had to stop Joe.

"That left a lot of shots open for me and Brandon. Luckily, I was knocking them down."

Certainly, it wasn't all luck. Miller was leading New Castle scorers with a 17.1 average, and Rowland was at 14.1. But each had *taken* just three or four 3s in the average game, and averaged hitting one.

So, Skipper, three in the first quarter? That was, indeed, a lifetime-best start, confirmed the smiling young Trojan who was christened, not nicknamed, Skipper Von Rowland.

237

A few points short

The real Rayl look-alike came off the New Castle bench to open the second quarter with a 3. Darnell Archey is a 5-11, 132-pound sophomore who all season averaged getting one 3 attempt launched every four minutes he was on-court — not Raylish but twice as fast as any other Trojan. It took him just 2:43 this time, and he hit it. New Castle led 18-9.

The lead stayed about there, through 32-24 after one more 3 by Miller a minute and a half into the third quarter. Kokomo's Aaron Alexander, a 6-2, 185-pound football wideout headed for Bowling Green on scholarship, turned an offensive rebound into a point, then twice slipped free for layups. The second one tied the game 32-32, an eight-point Kokomo run.

The New Castle answer was the same one the Trojans had to the game's only previous tie, 0-0: a 3-point basket by Rowland. Archey followed with one. So it was 38-32 when Kokomo opened the fourth quarter by springing 6-2, 218-pound Herman Fowler free for a driving basket. He wasn't free at the end of it all. Officials wiped away his basket with a charging call, foul No. 4 on Fowler. Right at the game's breaking point, Mawbey had to take out his best weapon. Fowler sat down and Mawbey jabbed a soft, frustrated kick at a table.

Archey jabbed back with a 3, his third in four shots, his team's 10th in 16 shots. The lead now 41-32, New Castle coach Curt Bell did unto Basil as Basil would have done unto him.

New Castle backed off with the basketball, spread out, killed some seconds, and ultimately forced Mawbey to leave the 2-3 zone and attack man-to-man.

"We knew if he was ahead, that's what would happen," Bell said. "I thought we did a nice job spreading the floor and handling the ball down the stretch."

The trailing team has no choice but to try to trap and steal and, if that hasn't worked, foul. First Miller, then Rowland put the victory away for the Trojans by turning one-and-one chances into two points.

"We've been pretty good at that," Bell said. "We've won a lot of games in the fourth quarter, because we've got five guys on the floor shooting 75 percent at the line."

The buzzer sounded and there were those numbers on the scoreboard: New Castle 49, Kokomo 36.

Neither one of them had matched its man in that 51-49 epic.

The nets come down

Neither coach cared, of course.

"We were a lot more concerned about winning the conference," Bell said. It was just the sixth time ever, and the third, in a third different role, for Bell: a player (under Sam Alford) in 1979, an assistant coach in 1990, and now the head coach (succeeding Alford when Sam left to join son Steve's staff at Southwest Missouri State after the 1994-95 season). Bell showed his exuberance by turning his players loose to cut down the nets after the game, rare for a regular-season game.

"I have to take my hat off to my kids," he said. "We had a game plan and they came in and executed it perfectly.

"You've got to shoot decently against a 2-3 or they'll never open it up at all. We stroked it pretty well early."

The Trojans may have stroked those 3s a little more often than Bell wanted. "I thought at times we were living out there a little bit," he said.

"We hadn't shot it as well of late, but we've got three or four awfully good shooters. Rowland did a great job early. He drilled them, and that meant they had to come out and defend him a little bit more. That left us a little more open in the post and helped us a lot."

Now the Trojans' goal was the state championship.

"Everybody wants to win it this year," Bell said, the imminent switch to class basketball in his mind.

"I'm totally against it, have been from the beginning," he said.

"I've just taken the attitude that we'll play and see what happens. There's not anything else to do. We're not going to quit playing basketball.

"I think financially it's going to devastate us. It takes away county ties and area rivals. I was at a game the other night between two pretty good small schools. There wasn't more than about 500 people there. That gives them an idea of what the sectional is going to look like in a year or two.

"But they voted that way, and if that's what they want . . .

"I just think it takes away so much nostalgia. So many good things have happened. I'd go along with what most people say: if it ain't broke, don't fix it. And it sure as heck isn't broke.

"I think 15 or 20 teams are capable, and we've played three or four of them. Kokomo is capable, Lafayette, Anderson — go down the line."

'I want this one bad'

Rowland's 20 points made him the only double-figure scorer on the floor. Kokomo's Matt Brady outscored Gaw, 9-8, in the centers' matchup.

Rowland looked ahead to the sectional tournament, which the Trojans had won every year of his high school career, every year since he was in third grade, actually.

His sights were longer-ranged: toward the State championship that only one other New Castle team ever had won (1932).

It wasn't unrealistic aiming. This Trojan team had just won a co-championship in the most prestigious league in Indiana, with the best record (19-1) in the history of a school that had forwarded All-Americans Kent Benson and Steve Alford to national-championship teams at Indiana. Never in their days or the state championship year had New Castle gone 19-1.

And this New Castle team was rated No. 1 or No. 2 in the state, depending on the poll.

"I want this one bad," Rowland said. "You get the last one, everybody's going to remember it. And we've got a shot."

He wasn't happy calling this one the last — the last before the teams New Castle has been used to playing in the sectional scatter into other classes and a new era of Indiana tournament play begins.

"Personally, I do not like the idea," Rowland said. "We're one of the few states that still have one-class basketball. They even made a movie of it."

There was no other 4A school in the New Castle sectional field, no 3A team, either. The field, as it has been for years, included 2A-sized schools Knightstown and Shenandoah, and 1A Blue River Valley, Morton Memorial and Tri. Shenandoah, the last of these schools to win a sectional (1988) and a Final Four team in 1981, was the only one of the five to vote against class basketball.

"I'm friends with some of the guys from the smaller schools," Rowland said. "They definitely want a change. I can understand that — that they would want a shot at it.

"But from my standpoint, I think one tournament is definitely the best way to go."

20

Muncie Central	77
Ind. Tech	61

February 22

MUNCIE CENTRAL		INDIANAPOLIS TECH
Eight: 1928, 1931, 1951, 1952, 1963, 1978, 1979, 1988	**STATE CHAMPIONSHIPS**	None
Nine: 1921, 1923*, 1927*, 1930*, 1948, 1954*, 1958, 1960*, 1970 (* lost in championship game)	**OTHER TIMES IN FINAL FOUR**	Four: 1929*, 1934*, 1952*, 1966* (* lost in championship game)
32: first 1921; one in '90s, 1994	**REGIONAL CHAMPIONSHIPS**	10: first 1929; most recent 1978
50: first 1917; four in '90s, most recent 1994.	**SECTIONAL CHAMPIONSHIPS**	19: first 1920; most recent 1978
None	**CONSOLIDATIONS**	None
No	**VOTE ON CHANGE TO CLASSES**	No
4A. (1,080; 67th of 95 in class)	**1997-98 CLASS (ENROLLMENT)**	4A. (2,196; 5th of 95 in class)
3A, Muncie South, Yorktown; 2A, Muncie Burris; 1A, Cowan, Daleville. Muncie South site and 1997 champion.	**1996-97 SECTIONAL OPPONENTS (1997-98 CLASSIFICATION)**	4A, Franklin Central, Indianapolis Arlington, Warren Central; 3A, Indianapolis Cathedral, Indianapolis Chatard. Franklin Central site, Indianapolis Cathedral 1997 champion
Anderson, Anderson Highland, Connersville, New Castle, Richmond	**1997-98 SECTIONAL OPPONENTS**	Franklin Central, Indianapolis Arlington, Lawrence Central, Lawrence North, Warren Central
11-11 (lost to Muncie South in sectional final, 78-53)	**FINAL RECORD 1996-97**	12-10 (lost to Indianapolis Chatard in sectional quarterfinal, 78-57)

A Night
with the
Romans

For years in Indiana high school basketball, they were the biggest and the best — Indianapolis Tech by far the biggest high school in Indiana, enrollment topping 5,000; Muncie Central the most successful, a state championship contender every year, it seemed.

In 1952, these two schools played for the state championship. They carried out their historically assigned roles: Muncie won, state champion for the second straight year, the fourth in its record total of eight championships; Tech lost, the third time it had reached the championship game, and fallen. A fourth time was to come in 1966, when Michigan City defeated the Titans. Only 14 Indiana high school teams have played in four or more state championship games. The other 13 all won at least once, all but hexed Tech.

Central and Tech were fellow members of the North Central Conference in 1952. The NCC has been Indiana's premier basketball league for 70 years. In 1952 and the years immediately to follow, it probably was the best high school basketball league in the country.

And 1952 was its ultimate year.

Ten teams in the league: Muncie Central won the state championship; all nine others were eliminated by NCC teams.

You can look it up. Tech, with 18 points from Trester Award winner Joe Sexson, beat Lafayette Jeff in the afternoon round at

Landon Turner (left), a star for Indianapolis Tech, guards Muncie Central's Jerry Shoecraft in a 1978 semistate game at Hinkle Fieldhouse. Turner led Indiana University to the NCAA title in 1981 before auto accident injuries ended his career. (Photo courtesy Indiana Basketball Hall of Fame)

the State; Muncie Central beat Kokomo and Lafayette beat Logansport in semistate championship games; Kokomo beat Marion in the afternoon round at the semistate; Tech beat Anderson, Lafayette beat Frankfort and Muncie Central beat both New Castle and Richmond in regionals. All 10 won sectionals. They were a combined 50-0 in the tournament against outsiders.

In 1992, Richmond beat Lafayette Jeff in overtime for the NCC's 25th state championship since formation in 1927. That doesn't include three before 1927 by future league members (Lafayette, 1916; Frankfort, 1925; Marion, 1926). The Richmond-Lafayette final was the eighth time both teams in the championship game were from the NCC.

Tech dropped out of the NCC in the '60s because it made more sense financially to cut out trips and play against the local teams, whose numbers were increasing every year. The Muncie Central series has continued.

244

Twins Tom (left) and Dick Van Arsdale starred for Manual High School, then went on to successful careers in the NBA. (Photo courtesy Indiana High School Athletic Association)

'One of my dreams and goals'

As sure as Tommy Lasorda's blood was Dodger blue, Frank Craig's blood is Titan green. Craig played for Tech, served in Vietnam, coached at junior high, freshman and JV levels in the city, then took over as head coach in 1984-85 on the retirement of his boss, the late Ernie Cline. The job, he said, "was one of my main dreams and goals."

Craig was on the court for one of Tech's biggest basketball victories. In the finals of the 1960 regional at Butler Fieldhouse, Indianapolis Manual with the Van Arsdale twins led Tech, 45-44, with three seconds to go. Jump ball, center court. Piece of cake for Manual: Dick Van Arsdale was jumping, and he tipped the ball to Tom, who clamped his strong hands on the ball, turned . . .

And was called for charging into Tech's great guard, Mel Garland. With one second left, Garland hit both free throws and Tech was the regional champion. "It was the last year you shot charging fouls," Craig said.

"I was 'the other guard' with Mel in those days. My job was to take the ball out of bounds and pass it in to him.

"What a great guy."

Garland went on to star for Purdue and was on his way to a standout coaching career when cancer killed him.

The very best, ever?

The scourge of Indiana basketball that 1959-60 season was Muncie Central, with a team that may have been the Bearcats' all-time best — maybe Indiana's best, though it's not on the roster of champions. Its forwards and big scorers were Ron Bonham and John Dampier. Bonham was a star on two national champions at Cincinnati, the 18th NBA draft pick in 1964 and a member of two NBA champions with the Celtics. Dampier played at Miami of Florida, and Jim Davis, the center, played eight NBA seasons after a college career at Colorado. Guard Jim Nettles was a state hurdles champion, a track and football star (defensive back) at Wisconsin, and an NFL standout with the Rams.

"They had *good* athletes," Craig said. But one of the few close games for Muncie Central along the way was a 48-44 semistate victory over Tech. Then, seeking to be the third unbeaten state champion after Bonham scored 40 and Dampier 29 in an after-noon wipeout of Bloomington (102-66), the Bearcats fell to the wiles of East Chicago Washington coach John Baratto — fell with an unimaginable thud, 75-59. It turned out Baratto had some pretty good players himself; four starters played Division I ball. But that Bearcat loss, at the time, was a more staggering upset than the one six years earlier to Milan.

Otherwise, state championship leader Muncie Central could have nine of them. Or 10. Or more. For Tech, with its four runner-up finishes, isn't the leader in those. Anderson is, with seven, but Muncie Central has five. For every one of those eight champion-ships, there is oh, so near a miss. In a 10-year stretch when the Bearcats did win two state titles there were agonies in 1953 (1952 championship team back, double-overtime regional loss to Rich-

John Dampier and Ron Bonham listen to coach John Longfellow during the 1959-60 season. Although the Bearcats were upset in the state tournament that year, many consider that team to be Muncie Central's best ever. (Photo courtesy Indiana High School Athletic Association)

mond), 1954 (Milan), 1955 (71-70 semistate championship loss to Oscar Robertson and Indianapolis Attucks), 1959 (64-62 semistate loss to eventual champion Attucks) and 1960 (the stunning rout by East Chicago Washington). Those two titles in the '50s so easily, so very easily, could have been seven.

Thumbs always down

Nowhere in this lore-loving state are there ghosts to match the ones at Muncie Fieldhouse.

It was built as part of old Muncie High School in 1928, its setting near downtown, just off the White River, its capacity so

Muncie Central's 1928 State Championship team included, front row (from left), Glenn Wolfe, Francis Reed, coach Raymond (Pete) Jolly, Ralph Satterlee and Carleton Walsh; back row, Charles Secrist, Hays Young, Eugene Eber, Robert Parr and Robert Yohler. (Photo courtesy Indiana Basketball Hall of Fame)

visionary it must have seemed ridiculous then: 7,000, bigger than all but a few college arenas around the nation.

It has aged gracefully, a 1983 facelift not changing the Roman Arena feeling. A high brick wall surrounds the playing area, far enough back on the sides to allow nine rows of rollaway bleachers running from wall-level to court. The Romans sit in permanent wooden bleachers above the wall, 15 rows of them all the way around, stretching to 17 in the corners, looking down into the arena. The Romans at Muncie Fieldhouse have their thumbs locked in a permanent down position. Eat 'em alive, Bearcats.

It's homecoming in Muncie Fieldhouse.

Honored guests are Silver Anniversary Bearcats, 1972 graduates including former Michigan player Tim Kuzma, introduced as "one of the great Bearcats of all time."

"Your *Bearcats* of *Muncie Central*" came on-court to the P.A. heralding and the school song, "Indiana, Our Indiana" — four-syllable Muncie Central fitting nicely into the Indiana places.

And NOW! On your FEET, as we pay TRIBUTE to EIGHT STATE CHAMPIONSHIPS and to BEARCATS EVERYWHERE!

It was one of those moments Shakespeare talked of in *King Henry V*, the "Once more unto the breach" segment that says: ". . . when the blast of war blows in our ears, then imitate the action of the tiger; stiffen the sinews, summon up the blood, disguise fair nature with hard-favor'd rage . . . "

If he had been writing in Muncie Fieldhouse this night, be sure he would have switched tiger to bearcat and let the rest stand. Kids in the third grade, grandmas in the 13th row, had their sinews stiffened and their blood summoned up, let alone the 12 uniformed, hard-favor'd-raging Bearcats.

You get the feeling neither Milan nor Hickory would have had a great chance here.

A license to shoot

Right away, Tech's Antwan Freeman zapped the Bearcats with a 3.

Craig brought senior Freeman onto his varsity as a freshman. "We haven't had more than one or two freshmen do that," he said. Freeman is a 6-foot guard with scoring skills and freedom to use them.

"We lost a couple of our starters after the City Tournament," Craig said. "Grades and personal reasons. One of them was our second-leading scorer. That put a little more on Antwan's shoulders. He's pretty much had a free rein."

Freeman had his season high in a semifinal loss to Indianapolis Cathedral in that tournament. "They beat us by eight," Craig said. "He scored 43 of our 53 that game."

So, Terry Thimlar, what do you try to do with an Antwan Freeman?

"Try to get him to come to Muncie Central," Bearcat coach Thimlar quipped.

"He's a player. We switch a lot, but we didn't switch with him. And any time he was being picked for, we had to open up and let the man through."

Usually that man was 6-3 junior Craig Zeigler. "He's a pretty good player himself," Thimlar said.

Muncie Central led just 28-21 at halftime, and a Freeman 3 brought Tech within 30-27. Boom, boom, boom; 3s by John Heinrichs, Zeigler and Heinrichs again popped Muncie Central out front 39-29, and Tech had lost contact. The Bearcats' margin topped out at 22 in the 77-61 breeze.

Craig wasn't shocked. The night before, Tech topped Indianapolis Broad Ripple, 89-88 — "our archrival, on our homecoming, for the conference championship. That was probably the most emotional game I've ever been involved with."

It was also sensational. Freeman scored 39. "We beat them in double overtime and Antwan hit about a 55-footer at the buzzer," Craig said. "We were down two with three seconds to go. We set a play, he turned around, took a dribble and hit it.

"Tonight, we just didn't recover. And Muncie Central wasn't bad. I wasn't surprised. We just never got back up."

Freeman had 22 Tech points, but it took him 27 shots to do it. He was to finish the year tied for seventh among state scorers at 25.5 a game. He'll probably go to a junior college, Craig said, though his ACT score was 23, well above the NCAA minimum. "His core grades were low. He just didn't do what he should do in the four-year period. He's aware of it.

"I have no doubts he'll make it. His priorities are right now."

'The best job in the state'

Terry Thimlar was pleased. He was three nights away from opening sectional tournament play against Cowan, and his 10-10 team had played well, particularly in shooting the 28-21 halftime lead up to 64-42 in 11 minutes. "We said at halftime we had to really concentrate on making the extra pass," he said. He had asked for that, sometimes angrily, in the first half, when time after time a Bearcat dribbled into the heart of the Tech defense and, when a

Former Muncie Central coach Bill Harrell directs the Bearcats during the 1988 State Tournament. (Photo courtesy Indiana High School Athletic Association, ©Mark Wick)

dropped-off pass was much the better choice, forced up a shot that missed. "We were taking it all the way to the basket," he said. "We said whenever a defensive guy comes over to you, someone's got to be open." Someone was, and got a lot of second-half layins.

Senior forward Alan Jones matched Heinrichs' 17 for Muncie Central, and senior guard Travis Wilson matched Zeigler's 15. Heinrichs, a 6-2 senior who had been in a shooting slump, was hot at the perfect time. Against Marion Friday and again against Tech Saturday, he hit five 3s. "Tonight he was 5-for-8," Thimlar said. The team was 9-for-20. "It kinda becomes contagious," Thimlar said.

Terry Thimlar is in his early 40s, but he's a coach who has been places and seems thrilled to be where he is — the NCC, Muncie Central, Muncie Fieldhouse, Indiana.

"It's the best job in the state," he said. "It just has tradition galore. You feel part of it. Tonight we had a Silver Anniversary team there. I told my players, 'There are guys out here who represent this program. Go out tonight and show them it's still going.' "

Muncie Fieldhouse doesn't hurt, either. "I don't know if there are ghosts, but it makes you play and practice hard," he said. "It makes you *want* to go to practice. It makes you want to carry on the tradition. The banners are there, the bleachers are there, the atmosphere is there, the old Bearcat fans are there.

"Last night at Marion, we didn't play well, it was on statewide TV, they pulled away from us at the end and won, but what a great place to play basketball.

"Then you go to New Castle — a great place to play basketball. It's all first class.

"I coached at the collegiate level. Some of the things they do in this conference you don't see as a visitor in Division I basketball. Only the class places do it — the Big Ten, the schools that have tradition. They know how to treat people."

A year with Larry Bird

Thimlar's dad, Hugh, was maybe the best player Royal Center ever had, on the best team the little Logansport-area school ever had before becoming the base for a consolidated identification-stripper, Pioneer, in 1963.

Hugh played for Tony Hinkle at Butler, then put the Hinkle System to work at Montpelier, Wolf Lake and Pike. It was Pike Township then, a rural school within Marion County, just outside Indianapolis. It's just plain Pike now, and huge. "I went to elementary school there when Dad coached there," Terry said. "I played at Pike for Ed Siegel (who stayed on for more than 20 years and just this year was inducted into the Indiana Basketball Hall of Fame).

"We won Pike's first sectional in 1972 (at Lebanon). Then we won the regional at Frankfort and got beat in the semistate at Mackey Arena. We cut down the first nets in the school's history. It was a great experience."

Growing up in a coach's home didn't really pull Terry into coaching. "Not in the beginning. I kinda wanted to stay away from it. I saw how difficult it was to be a coach and have a family. I love my family very dearly. I always wanted to make sure I could handle that. I didn't get married till two years ago, when I was 40."

Contacts got Terry Thimlar into coaching. His dad had gone to Fort Myers, Fla., to coach. Indiana State coach Bob King, a friend of Hugh Thimlar, visited the family and went away with two new assistants: Bill Hodges, who played for Hugh, and 21-year-old Terry, who joined the King staff as a student assistant. Terry left there to go on the Florida staff. King became ill after the 1977-78 season, Hodges was advanced to head coach, and Hodges brought Thimlar back as an assistant.

He was there for one of college basketball's all-time great joyrides. With Larry Bird, a first-team All-American the year before, showing a little bit more greatness every night, the Terre Haute school that had almost never even been noticed before went 33-0, finished the season ranked No. 1 in the country, and reached the national championship game before losing to Magic Johnson and Michigan State.

"My overriding memory of that year is how close the team became — how leaders like Larry, Carl Nicks, Steve Reed, Brad Miley, Alex Gilbert, every one of them understood their role," Thimlar said. "We did things together. We became one cohesive unit.

"Larry brought that in, and everyone bought into it. Larry was the first to practice and the last to leave. If your leading player is doing that, everyone else goes along."

Thimlar got out of coaching briefly ("I saw some things I just didn't like"), ran a health club in Indianapolis, then joined his still-active father as an assistant on his staff at Edison Community College in Florida. After two years there, he went out on his own for 10 years as a Florida high school coach, before the Muncie Central opening came.

He arrived just in time to see Indiana converting to what he thought he had left behind: class basketball.

"I think it stinks," he said. "I was in class sports in Florida. I saw how low interest was. I saw them go from four classes to five, and interest dropped; I saw them go from five to six, and saw it drop more.

"There are no rivalries. Your big rival in town may be 3A and you're 4A. You may play one time and that's it.

"Next year, we're going to have a lot of people come to watch us play in the sectional because we're in the toughest one (with Anderson, New Castle, Richmond, Connersville and Anderson Highland). There's a tough one down in the southern part of the state, too. But some of these smaller schools, I don't know how many people they're going to have at their games."

Damon Bailey of Bedford North Lawrence played to packed and sold-out houses throughout his prolific four-year career. He may have been the reason the State Finals were moved to the Hoosier (now RCA) Dome in 1990. Here he goes up against a Southport player as the largest audience ever to see a high school basketball game anywhere looks on. (Photo courtesy Bloomington Herald-Times)

The
Tournament

Jasper	**37**
NE Dubois	**34**
Pike Central	**48**
Forest Park	**30**

Sectional openers, Feb. 25

JASPER		PIKE CENTRAL
1949	**STATE CHAMPIONSHIP**	None
1934	**OTHER TIMES IN FINAL FOUR**	None
13: first 1934; one in '90s, 1996. Also in corporation, one: Ireland, 1963	**REGIONAL CHAMPIONSHIPS**	One as Pike Central, 1997. Others in corporation, three: Winslow 1950, 1951, 1954
28: first 1922; two in '90s, most recent 1996	**SECTIONAL CHAMPIONSHIPS**	One as Pike Central, 1997. Others in corporation, 12: Otwell 1969; Spurgeon 1928, 1929; Stendal 1931, 1932, 1939; Winslow 1923, 1924, 1941, 1950, 1951, 1954
Ireland 1970	**CONSOLIDATIONS**	Formed 1974: Otwell (Velpen 1937), Petersburg, Winslow (Spurgeon, Stendal 1966)
No	**VOTE ON CHANGE TO CLASSES**	No
3A. (723; 27th of 96 in class)	**1997-98 CLASS (ENROLLMENT)**	3A. (492; 84th of 96 in class)
3A, Pike Central; 2A, Forest Park, Oakland City Wood Memorial, Southridge; 1A, Northeast Dubois. Southridge site; Pike Central 1997 champion	**1996-97 SECTIONAL OPPONENTS (1997-98 CLASSIFICATION)**	3A, Jasper; 2A, Forest Park, Oakland City Wood Memorial, Southridge; 1A, Northeast Dubois. Southridge site; Pike Central 1997 champion
Gibson Southern, Pike Central, Princeton, Vincennes Lincoln, Washington	**1997-98 SECTIONAL OPPONENTS**	Gibson Southern, Jasper, Princeton, Vincennes Lincoln, Washington
7-15 (lost to Pike Central in sectional semifinal, 62-37)	**FINAL RECORD 1996-97**	22-4 (won sectional, regional; lost to New Albany in semistate semifinal, 70-52)

'Money' Time

Once the world knew Jasper as the home of Kimball pianos. The *world* — Kimball was right up there with Wurlitzer among the international biggies in piano manufacturing. No more. Kimball now makes pool tables. OK, that was for esthetic effects. It also makes office furniture, and business is good; employment in Jasper is as good as it was at its piano-making peak. That takes care of Monday through Friday in Jasper, but Friday nights and Saturday nights are for watching and celebrating basketball victories.

That's where the town's slump was this winter.

But it's sectional time, and Jasper is to tournament-time turnarounds as Milan is to miracles. In 1949, Jasper lost nine regular-season games, and not to a whole lot of state powers. Lost twice to Huntingburg, for heaven's sake. In those good old days, all Jasper ached any time that rivalry game got away; especially home-and-home. But that 11-9 Jasper team won everything the rest of the way, including a 62-61 state championship-game victory over Madison, despite a game-record 36 points by the Cubs' Dee Monroe. Ever since, Jasper — and heroes Leo "Cabby" O'Neill, the team's Hall of Fame coach, and 5-7 guard Bobby White, the surprise final-game hero with 20 points, and Jerome "Dimp" Stenftenagel, the best of the long line of Jasper Stenftenagels and a Hall of Famer — has represented hope for every team taking a mediocre record into the tournament.

257

Coach Leo "Cabby" O'Neill, above, and Jerome "Dimp" Stenftenagel helped Jasper to the 1949 State Championship. (Both photos courtesy Indiana High School Athletic Association)

Mediocre may overstate this Jasper season: 6-14, a year after reaching the semistate for the first time in 23 years and sending state-leading scorer Michael Lewis on to Indiana. This Jasper team has an IU name of its own. Faruk Mujezinovic, the Wildcats' 6-7 sophomore center, is a cousin and look-alike of Indiana senior Haris Mujezinovic (moo-yay-*zeen*-oh-vitch, and Bosnian, if you're wondering).

On this point-deprived night, Faruk led both teams with 11 points, but Northeast Dubois had the Wildcats down 31-19 with seven minutes left. Then, the team that had needed 25 minutes to score 19 points ran in 11 in a row, in two minutes.

The last of those came on a 3-point basket by 5-8, 150-pound senior sub Michael Denton. So it was 34-34 when Northeast Dubois survived a shot by Doug Wigand, but turned the ball right back; retrieved a miss by Mujezinovic, but gave the ball back on a charging call; rebounded another miss by Jasper guard Luke Dippel but turned the ball back again on a five-second closely guarded violation.

So now there were 63 seconds left, Jasper spread out and played for a last shot. Things went awry when the Wildcats put a play into motion with just under 10 seconds left. Suddenly, time was running out, and Michael Denton had the ball. During the season, Michael had played some in 15 games, taken nine shots all year and hit one, a two-pointer. His 10th shot of the year was the 3 he sank earlier in the fourth quarter.

So of course from the deep left corner he launched the game-winner and Jasper moved along, 37-34.

An along-in-the-years Northeast Dubois fan, seated in the top row, just under a press section, groaned at the loss but dealt with it Hoosier-style. He leaned back wearily, turned to some media types behind him and said almost accusingly:

"Now why in the hell would *anyone* want class basketball?"

It was wonderful, coming from a fan on the broken side of a heartbreaker. Even in defeat, even after a game played not very well, he treasured the heart 10 kids put on display, whatever 10 happened to be playing at any point of this game.

He had been there before. Hoosiers always have treasured sectional tournament competitiveness — nowhere in all Indiana any more so than in this particular sectional.

The last tournament of the kind the man had known all his life was under way.

A very good question

There has been talk of fading interest, of declining attendance in Indiana high school basketball. There hasn't been any of that here — fading interest or declining attendance. The Southridge sectional at Huntingburg annually ranks No. 1 or No. 2 among the 64 sectional sites.

They're proud of that at Southridge. "Every year, it's the same thing — it's either us or Anderson," Southridge athletic director Jim Bardwell said. Every year spans a long time, because 45 years ago, when the biggest high school gym in the state was 7,460-seat Muncie Fieldhouse, Huntingburg, a town of 4,600, built a gym that seats 6,214.

It was filled then and still is at sectional time. The teams in it all bore town names and interesting nicknames, among them the Ireland Spuds, the Dubois Jeeps (for a cartoon character, not the vehicle), the Holland Dutchmen, the Winslow Eskimos and the archrivals from seven miles apart, the Jasper Wildcats and the Huntingburg Happy Hunters. Consolidations eliminated all of those but Jasper. Huntingburg and Holland merged to form Southridge, and the rivalry with Jasper remained intense.

Before the gym, before the mergers, there were sectionals at both Huntingburg and Jasper. Gil Hodges, a "Boys of Summer" Brooklyn Dodger and manager of the 1969 Miracle Mets, was All-Sectional for Petersburg when it was runner-up to Huntingburg in 1940. Vance Hartke, later a U.S. senator, made All-Sectional as a guard on the Stendal Purple Aces when they won the 1931 tournament at Jasper. Paul Hoffman, Jasper '43, after a career at Purdue was the first Rookie of the Year in the fledgling National Basketball Association.

After the gym was built, Holland turned out two NBA players, Gene Tormohlen and Don Buse. The tournament scoring record, 47 points, was set by another future professional: Scott Rolen, who hit ten 3-point shots in getting his 47 in 1993 and four years later was a Rookie of the Year candidate with the Philadelphia Phillies.

Through it all, with great teams and great players or with less than great, this sectional brings them out — not just from Huntingburg/Southridge or Jasper but, as the filled-to-the-top Northeast Dubois section showed, from every team in the field. In the six are schools that next year will be scattered to 3A, 2A and 1A. As they were, under the income distribution system that has been standard in the state for years, the smallest sectional split any school received last year was $5,027 (Northeast Dubois), up to $8,039 (Jasper).

Now why in the hell *would* anyone want class basketball?

The vote among these schools was 4-2, against the change. Forest Park and Oakland City Wood Memorial said yes.

Pike Central was in the group saying no, though at the time it voted the school had never won so much as a sectional tournament.

This is a high school formed in 1974 as the amalgamation of what once were six different schools: Otwell, Velpen, Petersburg, Winslow, Spurgeon, Stendal.

Even splintered, those schools had their moments. Four of them won sectionals, and Winslow — when it entered the '50s with a 6-4 center named Dick Farley — aimed a whole lot higher than that. The Eskimos — named for their igloo-like gym, which was heated by a pot-bellied stove — won the regional for the first time in 1950, Farley's senior year. In the semistate, Winslow routed traditional state power Evansville Bosse, 75-55, but fell to another one, New Albany, 52-36 in the finals. Farley went on to be a star on Indiana's 1953 NCAA champions and a contributor to Syracuse's 1956 NBA championship. Even without him, coach Kern McGlothlin took Winslow to two more regional titles in the next four years, and both he and Farley are Indiana Basketball Hall of Famers.

A 'Farley' named Seitz

Pike Central came in sniffing its first sectional championship, because it may have another Farley.

Adam Seitz is this team's leader: 6-3, athletic, just a junior but well up on the list of state scorers with an average around 23 points a game.

"He goes to the hole so strong," Pike Central coach Brian Wahl said. "He's hard to stop because of his quickness. When they do drop off, he's capable of hitting the 3."

Seitz broke out for a dunk on Pike Central's first possession against Forest Park. Nothing else came so simply for the Chargers. It was the only basket Pike Central scored in the first quarter, and Forest Park's deliberate game had it ahead, 9-4.

First sectional games can bring out jitters that weren't there in regular-season games, Wahl knew, "especially when you're the favored team and you get down early. They spread you out; you're just working like crazy to get back into the game. That's why you work your butts off all year long, so you can be in shape to do something like that."

Seitz recognized the problem, though he didn't really share it.

"I wasn't feeling any pressure," he said. "This is my third year.

"But it was the first sectional for some people. I remember my first sectional as a freshman. My first free throw, I air-balled it.

"The pressure does get to you the first year — you don't realize it until you get in the game and everybody's yelling.

"But after the first quarter, everybody's OK."

Immediately after the first quarter, Pike Central was OK. The Chargers scored the first six points of the second quarter to go up, 10-9. Seitz had eight of the 10 points.

After senior Mark Wells' interception gave Pike Central the ball closing out the half, Seitz let the time run down and sank a 3-pointer at the buzzer for a 16-12 halftime lead.

Opening the second half, Seitz stepped into a passing lane, picked off a Forest Park pass and got the ball to junior Jared Thomas for a layup. The pullaway had begun. A dunk and a later three-point play by Seitz in an 11-point Pike Central run blew the margin up to 43-23 with just under two minutes left. It was the last scoring by Seitz, who scored 26 — more than the Forest Park total when Seitz's shooting ended.

"That's a typical game for him." Wahl said. He pinpointed the interception and breakout opening the second half. "He sees those things and reads those things," Wahl said. "He has played so much basketball."

Seitz finished the slow-paced game with just two fouls. Even in faster games, Wahl said, fouling hasn't been a problem for a man his team can't afford to lose. "He's pretty smart. He gets more aggressive on defense as the game goes on."

Wearing the same number (33) he wore at Indiana State and throughout his career with the Boston Celtics, Larry Bird of Springs Valley shoots over a Jasper defender. (Photo courtesy Indiana Basketball Hall of Fame)

Another southern Indiana basketball player grew up about 30 miles from Huntingburg. Springs Valley played in the Huntingburg sectional at one time, but not during the years Larry Bird's was a player there. Seitz, one of a million who would love to emulate Bird's success, has a better understanding than most of how and why it happened.

"He worked — hard," Seitz said. "He might not have been the prettiest player, he didn't jump the best, but his hard work paid off for him.

"I'm going to work on my shooting this summer, because I'll probably play college ball somewhere, and I'm going to be playing outside. I want to be able to shoot.

"Since my freshman year I think I've improved a lot. A lot of it is just mental, getting confidence. Just keep shooting it. Over this last summer that was probably my biggest improvement.

"Tonight, I was shooting pretty well. They were giving me the drive. I probably should have pulled up on some of those."

'The best sectional in the state'

Pike Central, a 3A school, won't be coming back to 2A Southridge for tournament play next year. "I guess we'll be at Washington," Seitz said. The Hatchet House is a big arena, likely to be filled by the first sectional involving neighborly rivals Vincennes, Jasper, Washington and Pike Central.

But Seitz lamented just a bit leaving the Southridge sectional. "This is a great atmosphere," he said. "Some people say it's the best sectional in the state. I have to agree with them."

Wahl said he is "definitely against the change (to classes). I really wish we had known more about what they were going to do before they had votes, not just say, 'We're going to classes. Do you want to do it or not?' Let's see where we're going, who's in what class.

"You see an atmosphere like this tonight — I don't think you're going to see it other places."

It may not survive even at Southridge, with a new mix involving teams from farther away.

"I don't think it's going to work," Seitz said. "I think they're going to try to come back to what we have now."

But not before he has moved on.

"They want to go to it, that's their decision," he said. "I guess we've just got to play."

Elsewhere in Indiana . . .

Games were played at all 64 sectional sites on this opening night of the 87th annual tournament.

At Crawford County, Cannelton's four-victory season ended characteristically. Tell City took out the Bulldogs, 66-62. McClintic was crushed after one more near-miss, but he bounced back and looked forward to his 12th season. "We've got our two leading scorers back," he said. "We played well (against Tell City). We got down 10-1 — we were awful shaky for some reason. They we turned it around and played them right to the end. I couldn't have asked any more."

The night's stunner was at Richmond, where Winchester knocked out the Red Devils, 49-42. Richmond, a first-game sectional loser for the first time in years, didn't win again after its victory at Marion. Winchester went on to its first sectional championship in 17 years.

Indianapolis Tech, playing its third game in five nights, lost 76-57 to an Indianapolis Chatard team it had defeated 11 days earlier. Rushville fell at Connersville, 64-46.

Western Boone repeated the victory over North Montgomery that introduced both — and Wingate, Thorntown, Homer Stonebraker *et al* — earlier in this trip. This time it was 56-48, the same margin as before.

Oak Hill and state scoring leader Jarrad Ogle (29.4 at the finish) lost 72-55 to Marion.

And Milan's hopes died right away. Lawrenceburg was a 75-62 winner.

All other teams you met lived on for another round. And so did one you didn't meet but — guaranteed — you will remember.

At Jeffersonville on this opening night, Charlestown (10-10) came from 11 points down in the last two minutes to get into overtime against Silver Creek (16-4, with one of the state's top players, Matt Renn). In the overtime, Silver Creek once again led, 70-69, with time running out. At the buzzer, Michael Frazier sank a 3 and Charlestown, not Silver Creek and Matt Renn, moved on.

Michael is a freshman.

Michael played less than a minute of the game.

And to reporters later, this modest young hero in surely his first interview said:

"They don't call me 'Money' for nothin'."

The line of the night, of the tournament, of the year.

22

Terre Haute S.	53
Terre Haute N.	42

*Sectional semifinals,
February 27*

TERRE HAUTE SOUTH		TERRE HAUTE NORTH
None	**STATE CHAMPIONSHIP**	None
Four as T.H. South: 1977, 1978*, 1979, 1991 (* lost in championship game). Others in corporation: T.H. Wiley two: 1924, 1931	**TIMES IN FINAL FOUR**	None as T.H. North. Others in corporation, seven: T.H. Garfield 1922*, 1947*, 1963; T.H. Gerstmeyer 1953*, 1954, 1956, 1957 (* lost in championship game)
10 as T.H. South: first 1973; one in '90s, 1991. Others in corporation, four: T.H. Wiley 1924, 1931, 1932, 1942	**REGIONAL CHAMPIONSHIPS**	Five as T.H. North: 1972, 1975, 1987, 1990, 1996. Others in corporation 13: Glenn 1951; T.H. Garfield 1922, 1939, 1947, 1952, 1963, 1967; T.H. Gerstmeyer 1945, 1953, 1954, 1956, 1957, 1958
16 as T.H. South: first 1973; three in '90s, most recent 1997. Others in corporation, 22: Honey Creek 1946; T.H. Normal 1920; T.H. State 1944, 1949, 1965; T.H. Wiley 16 (first 1924; last 1970)	**SECTIONAL CHAMPIONSHIPS**	12 as T.H. North: first 1972; five in '90s, most recent 1996. Others in corporation 29: Fontanet 1933; Glenn 1951; T.H. Garfield 16 (first 1922; last 1967), T.H. Gerstmeyer 11 (first 1941; last 1971)
Formed 1971: Honey Creek (Blackhawk, Pimento, Prairie Creek, Prairieton), T.H. Wiley, parts T.H. Schulte, T.H. State; Gibault 1977	**CONSOLIDATIONS**	Formed 1971: T.H. Garfield (Otter Creek, T.H.), T.H. Gerstmeyer (Fontanet, Glenn, Riley), parts T.H. Schulte, T.H. State. Previous schools in corporation: T.H. Rankin, T.H. Thornton
No	**VOTE ON CHANGE TO CLASSES**	No
4A. (1,497; 26th of 95 in class)	**1997-98 CLASS**	4A. (1,618; 14th of 95 in class)
4A, Northview, T.H. North; 3A, South Vermillion, West Vigo; 1A, Riverton Parke. T.H. South 1997 champion	**1996-97 SECTIONAL OPPONENTS (1997-98 CLASSIFICATION)**	4A, Northview, T.H. South; 3A, South Vermillion, West Vigo; 1A, Riverton Parke. T.H. South 1997 champion
Avon, Brownsburg, Mooresville, Northview, T.H. North	**1997-98 SECTIONAL OPPONENTS**	Avon, Brownsburg, Mooresville, Northview, T.H. South
18-6 (won sectional; lost to Bloomington North in regional semifinal, 58-49)	**FINAL RECORD 1996-97**	11-11 (lost to T.H. South in sectional, 53-42)

Dreams Along the Wabash

It's not as if Terre Haute is an island of basketball apathy in a sea of frenzy. "In Terre Haute, we *love* our basketball," Terre Haute South coach Pat Rady said. "We claim Larry Bird, even though he's from Springs Valley — he went to Indiana State here. We had Terry Dischinger, Charley Hall, Clyde Lovellette, the Andrews twins and Uncle Harold . . . there's such a great history.

"And great coaches — Howard Sharpe, Willard Kehrt, Gordon Neff.

"It would be awesome if we could get there and win it for the city of Terre Haute."

Getting there and winning it means the Final Four three weeks down the road. And the awesome part?

This Wabash River town of nearly 60,000 has known notability (native sons include playwright Theodore Dreiser and his brother, Paul Dresser, who wrote the state's very own anthem, *Back Home Again in Indiana*, and six-time Socialist candidate for president Eugene V. Debs) and it has known notoriety (well, some blushed at the time over what playwright Dreiser wrote, and Debs advocated, and there were always those rumors that Al Capone and friends of his knew their way around town).

What Terre Haute never has known is the jubilation, the pride of producing a state high school basketball champion.

Clyde Lovellette, a 6-foot-9 center, led Terre Haute Garfield to the 1947 state championship game, where Shelbyville, led by Bill Garrett (left, below with Ed Searcy of Indianapolis Attucks), upended the Terre Haute team. (Both photos courtesy Indiana High School Athletic Association)

It is by far the biggest Indiana city that hasn't had one. Northern Indiana neighbors Elkhart and Mishawaka, about 43,000 each, are next in line.

Four Terre Haute schools have played in the Final Four a total of 13 times — as early as 1922 (when Terre Haute Garfield lost in the finals to the last of the Franklin "Wonder Five" teams, 26-15, though Garfield's Babe Wheeler outscored Franklin's Fuzzy Vandivier, 13-12), as recently as 1991 (Terre Haute South, with future Big Ten Player of the Year Brian Evans of Indiana, beaten in the semifinals by Brebeuf and Evans' future college teammate, Alan Henderson).

Besides 1922, three other Terre Haute teams have lost in the championship game (Garfield, 1947; Gerstmeyer, 1953; South, 1978). Two of those are particular nightmares in Terre Haute.

In 1947, Garfield had a 6-9 junior center, Big Clyde Lovellette, the Big almost an official part of his name. He was to be an All-American at Kansas, the only player ever to lead the nation in scoring while playing on the national championship team (1952, when a little guard named Dean Smith was a teammate). He was to be the leading scorer on a gold-medal U.S. Olympic team (1952). He was to average more than 20 points a game in six of his 11 NBA seasons. A three-time All-Star, he was to play on two NBA championship teams (Boston, 1963, '64). He was to be elected to the national Basketball Hall of Fame, as well as to Indiana's.

And on the night of March 22, 1947, in Butler Fieldhouse he was about to make Terre Haute Garfield (31-0) the first undefeated state champion in Indiana history.

It didn't happen. He scored 25 points, but Shelbyville — the alma mater of Garfield coach Willard Kehrt — got 21 from its center, Bill Garrett, half-a-foot shorter than Lovellette, 23 from guard Emerson Johnson and won solidly, 68-58. Garrett was to go from there to the Indiana University campus, where he became the Big Ten's first black basketball player and an All-American.

Garfield lost in the sectional Lovellette's senior year and he wasn't even named Mr. Basketball. Another future IU star, Bobby Masters of state champion Lafayette Jeff, was.

Sharpie and his Black Cats

Garfield and Gerstmeyer were the city's bitter rivals then. Gerstmeyer flowered as a state power in the early 1950s, its first big star Bobby Leonard of Indiana's 1953 NCAA champions. Leonard's Gerstmeyer coach was Howard Sharpe, who was to stay on in the profession until he became the state record holder for victories, 755.

He'd have traded most of them for one little correction. Gerstmeyer was in the 1953 championship game with one of the most colorful groups ever to make it there. The Black Cats had twins playing at forward, Harley and Arley. The center was their uncle, Harold. The twins had been separated in class, Harley a senior and Arley a junior. Uncle Harold was a sophomore. In the State semifinals, Gerstmeyer had beaten Lamar Lundy and Richmond, and South Bend Central had taken out Bobby Plump and Milan on their first State run.

The Andrews twins were identical, and their uniforms played to the confusion of identification. Arley wore 34, Harley 43. In the state championship game, a second-quarter foul on 43 was recorded against 34. In the fourth quarter, Arley — though a junior already the state's career scoring record holder — drew what should have been his fourth foul and fouled out, because of the score book error. Harley, who officially had no fouls, played gamely, scoring 20 points (to Arley's six), but the game came down to Harley's semi-desperation shot from well above the foul circle in the final seconds. When it bounced away, South Bend Central was the champion, 42-41. Sharpe took teams back to the Final Four three of the next four years, once with future major-league pitcher Tommy John as the uniformed ball boy who led the Cats onto the Butler Fieldhouse court. But the man they called Sharpie never got to the final game again, in 37 years as a Terre Haute coach and a few elsewhere.

Garfield had another Lovellette-type star in Terry Dischinger, who went on to be an All-American at Purdue and start (as the only teenager) on the powerful 1960 Olympic team (Oscar Robertson, Jerry West and Jerry Lucas for headliners). When Garfield had him, Gerstmeyer had Charley Hall, who went on to be a good player

Twins Harley (43) and Arley Andrews led Terre Haute Gertsmeyer to the 1953 State Championship game against South Bend Central. An official scorer's error caused Arley to foul out of the game with only four fouls. (Photo courtesy Indiana High School Athletic Association)

on good teams at Indiana. Every year, there seemed to be a Garfield-Gerstmeyer duel for state notice.

In 1971, when Terre Haute realigned its high schools, Garfield and Gerstmeyer went together into Terre Haute North. The state shuddered. But it was rival South that was to achieve dominance before the decade closed out. South — its most distinguished ancestor high school 16-time sectional champion, two-time Final Four team Wiley — won 10 straight sectionals (1976-85) and became just the third school in history to win three straight semistates (1976-78, joining Lafayette Jefferson 1950-52 and Indianapolis Attucks 1955-57). The '78 South team got a miracle shot from guard Richard Wilson at the buzzer to go into overtime in the championship game but lost to Muncie Central, 65-64.

North has had less tournament success.

In 1997, when the Indiana basketball world was changing, Terre Haute North coach Jim Jones smiled and said quietly: "They're crying about class basketball. We haven't won."

It was a gentle reference to his whole adopted city's plight.

"Nobody says much about it, there's no pressure there, but we'd sure like to reward these fans," he said. "We've waited so long."

'Biggest mistake I ever made'

North under Jones had won four straight Terre Haute sectionals when its virtually annual tournament showdown with South came. It was in the second round, each cruising on opening night (North 57-40 over Northview, South 94-55 over South Vermillion).

North vs. South means Jones vs. Rady. They are two of just 18 coaches in Indiana high school history who have won 500 games, two of just four still active in this 1996-97 season (Jack Butcher of Loogootee and Bill Springer of Southport the others). Rady came in with 535 career victories, Jones 514 — 1,049 of those represented on the sidelines this night.

They play this sectional in Hulman Center, the downtown arena that Larry Bird graced with night-to-night brilliance during his three seasons at Indiana State.

Jimmy Jones was Larry Bird's first high school coach.

"Larry was a very good player as a sophomore, but he broke his foot — skinny, 6-1, 135-pounder," Jones said. "He was a guard then, but he could handle the ball. And he knew the game. He'd anticipate, steal, pass — he was the best player we had.

"We had a real good team when Larry was a junior — an outstanding team. We won 19 games."

But Gary Holland, Jones' assistant, coached Springs Valley in Bird's senior season. By Jones' choice.

"My children were beginning to come along, and I was also athletic director. I thought it was a good time to get out."

He became full-time athletic director.

"Boy," Jones said, 23 years later, "that was the biggest mistake I ever made in my life."

He's not even referring to missing that final season of probably the greatest small-school player in Indiana history, the choice of some as the greatest, period.

It was giving up coaching for athletic director, which he found to have demands of its own.

"If you're going to be that kind of a worrier, you might as well worry about coaching," he said.

"The next year, I didn't feel comfortable asking for my job back, so I went to Princeton (as coach)." After 11 years there, with the children raised, "My wife and I decided we'd like to live in a larger city — Evansville, Terre Haute, Bloomington or the Jeffersonville-New Albany area," Jones said. "The job here opened."

That was the summer of 1985. Rady already was well established with his South program after building a statewide reputation early in his career with successes at Bainbridge, Winchester and Shelbyville.

Rady and Jones are evidence that small schools haven't meant a basketball dead-end for potential coaches. Jones came from Oolitic, a bitsy town north of Bedford, known more for its limestone than its basketball, though it had its moments. One of them was Jones' junior year, 1954, when Oolitic won its first sectional championship. "It was a great thrill, a tremendous thrill," Jones

Terre Haute South coach Pat Rady (left)endures a tense moment. Below, Terre Haute North coach Jim Jones gives instructions during his team's 1996 regional game against Monrovia. (Rady photo courtesy Indiana High School Athletic Association; Jones photo©Michael A. Curlett, Terre Haute Tribune-Star)

said. "That's when I determined that I wanted to coach. My dad was a coach — never coached me, but I was around the gym a lot."

Oolitic is uptown compared to Rady's hometown.

"People say, 'You're against this (the change to classes) because you're from a big school,' " Rady said.

"I graduated from Roachdale High School. There were 24 in my class. We beat Greencastle in a semifinal game. The fire truck was waiting for us coming back to town — it was just tremendous.

"And I coached at Bainbridge (six miles down the road, if there had been a road).

"We had 200 in high school there. I remember we had games where people were lined up but couldn't get in — people were on ladders looking through the windows."

That was in the 1965-66 season, when Putnam County (Greencastle, with not quite 9,000 people, its metropolis) was a small-school power center. Cloverdale, which had reached the Lafayette semistate the year before, had its team back, guard Rod Hervey the leader. Rady's Bainbridge team had future Kentucky and NBA star Larry Steele. Fillmore, in between the two, had a Division I center, 6-8 Wayne Bright. Greencastle, with its all-time leading scorer, guard Mike Troyer, had one of its best teams of the era.

Purely by chance, the IHSAA chose that year to do some tournament rerouting. Just a tiny shift created a situation in which county rivals Bainbridge and Cloverdale, 15 miles apart, couldn't have met in the tournament until the state championship game.

And they darned near did.

Cloverdale went south and won the Evansville semistate to get to the State for the only time in school history. Bainbridge went north and won a sectional and regional. Rady's team lost in the semistate to East Chicago Washington, 78-74.

That Bainbridge-East Chicago Washington game was classic David and Goliath, the kind of matchup that class basketball not only will prevent but pointedly wants to. That's absolutely wrong thinking, Rady's experience tells him. "We *wanted* to play East Chicago Washington," he said.

"Larry Steele is living in Oregon now. Just a few days ago, he called and said, 'Coach, what are you *doing* out there? Out here they have classes, and nobody goes to the high school tournament, nobody knows who the state champion is. Do they know what they're doing?'

"Maybe in a while we'll get this back. I think they pulled the plug too quick. They didn't try to make it better. I don't think they've looked at what they could still save.

"I think we should have had a small-school tournament like Kentucky — not four classes, maybe two. Just have it for maybe the smallest 150."

Jones had different thoughts.

"I understand where the people are coming from," he said. "The small school never has a chance." But Jones would have preferred some surgery before amputation. "I would have liked to see them do something on the lower level first, the sectional or regional level," he said.

"For example, Riverton Parke played great tonight (what is now a Class 1A team lost a brisk semifinal game to 3A West Vigo, 52-45), but they don't belong in this sectional. Vincennes doesn't belong in its sectional. That's the two extremes. They could have made a level playing field. To me, the six-team sectional is the most unfair thing we have."

Six-team sectionals became the norm in the state, as soon as the entry numbers dropped to 384 statewide (six times 64). Jones isn't the only coach who hates six-team tournaments, because the setup guarantees that one team in the sectional championship game will be playing its third game of the week and the other its second. "I would rather you play in a four-team sectional and me in an eight, and meet in the regional," Jones said.

A leader named Lewis

But 1,000 victories' worth of experience wasn't being focused on anything but this semifinal game when North met South for sectional survival.

South had the game's most noted player. Junior guard Maynard Lewis has been a standout since Rady brought him onto the varsity as a freshman — to the varsity immediately at the start of the year, into the starting lineup by New Year's. "He can create, he can dish, he can hit the 3 — he's a heck of a player," Rady said. A few weeks later, Lewis said he would be signing in the fall with Gene Keady's program at Purdue.

North had a Team of the Future look. Jones started three sophomores, including team leader Alan Goff, a 6-2 guard. "Goff could play for anybody," Jones said. "We're going to be good, but they're about to wear my patience out."

One of the sophomores, 6-3 Justin Gilmore, opened the game with a 3-point basket, and the sparring had begun. Early in the second quarter, Goff worked free and sank a jump shot that put North ahead, 15-13. At that point, Lewis was 1-for-5. "I had jitters tonight I probably shouldn't have had," Lewis said. "I've been here three years."

He missed his sixth shot, too, but at the other end he intercepted a Goff pass and rushed the ball upcourt to get a 15-15 tie by setting up senior teammate Seth Dunlap's layup.

Dunlap broke that, the game's sixth tie, with a 3-point shot out of the right corner, and now South was rolling. Jones took a timeout, but Mark Raetz — whose dad, Dennis, is Indiana State's head football coach — worked free inside for two straight South baskets and Lewis came up with another interception and breakaway layup. It was an 11-0 run — "a good run," Lewis called it — to a 24-15 lead and Jones had to take a second timeout.

One of the year's strangest sequences came a minute later. North's Gilmore drew a two-shot foul. He missed both, but teammate Bryan Reed rebounded and missed. North's Terry Henry rebounded that miss and was fouled as he shot. Henry hit his first free throw, missed the second, but Reed again rebounded, missed, rebounded again and was fouled. He missed both, but Gilmore rebounded and missed, then Reed rebounded, drew a foul as he shot, and finally hit both free throws — seven North shots, four of them drawing fouls that produced eight free throws, six offensive rebounds, all in less time than it took you to read all that: 11.4 seconds, officially. The net result was five missed free throws but one more point than North would have had from the sequence if Gilmore had hit the two free throws that started it all. "I thought we were going to one-'em to death," Jones said.

South went to halftime up 24-20 and expanded that with a quick three-point play by Lewis, a charging-blocking foul decision going his way and preserving his basket. South went up 12 on a 3-point shot by Lewis four minutes into the quarter. North got within six early in the fourth quarter. Maybe they weren't the shots Rady would have preferred, but Scott Kluesner and Chris Cassell delivered 3-point baskets right at that point and South was out of reach again. "They're capable of shooting poorly, and our kids don't quit," Jones said. "So you always hope you've got a chance. But not tonight. We had 21 turnovers and didn't shoot the ball very well. Against a team of that caliber, that's payback time."

Raetz closed out the 53-42 victory with a free throw with six seconds left. "They've won this sectional four times in a row," Rady said. "I didn't relax until that foul shot."

A Mellencamp man

Lewis had 16 points and Dunlap 13 for South. Rady's first substitute was 6-1 guard David Lewis, Maynard's freshman brother. "He's going to be good," Rady said. This game, he didn't take a shot but pulled off two defensive rebounds. "He jumps better than I do," Maynard said. "He does the hurdles and sprints in track."

Gilmore had 11 points and Goff 10 for North, which finished 11-11 and keeps every scorer from this game. With more experience next year, Jones said, "We hope we'll be able to speed the game up a little, but we've got to watch our turnovers.

"We've gone about seven years here pretty daggone strong. We won 20 games four years in a row. We don't get a lot of recognition, but we've been very competitive.

"These sophomores would like to play in the Hall of Fame Classic their senior year. They deserve that.

"Our program is always going to be good because we work hard. We're a large school but we make it a small-school atmosphere. That's Terre Haute. Terre Haute is a big town with a small-town personality."

Remember, Jones is from Oolitic. He coached the self-labeled "Hick from French Lick." And this is the state that turned out John Mellencamp, who turned out *Small Town*. There isn't any question; from Jim Jones, those were compliments.

Elsewhere in Indiana . . .

Your newly adopted family had a pretty good night around the state: 25-7, two of the losses in rematches of games we all peeked in on earlier in the trip.

They came out as they did before. Anderson ran off 18 points in a row during a 57-45 victory over city rival Highland. Union (Dugger) rolled one more time against White River Valley, 78-40.

At Gary, both Roosevelt and Wallace were eliminated — Andrean ousting Wallace, 90-54, and Gary West outscoring Roosevelt, 84-74. Afterward, Roosevelt coach Ron Heflin announced his retirement.

Losses by Seymour (68-59 to Jennings County) and Fort Wayne Snider (70-62 in overtime to Fort Wayne Dwenger) weren't shockers. Neither was Pike Central's second-round rout of Jasper, 62-37.

But there almost was one at Greensburg. No. 3-ranked Batesville got 27 points from Michael Menser and needed them all to squeeze past Jac-Cen-Del, 71-69. Brad Borgman scored 26 for Jac-Cen-Del, which closed out a most unusual year: 0-3 against Batesville, 18-0 against everybody else. "That's your argument for class basketball," Menser said. "They're a *very* good ballclub. They're 1A. They would have done very well." Jac-Cen-Del was the one Ripley County school that voted for classes.

Bosse   **44**

Memorial   **32**

*Sectional Championship,
February 23*

EVANSVILLE BOSSE		EVANSVILLE MEMORIAL
Three: 1944, 1945, 1962	STATE CHAMPIONSHIP	None
Three: 1932, 1939, 1982	OTHER TIMES IN FINAL FOUR	None
12: first 1932; one in '90s, 1990	REGIONAL CHAMPIONSHIPS	Five: 1966, 1970, 1986, 1987, 1989
23: first 1930; three in '90s, most recent 1997	SECTIONAL CHAMPIONSHIPS	Seven: First 1966; two in '90s, most recent '96
None	CONSOLIDATIONS	None
No	VOTE ON CHANGE TO CLASSES	No
3A. (757; 20th of 96 in class)	1997-98 CLASS (ENROLLMENT)	3A. (668; 39th of 96 in class)
4A, Castle, Evansville Harrison, Evansville North; 3A, Evansville Memorial; 1A, Evansville Day. Evansville Bosse 1997 champion	1996-97 SECTIONAL OPPONENTS (1997-98 CLASSIFICATION)	4A, Castle, Evansville Harrison, Evansville North; 3A, Evansville Bosse; 1A, Evansville Day. Evansville Bosse 1997 champion
Boonville, Evansville Memorial, Heritage Hills, Mount Vernon, Tell City	1997-98 SECTIONAL OPPONENTS	Boonville, Evansville Bosse, Heritage Hills, Mount Vernon, Tell City
20-5 (won sectional; lost to Vincennes Lincoln in regional final, 63-57)	FINAL RECORD 1996-97	15-7 (lost to Evansville Bosse in sectional final, 44-32)

A Quiet Exit
in Evansville

In the Broadway musical *Annie*, Daddy Warbucks sings: "My speeches are greeted with thund'rous acclaim, at two universities bearing my name." Think of that. Two. That would set a person apart. So, consider a philanthropist Evansville once had — Francis Joseph Reitz, for whom in his grateful city there are no universities bearing his name but two high schools: Reitz (as in last rites), which long has been one of Indiana's football powers, and Reitz Memorial, which among its athletic alumni includes Don Mattingly.

Evansville also thought a lot of Benjamin Bosse, a mayor back in the days when mayors were beloved. Bosse High School, pronounced bossy, has the same longevity in association with basketball success as Reitz does with football.

The game was basketball as Mr. Bosse's school met Mr. Reitz's Memorial for a sectional tournament championship.

This may have been one of those occasions for some spinning in graves. The teams collaborated for a most unusual second quarter: no points at all, just one shot, which was neither a good one nor one that came at all close.

The game proceeded normally for a quarter, played out to a spirited 12-12 tie. Then it was as if someone hit the pause button. Action froze till the second half came, and then the game's pace was normal again. Bosse won quite handily, 44-32, which may explain and even glorify the decision to preserve the tie for as long as possible.

It wasn't, however, a one-team decision.

Memorial opened the second quarter by putting the ball in 5-7 guard Rico Maddela's hands and stationing him high on the court beyond the Bosse zone defense. "We did not do that with the intention of holding the ball for a quarter," Memorial coach David Hayden said. "We thought Bosse would come out and trap, and we'd backdoor them and get a layup.

"When they decided to pack back in, I thought, 'What the heck? It will just shorten the game. They have better athletes.'

"In retrospect, it wasn't a positive for us, but we were definitely in the hunt at halftime."

Bosse's "better athletes" might well have attacked as Hayden expected, except the approach wasn't original, even for this sectional tournament, so the Bulldogs were out there with a plan of their own.

"The first two games (against Evansville Harrison and Castle), everybody spread us out and we were chasing and chasing," Bosse coach Gene Ballard said. "They were getting easy baskets. We came into this game saying, 'Patience. Patience.'

"I said, 'If they want to hold it till there's two or three minutes left in the game, we'll do it.' Those people up there in the stands paid money, and they didn't come in here to watch those guys stand."

There was indeed a surly tone to a crowd chant of "Bor-ring, bor-ring," but it was mostly Bosse-based. Memorial ticket-buyers seemed kind of cheery about the whole thing as Maddela, 5-7, and Bosse defender Detrick Willett, 6-foot-2, who would have been about five weight classes apart if this were boxing, stared each other down from an unthreatening distance.

After nearly five minutes, Memorial injected just a bit of movement into the freeze and a Maddela pass flew right into the Bosse bench.

Now there was 3:14 left in the half, and at the Bosse end, nothing happened, either.

"Actually, we weren't stalling," Ballard said. "I wish I could take credit for saying, 'We're going to do it back to you.' We were just trying to figure out how to attack, because we needed to score on that possession to take the lead."

After 90 seconds of figuring, Bosse guard Michael Durrett threw the ball away, and Memorial took off on a scoring foray. Bill Blake's drive to the basket produced a shot forced up to try to draw a foul. It didn't work, the ball bounced out of bounds, Memorial retained it — and, after killing 90 more seconds waiting for a shot at the buzzer, turned it over.

Pointless quarter.

Levron: No. 2, and No. 4

Going in, this figured to be a scoring duel between two of the state's best: senior Levron Williams of Bosse and junior Clint Keown of Memorial.

Evansville has had some great high school athletes over the years, many of them doubling up. NFL Hall of Fame quarterback Bob Griese was a basketball player as well, not just at Rex Mundi High School but also at Purdue. Mattingly played football and basketball in addition to baseball at Memorial. Before World War II, Billy Hillenbrand came out of Memorial to be a consensus All-America tailback at Indiana. Bob Ford, leader of North's 1967 state champions, was All-Big Ten at Purdue. Calbert Cheaney of Harrison became the Big Ten's all-time leading scorer and 1992-93 College Player of the Year at Indiana. A young teammate of Cheaney's at Harrison, Kevin Brown, became the No. 2 player taken in the NFL draft after an All-America football career at Illinois, where Reitz products Don Hansen and Scott Studwell had been stars before him. The city has been a fertile talent garden for decades.

Levron (the accent on lev as in level) Williams came into this sectional championship game as maybe the best combination football and basketball player even Evansville ever has had: No. 4 all time among Evansville's career basketball scorers; No. 2 on the all-time football list in career rushing. A first-team *Parade* All-America tailback, Williams (6-4, 200) signed at Indiana and got assurances from both Hoosier coaches, Cam Cameron in football and Bob Knight in basketball, that he could try to double there, too.

This was not a game that maximized Levron's talents.

Nor Keown's. A 6-2 long-range gunner, Keown (*kee*-ahn) put up four 3s and sank two of them in the first quarter, then didn't score again till the fourth quarter. Williams scored two baskets inside in the first three minutes, then didn't shoot again till the fourth quarter. Their combined average entering the game was nearly 50 points.

Obviously, others decided this one.

The most decisive play of all came immediately after halftime. Bosse had possession, worked for a shot, and when Durrett felt himself open for a 3-point try, took it and hit. "I really didn't think about it — I noticed that I was wide open, so I just shot it," Durrett said. There were no special instructions, Ballard said. "I told them at halftime we needed to score. That's our problem: we haven't been able to get up on a team enough that can't stall on us."

It's amazing how big a three-point lead looked after that second quarter. Memorial needed the whole third quarter to score four points, and by then Bosse's lead was 28-16 — mountainous. Keown did score nine last-quarter points, but his team trailed by as much as 16 and never less than nine.

The tiebreaker opening the second half was Durrett's only 3-pointer. Bosse got three others, and 13 points in all, from another of those two-sport players. Tim Long was the quarterback with tailback Williams. In this championship game, he was Bosse's star.

Offsetting Keown's point total with Long's, a square-off of close friends, was a major plus for Bosse. Ballard didn't seem surprised. "Tim's shooting about 38 percent on 3s," Ballard said. "He's a great player. He and Michael I think are two of the finest junior guards in the state, as a combo."

Long had been getting himself ready for this one for a while.

"Our three state championship trophies (1944, '45 and '62) are just outside the office at school," Long said. "I go back there and look at them all the time — the trophies and the team pictures on the wall.

"I've always thought, 'I want to be up there some day.' I'm going to get my chance.

Jack Matthews of Bosse scores in the Bulldogs' 37-35 victory over Broad Ripple in the 1945 Final Four semifinals. Bosse went on to win its second consecutive state championship. Ironically, the only players not shown here are Bosse star Broc Jerrel and mental award winner, Max Allen, of Broad Ripple. (Photo courtesy Indiana Basketball Hall of Fame)

"This is special. We were talking today — we're going to go down in the history books as the last team to win this sectional. That's something no one else can say and no one can take away from us.

"As a team, it feels great."

Options, please

With its rich basketball history, Bosse may be the Evansville school most miffed by the change to class basketball. It's headed not for the biggest enrollment group, 4A, but for 3A.

Ballard doesn't understand why a school can't voluntarily "play up" — go against bigger schools, if it wants.

"I definitely would be in favor of that," he said.

"Look at our schedule. We play North Central, Terre Haute North, Terre Haute South, Jeffersonville, New Albany. Why do we have to go play 3A schools?

"Memorial's the same way. They'll be 3A. We'll both be traveling to Boonville (for the 3A sectional) next year. I'm really excited about that.

"Look at tonight. Where are all the 4A schools?"

Reitz, Harrison, Central and North are the Evansville schools that will fill up the new Evansville 4A sectional, along with neighbor Castle. It's one of three 4A five-team sectional fields; the next-closest 4A school is Bedford North Lawrence, 100 miles away.

Bosse and Memorial will be in a 3A sectional with Heritage Hills, Mount Vernon and Tell City at Boonville. Each played just one of the four this year.

Ballard isn't looking forward to leaving spacious Roberts Stadium, though its size wasn't needed this time. He played at Bosse the same years Ford was at North (1966-68), and another future Purdue star, Larry Weatherford, was a teammate of Ballard's at Bosse. "I've played in this place when there were 13,000 people — no aisles, just people from the first row straight to the ceiling," he said.

"I told the kids before we came out that this will be the last sectional in Roberts Stadium. People are going to look back as part of history and want to know who won that last sectional."

Hayden said Memorial voted against the change. "I don't like it — I definitely like the system we have now," he said. His high school alma mater, Evansville Mater Dei, will be playing 2A, nearly 60 miles away at Southridge.

Tough night with pals

Ballard would have preferred a better showcase game for Williams, whose nine points came with just six shots. "He's an All-State player, no doubt in my mind," Ballard said. "He has been starting for four years. Last year he averaged 23.4, about 13th in the state. This year he's averaging 19 and we're a better basketball team.

"He doesn't force shots. He's shooting 63 to 65 percent, over four years. He assists, he rebounds, he plays defense."

Hayden felt as disappointed for his own star, Keown, whose final scoring average (27.1) was second in Indiana, topped by only Oak Hill's Jarrad Odle (29.4). Both Keown and Odle are juniors.

"I have to give credit to their defense," Hayden said. "Keown didn't shoot well either night against them.

Members of Evansville Bosse's second straight state championship team in 1945 were, front row (from left), Bryan "Broc" Jerrel, Alfred Buck, Don Tilley, Jack Matthews and Norman McCool. Back row, Norris Caudell, Julius "Bud" Ritter, Bill Butterfield, Jim DeGroote, Gene Whitehead and coach Herman Keller. (Photo courtesy Indiana High School Athletic Association)

"He's good friends with a lot of their guys. It's a personal thing, in some ways.

"But he's a great player."

Bosse is more than an athletic rival for Keown. "I grew up with a lot of them. Tim Long is one of my best friends.

"This was a special game, the last sectional championship. We came out the second half and I don't know what happened. We were going to attack — just take good shots. Unfortunately we were not hitting tonight, especially myself."

That wasn't happenstance.

"Bosse has a lot of great athletes. Everywhere I went, all five players knew where I was. They were single- or double-teaming me. It was hard to get a good look at the basket.

"We knew before the game we couldn't run with them. I don't think anyone in the state can, to be honest.

"It's a tough game to accept. But I'm all for Bosse. They're a great team. We know we got beat by the best. Hopefully they'll go far in the tournament and represent Evansville well.

"I've battled with Levron for three years now. He's an exceptional athlete."

Elsewhere in Indiana . . .

All that sectional tournaments at their best have brought out over the years — peak effort, unintimidated irreverence, indomitability on both sides — lit up the night at Bedford when the two Bloomington schools met for the second time, for tournament survival.

North came in No. 1 in the state and 21-1, South unranked and 13-8, one of the losses 60-55 at North, you will remember. South had been 7-8 before winning its last six games. Coach J.R. Holmes had his team ready. So did coach Tom McKinney of North, which had never won a sectional played at Bedford.

The two teams stood dead-even, 27-27, after 28 unyielding minutes. South's sophomore leader, Jon Holmes, broke the tie with a 3-point basket, three huge points that knifed into North's confident elan. Jeremy Sinsabaugh was the Cougar assigned to Holmes. "I had just come off a pick, he pulled up real quick, I was getting there, but . . . it was off me," Sinsabaugh said. "Their crowd went crazy and I was like, 'This can't happen. We've *got* to win.' " Kueth Duany of North said, "I looked up at the scoreboard and said, 'Man, this has been too good a season for it to end now.'" Duany's 6-6 partner in North's inside game, Djibril Kante, said, "We wanted to beat South. They beat us in the sectional last year. We couldn't let them do it again."

And then it was 30-30 with 40 seconds left when South sophomore Adam Schaeuble fouled Kante, the gamelong strategy that J.R. Holmes had discussed a month before: make a mediocre free-throw shooter earn his points. "It was pretty obvious — sometimes they were just grabbing me," Kante said. "I guess I did shoot 40 percent during the season, but I think I'm a better free-throw shooter than that.

"From what I hear, when I go to the free-throw line, everybody's thinking, 'He's not going to hit them anyway. Who cares?'

"Then I went up there and hit them. It felt good."

Peppery North guard Mario Wuysang remembers thinking: *Djibril is hitting free throws. We're going to win this game.* "I was proud of him."

Now it was 32-30 and Holmes had the ball for South, a 3-point artist one 3-point shot away from winning the game. Sinsabaugh was the defender, as time ran down. "I just tried to stay down — keep my feet and move with him," he said. "They picked for him all across the court. I knew he was going to go up for a 3. I was pretty close on him, but he's got a really tough shot to block." Duany came into the scene. "He came off a screen and I jumped up there," Duany said. "We knew who wanted to shoot. He knows I have long arms. He couldn't shoot over me. I had my arms up, moving everywhere. He picked up the ball." Holmes went to Plan B. He dropped a pass off to sophomore Schaeuble, who tied the game with a 10-foot baseline shot.

Sinsabaugh opened the overtime with a 3-point basket, delivered an old-fashioned three-point play later, Kante hit two more free throws and North survived, 48-39. Kante, a 42-percent free-throw shooter during the season, was 8-for-8 against the South challenge, 36-for-44 for the whole tournament, 82 percent.

The neighborhood duels were similarly brisk and disrespectful all around the state.

At Jeffersonville, Charlestown continued the upset swath it had started with Michael "Money" Frazier's winning basket against Silver Creek by stunning Jeffersonville, 54-52. It ended Jeffersonville's string of six sectional championships, running to another Charlestown victory in 1990.

Harrison repeated its November victory over Lafayette Jefferson, 76-62. Marion denied Madison-Grant's spirited try for a second straight sectional championship, 81-75. Muncie Central was taken out resoundingly by strong city rival Southside, 78-53. Both teams met in Chapter 1, Crawfordsville and Greencastle, lost in the championship round — Crawfordsville to Thorntown legatee Western Boone, 52-38, and Greencastle to Rockville, 65-52.

24

Plymouth	36
Warsaw	32

Regional, March 8

PLYMOUTH   WARSAW

PLYMOUTH		WARSAW
1982	**STATE CHAMPIONSHIP**	1984
None	**OTHER TIMES IN FINAL FOUR**	Three: 1981, 1992, 1996
Seven: 1970, 1973, 1977, 1982, 1983, 1995, 1997	**REGIONAL CHAMPIONSHIPS**	11: first 1923; three in '90s, most recent 1996. Also in corporation: Atwood 1922
26: first 1926; five in '90s, most recent 1997	**SECTIONAL CHAMPIONSHIPS**	33: first 1923; seven in '90s, most recent 1997
Inwood 1922, West Township 1965	**CONSOLIDATIONS**	Atwood 1962; Claypool, Leesburg, Silver Lake 1966
No	**VOTE ON CHANGE TO CLASSES**	No
3A. (808; 11th of 96 in class)	**1997-98 CLASS (ENROLLMENT)**	4A. (1,439; 32nd of 95 in class)
2A, Bremen, Glenn, LaVillea; 1A, Culver, Oregon-Davis. Plymouth site and 1997 champion	**1996-97 SECTIONAL OPPONENTS (1997-98 CLASSIFICATION)**	3A, Culver Military, Rochester, Wawasee; 1A, Argos, Triton. Warsaw site and 1997 champion
Culver, Mishawaka Marian, New Prairie, South Bend St. Joseph's, South Bend Washington	**1997-98 SECTIONAL OPPONENTS**	Concord, Elkhart Central, Elkhart Memorial, Goshen
23-3 (won sectional, regional; lost to DeKalb in semistate semifinal, 76-52)	**FINAL RECORD 1996-97**	19-5 (won sectional; lost to Plymouth in regional semifinal, 36-32)

Pilgrims' Pride

Warsaw and Plymouth, linked by 26 miles of U.S. 30 in northern Indiana's lake country, have always been rivals. In everything. In basketball, though, the stakes shot up when Warsaw, under a young coach named Al Rhodes, made its first trip to the State in 1981. The very next year, Plymouth, under coach Jack Edison, won a surprise state championship the first time it had even been in the Final Four. Two years later, 1984, Warsaw won its first state championship.

Certainly those three events were related, Rhodes feels. "I think we let Scott Skiles know that he could get to the State. And after Skiles won the championship, I think that let Jeff Grose know that he could do it. Skiles was kind of Jeff's hero." Skiles and Grose were tough, high-scoring guards who led those championship teams — and in the process, sharply elevated sights in both programs.

"Fierce" is the word Edison gives, "tremendous" is the Rhodes choice to describe the rivalry since the championships. The same thing has happened in both communities. Immediately after that first run to the State, Edison said, "A lot of our people said, 'This is a once-in-a-lifetime happening.' " By the next March, "They kinda changed their mind." Awe had changed to annual expectation. Now, every year at Warsaw and Plymouth starts with state championship hopes, and every team gets comparisons with that champion of yesteryear. "It's tougher and tougher for our community to be happy," Rhodes said. Edison and Rhodes have apparently been the perfect coaches to handle the situations because both programs have boomed, consistently. "In the '90s, we've won over 85 percent of our games," Rhodes said. That includes returns to the Final Four in both 1992 and '96.

And this is Plymouth's year to take a shot at it.

If it can get by Warsaw in the regional.

Welcome to Huntington

They played this regional in Huntington. For Indiana, basketball began in Crawfordsville. For me, everything began in Huntington, especially a love that is, deeper than love, a genuine reverence for the state tournament — from sectional on.

The Huntington County where I grew up had 15 basketball-playing high schools and — no, no Indian outposts, unless you count the Banquo Indians. They were the Ghosts throughout the professional residency of a Shakespeare-conscious Huntington sportswriter named Cassius (honest — the lean and hungry part I can't swear to) Keller. They called him "Cash" and before he left on a distinguished journalism career that ultimately took him to Washington he had named most of the Huntington County teams. He was hardly out of town before the Banquo natives switched Ghosts to Indians, which was probably good because in Huntington County it was pronounced *bann*-ko, not at all like *Macbeth*'s noble *bann*-kwo, anyway.

There are 12 townships in the county. Each had a high school, 10 of them only one. Rock Creek Township had two, because the town of Markle wanted its own. The very first basketball game I covered, as the 18-year-old sports editor of the *Huntington Herald-Press*, was Banquo vs. Markle Nov. 3, 1954. Banquo won, 39-27, and it was statewide news. The victory ended a 56-game losing streak that was the state's longest. Markle went on to lose 39 straight.

The township of Huntington had three teams: the city team, Huntington; Huntington Township, its district the land in the township on all sides of the city limits, and Huntington Catholic.

Huntington's biggest basketball moment came in this game in 1964. The Vikings beat No. 1 Columbus in the afternoon game but lost in the championship to Lafayette, 58-55. Columbus' Jerry Newsom (41) and Steve Hollenback (45), and Huntington's Mike Weaver (beside Newsom) and Mike Shumaker (right), were Indiana All-Stars. (Photo courtesy Indiana High School Athletic Association)

That's 15 schools where now there is one. At sectional time five players now are starters where once there were 75. It's a mystery of life. Where are those other 70 players? When there were 15 teams, always there were four or five that were pretty good. Almost every team had at least one player who was excellent; some, three or four. About 30 players each year carried double-figure scoring averages. There were 6-5 centers, sometimes 6-7 and 6-9. There were 6-4 guards. There were shooters, lots of them. *Where have you gone, Billy Glendenning?*

Bill Glendenning. Darwin Stouder. Garl Bockman. Phyl Stouder. Merritt Hethcote. They were more than the starting five; they were 20.8 percent of the student body of Monument City High School in 1953. Of the 24 boys and girls in school, 10 suited up for the sectional tournament, but only seven got into games, six at times, five when things were really tight. The '53 Monument City Greyhounds got a draw that maximized their strain, forcing them to play four games in 35 hours to reach the sectional tournament championship game. They got there, and they took on the big school of the tournament, Huntington, on Huntington's court (Community Gymnasium). It was a splendid game. It went into overtime. This was a year before the Milan-Muncie Central finish, but the overtime's final seconds wound down in the same way: a guard, Monument City's Glendenning, in Bobby Plump's ultimate role, holding the ball almost the whole three minutes of the overtime in a staredown with Huntington defender Bud Stringfellow, who was in Jimmy Barnes' role.

Now, understand this about Monument City's five: they could play. Glendenning was a 6-foot athlete who was his school's one-man track team, State-meet caliber in both the 100-yard dash and long jump. Stouder was a 6-2 Charles Barkley, more svelte than Barkley and legendarily muscular; *mano a mano*, Barkley would have called *him* Sir. Darwin's little brother was Phyl, short for Phylbert. He was a 6-foot version of Darwin, a robust guard. Bockman was 6-4, monstrous at the time for a forward, which he could be because Darwin played, and filled, the post.

Stringfellow also was a State meet sprinter. These were two excellent athletes eyeball-to-eyeball in a confrontation the state didn't even know about.

When the clock dipped under 10 seconds, Glendenning faked, drove (left, memory says, not right a la Plump), shot and missed, but Stringfellow fouled him. The clocks were on Community Gym's sides, sweep-second, not digital. One said there were three seconds left; the other showed four. Glendenning missed, then made: 38-37, three or four seconds left. There was one Huntington pass to near midcourt along a sideline; a catch, a dribble and a launch by left-handed Ron Crawley. If the 50-foot shot had been a foot longer, it would have swished. If it had been an inch longer, it would have gone bounding away, off the rim, and the state would have heard about one of its all-time smallest sectional champions. It barely ticked the rim and dropped straight down. Running in from the right was Bill Bond, who caught the ball in stride, eased it back over his head, and his shot rolled 'round and 'round and 'round and dropped through.

Basketball for breakfast

Huntington has had its share of scandals. A mayor there once ran the town from jail, but the fellow was both a newspaperman and a lawyer so when politician was added to that mix, what would you expect? A local beauty was linked with George Gershwin in Huntington talk that seemed confirmed when Gershwin came out with a song named *Fare Thee Well, Annabelle*, which jibed. A local lady wrote a book about an unwed young mother who her shamed, aristocratic family kept hidden with her baby in an upstairs loft. The baby turned out to be Shirley Temple who suspected Ronald Reagan was her illegitimate father in parts the two played in the film adaptation of *That Hagen Girl*. It was probably Hollywood's biggest bomb of 1947, not to mention one of Huntington's enduring gossip generators.

But none of those things stirred the city like The Rape of Monument City. For six days, the *Herald-Press* was full of letters to the editor, letters that decried the theft and that rebutted with outrage; letters that detailed experiments that proved all that couldn't be done in three (or four) seconds, and letters about tests that proved indeed it could. One man said he listened to the game on radio and his wife "was popping corn. She made two trips through the three rooms to shake the popper after the last three seconds of play was in progress, and she was back to the radio in time to get the final shot." A woman warned the game's timer "a payday is coming for you, buddy, when you have only three seconds to enter the pearly gates, then you can't make it seven." The vituperation was not one-way, and it heated as the week (and the letters) progressed. Finally, the beleaguered editor suspended access to his pages and the writing stopped. The city vs. county bitterness didn't. At sectional time in the immediately following years — talk about fun!

A 16-team sectional needed 15 games to sort out a champion. That meant two games on Wednesday and Thursday nights (starting at 7 and 8:15), then eight on a marathon Friday and three on Saturday. Friday's came in three sessions: morning games at 8:30, 9:45 and 11; afternoon at 1:30, 2:45 and 4, and evening at 7 and 8:15. The evening games matched the winners of the day's first four games. Monument City was in the 11 o'clock game. Exposing players to four games in two days was a dangerous absurdity. Giving spectating kids 15 games to watch in 76 hours — talk about fun!

And basketball, and popcorn, and hot dogs, at 8:30 on a Friday morning, with schools silent — talk about fun!

Then the mergers began. In Huntington County, first to go was Monument City (that sectional championship game its last), then Banquo, then Markle, then TV sportscasting superstar Chris

Schenkel's hometown alma mater, Bippus. In 1966, the nine sur-
viving rural schools joined Huntington in forming Huntington
North, which exists to this day as a strangely named entity because
there is no Huntington South, East or West. Just Huntington North.
Not Huntington County High School, which it really is. Just Huntington North. Ultimately, Huntington Catholic gave in to funding
problems and joined, too. By then, there not only wasn't a Monument City High School, there was no Monument City. The town
had been evacuated, its cemetery moved, when the old site was
buried under the waters of one of the three flood-control reservoirs
the Army Corps of Engineers built in the '60s to make life down
the Wabash safer and summer life in Huntington County more re-
freshing.

*Where **have** you gone, Billy Glendenning?*

Tiger time

They don't play at Community Gym anymore. They play at
the new high school's handsome gymnasium which is, at least, on
the city's north side. Huntington North was in a hosting, non-com-
bat role when Warsaw met Plymouth. The Vikings had been taken
out in their sectional championship game by high-scoring Northfield,
which would play Columbia City sectional winner Tippecanoe Valley this day when Warsaw and Plymouth finished.

Everything in advance pointed to Plymouth — 21-2 to
Warsaw's 19-4; No. 15 in the rankings to Warsaw's No. 31; an 87-
66 winner when the two first met just three weeks before.

Plymouth also had Nick Wise, who averaged seven points a
game as a freshman and starred the next three years — every one
of those four Plymouth teams he played on a 20-game winner. A
6-3, 190-pounder, Wise also had college offers as a football tight
end, and he stood out in baseball, too. "Growing up in Indiana,
my first love has always been basketball, and that's what I'm
leaning to (for college)," he told Matt Kopsea of the *South Bend
Tribune* the week of the regional. "Just a great kid," Edison called
him. "Real quiet."

Nick was quieter than he wanted to be when Warsaw shot out
to an 11-2 lead. Tom Krizmanich, a 6-4 senior whose 20.9 scoring

average indicated he could offset Wise (21.7), was more than doing that in leading the early Tiger surge.

Edison, a look-alike of former NCAA executive director Dick Schultz, has been turning out Plymouth basketball teams for 24 years now. This is the 15th that has operated under the post-State championship expectations. He does not panic easily, nor does he expect his teams to. The bad start did not elicit even a blink from him, let alone a timeout. The 11-2 early hole "was the pleasing part of the game for me," Edison said. "We didn't seem to get impatient. I'm always interested to see how we play when we don't get a good start. Do our shooters still have their confidence? From the field? From the line? Is our defense still pretty strong and playing smart, where you know where their key people are?

"I thought we were doing some pretty good things. We just missed some high-percentage shots."

In the second quarter, Plymouth sub Chris Davis hit his second straight 3-point shot and the game was tied at 18. Then Wise, 2-for-8 at the time, hit a jump shot and Plymouth was never to be caught again.

Scared some, challenged a lot, but never caught.

Plymouth's lead reached 29-23 on a basket by 6-4 senior Matt Cramer with 5:38 left in the third quarter. The Pilgrims didn't score again for more than a quarter, but points were not coming fast at either end. Warsaw, which took eight shots and missed them all in the third quarter, was outscored in that eight minutes, 4-3.

Edison said whoa to that kind of pace. On Plymouth's first fourth-quarter possession, with Warsaw in the zone defense it had played most of the game, the Pilgrims — up 29-25 — backed off on offense and held the ball. On the Warsaw sidelines, Rhodes waved for his players to stay back and stick with the game plan: "Play zone and put a crowd around Wise and (No. 2 Plymouth scorer Brian) Wray," he explained it. "Basically, it was successful."

For almost two minutes, all was quiet on the court and loud in the stands. Edison had his loyalists' passionate backing. Then Warsaw guard P.J. Wiley sprang suddenly at Plymouth's Davis, stole the ball and dashed to a layup that tightened the game to 29-27.

Since being named coach in 1981, Al Rhodes has taken Warsaw to the State Tournament four times, winning it in 1984. (Photo courtesy Indiana High School Athletic Association, ©Mark Wick)

The noise in the Plymouth stands changed to an uneasy rustle, Edison's stall not quite so popular.

"What," Edison was asked afterward, "were you thinking when you backed off on offense and they scored?"

"I was thinking, 'Why did we back off?' "

That was Edison humor. He knew why. "We had two guys on the bench (Wise and Wray), and Brian had three fouls," Edison said. "We thought we'd get two minutes more rest for them. I thought if they came out of their zone, I'd call a timeout. But I didn't get it called in time. They got a great steal."

Warsaw got the ball back one time with a chance to score, but before the Tigers could get a shot up, 6-2 junior reserve Kent Stackhouse intercepted a pass. Wise scored, then after another turnover, Stackhouse did. Now it was 33-27, and Plymouth shot nothing but free throws the rest of the way in winning, 36-32. It wasn't really easy. Plymouth missed seven free throws in the last three minutes-plus, twice escaping 3-point shots by Warsaw when the lead was 35-32 in the long final minute.

Programmed to win

"To miss free throws like we did and still hang in against a quality team like Warsaw, we had to do some pretty good things," Edison said.

Wise had 14 points, though hitting just six of 22 shots. Krizmanich led Warsaw, but he scored just nine points, hitting four of 12 shots. It was not a shooters' game for teams that came in shooting .525 (Plymouth) and .573 (Warsaw) for the full season. This day they were .341 and .333. "They play great half-court defense," Rhodes said. "In the second half, we had real trouble scoring."

"Warsaw's defense took us out of a lot of things," Edison said. "Fortunately we were pretty patient and didn't force too many things."

"As great a program as they have, as determined as they come to play and as smart as Warsaw plays, it's just difficult to beat them once. Twice in one year? I don't know if we've done that for a while."

Probably not. Warsaw, in the 17 Rhodes years, stands 317-105, a three-to-one ratio of victories to defeats. Numbers compliment both programs. In 1995-96, counting records of varsity, JVs and freshmen, Plymouth had the most successful program in the state. Rival Warsaw was third. And for the decade of the '90s, Warsaw has passed Bedford North Lawrence for first in the state in the same kind of grading.

Al Rhodes grew up north of Warsaw. He played at Penn High School for Jim Miller, who had taken Cloverdale to the 1966 Final Four and gone to Penn from there. Rhodes as a junior and senior played on Penn teams that lost close sectional tournament games to Elkhart. Then he went to Tri-State College at Angola, and stayed in the town for a year to coach the Angola High JVs under coach Basil Mawbey.

Miller moved to Warsaw, Rhodes went there as JV coach, and four years later, in the 1980-81 season, he moved up to head coach when Miller went to Huntington. That first year, Warsaw went to the Final Four for the first time and started all this.

King of the driveway

Jack Edison has the mien of a scholar and the modesty of a monk. His reaction to the brilliant 28-1 run his 1982 team made to the state championship was:

"Why me?"

That taste of Hoosier existentialism is the part of winning the ultimate championship that Edison calls "the most humbling, and almost difficult to accept. People you've admired and looked up to your entire life haven't had the good fortune to be there, and you know they're 10 times the coach you are." ("Why me — that's exactly the feeling you get," Ben Davis coach Steve Witty said at another time, when he heard the Edison comment. "Jack is absolutely right about that.")

The '82 championship made Plymouth, a town of 8,000, the smallest since Milan to win a State. Edison started smaller. In the early '60s, at the same time Bruce Whitehead, the Crawfordsville athletic director who headed the IHSAA's class basketball study committee, played at Madison Township in the South Bend sectional, Edison played at Greene Township. "We had less than 200 kids," he said. The giant in that tournament, Edison said, was "South Bend Central — Mike Warren and people like that."

That experience, high school underdog heading into a sectional that included an overpowering team, influences Edison's standing on the class basketball issue. "The thrill of just being able to have a goal of beating a team like that to me overshadows anything with the class system," he said. Yes, he knew as a high school player his team was outmanned by that South Bend Central team that went to the 1963 state finals. He also remembers how he felt: Boy, if we get a chance to play these guys, we're going to beat 'em.

"I beat them a lot of times in my driveway."

Edison went to nearby Bethel College, then joined the Plymouth system, "but not as a basketball coach. I started out helping with wrestling — you're young, you'll do anything." He got into basketball as assistant freshman coach and worked his way up to JV coach. Steve Yoder, a Plymouth High product who a few years later was to be head coach at Wisconsin, left the Plymouth job to enter college coaching at Furman. "They asked Bill Nixon, who was the head baseball coach, to take the basketball job and he said no way," Edison said. "They asked me, and after a couple of days I said, 'I'll try it.' "

That was 1973. When his ninth year came around, he wasn't thinking state championship. The previous four years, his team

Plymouth legend Scott Skiles takes a shot against Gary Roosevelt in the 1982 State Championship game. The Pilgrims won 75-74 in double overtime in a game considered one of the tournament's all-time classics. (Photo courtesy Indiana High School Athletic Association)

hadn't made it through the sectional, though it was played at Plymouth. The '82 Pilgrims won their first 19 games, then lost their last regular-season game at home to South Bend LaSalle. "Our goal — mine, anyway — was winning the sectional," he said. In the regional finals, Elkhart Memorial had the Pilgrims 15 points down. "We were really a long way from being a state championship team then," he said, "in my mind."

In the semistate, the Pilgrims outlasted Marion in overtime, then got even with South Bend LaSalle, 77-71. They were in the State tournament — and starry-eyed, maybe? "I was," Edison said. "Fortunately, the kids weren't."

The "kids" included Skiles, a chunky, brazen guard who was about to show the state the fire and grit and astonishing scoring skill that would carry him through an outstanding career at Michigan State and on to the NBA. That Plymouth team also had a guard, Phil Wendel, who won the Trester Award at the '82 State, and two other starters who won awards at least as important. "Barry Peterson was valedictorian that year and Todd Samuelson was the next year," Edison said.

"I don't think we went into the State feeling that we didn't have a chance, but we certainly weren't overconfident," Edison said. "There's a lot of media attention all week long — the kids are all over the papers and TV. I really felt like they took that all in and when it was time to practice, they were ready. Maybe being good students helped."

Plymouth's semifinal matchup was Indianapolis Cathedral, "the best team in the state," Edison felt. "They had Ken Barlow (6-9), Scott Hicks and Shelton Smith, three Division I players. I just didn't see how we could match up with them.

"I don't know who matched up with Barlow yet."

Barlow had 22 points, his future Notre Dame teammate Hicks had 18, but Skiles scored 30 and Plymouth moved on, 62-59.

The championship game with Gary Roosevelt is one of the tournament's all-time classics. Plymouth won 75-74 in double overtime, with 39 points from Skiles, matching Oscar Robertson's final game in 1956 as the most ever scored — still — by a winning player in the championship game.

"The first time I sat down and watched a tape of that game, I had trouble believing it was the same game I had seen," Edison said. "We're four points down with just under 20 seconds left, and don't have the ball. I thought, 'There's no way.' I never felt it at the time, but I really felt futile watching it.

"Skiles hit one right at the buzzer in regulation time." From how far out? "Well, it would have been a 3 now. Actually it gets longer each year. By now, it's about 40 feet."

Returning to coaching right after that he found "really . . . interesting. A challenge. Expectations have changed now. You've got to watch that you don't put those expectations on a team — that you don't compare teams, or players.

"Especially with a guy like Skiles."

After the unattainable

That matter of Life After a Championship — in subsequent coaching, does that title become a plus or a minus? "That's an interesting question," Rhodes said. "At times after you've had a team that played basketball that well, you get into periods of frustration: 'Why won't these guys listen as well as the State champion team did?'

"But that's why I hate the new tournament. I have always appreciated just how high a goal the State championship in Indiana was. To most people, it seemed unattainable.

"I remember in '81 people told me, 'You'd better enjoy it, because it's probably the only trip to the Final Four you'll get.' I figured if I could get there once, I could get there again, and again. I just have to convince young people to play basketball the right way."

And it's never easy. Nor the same, year to year.

"We've felt as coaches our last four teams have been fundamentally sound," Edison said. "This group . . . oh, my.

"We've kind of adapted to them a little bit, and that concerns me."

The Pilgrims got off their post-Warsaw high, jumped out 15-0 on Northfield, and then hung on. But they won, 65-55, the 88th winning game for Nick Wise. They were back in the Sweet 16 for the second time in his four seasons, the third time since The Season, 1982.

Elsewhere in Indiana . . .

This is the round where the People's Choice died, where the Batesville dream ended not identically to last year but painfully close.

Again it was New Castle that outlasted the Bulldogs in a splendid game. Last year, the Trojans won on a 3-point shot at the buzzer, 63-62. This year, they were the No. 2-ranked team in the state, going against No. 3 Batesville, and New Castle won in overtime, 61-58. Each game, of course, was on New Castle home ground, at Chrysler Fieldhouse.

Batesville's Melvin Siefert became one more coach wondering how a game would have come out, how many more small-enrollment teams might have advanced farther in the tournament, if the IHSAA had given in years ago and abandoned the practice of playing two games in one day — the format for regionals, semistates and the State, for both boys and girls tournaments.

New Castle had beaten Winchester, 56-37, and Batesville beat Connersville, 57-39, in first-round games. At night, Siefert said, "I don't think we played as well as we could have played. I think playing the second game in the morning, short rest, had a little bit to do with it. Our two main shooters shot about 32 percent in the evening game. If we'd had fresh legs, I think we would have had a different result.

"But the atmosphere — there's no substitute for that. Absolutely none."

Batesville tied the game in regulation time with two free throws by Menser at 0:04. Menser opened the overtime with a 3-point basket. "It gave us the momentum — for about five seconds," Menser said. New Castle countered. With about 10 seconds left, 6-8 Joey Gaw of New Castle tipped in the basket that teetered the Trojans on top, 59-58. Batesville hurried the ball downcourt, hoping to give Menser one more chance. New Castle shut him off and when the Bulldogs tried to go elsewhere, Gaw slapped the ball loose, recovered it and drew a foul — Menser's fifth. Gaw, who hit the free throws at 0:02, had 17 points and Skipper Rowland 23 for New Castle, Menser 21 for Batesville.

Weeks later, Menser hadn't watched the game on tape and didn't anticipate ever doing it, but he did see those last seconds on a highlight tape, did see himself drop to the floor after that foul, "knowing that was my last play in high school basketball. It was a sad feeling."

The feeling didn't ease up quickly. With his school on spring break, he (like Siefert) went to Florida, missing the state tournament for the first time in years. "It gave me time to think about things," Menser said. It put him in a different sort of leadership role, easing teammates through the disappointment. "It was easier for me because I still have a career with Indiana State. For some guys, it was really rough."

That, to Melvin Siefert, was Michael Menser off the court doing what he had done on basketball courts for four years. "He makes the other players so much better. Without a doubt, he's valuable — even if he doesn't score. He makes the other guys play so much harder.

"We were 26-2 this year, 85-16 his four years."

Ultimately, Menser could appreciate all that he was a part of, even that last high school game.

"Intensity" was his one-word description of the game. "The whole game was back and forth. Every shot was crucial. You knew it was going down to the wire. And it went overtime. Some games you feel like you will pull away, but there was no way anybody was going to in this game. It makes you nervous. There's added pressure every play."

It was, in other words, the game he had been preparing to play, the game he had been dreaming of playing since his romance with basketball started in his days as ball boy for Batesville teams: his outstanding team against another just as good, for tournament survival.

"You'd like to go farther in the tournament," Menser said, "but I can look back and feel like I had an awesome career. I was just a hair short.

"I never would have dreamed of doing all the stuff that we did — we won four conferences, four sectionals, one regional, the Hall of Fame tournament. Then, to be an Indiana All-Star, that's a lifelong dream." Siefert passed the word to him that he would be on the Indiana team playing Kentucky's All-Stars in the series the states started in 1940. "Since I was 8 I've seen every All-Star game," he said. "I got all the autographs. The year Damon Bailey played (1990) was exciting — to be able to walk down and get his autograph."

In class basketball, of course, there might have been a state championship at the end for Michael Menser.

"Oh, no, I'd rather go out like this," he said. "It hurt really bad. But being in New Castle in front of all those fans — they had to bring in extra bleachers — playing No. 2 against No. 3, there's just no way class basketball is ever going to be able to match that."

"In two years, I look for them to go back to what we have now," Siefert said.

Ben Davis reign ends

At Terre Haute's Hulman Center, top-ranked Bloomington North was 14 points behind Terre Haute South with 14 minutes to play but charged to a 58-48 victory, despite 19 points and 10 rebounds by the Braves' Maynard Lewis. North's Mario Wuysang called it "my most fun game. We were down 14 and I didn't feel nervous or scared at all. And I had a good game (14 points off the bench, high for the Cougars). There was a little trash-talking — not from Maynard, a couple of their other guys. It got me excited. They were a tough team."

The Cougars trailed again (22-19 at halftime) in the regional championship game against probably the best genuinely small-school team in the field: Union of Dugger, 81st in enrollment among the 96 in 1A. Jared Chambers solidified an Indiana All-Stars spot with 25 points. "They couldn't stop him," said Chambers' teammate, point guard J.T. Golish, who directed an offense that committed only seven turnovers against the strong North defense. But North had four double-figure scorers and won, 62-51, following up on an earlier 80-62 victory over a team that finished 21-4. North coach Tom McKinney called Union "one of the three best teams we faced."

This round's shocker came at Anderson, where Delta won its first regional by ending the Indians' state-championship dream in the final game, 56-48, after No. 5-ranked Anderson had outrun No. 6 Muncie Southside, 76-66, in the second game of the morning round. Junior guard Patrick Jackson made himself a new name to remember with 25 points in a head-to-head duel with Anderson star Eric Bush (14 points).

Unranked Indianapolis Cathedral was the team of the day, ending No. 10 Ben Davis' hopes for a third straight state championship, 53-45, and following up at night over No. 7 North Central, 66-62, despite Jason Gardner's 25 points. Ben Davis coach Steve Witty called Cathedral "just outstanding" and gave his team a valedictory. "We were 18-5 and won our sixth straight sectional. There is a perception that this team failed. We've always told our teams that all they have to do to carry forth the Ben Davis tradition is become the best team they can become. I think this team for the

Union's Jared Chambers fights for the ball between Djibril Kante (33) and Kueth Duany (41) of Bloomington North in the Terre Haute Regional championship. (Photo courtesy Bloomington Herald-Times)

most part did that. As I look back on the year, maybe this team didn't have the mental toughness it needed to deal with expectations, people talking 'Three-peat,' things like that."

Mitchell's bid to make this North Central's first Final Four team lost some steam shortly after the two victories over Ben Davis, he felt. Dealing with the No. 1 ranking "probably" had something to do with that. "The coach probably didn't know how to handle it as well as he should have. I'd never been that route before. I'll know next time. I don't know that we 'peaked.' The attitude of this

Union freshman Brody Boyd passes the ball as Jeremy Sinsabaugh tries to get a hand on it during Terre Haute Regional play. (Photo courtesy Bloomington Herald-Times)

team was much better than it has ever been on teams I've played on or coached. But I think when you're trying to chase something that big, the margin for error is so small."

Vincennes got 23 points from Charles Hedde and ousted Evansville Bosse, 63-57, at Roberts Stadium. In a splendid square-off of Big Ten recruits at Fort Wayne, Purdue-bound Cameron Stephens of Fort Wayne South tied the game with a basket, then

Indiana signee Luke Recker drove the length of the court and dropped off a pass for the untying basket at the buzzer as DeKalb edged the Archers, 54-52.

Adam Seitz hit two free throws with five seconds left and scored 20 points as Pike Central won its first regional championship and denied little Barr-Reeve its first, 39-37. In the IHSAA survey that assigned 1997-98 classes, Barr-Reeve was just 30 students and six positions above Union of Dugger in 1A. Even with their enrollments added together, they'd still be 1A.

Four other teams you know won their way to the Sweet 16: Franklin, Harrison, Kokomo (59-52 over Bellmont after beating Marion, 63-50) and New Albany (ending Charlestown's charming four-victory tournament run, 72-53).

25

Delta	59
Ind. Cathedral	**48**

Indianapolis Semistate,
March 15

INDIANAPOLIS CATHEDRAL		DELTA
None	**STATE CHAMPIONSHIP**	None
1982	**TIMES IN FINAL FOUR**	1997* (* lost in championship game)
Two: 1972, 1982	**REGIONAL CHAMPIONSHIPS**	One: 1997
Seven: 1971, 1972, 1982, 1992, 1994, 1995, 1997	**SECTIONAL CHAMPIONSHIPS**	Five: 1980, 1985, 1989, 1993, 1997
None	**CONSOLIDATIONS**	Formed 1967: Albany, Desoto, Eaton, Royerton
No	**VOTE ON CHANGE TO CLASSES**	No
3A. (796; 14th of 96 in class)	**1997-98 CLASS (ENROLLMENT)**	3A. (700; 32nd of 96 in class)
4A, Indianapolis Arlington, Indianapolis Cathedral, Indianapolis Tech, Warren Central; 3A, Indianapolis Chatard. Franklin Central site, Indianapolis Cathedral 1997 champion	**1996-97 SECTIONAL OPPONENTS (1997-98 CLASSIFICATION)**	4A, Jay County; 1A, Monroe Central, Union City, Wapahani, Wes-Del. Jay County site, Delta 1997 champion
Brebeuf, Danville, Indianapolis Chatard, Indianapolis Scecina, Plainfield	**1997-98 SECTIONAL OPPONENTS**	Blackford, Elwood, Mississinewa, Muncie Southside, Yorktown
17-8 (won sectional, regional; lost to Delta in semistate semifinal, 59-48)	**FINAL RECORD 1996-97**	24-5 (won sectional, regional, semistate; lost to Bloomington North in state championship game, 75-54)

Delta Was Ready

Paul Keller was doing his best to play the Gene Hackman *Hoosiers* role — the cool, steadying coach easing his team through the awe of a first appearance in hallowed Hinkle Fieldhouse. The problem was Keller was as awe-prone as any of his Delta players.

Delta practiced there the day before the school's first semistate appearance. "We really were excited about going there," Keller said. "We let the kids have a little fun before we started practice. Somebody brought a tape measure — the whole Hickory bit.

"We were downstairs in the tunnel, in the old locker room — it was just everything that as a high school player in Indiana you can dream of.

"When you practice in there, the sound just reverberates. Boy, when they get to yelling . . .

"When I left that place, I just had fallen in love with it. That is just such a neat place.

"I was there in '93 with a kid in the slam dunk competition. I remember that night, sitting on that floor as a judge, going back up to my wife and saying, 'I would give anything to bring a team in here.' "

And here he was, in the semistate at Hinkle, with a formidable job.

Cathedral — mighty tough

Indianapolis Cathedral in one impressive day had taken out both two-time defending state champion Ben Davis and the North Central team that had spent almost the entire season ranked No. 1, or very close.

"Let's talk two weeks," Cathedral coach Peter Berg said. "In the sectional, we beat the city champs (Arlington) on Thursday, the county runner-up (Franklin Central) on Friday, the defending state champ (Ben Davis) the next Saturday afternoon and the county champ (North Central) that night. The kids really came together and accomplished something special. We're very proud of them."

Those last two state-shaking victories were at Hinkle Fieldhouse. Keller knew Berg's team would be ready, though it wasn't any more tournament-suave than Delta. Cathedral hadn't been in a semistate since 1982, before any of the present players were in kindergarten. This was just the third regional championship in school history, No. 3 coming on the 25th anniversary of No. 1.

Cathedral's renown is for football. Say that in past tense and say it again in present. The Irish just last fall had the first 14-0 season in a long and glorious history, winning the Class 4A state championship.

The heart of that championship team is on the basketball team. Maybe the best of the doublers is 6-5, 230-pound junior forward/tight end Rylan Hainje, "big-time" in football, the reports on *Hane*-jee say, and very good (a team-leading 14 points a game) in the sport Berg and Keller teach. If he is the best of Cathedral's doublers, 6-1, 220-pound senior forward/tailback Devin Schaffer isn't far back, after rushing for 1,700 yards (he signed with Indiana) and averaging 12 points a game on this team. Zach Fox, a 6-1 junior guard/quarterback, passed for more than 1,000 yards — and 100 points, as the No. 2 man on the basketball team in assists. His primary football target, even more than Hainje, was 6-5 junior forward/split end A.T. Simpson, who came off the bench in this sport but was the No. 4 scorer and the team leader by far in assists. He's another name expected to be big on football recruiters' lists.

That football strength and toughness were vital in answering the raw physical demands of the Ben Davis-North Central one-day double a week before this. That was impressive, but no more than the extra part: Schaffer was the only senior who played any sort of major role. Plan on Cathedral prominence — in Class 3A — in the new year and the new world.

Delta's in there, too. And both schools voted against the switch to classes. These are two basketball-proud institutions with backgrounds not so rich as their futures.

Meet Patrick Jackson

Delta's future — going into this game, this tournament round and whatever comes afterward through March 1998 — is Patrick Jackson.

Patrick is a junior, listed at 5-10 and 150 pounds though on a basketball court he looks capable of a career switch to jockey. On a court he also looks unlikely to be switching sports for a while. He has found his game.

"Patrick has been a secret," Keller said. "I've been thrilled that we've been able to do so well. It gets him a little more exposure. He's just a top-notch kid, too.

"I haven't seen all the guards in the state by any means, but there isn't any that I have seen that I'd rather have. He can do so many things — shoot the 3, penetrate and finish. He has great body control; he's a great ball handler. He's got the whole package.

"It would be nice if he was 6-2, but he has a heart that makes up for that. He's willing to go in there and mix it up with the big boys."

Patrick's older brother, 6-1, 195-pound senior Roosevelt Jackson, is the Eagles' center, the one Delta player with a Cathedral look.

The Jacksons "have some cousins in Anderson," Keller said. "When Patrick was 12, he played with Eric Bush and a couple of the other Anderson kids."

Delta got to this Cathedral game by beating Anderson at The Wigwam in the regional championship game, 56-48. There, matched directly with the quick-handed Bush and cohort Tyson Jones, "Patrick played great — he and Billy Lynch did a terrific job. They just did not turn it over.

"It was a one-point game at the half. In the third quarter, we got Anderson down seven, but they made a run and caught us at the end of the third quarter. Patrick hit a 3 to start the fourth quarter and they never caught us."

'I just stood and looked around . . . '

This is Paul Keller. This is his feeling for Indiana's basketball tournament, for one of its citadels.

"I've been a varsity coach for 12 years and I don't think I ever wanted to win a sectional as much as this year," he said.

"I wanted to go to The Wigwam one more time."

And he got there. And then he won.

"When we walked out after winning there, I went back in. The lights were down, there were a couple of janitors there, I just stood and looked around . . .

"It was an incredible feeling.

"It was such a thrill to come out of there with a championship."

Delta is not a community. It's a school corporation about five miles northeast of Muncie, formed by the merger of four community schools: Albany, Royerton, DeSoto and Eaton. All of those played in the Muncie sectional. None ever had won a sectional championship.

Paul Keller had.

His school, also located in Delaware County near Muncie, was Yorktown, whose own Oscar Robertson, Larry Bird, Fuzzy Vandivier — basketball exemplar, the greatest, ever — was Bruce Parkinson. Bruce might quarrel with that. His father, Jack, also played at Yorktown and went on to a splendid, war-interrupted career at Kentucky. Jack Parkinson, elected to the Indiana Basketball Hall of Fame in 1996, died less than a year later. Cliff Barker followed Jack Parkinson to Kentucky and also is in the Indiana Basketball Hall of Fame. Bruce isn't in that Hall yet; that will happen in a year or two, surely not much longer. He was that good at Yorktown, even better as a four-year leader on excellent teams at Purdue. There's a third-generation Parkinson coming along. Bruce's son, Austin, playing at Northwestern High just outside Kokomo, was able to make as much impact on his team as any freshman in the state did during this winter.

Bruce Parkinson predated Paul Keller by two years at Yorktown. And by one great victory.

The making of a coach

In 1972, Parkinson's senior year, Yorktown beat Muncie Central in the championship game of the Muncie sectional. It was the first time — ever — that a "county school," a team from outside the city of Muncie, had won the sectional tournament at Muncie Fieldhouse.

There was a time when little Burris, the Ball State Teachers College laboratory school, had some great teams. The Owls won six straight Muncie sectionals from 1939 through '44. In both '39 and '42, Burris reached the Final Four, and the '42 team lost to Washington in the state championship game. Burris has not won a sectional since 1947, a 50-year gap now. Muncie South came in as a budding power in the 1960s and still is one. Short-lived Muncie North won three sectionals between 1974 and '84.

Central has always been there. Always the Bearcats. Always the team to beat — so much so that when Muncie Central won, there was a tendency to take it as the expected outcome and line up behind the Bearcats as they went against the rest of the state. "Once they got out of the sectional I think everybody in Delaware County kinda looked up to them," Keller said. "When I was an eighth-grader, I remember watching them play in the 1970 semistate."

And he remembers, he will always remember, sitting in the stands as a sophomore and cheering that Parkinson-led Yorktown team to victory over the vaunted Bearcats. That night, he said, "Our community at Yorktown — we did everything but burn the town down.

"It was the biggest thrill of my life, at that point. Fantastic.

"I think it's really when I knew that this was going to be my profession. I just totally fell in love. I had always loved the game, but this just took it to a new level."

More than a championship

Winning in the Fieldhouse was part of it. "Oh, yeah, no doubt about it," Keller said. "What they're missing in this class thing is the excitement and the thrill that you feel with the opportunity to play a big school in a big arena. There's a lot that they don't seem to understand.

"They decided that the state champion is the only one getting satisfaction in the tournament. I think they're just totally off base.

"We're really more and more getting principals who have never been coaches, which is fine. But they're making decisions about athletics and they never have experienced what's going on down here.

"You just can't tell me that Winchester would trade beating Richmond and winning the Richmond sectional for even a semistate berth at the Class A level. That's the epitome of why it's called Hoosier Hysteria. Anything can happen.

"They're missing the point. The hierarchy of the state thinks if we can't give them some kind of ring for a championship, they're not getting enough. But they are getting enough. Those kids cherish that.

"In our whole county, there isn't anybody in coaching who is in favor of this. And yet we have Phil Gardner heading it up, and he's the principal at Wes-Del right here in Delaware County."

A year after the Parkinson team's victory, Keller was on another Yorktown team that repeated as Muncie sectional champion. "Our team in the sectional played Muncie Central, Muncie North, which I think was ranked sixth in the state at the time, and Muncie South — we had to beat all three to win."

Yorktown has won one sectional since then, in 1986. The school was not tiny. "We had 240 in our graduating class," Keller said. "We were the biggest class they had ever had. I think the school was around 800."

After graduation, Keller picked up his degree at Ball State and began his career as freshman basketball coach and assistant football coach at Shenandoah, a Henry County consolidation (of Middletown, Sulphur Springs and Cadiz). He was there in 1981 when Bob Heady took the team all the way to the Final Four, the only time it or any of its predecessors ever advanced past the regional.

He was an assistant coach at Delta for three years before getting his first head coaching chance at Wapahani, in the same county. After seven years there (and two Blackford sectional championships), he returned to Delta as head coach. His first year there — back to the heights. "We won the (Jay County) sectional and beat Muncie Central in the afternoon game at the (Anderson) regional."

Beating the Bearcats was one more thing that had never happened at Delta or any of its ancestor schools.

"Oh, my — you talk about a big win," Keller said. "I can't tell you how many people came to me and said, 'I've wanted to beat Muncie Central all my life. And we've *done* it!'

"Phenomenal."

Going to work, gloriously

The Bearcats and the Fieldhouse, Anderson and The Wigwam were out-of-mind experiences when Keller sent his Eagles against Berg's strong Irish in the first morning game at the Hinkle Fieldhouse semistate.

They built the place in the mid-1920s. Michelangelo couldn't have improved much on the building's ceiling, really a sky-high roof with rows of windows at the peak that in morning and early afternoon bring in sunshine as an art element. Spectators see brilliant, almost blinding reflections on the court, but players don't. Players can look up and up and up into the bleacher rows on the west side and see faces and heads backlit so deftly it has the appearance of a Norman Rockwell painting. It's a great place to see basketball played. In morning and early afternoon, it's also a glorious place.

Delta edged ahead on junior Tyce Shideler's free throw, applied a full-court press and forced a turnover that blossomed into a

3-0 lead. Then Cathedral began to use its big-body edge. Pass after pass put pressure on Delta's defense around the basket. Cathedral shot ahead 12-8 and Hainje had eight of the Irish points.

"Physically obviously we didn't match up at all," Keller said. "We knew that Hainje was really an outstanding player."

Closing out the quarter, Delta pressed twice and forced two backcourt turnovers. "I felt that was a little bit of a weakness on their part and it's one of our strengths," Keller said. "My guards are good anticipators."

Cathedral went nearly the first six minutes of the second quarter without a basket. The inside game that figured to be so dominant wasn't there. "We started out establishing what we wanted to do and got away from it," Berg said. "We just weren't as well prepared for their pressure as I thought. That's coaching, but it's also very difficult to simulate what Delta has — players who do a fine job of playing their roles and playing disciplined."

The other Irish problem was corralling quick, slippery Patrick Jackson. Jackson's basket from just inside 3-point range put Delta up 21-14. Finally, Hainje got the ball in operating position and delivered a three-point play. Jackson pulled a defender to him above the foul circle, freed himself with one-on-one moves and scored again. But, just before the half, Schaffer — "our leader," a Cathedral assistant coach called him — tried a 3-point shot that caught no rim and the inevitable jeer from Delta's fans: "Airball!" However, Cathedral recovered the miss, Schaffer got the ball again and with the chant still ringing, sank a 2-point shot that sent the Irish to halftime down just 23-21.

A different game

Each team had found what worked and what didn't work by then. Delta had learned the most: Jackson couldn't be contained, and Hainje, good as he is, couldn't operate well inside what amounted to a five-man jam. Delta's defense had been beaten early by plays designed to get Hainje freedom for a pass. A Cathedral guard cutting through would get attention — hedging was Keller's term — from a Delta big man, and that benefited Hainje, who had 10 of his eventual 19 points by halftime. Keller told his team:

"Let's not hedge any more until they prove to us that they want to hit the cutter."

Cathedral's counter was to take the shots being given outside. When quarterback Fox and strong safety Eddie Freije hit 3s opening the second half, Cathedral moved ahead, 27-25. "You have to make your choices defensively," Keller said. "You look at some people and say, 'Let's have this young man shoot the ball a little more than he's used to.' If he wants to shoot it, we think we can live with that." Guards Fox and Freije had been combining to take only about three 3-point shots a game, and hitting them at less than 30 percent. They were to take four more after their boom-boom start and hit just one. Schaffer didn't get a second-half shot to drop, in four tries. Simpson didn't get one in all day.

Meanwhile, Hainje didn't get a third-quarter shot. "They were dropping people in on him," Berg said. "They gave us some shots and we didn't hit them.

"Any time a guard passed in, they had five guys in the lane. It's hard to play two-on-five."

Delta got to the fourth quarter up 34-32 and both coaches knew it was a significant edge that magnified Jackson's importance. The score was 36-34 when he caught his defender playing back a step and sank a 3. It was 39-37 when the defender moved up and Jackson beat him with another one-on-one move for the last basket of his 23-point game. Down 43-37 with 3:36 left, Berg took a timeout and applied some full-court pressure to Delta. Twice in a row, after Cathedral had pulled within 43-40, Delta got the ball downcourt to Roosevelt Jackson for layups. Now it was 47-40 with 2:25 left and the team that had beaten Ben Davis and North Central was headed for the sidelines to join them.

"When our kids get that lead, they've got every confidence in the world that we're going to be able to hurt the opponent," Keller said. "Now they have to guard 42 feet in half-court, because we have five people on the court who can all take care of the ball, who have pretty good timing on where to pop and keep the floor spaced."

From 43-40, Delta made its coach's point. The Eagles outscored Cathedral 16-8 and scored at least a point all nine times they had the ball.

Berg was philosophical: his team simply wasn't set up to play a Delta. "We put a lot of stake on the city championship and the sectional and regional," he said. "We had not played a team of that caliber with that style of play all year. We primarily played teams that were very athletic and crashed the boards hard.

"They have 3-point shooters and guys who can drive. They don't hurry. That's pretty tough to play against when you're used to being the one that controls tempo. When they turn the screws down on you, it's tougher."

It wasn't a matter of his team's failure to refocus after its emotional joyride of the previous weekend, Berg said. "Delta would have been very tough for us to play even if they were the first-round sectional opponent.

"Our kids are very disappointed. They're competitors. They love a challenge. They were looking forward to playing another week. I don't mean they were looking ahead, they just wanted to play the whole thing out."

And so did Delta. Keller sent his players off for the between-games break and noted: "We're not going to talk about being tired. My lands, you're playing for a chance to go to the Final Four!"

Elsewhere in Indiana

In other semistate openers across the state, moving along were Bloomington North, 52-50 over Vincennes Lincoln; DeKalb, 76-52 over Plymouth, and LaPorte, 75-64 over Harrison.

At Evansville, Vincennes trailed No. 1-ranked Bloomington North 27-15 at halftime but took its first lead at 50-49 with 1:05 left on a reverse layup by Derek Cardinal. It was 50-50 and Vincennes was playing for a final shot when Cardinal, with North's Ryan Reed pressuring him, had the ball bounce off his leg and out of bounds, with nine seconds left.

North's play was to get the ball to Kueth Duany moving up the left side of the court. Vincennes coach Gene Miiller didn't care who had the ball; his team still had two fouls to go before North would shoot a one-and-one. Two fouls out on the court would pretty much exhaust the nine seconds, Miiller reasoned. But nobody got to Duany before he put up an eight-foot shot from the left side. It missed, but North's Jeremy Sinsabaugh ran in from the right side, got the rebound, missed, and was in the right spot when Ryan Reed got a hand on that rebound and tipped it his way.

"I grabbed it, gathered, and put it up again," Sinsabaugh said.

"It took forever to go in.

"I banked it, it hit the front of the rim, the back, the front again, then it dropped in.

"I looked at the clock and saw 0:01, then zero . . . I ran down the floor and jumped in the air . . .

"It was probably the best feeling I've ever had."

And one of Miiller's worst, on behalf of his team. "We played them well . . . *really* well the second half. We just weren't able to make the play when we really needed to. I told our kids in the locker room that I couldn't have asked any more from them. They left everything they had out there on the court. To come back from 12 down against the No. 1-ranked team in the state, and to actually take the lead — that shows you the heart and guts this basketball team had."

At Fort Wayne, DeKalb's Luke Recker had 27 points, 10 rebounds and seven assists, and he was 5-for-10 on 3-point shots in a virtuoso performance that Plymouth coach Jack Edison didn't exactly enjoy, but admired.

"You saw how multitalented he is," Edison said. "His defense — how many deflections he gets, how much he takes away from your offense . . .

"I think IU will look for him to get the ball to some people. Today, you saw he can. He keeps the other players in the game."

Plymouth's Nick Wise closed out a 1,617-point, 88-12 career with 19 points, and Brian Wray scored 24, but the other Pilgrims went 2-for-17. "I haven't seen five guys with as much defensive savvy since the Argos teams of the '70s," Edison said of DeKalb.

At West Lafayette, LaPorte couldn't stop Josh Whitman (31 points), but Harrison couldn't work the 3-point magic that had been its outside complement. Adam Tesch, Brent Mason and Pat Colletto combined to go 4-for-25 on 3s and 8-for-41 overall. Greg and Ben Tonagel combined for 41 points as the Slicers won 65-62.

Franklin	71
New Castle	**65**

*Indianapolis Semistate,
March 15*

FRANKLIN		NEW CASTLE
Three: 1920, 1921, 1922	**STATE CHAMPIONSHIPS**	1932
Four: 1912*, 1939*, 1973, 1974 (* lost in championship game)	**OTHER TIMES IN FINAL FOUR**	Three: 1967, 1971, 1984
12: first 1921; one in '90s, 1997	**REGIONAL CHAMPIONSHIPS**	16: first 1926; five in '90s, most recent 1997
43: first 1918; four in '90s, most recent 1997. Others in corporation, 2: Union Township 1952, Hopewell 1916	**SECTIONAL CHAMPIONSHIPS**	52: first 1915; all eight in '90s, through 1997
Providence 1907, Needham 1927, Hopewell 1936, Needham Township 1939, Masonic Home 1944, Union Township 1963	**CONSOLIDATIONS**	None
Yes	**VOTE ON CHANGE TO CLASSES**	No
3A. (838; 5th of 96 in class)	**1997-98 CLASS (ENROLLMENT)**	4A. (872; 93rd of 95 in class)
4A, Center Grove; 3A, Greenwood, Roncalli, Whiteland; 1A, Indian Creek. Greenwood site, Franklin 1997 champion	**1996-97 SECTIONAL OPPONENTS (1997-98 CLASSIFICATION)**	2A, Knightstown, Shenandoah; 1A, Blue River Valley, Morton Memorial, Tri. New Castle site and 1997 champion
Beech Grove, Brown County, Greenwood, Roncalli, Whiteland	**1997-98 SECTIONAL OPPONENTS**	Anderson, Anderson Highland, Connersville, Muncie Central, Richmond
24-3 (won sectional, regional; lost to Delta in semistate final, 61-54)	**FINAL RECORD 1996-97**	24-2 (won sectional, regional; lost to Franklin in semistate semifinal, 71-65)

Guys
Named Joe

When comedian Rodney Dangerfield made "no respect" into a *shtick* that stuck, sports found a motivator. In 1994, Arkansas went into the NCAA tournament No. 1-ranked in the land in the coaches' poll. It was given a No. 1 seeding by the NCAA. At the Final Four, Razorbacks coach Nolan Richardson's recurring theme was that he and his team did not get proper respect.

Is there a ranking or a seeding higher than 1?

It is a theme played out *ad nauseam*. Once there was a charm in underdog status, in a chance to make doubters look bad, even in tricking people into overlooking an opponent more dangerous than billed. Lying in the weeds was a term for it, and it wasn't demeaning. "Overdogs" for years have envied that status.

Franklin coach Dave Clark quietly made it work for him this year and this game.

His Grizzly Cubs took a 23-2 record into the semistate, a 10-game winning streak. Going into the sectionals, 10 of the polls' Top 20 teams had lost more than two games. By this point, two weeks into the tournament, 12 of the season-ending Top 20 had been eliminated. Franklin wasn't in the Top 20 all year long. At 17-2 when the last poll was taken, the Grizzly Cubs weren't close to the Top 20; the pollsters gave more votes to 33 other teams.

Dave Clark must have smiled when he saw that.

He had his tournament theme.

And now was the time to use it. In the Indianapolis semistate, two victories away from the Final Four, he was taking his team against No. 2-ranked New Castle, which was about to play its first tournament game away from the comfort of its home arena.

Even in the tournament's *newspeak*, it was 3A Franklin against 4A New Castle. Never mind that these schools were just 34 students apart in the IHSAA survey, New Castle 93rd in the state and Franklin 100th. The 4A-3A cutoff line was in between them. If there is a next time for such a survey, fast-growing Franklin almost certainly will be 4A. More static New Castle might not be.

But that's another day. This one, it is 3A, unranked Franklin (23-2) against 4A, No. 2-ranked New Castle (24-1). Franklin, co-champion with Mooresville in the Mid-State Conference, against New Castle, co-champion with Anderson in the mighty North Central Conference. On a neutral court.

It was Franklin, lying in the weeds, its coach smiling.

A Grizzly, not a Cub

There was a microcosm of the overall situation in the matchup at center: Two 6-8 guys named Joe. Joey Gaw of New Castle was All-NCC, a Top 40 candidate for the Indiana All-Stars, already assured of a Division I college future by the Drake scholarship he had signed in November. Joe Hougland of Franklin had some games when he wasn't All-Franklin.

This wasn't one of those. Hougland this day was more of a Grizzly than a Cub.

He was almost too aggressive early. He missed his first three shots and New Castle opened an 11-3 lead. Clark made a defensive alteration, changing from man-to-man to a 1-3-1 zone a little earlier than planned, but not much. In the week of film-watching, Clark said, "We didn't think they attacked a 1-3-1 real well. We kinda held that back."

But at least as important was what happened at Franklin's offensive end of the court. Hougland scored seven straight Franklin points, five of them with offensive rebounds. He put Franklin in position for Mark Pitcher's basket three seconds ahead of the buzzer to give the Cubs a 14-13 first-quarter lead.

At that point, Hougland had eight rebounds, Gaw none.

Then Franklin opened the second quarter with a 10-0 blast. New Castle, so deep in deadly shooters it still was bringing one of its best, sophomore Darnell Archey, off the bench, made just one of the 10 shots it tried in the second quarter, and the Trojans found themselves looking at each other wide-eyed in their locker room at halftime, down 30-17.

Their 3-point shooters were 0-for-9. Their two big men, Gaw and 6-5 forward John Bryant, had no rebounds. Hougland had 11, plus 13 points, five more points than Gaw and Bryant together. "When we had our run to get the lead, it was basically one shot, one-and-done, for them," Clark said. Hougland was the main reason, though 6-3 forward Michael Whitted also helped.

"We felt we had an advantage inside," Clark said. "We thought our two were quicker and more athletic than their two were."

Still, New Castle coach Curt Bell, who was to resign at after the season, replaced by University of Evansville assistant Steve Bennett, said, "If I could explain that second quarter, I'd be a lot smarter than I am. I felt like I was in the Twilight Zone. I don't know if we were shell-shocked or what. I didn't get too upset. I just told them: 'Here's what's happening out there. You're either going to get it together or you're not.' "

For want of a dunk

The Trojans tried. Their offense became quicker and sharper. Their defense became full-court. Franklin went to Hougland right away for its first basket of the second half, but now Gaw was matching him and the big New Castle fan following was aroused.

Franklin led 36-24 when guard Brandon Miller finally hit the first New Castle 3. Chad Bell scored inside, so it was 36-29, Hinkle Fieldhouse aroar, when New Castle's pressure for the first time produced a midcourt steal. Suddenly, there was Gaw out front, headed for the dunk that — with almost 13 minutes still to play — would bring New Castle within five and . . .

Gaw's dunk rimmed out.

There still was all that time left, but most of it was gone before New Castle ever got as close as seven points again. When Skipper Rowland hit his one 3 of a 17-point performance, New Castle was within 68-65 with 50.6 seconds left. But the Trojans didn't hit another shot and Franklin widened its margin with free throws.

Bell was dragged through the what-ifs, starting with Gaw's missed dunk at 36-29. He played down the significance. "He just missed it. I don't know if he didn't have his legs or what."

It was, he admitted, "a big momentum-changer for us. If he dunks it, it not only cuts into their lead but the emotion is great . . . it's down to five, and we're playing pretty well. Defensively we were doing a pretty good job full-court, scrambling them.

"We just could not score consistently until the fourth quarter."

A day undreamed of

Gaw made the plays that got New Castle past Batesville and into the semistate. Hougland took his turn at stardom in this one.

"I'd have to say as far as overall play, board play and offensively, it was his best game," Clark said. "He has been inconsistent — he has scored 30 and 20 points, and he has had games where he scored four or five points. We've been after him all season long. You get in this situation, all it takes is one bad game.

"He came ready to play."

Hougland had 22 points and 14 rebounds, to 17 and 4 for his matchup, Gaw. "I was impressed," Bell said, making it clear that Hougland hadn't been overlooked in defensive planning.

"A lot of times, what you work on during the week doesn't get done that day," he said. "We knew he was a nice player, but if you let him double his scoring average, you're in trouble.

"I thought Joe (Gaw) came out and played real well early. We had a long stretch where we just didn't have much out of him. And we got beat so bad on the boards the first half. You just can't shoot that poorly and get beat on the boards and expect to win.

"Archey and Rowland have shot the ball so well all year. I'd never dream that they'd be 3-for-20 together. I'd never dream we'd have trouble scoring, and for three quarters we did.

"Give them credit. They got out in their 1-3-1 and did some things well."

Clark felt his team "got out on them and at least rushed the shots. They like to dribble, penetrate and kick to their shooters. They couldn't do that well in our 1-3-1.

"I thought we did a good job keeping them away from the arc. Archey and Rowland are spot-up type shooters. We thought we had to run them off the line and make them put the ball on the floor.

"We knew they were going to make a rush sooner or later. We were just hoping we could hold them off."

The respect thing

There was that matter of Franklin's poll omission. "We were thinking, 'Shoot, we're 23-2 and we don't play a terrible schedule — maybe not a North Central-type of schedule,' " Clark said. "Our kids all year long have felt like we were slighted a little bit. That's been a big approach to us."

"I don't understand why they weren't ranked," Bell said. "I don't vote.

"Watching tape, I thought they were a quality team. I think they're a definite Top 20 team, and should have been all year. Five guys averaging in double figures, they won 23 games, they played some pretty good people — I liked them. They reminded me of our team last year, no one guy you can pick out and say, 'You've got to shut this guy down.'

"The sad thing to me is you won't see this kind of thing any more — close to 12,000 in here, for schools of different levels. You lose this atmosphere, and it's really sad.

"Yes, we're disappointed because we lost a game, but Indiana is going to lose a lot more, starting next year."

Elsewhere in Indiana

Noblesville and Kokomo used opposite ways of joining Franklin and New Albany in second-game semistate victories.

At West Lafayette, Noblesville got 44 points from junior guard Tom Coverdale in pulling away from Gary West, 92-78.

Coverdale hit 14 straight free throws in the last quarter, when Gary West was trading "frees" for 3s in a 69-point scoring orgy — 36 of those last-period points Noblesville's.

"We let them get away in the third quarter," Gary West coach Ivory Brown said.

Coverdale's 44 was the sixth-highest point total in semistate history, behind:

Steve Alford, New Castle .... 57 vs. Indianapolis Broad Ripple, 1983
George McGinnis, Ind. Washington .... 49 vs. Jac-Cen-Del, 1969
Jim Ligon, Kokomo .... 47 vs. Elkhart, 1962
Rick Mount, Lebanon .... 47 vs. Logansport, 1966
Terry Fuller, Anderson .... 47 vs. Gary Roosevelt, 1990
Kojak Fuller, Anderson .... 47 vs. Ben Davis, 1993

He hit 12 of 14 shots, including the only 3-pointer he tried, and he was 19-for-22 on free throws.

At Fort Wayne, Kokomo threw a little Basil Ball at a 25-1 East Noble team and came shockingly close to a shutout.

East Noble had no points at all at the end of the first quarter and just five for the first half.

Kokomo hit its first five shots, led 17-5 at halftime, and pushed the margin as high as 15 in the second half. The Wildkats took just 24 shots in the game and hit them at a .625 rate. "We were awfully efficient, offensively," coach Basil Mawbey said. Guards Michael Gaines (14) and Joe Sanders (11) did the Kokomo scoring, and center Chad LaCross (16) had nearly half of East Noble's.

At Evansville, New Albany took out another People's Choice team — Pike Central. The Bulldogs did it solidly, pushing out to an 18-8 first-quarter lead and crushing Pike Central's comeback attempt with a 22-point blitz in the first four minutes of the fourth quarter.

New Castle standout Steve Alford goes for two of his Semistate-record 57 points against Broad Ripple in 1983. (Photo courtesy Indiana High School Athletic Association, ©Jerry Clark)

Junior Adam Seitz led the Pike Central comeback try with 18 points, while Reggie Wheeler — blanked when Jeffersonville gave this 23-3 New Albany team its first defeat back in January — stung Pike Central for 25 points.

27

Bloomington N.   68
New Albany   59
*Terre Haute Semistate,
March 15*

BLOOMINGTON NORTH		NEW ALBANY
One as Bloomington North, 1997. Others in corporation, one: Bloomington High 1919	**STATE CHAMPIONSHIP**	1973
None as Bloomington North. Others in corporation, three: Bloomington High 1918, 1922, 1960	**OTHER TIMES IN FINAL FOUR**	8: 1911, 1950, 1952, 1955, 1959, 1980*, 1994, 1996* (* lost in championship game)
Two as Bloomington North: 1982, 1997. Others in corporation: Bloomington High 10 (first 1921, last 1971)	**REGIONAL CHAMPIONSHIPS**	15: first 1936; three in '90s, most recent 1997
10 as Bloomington North: first 1976; two in '90s, most recent 1997. Others in corporation, 28: Bloomington High 25 (first 1915, last 1971), Bloomington University 2: 1946, 1972; Unionville 1966.	**SECTIONAL CHAMPIONSHIPS**	41: first 1925; all eight in '90s, through 1997
Formed 1972 (Bloomington University, Unionville, part of Bloomington High)	**CONSOLIDATIONS**	None
No	**VOTE ON CHANGE TO CLASSES**	No
4A. (1,026; 70th of 95 in class)	**1997-98 CLASS (ENROLLMENT)**	4A. (1,774; 9th of 95 in class)
4A, Bedford North Lawrence, Bloomington South; 3A, Brown County, Edgewood; 2A, Eastern (Greene County). Bedford-North Lawrence site, Bloomington North 1997 champion	**1996-97 SECTIONAL OPPONENTS (1997-98 CLASSIFICATION)**	4A, Floyd Central; 2A, Eastern (Pekin); 1A, Graceland Christian, Lanesville, South Central. New Albany site and 1997 champion
Bloomington South, Columbus East, Columbus North, East Central, Martinsville	**1997-98 SECTIONAL OPPONENTS**	Bedford North Lawrence, Floyd Central, Jeffersonville, Jennings County, Seymour
28-1 (state champion)	**FINAL RECORD 1996-97**	23-4 (won sectional, regional; lost to Bloomington North in semistate final, 68-59)

From the South: North

It rarely works out so well. It wasn't true in any other semistate. But at Evansville, the teams that had been considered southern Indiana's best for most of the year, Bloomington North and New Albany — each of them at some time during the year No. 1-ranked in the state — were playing for the semistate championship.

It was a matchup of contrasting tournament histories. New Albany, defending champion of this semistate, had won it eight times, the most semistate titles by any team south of Anderson — Indianapolis included. Bloomington North, trying for its first, already was farther than any predecessor from its school had gone — not counting old Bloomington High, part of the North ancestry.

New Albany-Bloomington North was a game even the players looked forward to. After they had won their morning game with Vincennes, North's players watched a little of New Albany-Pike Central and left with the game in progress. On the way out, North's Kueth Duany and New Albany's Chad Hunter, on the court at the time, caught each other's attention. "We made a little eye contact and smiled at each other," Hunter said. "I played against him in AAU ball last summer. We were just looking forward to the game."

One for the Crazies

In the game's fifth minute, the score an unexciting 4 to 4, Djibril Kante of North caught a pass near the basket, wheeled to his right much more quickly than Hunter expected and slammed the ball through with an explosive, electric two-handed dunk.

Now, dunks are not unanimously admired, perhaps because they are not unanimously attainable. John Wooden, who certainly never made one, had several denied him when college rulesmakers outlawed the dunk after Wooden had Lew Alcindor for a year at UCLA. When the dunk came back in 1976-77, not only was Alcindor out of college play but so was Wooden, who all along had supported the anti-dunk rule. Wooden once proposed giving just a point for such a basket. Others see whole evenings of ESPN's *SportsCenter* with nothing but dunks and 3-point shots and wonder at a one-time team game's descent into flamboyance. Probably, none of the wonderers ever dunked a basketball, either.

This one by Kante, so very early in so very big a game, a lightning smash to the face that signaled the end of the sparring and the start of the fight, lit up this night.

"That," North's Ryan Reed recalled afterward, "was probably the thing that said, 'We can *do* it.' " Reed is a great believer in the inspirational power of a well-timed dunk. Even teammates of the dunker, he said, "get this real high feeling, really pumped up."

Duany recreated the play from memory: "Djibril and I were in the post. He made a nice spin move on his man. I didn't know what he was going to do. He went up and dunked it.

"A dunk just picks everybody up — especially the crowd, the Cougar Crazies, we call them. And once they get into it, they get us going.

"Djibril and I have a little contest between ourselves. I thought, '*I've* got to get one now.' "

Even on the Cougar bench, it was igniting. "It was kind of a sluggish start for both teams," Mario Wuysang said. "All of a sudden, Djibril gets the ball, spins — I look out there and the *rim* is bent down.

"I jumped up and yelled 'Yes!' The whole bench did. It pumped us up.

"I was confident from then on. 'OK, *that's* how this game is going to be.' "

A long way back

It's not as if New Albany saw the dunk and dived right into a tank. The Bulldogs had not just scoring leader Hunter but also Ricky Wright and Reggie Wheeler, all key performers in the drive to last year's state championship game. They were down just 10-7 till the North lead doubled when David McKinney beat the first-quarter buzzer with a 3-point basket.

It was the first of those in the game for the Cougars. Duany hit two of them 90 seconds apart to shoot North into a 25-14 lead. It was 29-17 at halftime, and New Albany was reeling.

"We seemed a little timid at first, not with a lot of intensity like we've been doing in the tournament," Hunter said. "I think we came out a little laid back, too relaxed, and they capitalized on it.

"At halftime, we made a couple of adjustments and came out and played well."

New Albany's big adjustment was to pick up the game's pace and challenge the Cougars with full-court pressure. Marcus Frazier hit for New Albany; McKinney answered with a 3. Hunter hit two free throws for New Albany; Jeremy Sinsabaugh beat the press with a 3. Hunter scored from the baseline for New Albany; Duany hit a 3. New Albany had come out sizzling, scoring three straight times, but its deficit grew from 12 to 15. "They were scoring but we were scoring better," Sinsabaugh said. "But I also knew they were a talented team and they could come back."

The North lead peaked at 40-23. Then the press began to work. Three straight times North turned the ball over, and the lead melted to 41-32. "Definitely there was some frustration, but they threw a pretty good press on us — big, long arms," Sinsabaugh said. "They're a talented team."

North coach Tom McKinney took a timeout, but the turnovers continued. So did the New Albany surge. Duany got his dunk, after picking off an offensive rebound, but New Albany kept coming. At 45-40, McKinney hit his third 3, but the quarter ended and the Bulldogs kept coming — to 48-46 after Wheeler's 3.

Duany drove the middle for a basket that put North up 51-48. Wheeler tried to fake Duany into the air, couldn't, and still, somehow, with Duany almost eye to eye, sank a remarkable shot from the deep right corner.

It was 51-51, North's once-huge lead gone, New Albany's once-steep mountain climbed. For both teams, the Final Four now was a six-minute game away.

Flashing through Duany's mind was one question: "What's happening to us?"

"We came out ready to play, doing everything right," he said. "Then all of a sudden in the third quarter, we got careless. We acted like the Harlem Globetrotters, playing around. We were throwing long bombs.

"They had a good team. They didn't want their season to end. They put a press on us and we panicked. Coach is usually calm, but when we came over there (at the timeout), he was intense. We went, 'Whoa! We'd better do what he wants.'

"He wanted it more than us, probably. He wanted it bad."

Block party

One of the Cougars' senior dependables, Ryan Reed, broke the tie with a baseline drive to a basket. He could have had a three-point play, but he missed the free throw. Duany shot upward to pick off the rebound and took it back up for a four-point sequence and 55-51 lead.

It was 57-53 when Kante made his second critical play. Hunter, a four-year player and the No. 1 scorer in talent-rich, basketball-rich New Albany history, knew it was step-up time.

And the ball was in his hands, near the basket. "I just wanted to get in position where I could score," Hunter said. "He tried to drive on me," Kante said. "I bumped him with my body. They could have called a foul." Hunter never argued for one. "Unfortunately, he was able to time my shot and get the good block."

It was more than that: like his dunk earlier, it was a play magnified by timing — a play not everybody could make, at a point in the game when it reverberated with overtones.

Overtones of finality.

Reed recovered the ball; at exactly 3:00 McKinney hit two free throws, and at 59-53, North was moving out. The Cougars scored on every possession the rest of the way, never let New Albany get closer than six, and won their first semistate, their first Final Four trip, 68-59 — a 17-8 victory in that closing six-minute game within a game.

"I think it was just Coach yelling at us in the timeout," said Duany, who scored 19 points and had a smothering block himself a minute after Kante's. "Once Coach got in our heads, we came down to earth."

Sinsabaugh (who matched Kante's 11 points, while McKinney had 14) said all he tried to think after the lead was gone was: "Just capitalize on each opportunity you have — especially now, when all the possessions are really critical.

"Down the stretch, when it was tied, we made the most of almost all our plays. But we had poise through the entire game, I thought."

Marr-ee-ohhh

Bloomington North had between 2,000 and 3,000 fans at this game, 120 twisty, two-lane miles from home. A whole lot of them made it onto the court afterward. A mob of students hoisted popular senior guard Wuysang onto their shoulders and bobbed him around like a cork in an ocean, all the while joyfully, not especially artfully shouting the sing-song chant they had come up with just for him:

"Marr-ee-ohhh . . . uh-ohhh . . . Marr-ee-ohhh . . . uh-ohh. . ."

It's a version of the guards' chant in *Wizard of Oz*. "I think they began that in the sectional," Wuysang said. "I didn't hear it till then. They did it the first time when I checked into the first sectional game. It made me nervous at the time. I felt like I *had* to produce. But that's what I like to do. I like to score.

"Then when I scored, they kept on doing it.

"Two girls at school tell me they made it up. I don't know why they do it. I guess they like me.

"It makes me feel good. It really gets me playing.

"So why stop?"

Especially on this night.

"It was such a great feeling. The kids rushed the court, lifted me up and did that.

"We knew we were in the Final Four, going to the Dome.

"Oh, it was great. Unreal."

No hurry to dress

Other Cougars were in clusters around the playing floor, talking to interviewers, exchanging hugs with their excited fans, taking their turns at cutting down the nets.

And in a locker room, maybe 200 feet away, there was no singing.

"I kept my jersey on," Chad Hunter said. "I just didn't want to take it off. It's been a long run for me, four years — so long this has become a family to me.

"Now I must move on."

The man who scored 1,463 points and played on a state runner-up team and a couple of others that at one time were ranked No. 1 in the state is moving on to Indiana State. He had 21 points in his final game, leading a team that finished 23-4 — 47-8 for its two years under coach Don Unruh, 92-15 for the four years that Hunter played.

"We made a real good run," Hunter said. "We thought we were going to be able to take control of the game — hopefully they wouldn't be able to withstand it. But they did.

"You can't take anything away from them. Those guys are very talented, and they play hard. They play to win. I wish the best for them.

"We came out a little slow at the start. Against a team like Bloomington North, you can't do that. You've got to get right on them and stay on them. They made the game theirs.

"We watched tapes on them. We knew they were good. We didn't think they would be able to handle our pressure. And they hit big shots when they needed them.

"Duany has improved a lot since last summer. You can tell he's been working. He's going to be an outstanding player.

"They've got a great team, they've got great athletes, and they've got a great chance of winning."

Elsewhere in Indiana

Evansville was the one semistate operating on Central time, the others all on Eastern, so the "Final Final Four" field was set as soon as this one was decided: Bloomington North vs. Fort Wayne winner Kokomo; Indianapolis winner Delta vs. Lafayette winner LaPorte.

Delta

Delta joined Bloomington North as a first-time State team, overtaking Franklin, 61-54. "Franklin really came out strong and shot it well (8-for-9 in taking a 23-9 first-quarter lead," Delta coach Paul Keller said. "They got us on our heels. We didn't expect them to run the floor as much as they did. I was just telling the kids, 'Chip away at it.' We had a great second quarter (pulling to within 35-33 by halftime)."

It was another Patrick "Petey" Jackson show — 27 points, including five 3-pointers, and he directed an offense that had just seven turnovers in this game, 15 for the day. But in a game when the four other starters scored just 11 points, Delta got 12, including 6-for-6 on fourth-quarter free throws, from 6-foot senior sub Chad Oakley, who had averaged just under four points a game going into the biggest one he had ever played. "It definitely was a surprise," Keller said. "He really never shot as much as he did here."

Mark Pitcher, the only starter Franklin coach Dave Clark had back when he started building this 24-3 team, closed out a grand career with 21 points.

Keller struggled with reality. "You dream of winning sectionals," he said. "When I went to Delta, my dream was to win a regional.

"We've just gone past that. It's an awesome feeling."

LaPorte

Keller was no more thrilled than LaPorte coach Joe Otis. Two years after a team with the same nucleus as this one went 3-19, his aged-under-fire team topped Noblesville, 69-59, to get to the State for the first time in 53 years.

The Slicers did it shooting — 26 of their 47 shots from 3-point range, 10 of them good. "That is the chemistry of their team," Noblesville coach Dave McCollough said. "They have three guys who can do that."

Brothers Ben (20 points) and Greg (14) Tonagel and forward Chris Bootcheck (17 points) were the three McCollough had in mind. His own junior star, Tom Coverdale, surely a bit weary from the 44-point second-game effort that got Noblesville by Gary West and into the championship game, had 20 for his 22-5 team.

"This was a big statement for us," Otis said. "Those (Harrison and Noblesville) were two really good teams.

"We have an exceptional group of kids. They endured the most painful season in LaPorte High School history. Even though they were young, they hated losing. Ben Tonagel wrote on the bottom of one of the team posters: 'LaPorte High School, State Champs 1997.'

"They have a sense of humor like mine — kinda smart-alecky. Greg Tonagel filled out a newspaper survey asking for the best Coach Otis story. He said, 'Any one that's less than 15 minutes long.'

"Maybe that's why we're still around. They don't fear anybody.

"We've gotten a lot better in the last month. Successful teams do that at tournament time." LaPorte moved on at 22-4.

Kokomo

Nobody played better in the semistate round than Kokomo, which followed its defensive gem against East Noble by shutting down DeKalb and Mr. Basketball Luke Recker, 69-46.

The Wildkats (23-4) led 37-17 at halftime, after letting East Noble score just five first-half points earlier in the day.

Recker closed his high school career with a 21-point game, but he labored to get them against Kokomo coach Basil Mawbey's 2-3 zone. Recker was 4-for-17 on 3-point shots. "I saw other teams trying to double-team him," Mawbey said. "All that did was let the other players get easy layups. We just had to make sure he had hard shots."

Kokomo point guard Michael Gaines had the primary defensive role against Recker, and starred on offense, too. Recker called Gaines "a great kid, a great point guard, a great catalyst. When they got that big lead, it was hard to come back on them because he is such a good point guard."

Recker's coach, Cliff Hawkins, said the Kokomo zone "forces you to shoot from the outside and we're not very good from there (the other DeKalb 3-point shooters were 0-for-8). We needed a full-court game. We needed to make them play differently, but they never had to because they were in control the whole time." DeKalb bowed out 25-4.

Gaines had 15 points and five assists. The Wildkats' sturdy offensive leader, Herman Gaines, hit seven of the eight shots he took and scored 20.

Kokomo shot .560 against DeKalb and .581 for the day. Mawbey, the one coach in the "Final Final Four" who had been there before (winning with Connersville in 1983, returning with Kokomo in 1989), is renowned for that zone defense. On this day, he said with a smile, "We played awfully well offensively, too."

28

Bloomington N. 50
Kokomo 43

State semifinals, March 22

BLOOMINGTON NORTH		KOKOMO
One as Bloomington North, 1997. Others in corporation, one: Bloomington High 1919	**STATE CHAMPIONSHIP**	1961
None as Bloomington North. Others in corporation, three: Bloomington High 1918, 1922, 1960	**OTHER TIMES IN FINAL FOUR**	Seven: 1925*, 1941, 1944*, 1959*, 1962, 1989*, 1997 (* lost in championship game)
Two as Bloomington North: 1982, 1997. Others in corporation: Bloomington High 10 (first 1921, last 1971)	**REGIONAL CHAMPIONSHIPS**	32: first 1925; four in '90s, most recent 1997. Also in corporation: Kokomo Haworth 1970
10 as Bloomington North: first 1976; two in '90s, most recent 1997. Others in corporation, 28: Bloomington High 25 (first 1915, last 1971), Bloomington University 2: 1946, 1972; Unionville 1966.	**SECTIONAL CHAMPIONSHIPS**	66: first 1916; last seven in '90s, through 1997. Also in corporation: Kokomo Haworth two, 1970, 1972
Formed 1972 (Bloomington University, Unionville, part of Bloomington High)	**CONSOLIDATIONS**	Kokomo Haworth 1984
No	**VOTE ON CHANGE TO CLASSES**	No
4A. (1,026; 70th of 95 in class)	**1997-98 CLASS (ENROLLMENT)**	4A. (1,527; 22nd of 95 in class)
4A, Bedford North Lawrence, Bloomington South; 3A, Brown County, Edgewood; 2A, Eastern (Greene County). Bedford-North Lawrence site, Bloomington North 1997 champion	**1996-97 SECTIONAL OPPONENTS (1997-98 CLASSIFICATION)**	3A, Western; 2A, Eastern (Howard), Maconaquah, Northwestern, Taylor. Kokomo site and 1997 champion.
Bloomington South, Columbus East, Columbus North, East Central, Martinsville	**1997-98 SECTIONAL OPPONENTS**	Harrison, Lafayette Jefferson, Logansport, McCutcheon
28-1 (state champion)	**FINAL RECORD 1996-97**	23-5 (won sectional, regional, semi-state; lost to Bloomington North in state semifinal, 50-43)

Nay, Wildkats

Kokomo is a Native American word that means high school basketball. OK, if you want to be picky, it really doesn't. Kokomo was a great Miami chief and the original village was on a Miami reservation. But to modern Americans and some not so modern, Kokomo *seems* to mean Indiana high school basketball.

Consider that:

■ In 1944, when boys book author John R. Tunis wanted to extend his series into high school basketball, he came to Kokomo and wrote *Yea! Wildcats!* As Milan in 1986 became Hollywood's Hickory, Kokomo High became Springfield for Tunis, but it was the Wildcats all the way — or, almost. The star of that Kokomo team was 6-5 center Tom Schwartz. "John stayed in our home with my parents and me for a couple of weeks," said Schwartz, Indiana's Mr. Basketball in 1945. "He did a lot of things with my dad. He sat on the bench with us every game till the final game, with Evansville Bosse." Tunis took great liberty with the story line but didn't even change the names of the teams Kokomo met down the tournament trail. "Springfield" had Muncie semifinal victories over Muncie Burris and defending state champion (in the book as well as in actuality) Fort Wayne Central, an upset of No. 1-ranked Anderson in the afternoon round at the State and a loss in the championship game to Evansville Bosse, with its little backcourt star — Broc Jerrel in real life, Jerry

Kates in the book. There was no problem recognizing the players. Tom Schwartz became Tom Shaw, Kokomo's Walt McFatridge was Springfield's Walt MacDonald, John Leslie was John Little, Chuck Farrington was Chuck Foster, and, in a mild switch of tactics, Gene Turner was Jim Turner.

■ In 1980, noted national writer Herbert Warren Wind came to Kokomo and wrote a story that ran on 25 pages of *The New Yorker* — a story about basketball and Indiana. "Not long after basketball was invented," Wind's story began, "the game became particularly identified throughout the country with the state of Indiana. I know that when I was growing up, in the late 1920s and '30s, in a basketball-oriented town in southeastern Massachusetts, somehow or other the word reached us that Indiana was *the* hotbed of the game — that it was played with more intensity there than anywhere else and was also played better." The arrival of Larry Bird on the national scene had alerted Wind that Indiana still must be special. (Actually, Bird made all of Boston Indiana-conscious. April 3, 1982, the Kennedy clan came to Bloomington for the marriage of RFK Jr., and Emily Black. Of course, there was a Kennedy touch football game, after which a Hoosier participant suggested that next time the game should be basketball. "Oh, yeah," said JFK and RFK nephew Stephen Smith, Jr., "I guess basketball *is* the big thing in Indiana since Larry Bird.") Herbert Warren Wind reacted to his Bird-Indiana connection by going to Kokomo in January to check things out for his *New Yorker* story. He spent a few weeks with the Wildcats (they didn't use the Kokomo K in Wildkats then) and stayed in touch through the tournaments. Kokomo's 19-4 season ended with a 55-54 regional loss to what Wind called "a newly consolidated high school close to Muncie," Delta.

In 1980, Basil Mawbey was in his 10th year as a head coach, his first at Connersville. Basil had been around: a graduate of Deedsville High in northern Miami County and of Ball State, a head coach at West Washington way down south, at Delta (is this the other place all roads lead to?), at Angola in the state's northeastern corner, then at Connersville in the state's southeastern quadrant. In his first Connersville season, he had a regional champion that lost by eight points to eventual state champion Indianapolis Broad Ripple, but his best team was coming. A couple of 1980 freshmen, twin brothers Mike and Chris Heineman, were to lead Mawbey's fourth Connersville team to the 1983 state championship.

Three years after that, with a 144-31 seven-year record at Connersville, he took the job at Kokomo, a county away from where he grew up. His average season there has been 19-5, so things haven't changed much since Herbert Warren Wind blew through.

A day for D

They have changed a lot since Jimmy Rayl. Rayl once hit the basket that won a semistate game, 92-90. In winning the Fort Wayne semistate the week before this, Mawbey's Wildkats playing their "Basil Ball" scored 116 points and gave up just 82 — in *two* games.

In the first half of those two games, East Noble and DeKalb scored 22 points combined against Mawbey's 2-3 zone defense: 32 minutes, 22 points, by teams that were 50-4 going into their Kokomo games.

"I've known Basil for a long time," North coach Tom McKinney said. "His teams play great defense." And slow offense? "Basil," McKinney put it, "has a philosophy that we're not afraid of close games, we're going to play the game this way, and if you get behind a few points, we're going to shorten the game."

The two's relationship did go back a long way. Mawbey's state championship team at Connersville lost just two games; one of those was 78-68 to McKinney's Franklin team, by far the most points that a Mawbey team allowed in a game.

Mawbey told of taking teams to Bloomington in November to watch Indiana coach Bob Knight's teams at work. He'd keep his team there overnight, and McKinney has given him practice time on North's court, he said. "A trademark of Tom is they're a very good defensive team," he said. "One time down there I watched them practice. It looked like they were going through a Marine training camp. I know they're going to play awfully hard."

In a state that has revered its shooters and loved shoot-outs, this "Final Final Four" was to begin with a game where points did not figure to be abundant.

Twins with hard noses

North's Ryan Reed scored the game's first basket. The play was not distinguished so much by the shot as by the move Reed made to get himself open and the perfectly timed pass from Djibril Kante that made the basket easy. The deft, quick, short inside passes that changed a clogged post area into an open layup by this point of the tournament run had become a Cougar trademark, and an indication of how far and how fast Kante was developing in his role.

As much of a trademark was Reed's scoring the first basket.

Final Four pressure, Kokomo's stiff defense, the vast space that is supposed to make shooters hate the downtown Indianapolis building built and financed as the Hoosier Dome — if any player on the court was capable of playing right through all those things it was Ryan Reed.

Or Matt Reed. Who really could tell the difference except by peeking at the uniform numbers (Ryan 25, Matt 45)?

They're the twin sons of two X-ray technicians, and the way they play keeps their parents busy. Ryan played most of the year with a sore left ankle and tendinitis in the left knee. The last regular-season game against Seymour, he injured the other ankle. Matt had a much more scary injury the year before: a cracked neck vertebra. He got up from the injury, shot the free throws, stayed in the game and scored 18 points including the game-winning, last-second basket — against rival South. Then he checked it out. He missed a few games, returned and wore a neck brace so he could play out the season. The day after it ended, he was playing basketball with friends and shattered an ankle. "Last year was rough," he said. "They're pretty hard-nosed kids," McKinney said.

They're mirror-image twins. Robert (for their father) Matthew Reed is 18 minutes older, left-handed, parts his hair on the left. William (for their maternal grandfather) Ryan Reed is right-handed, parts his hair on the right. "My grandparents can't tell us apart,"

Ryan said. Matt's theory is the reason the two rarely play together — Ryan a seasonlong starter their senior year, Matt usually the first player off the bench — is "the coaches can't tell us apart. They don't want to mix us up."

They do compete — fiercely, against opponents, though both deny there's anything special about the way they play. "Even in seventh and eighth grade, people said, 'Boy, those Reed boys hustle,'" Matt said. "I've always thought, no, we don't. I'm not athletic — Jeremy Sinsabaugh is athletic. Everything I've done my whole life I've had to work for — in classes, in sports, everything." Ryan said, "I just don't know how to play any other way. I'm not a Larry Bird just dead-eye shooting the 3. I'm not 6-8 and 230, just ripping the rim down. I've got to find my own little place where I fit in.

"I'd say a whole lot of twins are competitive."

Holding hands and walking

With them, it all started at home. "Everything as we've grown up — tests, soccer — I didn't care if I beat anybody else, but I wanted to beat him," Ryan said. Their rivalry is so intense they never play against each other. Not even the first times they played this thing, the Final Four. "When we were little, we'd pretend we were in the State tournament — he'd be Michael Jordan and I'd be Magic Johnson," Ryan said. "That little bar that goes with a curtain, we'd go up and dunk on that for hours.

"But we always made sure we were on the same team. When we got older, we'd play on our outdoor court — 3 . . . 2 . . . 1 . . . last-second shot for the State championship. Together. Because every time we went against each other, a fight would break out.

"In practice sometimes, we'd be on opposite sides and I'd say, 'Hey, I can't guard him. There'll be a fight.' "

Indeed, when coaches had dared to pit them against each other, there had been some fights — "not in high school, but in junior high," Matt said. "Oh, there'd be a brawl. On the court, we had each other's moves down. Neither one of us was going to score and there'd be blood shed. Even in the backyard, one of us would make a move and there'd be a shove: 'How do you like *that*? I know that move. Try that other one you like so much.'

"In junior high, our coach had a rule: if you got in a fight, you had to walk around the court holding the other guy's hand. I don't know how many times Ryan and I held hands and walked around that court. Regularly. 'Well, it's 3:30, the Reeds will be going by here holding hands in a minute.'

"We had a drill called Four Corners. The guys diagonally across from each other were on the same team — the coach would roll a ball out, two guys would go for the ball, and the one who got it would kick it out to his teammate for a layup. Oh, that was my favorite drill. The other guy would always *let* me get the ball. Unless it was Ryan. Then the ball would never come out. We'd both have a hold on that ball, rolling around on the floor."

"When we're playing against each other it's bad," Ryan said. "But when we're on the same team, I can throw no-look passes and *know* where he is."

"It's a lot of fun," Matt said. "I wouldn't change (being a twin) if I could. You get away with a lot of things. 'I didn't do that, it was Ryan. Durn him. Trying to get me in trouble again.'"

"I don't know what it's like not being a twin," Ryan said. "But I think being a twin's got way more pluses than minuses. That's my best friend in the whole world."

Those two had to wrestle with a situation in which Ryan started and Matt didn't. "This year, it *was* hard — junior year starting, senior year sitting," Matt said. Djibril Kante's development had left room for just one Reed on the front line. "It was real hard to cope with. I actually had people say, 'Your brother's a lot better player than you, isn't he?' To morons like that, I just said, 'Yeah, he is.' But it bugged me."

"We talked it out and both came up with the same thing," Ryan said. "I didn't know why I was starting in front of him, but I was. He made a lot of plays for us." At Anderson, Ryan was virtually out of the picture that game because of his ankle injury. "Matt just stepped up," Ryan said. "He was making plays all night. He fouled out. We thought about putting my brace and my jersey on him and letting him play."

That probably isn't altogether a joke. "We switch classes every April Fool's Day," Ryan said. "We just got caught once. In seventh grade. Our history teacher was a twin himself."

Ryan was the one who put North onto the scoreboard 32 seconds into the Final Final Four.

Colt on the loose

Matt came in for Kante with 2:33 left in the first quarter and Kokomo leading, 8-7. The Cougars were having an awful time scoring. Kueth Duany, his whole family in the stands — even brother Duany, whose Wisconsin season was over — was feeling the biggest load and shooting the worst. He tried two inside shots, two 3-pointers, even two free throws and didn't hit a thing in the quarter that ended with Kokomo leading, 10-7.

Herman Fowler was the Wildkat North couldn't handle. Fowler looked like a tall Joe Frazier at 6-3, 220. Mawbey joked that he "probably could start for the Colts." Mentioning Fowler tended to put Mawbey in a merry mood, because he had represented one of the major question marks when Mawbey went to work with his new team in October. "He had been a post-up player," Mawbey said. On this Kokomo team, he had to move to the perimeter. "That probably has been the key to this team, his adapting and doing an excellent job," Mawbey said.

He had six of Kokomo's 10 points in the first quarter. He opened the second with a 3-point basket, added another two minutes later, then faked the next time downcourt and got himself a jump shot that he hit. Kokomo had the Cougars down, 20-10. Fowler alone was ahead of them by four.

There had been one Kokomo storm cloud. In between Fowler's 3s, center Matt Brady drew his second foul and sat down. Fowler's second came just after his jump shot. He also went out, with 3:57 left in the half. Kokomo didn't score again before halftime, turning the ball over six times in that stretch.

Duany drew his third foul with 2:07 left. He still hadn't scored, 0-for-7 now, plus the two missed free throws. But he had helped with his defense, the phase that had taken over this game. Even with the long, long dry spell, the Kokomo lead shrank to just 20-16 at halftime.

Final Four MVP Jeremy Sinsabaugh launches a three-point basket against Kokomo. (Photo courtesy Bloomington Herald-Times)

Mawbey knew the Wildkats had missed a chance to bury North. He teaches a disciplined game and coaches that way. He always takes a major player out with two first-half fouls, to be sure he has him the second half. As absolute as that rule is for him, he admitted that during that flurry of second-quarter turnovers, he did look down the bench at Fowler, considering taking a timeout and returning him for the last minute and a half. "But we're up five," he said. "We've got very good penetrating guards out there — we should have been able to take it to the basket. We did. We got a travel and two layins inside that didn't go in.

"At halftime, with Fowler with two fouls and Brady with two, I thought we were in good shape."

Sinsabaugh, on a roll

North needed halftime. The combination of Dome and Kokomo zone had the Cougars wondering. "They say as big as it is it's a great place to play," Duany said of the huge arena. "I didn't like it."

"We were 0-for-10 on 3-pointers," Tom McKinney said. "Everybody talked about playing in the Dome. I said, 'Keep shooting. They'll fall.'

"The only thing I told Jeremy (Sinsabaugh) was, 'Let's move the ball a little bit before we shoot it.' I liked the tempo of the game. On videotape, I watched teams pass the ball 18 or 20 times against their zone, all on the perimeter, and then take the shot they could have had on the first pass."

Mario Wuysang had missed two of those 3s and hadn't scored. "Usually against a zone you get shots," he said. "It was hard for us to find them." Sinsabaugh also was scoreless at halftime, 0-for-3, all the shots 3s. "I don't know if it was the big gym — I think it was just nerves," Sinsabaugh said. "All I know is I couldn't shoot a lick."

Sinsabaugh dutifully moved the ball inside to Djibril Kante for a basket opening the second half. Kokomo's Aaron Alexander countered with his first basket. Then, from the right wing, Sinsabaugh fired a 3.

"That shot was the ugliest thing I've ever seen," Sinsabaugh said. "It bounced up and fell back in." Up? It shot off the back of the rim way high into the air, the clunk so hard the ball would have cleared the first wave of inside rebounders if normally directed. Somehow, this one, like a pop fly in a phone booth, plunked straight down into the basket.

Shooters have a remarkable ability to strip away everything else and remember "I shot, and it went in." Like a golfer penciling onto his card a lucky par, they don't ask how, they ask how many.

So, of course when Sinsabaugh got open again seconds later, he forgot all that first-half misery and couldn't wait to get another 3-point shot up. "Oh, yeah," he said, "the shooter's mentality is to shoot it until you hit. If you miss, keep shooting until you hit. Now I'd hit, so I'd keep shooting till I missed."

"Everything after that first one was all net."

Mawbey took a timeout after Sinsabaugh's second 3 tied the game at 24. Already, he'd had to pull Brady again. He drew his third foul barely over a minute into the second half.

After the timeout, Sinsabaugh hit another 3. Kokomo's 13th turnover was a charging call against Fowler, his third, and North followed with a David McKinney pass that Duany turned into a dunk — at last, his first points of the game. It was 29-24. But Fowler had stayed in with his foul peril; he powered up a basket that became a three-point play and drew Duany's fourth foul, then hit another basket to tie the game.

'It was like they didn't see me'

Now there was 2:30 left in the third quarter.

Tom McKinney ordered a stall. His son, David, backed to the right side of the court near the center stripe, put the ball on his hip, and — with Kokomo still back in its zone — let the seconds tick away. Into minutes.

With both Duany and Kante on the bench, McKinney said, "we had a mismatch on the floor — we had three guards and they had three forwards. I made the decision: let's play it right here."

This was Basil Ball and Basil was "very happy — we're getting rest for Herman and also getting Brady to come back in fresh the fourth quarter with two fouls to go."

With time nearing 0:10, David McKinney — who hadn't moved, himself or the basketball, all that time — made one pass, got the ball back and slipped it to Ryan Reed just above the foul line. His jump shot was perfect. Kokomo hurried the ball downcourt and Alexander got an open shot to tie from close range along the baseline. It missed. "Reed stuck it in from 15 with Eric Farrell coming at him," Mawbey said. "It was a tough shot. Then Alexander was wide open from four feet and it didn't drop down.

"Key plays like that happen. Sometimes you get the ring, and sometimes you don't."

Wuysang, scoreless since the Vincennes game in the morning round of the semistate, sank a 3 opening the fourth quarter and Kokomo never caught up. It was 37-34 when Brady picked up his fourth and fifth fouls just a few seconds apart. The day was over for Kokomo's leading rebounder and No. 2 scorer, who scored just two points and played an official 10 minutes.

He left amid a Wuysang flurry. The North senior guard came up with a loose ball and got it to Sinsabaugh for a 3. Wuysang intercepted a Brady pass and took the ball to the basket to draw Brady's fifth foul. He intercepted another pass, resulting in a North free throw, then stole the ball one more time and got it to Ryan Reed for a layup. "It seemed like the ball just started coming to me on defense," Wuysang said. "It was like they didn't see me and just kinda gave it to me. One pass even hit me in the chest.

"But there were so many people out there. I was pumped up, and when I'd make a basket, our crowd would just go crazy. That was the best feeling of all."

Fowler still had two 3s left, the second pulling Kokomo within 45-40 with 1:35 left. That's as close as the Kats got on a day when Fowler scored 27 points and all his teammates managed 16. "We couldn't stop him," McKinney said. "I thought we played pretty good defense overall."

"They did a nice job defensively," Mawbey said. "They're very physical. Wuysang played awfully well in that stretch. There were just a lot of little things that went their way.

David McKinney held the ball for more than two minutes as Bloomington North set up a last-second shot to close the third quarter against Kokomo.

Mario Wuysang (13) cashes in a steal during a fourth-quarter flurry that saw him open the period with a three-point field goal and finish with 10 points. (Both photos courtesy Bloomington Herald-Times)

"When Brady went out, I think our kids dropped their heads a little bit, knowing the big man wasn't in there. There was a lot of contact down low. He ended up with a lot of fouls, as did Duany.

"Fowler was exceptional. I really think in the last eight to 10 games he has developed into an all-state player. He's very physical, he hit four out of eight 3s, he hit free throws — just a great job."

Sinsabaugh had 15 North points, all in the second half. Wuysang had 10, all the last quarter. Ryan Reed had 13 points, a basket a quarter, steady throughout. What would you have thought, McKinney was asked, if you had been told before the game Duany would score just two points?

"Fortunately," McKinney said, "nobody told me that."

29

Delta   **57**

LaPorte   **56**

*State semifinals,
March 22*

LAPORTE		DELTA
None	STATE CHAMPIONSHIP	None
Two: 1944, 1997	TIMES IN FINAL FOUR	1997* (* lost in championship game)
Seven: 1925, 1926, 1930, 1939, 1944, 1991, 1997	REGIONAL CHAMPIONSHIPS	One: 1997
22: first 1925; four in '90s, most recent 1997	SECTIONAL CHAMPIONSHIPS	Five: 1980, 1985, 1989, 1993, 1997
Kingsbury, Mill Creek, Stillwell 1964; Union Township 1965	CONSOLIDATIONS	Formed 1967: Albany, Desoto, Eaton, Royerton
No	VOTE ON CHANGE TO CLASSES	No
4A. (1,519; 24th of 95 in class)	1997-98 CLASS (ENROLLMENT)	3A. (700; 32nd of 96 in class)
4A, Michigan City; 3A, New Prairie; 1A, Michigan City Marquette, Westville. Michigan City site; LaPorte 1997 champion	1996-97 SECTIONAL OPPONENTS (1997-98 CLASSIFICATION)	4A, Jay County; 1A, Monroe Central, Union City, Wapahani, Wes-Del. Jay County site; Delta 1997 champion
Chesterton, Hobart, Michigan City, Portage, Valparaiso	1997-98 SECTIONAL OPPONENTS	Blackford, Elwood, Mississinewa, Muncie Southside, Yorktown
22-5 (won sectional, regional, semistate; lost to Delta in state semifinal, 57-56)	FINAL RECORD 1996-97	24-5 (won sectional, regional, semistate; lost to Bloomington North in state championship game, 75-54)

The Final Finalist

There was, in the air at this State finals, a restrained but unmistakable anger. One of the reasons nearly 28,000 people were here this day where 21,000 had come the year before was the pulling power of passion, of believers disenfranchised, unable to do anything but glower as they watched something sacred to them desecrated in the name of improvement.

There were posters and T-shirts and ballcaps at the same time hailing this day, this gathering, and railing about why this 87th tournament had to be the last of its kind. Among the 28,000, there must have been thousands who were all for the change that was coming — simple percentages say that. But those people didn't wear T-shirts or wave signs. There was no outward celebration, only regret, of the unofficial title given to this: the Final Final Four.

For a day awash in so much sentiment about Final Fours past, this tournament had worked down to a foursome with a notably new look. Three of the four combined for a history of just one past Final Four trip: by LaPorte in 1944, the 53-year gap between its advancements the longest ever for a two-time Final Four team. First-timers Bloomington North and Delta were relatively new schools, in their 25th and 30th years of existence. Kokomo, a one-time winner and seven-time Final Four team before this day, had been the only veteran of these doings. And now it was gone, the Final Final Four down to a title-less three.

355

Actually, for a tournament accused of having evolved into an aristocracy closed to all but the same year-to-year high-enrollment regulars, this field was more normal than the one of a year ago. The four big schools in that one — Ben Davis, New Albany, Lafayette Jeff and Warsaw — represented the first time in 35 years all Final Four teams came in with at least one State championship, just the third such field in the 62 years of semistates.

By contrast, this year's four with three non-winners and just one former champion was the sixth like that in the last 10 years. And with Kokomo's loss the winner now was sure to be the seventh first-time champion in nine years — more first-time winners in so short a period than in even the first nine tournaments, or in any such stretch in the next 50-plus years.

This is a monopolized tournament?

Historian, hysteria, hysterics

No one was happier to be a first-timer at this party than LaPorte coach Joe Otis.

This day, this week brought Joe Otis out in all his hues. And there are many. Joe is a coach. A teacher. A historian. A poet. A sentimentalist. A writer. A comedian. Maybe a bit out of step in every one of those fields, willingly. Probably a Mort Sahl devotee in his early days — the '60s political satirist's wry stiletto wielded anew and applied deftly, often, by the coach of, of all names, the Slicers.

Dozens of coaches felt deeply aggrieved by this massive change they were powerless to stop. Joe Otis was their Bob Dylan, giving their song of outrage lyrics.

Before the class basketball vote, Otis composed "To the Keepers of the Flame," an open letter to the IHSAA's Board of Control seeking to save "the crown jewel of high school sports tournaments in any state." He mentioned his background, born in Canada ("just like Dr. Naismith") to a Hungarian mother ("so I am the immigrant child of an immigrant"), named for a Hungarian grandfather whose three sons "fought in WWI and WWII, with the 'bad guys.' I know in my heart that they were good people who were given a difficult

Coach Joe Otis led his team from the "most painful season in LaPorte history" to the Final Four in 1997. (Photo courtesy Indiana Basketball Hall of Fame)

task. And I know in my heart that the IHSAA administrators, board members and class study committee members are also good people who have been given a difficult task.

"Win or lose, I hope this debate does not sink to the level of the Republican Primary."

That is Joe Otis: high-principled, capable of lofty expression, incapable of repressing a sassy sense of humor.

That letter failed in its purpose, so Otis composed a follow-up work: "Joe's New Tournament."

Its premise was that the new spirit of increasing opportunities for success could be met far better than this change that will add just eight-tenths of one percent of Indiana's basketball-playing schools to the champions' list. "Joe's new tournament" proposed 64 classes of six teams each, with 64 state champions — and 64 Trester Awards.

"Your first victory makes you a sectional champion; second, a regional champion; third, a semistate champion; win four and crown yourself State Champs! You've earned it. Start building those trophy cases today."

There was more, of course: a Competitive Adjustment Factor in each game ("enrollment differential times tax base times average height and weight per player, divided by seating capacity of gym minus the number of advanced degrees by faculty — plus any team playing a defending state champion will receive 10 points)," and the FFQ, Fabulous Fourth Quarter, in which all points are tripled. He offered a sample of news coverage to come: "Tiny Moonville (enrollment 112) upset mighty Tigertown (enrollment 116), 176-175, in the 2A state championship game. Trailing 175-164, Elmer Shotwell canned his sixth nine of the FFQ and was fouled with no time on the clock. He calmly connected to complete the 12-point play."

There were four pages of details, including a double elimination-plus one plan, giving any team that loses its first two games a third chance. And, since Joe's tournament was solely for boys basketball, a P.S.: "If you are having trouble coming up with a new tournament format for *your* sport, go talk to the slow-pitch softball guys at the park some summer weekend. They probably don't even realize they are on the leading edge of tournament reform."

Driving and musing

Joe Otis drove a van back to LaPorte from West Lafayette after the semistate victory over Noblesville, the net-cutting, the interviews and the celebrating.

"I had most of the team with me," he said. It's an 83-mile trip. It was a mellow evening, and his mind drifted in a reverie of playbacks. "We went through Medaryville," he said. "I saw my first high school basketball game there, at the American Legion Hall. My cousin took me. I was about 7." Medaryville no longer has a basketball identification. The school merged with Francesville to form one of those directionally anonymous schools, West Central, in 1967.

LaPorte's Ben Tonagel shoots over Delta's Nathan Calvert during the afternoon session of the 1997 State Tournament. (Photo courtesy Indiana High School Athletic Association, ©Mark Wick)

About 15 miles uproad, the Otis van crossed into LaPorte County and got a police escort all the way to the school gym. It was nearing midnight by then but LaPorte wasn't sleepy. "There were 2,300 at the gym — really pumped up," Otis said.

While he was driving, and musing, he was listening to his players chatter. "They talked like champions," he said.

He had watched them grow into that status — kids who two years ago he had been forced to play before they were ready in "the most painful season in LaPorte history," just two regular-season victories. Three of his junior starters now, guards Greg Tonagel and Jeff Ballard and forward Nick Bernel, were freshmen on that team, and Ben Tonagel and Jeremy Hoehne, sophomores then, also played. "Ballard and Bernel came up the last five games and played in the sectional," Otis said. "Ballard started those games. Greg had started all along. He's a great talent.

"Ballard and Greg have April birthdays — I wish their parents had delayed their start of kindergarten, but I can't say much about that now. But in that sectional they were 14 years old, starting in the backcourt. We actually won a game in the sectional to up our win total to three before we got beat by Michigan City."

Jack Armstrong and friends

Otis puts his mind on free-flow in talking about those kids:

"The Tonagels' dad played a little bit at Purdue, so they have always been in love with Mackey Arena. They were thrilled enough that they played really well . . . The best thing about them is they have two younger brothers. I'm not going to run out of Tonagels for a while . . . Ben Tonagel is very strong — 6-3, 180, bench presses 225. He hit two 3s against Plymouth that were probably 30 feet out. Their kid guarding him went to Jack Edison and said, 'Where *do* you want me to pick him up?' Phenomenal shots. He's probably 4-for-4 from beyond 25 feet . . . Great kid. If they remake *Jack Armstrong, All-American Boy*, he should get the lead . . .

"Greg is a very smart player but sometimes he thinks he's Michael Jordan. He has to remember he's Greg Tonagel. He had a great day in Lafayette and a tremendous regional . . .

"Chris Bootcheck (the highest-scoring non-Tonagel on the team at 13.9 a game) is an outstanding baseball prospect, heavily recruited as a pitcher. He's a true thoroughbred — he can run all day long. I'd love to see him run the 400 meters, but I don't think (seven-time state champion baseball coach Ken) Schreiber is going to loan him out to the track team . . .

"Billy Spence, our little left-handed guy, is a hog farmer . . . has his own gym. His uncle bought the old Mill Creek School (a rural high school merged into LaPorte in 1964) . . . He can fill it up on 3s (58.8 percent for the year) . . . I guess it helps to own your own gym . . .

"We started 13-0. You kinda think you're unbeatable at that point. Then we lost four of our next five . . . We never panicked. We've started the same five guys all year long. I've never done that in my coaching career. We had a plan in mind and it worked out.

"We've brought our kids down to the State every year. The first time I was there was in 1967 as a (Valparaiso High) freshman. We sat in the top row at Hinkle Fieldhouse. Sparrows were flying around. I didn't even realize I was in the cheap seats, I was so excited to be there. Bob Ford (of champion Evansville North) broke Oscar Robertson's Sweet 16 scoring record that year. That's the glory of our State tournament — magnificent performances in the Final Four by legendary players."

As a Northwestern sophomore, Otis recalled, "I had to guard Ford in a box-and-one. Only time in my life I've thrown up. I started three games that year and that was one of them. I held him to 11 points and we won — knocked them out of the Big Ten race. That was my biggest thrill as a college player."

The world according to Virgil, and Tex

Otis played as Joe Hill in setting the Valparaiso career scoring record, 1,111 points, under his first big coaching hero, Virgil Sweet, at Valparaiso. Friday night, his team through its Dome workout, Otis called Sweet. "Now I'm ready," he said. He remembered Sweet's off-court counseling "about self-discipline, working hard, being ambitious, wanting to be somebody. He always said, 'Nothing good happens after 11 p.m.' At the time, I thought that was a foolish, adult-type thing to say. Now I'm saying it, because I don't know how many times I've picked up the paper and seen where high school kids get in trouble, and it's always at 1:53 or 3:30 in the morning."

The name thing? Otis' father and mother, who had divorced, remarried later in his life and he retook his father's name. His dad was a military man. "I'm the only guy 45 whose father was injured in Vietnam," he said.

Otis played at Northwestern under his second big coaching hero, Tex Winter. "The guy's a genius, and not just on X's and O's," Otis said. "I'm a history person. I loved to ask him questions. At Kansas State he had won eight conference championships in 16 years. 'You were like (Ohio State's) Fred Taylor,' I said. 'Why did you leave?' He said, 'I got up one morning, looked in the mirror and didn't like the person I had become. I had to browbeat them so badly to get them up to fans' expectations that it stopped being fun.' I really gained from being around him and gaining that perspective, that there is more to the game than just what happens on the floor." Tex Winter is a big name in basketball even today, the assistant coach who contributed his triangle offense to the Chicago Bulls' greatness. "He taught everything — footwork, faking," Otis said. "He made a believer out of me." So you run the Tex Winter triangle? "Not much. Actually, I run a lot of (Bob Knight's) motion. I'm in Indiana."

Cold chills and dreams

Paul Keller also had taken his Delta team back to a packed gymnasium after its semistate victory — "over 2,000 people, at midnight. I asked everyone who had played basketball in Delaware County to stand up. I told them, 'This is not just for us as a team or even our student body, but for all who have ever played county basketball and come up a little bit short.' "

Even then, in the exhilaration of history, there was a pall. A 37-year Delta High math teacher, Van Estes, had watched the semistate games on TV at his home, and died. "That's the two extremes," Keller said. "We ran the gamut this week." The funeral was Wednesday. Each Delta player wore a black ribbon around a shoulder strap at the State.

All week, Keller, as much of a traditionalist as Otis, was steeling himself for an emotional weekend.

"I'll tell you when I really get the cold chills — when I see my team go on the floor for warm-ups, say at the regional or the semistate. I don't trail my team out. I like to just stand there and watch those kids, and listen to that crowd, because I know what a thrill it is for the kids — and what a thrill it is for our community, to see their kids go on the floor.

"I've always told my players, in the years when we've won sectionals: 'You're going to feel like you've never felt before when you go on the floor in the regional. Your hair is going to stand up on the back of your neck.' Nobody ever has said, 'Coach, you weren't right.'

"I think I've enjoyed that as much as winning, just that real sense of pride at that moment.

"I'm not sure I can fully appreciate what this means now. I had dreamed about making it to Hinkle, but I really never could see myself at the Final Four.

"I just never sat down and dreamed about winning the State championship."

At 0:32, a new leader

"Jack Armstrong" came out firing. Ben Tonagel hit the game's first shot, then sank a 3, and after Jeff Ballard had scored, followed up brother Greg's miss with a rebound basket. The game wasn't two minutes old and, down 9-2, Paul Keller was forced to take timeout.

It got worse, 18-4 on the way to a 20-9 ending to the first quarter. "I wouldn't say I panicked, but I was certainly very concerned," Keller said. "The positive thing was we have been there before."

In his own huddle at the quarter, Otis made that very point. "Don't be thinking you're going to run roughshod over these guys," he told his players. "They're going to rally. We've seen it on tape."

The irony, he said, was "we are not a quick-starting team. Today we had the best start we've had since early in the year. It looked like things were going to go our way."

Patrick Jackson was 1-for-6 at that point, and he dropped to 1-for-8 with two quick misses opening the second quarter. He contributed a 3-point basket to a run that pulled the Eagles within 25-20. Junior Tyce Shideler had taken over Delta's scoring load, hitting his first four shots in the second quarter. "He's the best I've ever had at taking the ball to the basket and being able to shoot with either hand to finish inside," Keller said. LaPorte, with 12 points from Ben Tonagel, went to halftime with a solid 32-24 lead.

"We weren't very happy," Keller said. "I didn't feel we were digging in defensively, and we weren't getting some loose balls I thought we had a chance to get. I told them we didn't want to go out with an effort like we had the first half — 'If we're going to lose, let's lose getting after them.' "

Sophomore Rod Robbins started the "getting after them" by coming off a screen and sinking a 3-point basket from straight out front. That shot didn't just happen. Keller charted it for a player he called "an outstanding shooter — 51.6 percent on 3s and 90.3 on free throws."

When Patrick Jackson hit a 3 three minutes later, Delta was within 36-35. Greg Tonagel countered with one, and the Eagles didn't catch up until Shideler hit two free throws with 1:28 left in the quarter for 39-39.

Delta kept moving and put itself in the position that had paid off so often in this tournament drive: ahead late in the game, spread offense, five good ball handlers and good free-throw shooters ready for an ice-down. But this time, leading 55-51, Robbins (.903) missed a one-and-one and Roosevelt Jackson (.767) missed two free throws. With 32 seconds left, Ben Tonagel — the senior with NBA range — hit a 3-point shot that nosed LaPorte out front, 56-55.

P.J. time

Keller went back to the play he used opening the half: Robbins off a screen for a straight-out 3-point try. "We thought they might jump out on Patrick," Keller said. "Robbie opened up and had a real good look at the basket. It just didn't happen to go." LaPorte rebounded, and with 13.2 seconds left, Jeff Ballard had a one-and-one, but he missed. Now, with 9.7 seconds left, Delta at a timeout was planning how to get the ball in Patrick Jackson's hands: the ball out of bounds just past the free-throw line at LaPorte's offensive end. In the other huddle, Otis knew what he hoped to avoid: Jackson with the ball, on attack.

Delta set up for the pass-in, and LaPorte took timeout. "We wanted to see what alignment they were in, and it backfired," Otis said.

Otis' plan was to double-team Jackson in backcourt or midcourt and force the pass-in to someone else. It might have worked against anyone but the quickest, slipperiest target on the court. Jackson split the defenders, caught the pass on the fly racing upcourt, and seven of the 10 players on the court were non-factors as Jackson bolted in from the right side — with Shideler deep on the left side and only Chris Bootcheck left to play goalie.

Jackson went for the basket, Bootcheck slid over, and Jackson — making a play that looks easy only when a top guard is doing it — dropped off an exactly-the-right-instant pass to the man Keller had called the best finisher he ever had.

Shideler lived up to his role. He caught the pass and laid in the basket that put his team ahead, 57-56.

The play's only fault from Delta's standpoint was that it was too fast. LaPorte took timeout with 4.5 seconds still to play.

"My biggest concern was they would shoot very early and we would forget to rebound," Keller said. "I've seen games lost where someone throws up a prayer, everybody thinks it's over, it hits the bankboard and a teammate lays it in."

Greg Tonagel came up the right side but, double-teamed, had no choice but to give up the ball with a cross-court pass for Ballard. Rushing to catch and put up a desperation try, Ballard bobbled the pass and the buzzer sounded.

"We actually had some good defensive plays in that 4½ seconds," Keller said. "We were trying to make the offensive player reverse his direction. Billy Lynch did a great job coming over to challenge the pass Greg Tonagel tried to make."

Shideler had matched Ben Tonagel's 21 points. Jackson had won a splendid backcourt duel with Greg Tonagel, 16-10.

Exit lines for a poet

Otis showed the same poise and class going out as he had in getting his team farther than the school had been since the Roosevelt presidency. "I have no regrets about the way we played or the way I coached, though I got outcoached in the last situation, there's no question about it," he said. "He adjusted and anticipated what we intended to do when we called that timeout.

"Bootcheck, bless his heart, tried to do everything he could. He came up to help, Patrick threw the perfect pass, it was an easy layup, and we were stuck with 4.5 seconds to try to put a final touch on our dream.

"It was a great ride for us. I want to thank my high school coach, Virgil Sweet, for bringing me here 30 years ago. And I want to thank all my teachers for giving me a poet's appreciation of the beauty, in particular, of this tournament.

"This is the end of the single-class tournament. Part of its attractiveness is the Shakespearean element to the endings, like what happened to us today. It was devastating . . .

"But we'll always be able to say we were in the final Final Four. I think it's a great tribute to our kids, our coaching staff and everybody associated with our program.

"We were 3-19 two years ago. It would have been easy for these kids to be turned off on basketball. They just worked harder."

He thought of one in particular.

"My great regret was that I wasn't able to get Jeremy Hoehne in. He makes it hard for the other kids to complain, because he's a senior and he doesn't get to play that much, but he has always worked his tail off."

And he thought of one other person: himself.

"The great benefit for me is I get to retire this orange jacket."

During the tournament Otis had worn a Lou Henson-style bright orange blazer, which he traditionally had saved for annual rivalry games with Michigan City. His first season, LaPorte had beaten the Red Devils twice, a 17-year first. The blazer had been in on more than its share of victories over the rivals since, including one in the sectional this year. "It's a good-luck charm, it got me here," Otis said. "It's time to retire it."

30

Bloomington N.   75
Delta   54

*State championship,
March 22*

BLOOMINGTON NORTH		DELTA
One as Bloomington North, 1997. Others in corporation, one: Bloomington High 1919	**STATE CHAMPIONSHIP**	None
None as Bloomington North. Others in corporation, three: Bloomington High 1918, 1922, 1960	**OTHER TIMES IN FINAL FOUR**	1997* (* lost in championship game)
Two as Bloomington North: 1982, 1997. Others in corporation: Bloomington High 10 (first 1921, last 1971)	**REGIONAL CHAMPIONSHIPS**	One: 1997
10 as Bloomington North: first 1976; two in '90s, most recent 1997. Others in corporation, 28: Bloomington High 25 (first 1915, last 1971), Bloomington University 2: 1946, 1972; Unionville 1966.	**SECTIONAL CHAMPIONSHIPS**	Five: 1980, 1985, 1989, 1993, 1997
Formed 1972 (Bloomington University, Unionville, part of Bloomington High)	**CONSOLIDATIONS**	Formed 1967: Albany, Desoto, Eaton, Royerton
No	**VOTE ON CHANGE TO CLASSES**	No
4A. (1,026; 70th of 95 in class)	**1997-98 CLASS (ENROLLMENT)**	3A. (700; 32nd of 96 in class)
4A, Bedford North Lawrence, Bloomington South; 3A, Brown County, Edgewood; 2A, Eastern (Greene County). Bedford-North Lawrence site, Bloomington North 1997 champion	**1996-97 SECTIONAL OPPONENTS (1997-98 CLASSIFICATION)**	4A, Jay County; 1A, Monroe Central, Union City, Wapahani, Wes-Del. Jay County site, Delta 1997 champion
Bloomington South, Columbus East, Columbus North, East Central, Martinsville	**1997-98 SECTIONAL OPPONENTS**	Blackford, Elwood, Mississinewa, Muncie Southside, Yorktown
28-1 (state champion)	**FINAL RECORD 1996-97**	24-5 (won sectional, regional, semi-state; lost to Bloomington North in state championship game, 75-54)

The Last
of Their Kind

It was for the State high school basketball championship — for a truly special Indiana high school basketball championship. It was the biggest game in either school's history.

But as attuned as both Tom McKinney and Paul Keller are to the history and tradition of the sport they teach, they knew this game had to be approached as all the rest had: as a basketball game that would be won or lost by plays made and chances missed. They never had been in a situation remotely like this one before this tournament season began, but they tried more than anything else to emphasize to their teams:

This is not just another game, but it has to be played that way.

New name on the list

Very big in the planning of both was the littlest man in the two starting lineups. This tournament's capacity for creating its own heroes was demonstrated one more time by Patrick Jackson.

The tournament, particularly the Final Four, had no bearing at all on the everlasting renown, the stature inside the state and out, many of Indiana's greatest high school legends have achieved in the game. Steve Alford and Rick Mount never got to the State. Larry Bird never came close. They did all right. So, in other eras,

369

did any number of future college All-Americans, national champions and NBA players who never made this tournament's "Broadway" — the State finals, the Final Four.

A few great Indiana players, their stature already recognized before they ever reached the State, magnified their standing by what they did there: Oscar Robertson, George McGinnis, Damon Bailey, Glenn Robinson.

But the tournament "made" some players, made their names recognizable throughout Hoosierland not just for a moment but permanently — names such as Homer Stonebraker, Fuzzy Vandivier, Johnny Wooden, Dave DeJernett and Jack Mann, George Crowe, Charley Harmon and Jim Riffey, Broc Jerrel, Jumpin' Johnny Wilson, Bill Garrett and Emerson Johnson, Clyde Lovellette, Dee Monroe, Jack Quiggle and Arley, Harley and Uncle Harold Andrews, Bobby Plump and Ray Craft, Tom Bolyard and big Mike McCoy, Billy Keller, Bob Ford, Steve Downing, Jim Bradley, Pete Trgovich and Junior Bridgeman (Ulysses then), Dave Colescott, Jack Moore and Ray McCallum, Doug Crook, Scott Skiles, Lyndon Jones and Jay Edwards, Shawn Kemp and Chandler Thompson, Eric Montross, Jaraan Cornell, Damon Frierson and at least that many more.

And, now, Patrick Jackson.

A job to do

Chances are Tom McKinney had never heard of Patrick Jackson before this tournament began. This night, as he made his game plans, Delta guard Patrick Jackson was by far his biggest concern.

"We wanted to stay in front of him," McKinney said. "We saw them play Anderson, and Jackson just goes around *Anderson's* guards. We saw that and said, 'Give him a step or two. Stay in front of him.' " Somehow.

The instructions went to senior Jeremy Sinsabaugh, "our best athlete," McKinney said. "He is our quarterback in football and he plays center field in baseball — very strong, very quick. We were planning to alternate him and Wuysang on Jackson."

Above, Shawn Kemp jams over Muncie Central's Sam Long in 1988. At left, future Purdue star Jaraan Cornell of South Bend Clay in 1994. Below, from left, Dan Howe, Mike McCoy and Tom Bolyard led Fort Wayne South to the 1958 title. (Photos courtesy Indiana High School Athletic Association, Cornell photo ©Mark Wick)

Delta's Patrick Jackson, right, guards Mario Wuysang of Bloomington North. (Photo courtesy Indiana High School Athletic Association, ©Mark Wick)

In their minds, in the few hours they had to prepare for this game, the Cougars drew on their one common experience: Anderson, and its outstanding guard combination, Eric Bush and Tyson Jones. Jackson's strong game against them impressed North.

Ironically, North's one loss of the season, in overtime at Anderson, was one game when Sinsabaugh wasn't a prominent factor. He was sick that night. Wuysang started, and loved it. Wuysang played his senior year as a consummate team man, the trademark smile never leaving his face though his off-the-bench role wasn't the one he'd have liked.

Reconciling himself to not starting "was real tough," Wuysang acknowledged. "I've played varsity since I was a sophomore, and I've started four games in my whole varsity career. It's hard, but I don't think of it as a negative thing. I love the game. I'm just going to play hard and contribute however I can."

That night in Anderson, everything was there. He was playing in The Wigwam ("I'd heard so much about it and when I finally got there, it was great"), against "big-name guards — everybody knew about them; they were supposed to be so quick." And face-to-face, on the floor: "They *were* good. But I had no doubt in my mind I could hang with them. I was real ready to play."

And at the end of regulation time, it was Wuysang's 3-point shot that temporarily saved the Cougars and sent them into overtime. He scored 18 (Bush 23 and Jones 12) and Anderson won, 81-76.

That experience went through Wuysang's mind as he prepared for the state championship game. "Bush is very quick, one of the quickest people I've guarded," he said.

"He and Jackson."

Sinsabaugh was healthy this night. The pressure games he had spent with one-on-one responsibilities against crosstown rival Jon Holmes had helped prepare him. Always, except for that one night when he was too sick to do the job, he drew the tough guard, the quick guard. Now, for the state championship, he was drawing the quickest guard.

Struggling stars

McKinney also hoped to get his best offensive weapon going. Kueth Duany hadn't just shrugged off his 1-for-11, two-point game against Kokomo. "I was like, 'Man. All these people here and I'm not showing how good a player I really am. I know I'm better than the performance I put out there,'" Duany said later. "All those people" included a lot of Duanys. Brother Duany, his own season at Wisconsin over, "came in the night before. We talked for a long time. He told me not to be nervous." That didn't work. "I was *so* nervous. I wanted to put a good show on for my family. They were all there. My sister (Nyagon, a freshman player at Bradley) hadn't been to a game all year." Of course those aren't the priorities a coach would want a player thinking about. But the Wal Duany family is big and close, and no one knew that better than McKinney.

So nobody — coach, player or family — was pleased when the game's opening play was a traveling violation by Duany.

Ryan Reed scored the game's first basket. Nothing new there.

But once again, the significance wasn't so much in the basket as in its creation. Delta obviously came into the game respecting North's size edge inside and planning to maximize opportunities. Call it cat-and-mouse, call it Milan, call it prudence, the Eagles on their first possession sought to prove the coaching adage that any defense breaks down with enough passes. Plan A was to spring Patrick Jackson, and go elsewhere if someone else got free first. Jackson bobbed and cut, got the basketball a couple of times but gave it up, ducked in and around screens while passes went elsewhere, but Sinsabaugh was sticking close. And nobody else got open. The patient Eagles made five passes . . . 10 . . . 15 . . .

The 19th pass of their opening possession was one that Ryan Reed saw coming, intercepted on the run near midcourt and turned into an unchallenged layin.

Then, for five minutes, nobody scored.

This wasn't Bobby Plump with the ball on his hip and action frozen. Delta still was working hard to get premium shots and still being denied by a North defense that would not break down. One time Jackson squared off with Sinsabaugh for the one-on-one jitterbugging that had been freeing him for big baskets throughout the tournament. When Jackson made his feint and cut quickly the other way, Sinsabaugh's own athletic skills, from a position slightly farther back than usual, let him punch the ball loose on Jackson's first dribble, and David McKinney snatched up the loose ball.

But Delta was playing strong defense, too. These teams playing for the state championship went up and down and up and down and up and down and up and down and up and down and up . . . six

Djibril Kante, a 6-6-junior who teamed with Kueth Duany to give Bloomington North a powerful inside defense, swats away a Delta shot in the championship game. (Photo courtesy Bloomington Herald-Times*)*

straight possessions by Delta (four missed shots, two missed free throws and three turnovers), five straight by North (six missed shots and another turnover, by Duany), before Sinsabaugh got a step on his man and banked in a shot.

Matt Reed had come in by then. He hit a free throw, then an ugly baseline heave just ahead of the buzzer, and North led at the first-quarter break, 7-0.

That's right, nothing: zero for plucky, The Last People's Choice Delta in the first quarter of the state championship game — 0-for-5 shooting, five turnovers. It would have been more embarrassing

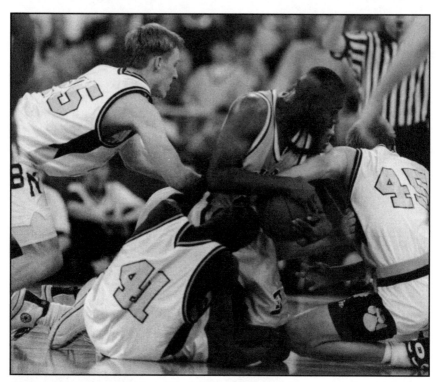

Roosevelt Jackson (with ball) of Delta struggles for possession with, from left, Ryan Reed, Kueth Duany and Matt Reed of Bloomington North. (Photo courtesy Bloomington Herald-Tmes)

for the stunned Eagles if the North point total had been normal. Delta was closer to this team than it had been to Franklin and LaPorte after the first quarter in its last two victories. Still, David McKinney confessed, "After the first quarter, we thought we should win the game. I didn't feel we had played too well yet and we were up 7-0."

North didn't wait around after that. The Cougars put together a championship-worthy second quarter. Wuysang came off the bench to hit two 3s. Sinsabaugh hit one and had nine first-half points. Ryan Reed had three second-quarter baskets and eight points at the half.

But with 30 seconds to go in that half, Duany still hadn't scored. Neither had Jackson.

The North lead was 16-9 when Duany put up his first shot, a 3-point try, and McKinney barked from the sideline: "Get the damn ball inside!" Seconds later, Duany drew his second foul, but McKinney stayed with him. "I was telling myself not to get down and just keep playing hard," Duany said. He did feel he was part of the reason Delta still wasn't in double figures. "I was having a bad *offensive* game," he said. Defense was another matter.

A 12-0 Cougar burst after that one Duany miss opened a 28-9 lead. Delta's huge fan following kept chanting, "We believe!" But this one was getting harder and harder to believe. 28 to 9? And, still, zero for Patrick Jackson?

With 15 seconds left in the half, Duany faked a jump shot and opened himself a drive to the basket for a layup, just his third and fourth points of his long day, and North was up 30-14. At the other end, a second before the buzzer, Jackson hit a 3-point basket.

Those streaks were over, but obviously Sinsabaugh had done quite a containment job. "Jackson is tremendously quick," David McKinney said. "I think the first game drained him a little bit. But Jeremy is an athlete."

The MVP

Sinsabaugh's offense wasn't bad, either. Delta scored first opening the second half to get within 30-19, but Sinsabaugh drove the baseline to score for North, then hit a 3. He had 14 points, all he was going to get in this game, all he needed to make him the championship game's Most Valuable Player.

From now on, for the rest of his life, when players anywhere talk of being "in a zone," Sinsabaugh will remember those last two baskets, this whole day, his "zone." In just over the regulation length of a ballgame, from the time his first 3 fought its way through the basket against Kokomo till this one against Delta, he had scored 29 points — in the Hoosier crucible, the State tournament.

"I can't even explain how that felt," he said. "I don't have the words — I guess Utopia is the closest. To have all the crowd into it, and us hitting, and them not hitting, and us winning, and it's the State tournament . . .

"It can't get a whole lot better than that in Indiana."

377

Stars untracked

The lead now was 35-19. "We've got to keep it on," Sinsabaugh told himself.

Wuysang entered and immediately delivered a blind pass to Ryan Reed for a basket. Djibril Kante dropped off a post pass to Reed for another score. North had its biggest lead, 39-19. Realistically, ring measuring could have started about then.

But not within McKinney's sight. Respect for Delta was part of it, but memories of fast dissipation just seven nights before against New Albany made him keep the pedal down. He wanted more, wanted a knockout, and suddenly Delta showed why he was anxious. The Eagles scored on seven straight possessions — 14 points in three minutes, after getting just 19 points in 19 minutes.

North was scoring, too. Indeed, Duany finally looked untracked. One more time he faked an outside shot and earned himself a layup. "It was easy, and I thought: 'Why haven't I been doing this all day?' " he said. Next trip, his man dropped off and he hit a 3. His game was in synch. Horrible start and all, he was to finish with 17 points, tying Ryan Reed for team high.

But McKinney was nervous. "I didn't like the idea that we were trading baskets," he said. "That's never a good thing." North's third-quarter lead was 50-35. The ominous thing to McKinney was that, Sinsabaugh and all, Patrick Jackson was starting to warm up. "Obviously Coach Keller said, 'Jackson, jump in here, we've got to have you. You've got to be more offensive-minded,' " McKinney said. "We tried to give him more cushion than anybody we've played, but even at that he kept driving." Jackson was to finish with 13 points, as did sophomore Rob Robbins.

'Wasn't over, but you knew'

The closest Delta got was 52-39, when Tyce Shideler rebounded a Jackson miss and scored.

Ryan Reed answered with a three-point play off an offensive rebound. Kante cashed in a rebound. Duany scored six straight North points. The Cougars were up 63-45 with 3:47 left, and the new champion had been determined — in the mind of everybody but the locked-in McKinney.

Bloomington coach
Tom McKinney
maintained his
intensity right to the
finish in the Cougars'
state championship
run. (Photo courtesy
Bloomington Herald-
Times)

"We figured we had won," Kante said of that point in the game, "but Coach wouldn't let us celebrate." So the well-coached Cougars darned well didn't. Still, Kante said, "That feeling — the game wasn't over, the season wasn't over, you were still playing, but you knew you had won . . . that was *great*."

"I looked at the scoreboard and thought, 'They *can't* come back in this short a time,' " Duany said. "I looked at Mario and said: 'We did it!' "

On the floor, with one quick exchange of glances, longtime friends David McKinney and Jeremy Sinsabaugh ran up a victory flag. "I looked over at him, we caught eyes — 'We did it!' " Sinsabaugh said. Not a word had been said: just eye contact between the two. McKinney's version: "We were in backcourt, about the circle, we looked at each other and kinda shook our heads — 'We're finally going to do this. It's really happening.' We were both just kinda in awe."

Kante hit two more free throws to make the lead 69-47 with 1:36 left, and Tom McKinney took a timeout. To empty the bench, obviously.

No. To keep barking about concentration.

Later, he gave that timeout a poignance. He knew this team had realized the dream he had carried since the disappointing day at Hinkle as a sophomore reserve on a powerful, unbeaten, No. 1-ranked Columbus team that lost, the dream he said he shared that night with the girl who was to be his wife: that someday he would win a state championship. He knew the chaos that would come with the buzzer. The timeout gave him one last minute with this team.

His players, oblivious to anything but the oddly timed timeout, were respectful but amused. "I was like, 'What's he thinking? Why did he call this timeout?'" Duany said. "I was just smiling."

At that timeout, Ryan Reed recalled, "Coach said, 'Get back out there and play defense.' He'd get that serious face on like they were within two points. I looked up at the score and thought, 'Why am I all stressed out? This is *great*.'

"I'm never a person who likes to showboat, but I did feel like it."

Sinsabaugh's memory: "We were standing by the huddle with him, and he stepped in real quick and said: 'I want this so bad. Let's go.' I'm thinking, 'My God. We've *got* it.'"

Finally, with 1:09 left and Kante shooting two more free throws, the substituting started. First Duany came off to a wild succession of hugs. Then, after the free throws, Kante left (the man who had started the tournament as an automatic fouling candidate and sub-.500 shooter was 6-for-6 in the state championship game). "When Djibril came out, we went to the end of the bench and we were hugging," Duany said. "We looked at the (huge arena) screen, and we were on it.

"I knew where my whole family was. I gave them a wave. This championship meant a lot to my mother. She's been there every game. My father played some basketball (in their native Sudan). My mother played team handball, which is a lot like basketball.

"After the buzzer went off, I went over and hugged her."

Ryan Reed, Jeremy Sinsabaugh and David McKinney, son of Bloomington North coach Tom McKinney, celebrate the victory. (Photo courtesy Bloomington Herald-Times)

The coach's kid

At 0:38, Sinsabaugh came out, with Ryan Reed and David McKinney.

The all-out celebrating had begun. Tom McKinney still had his great, stone game face. But it was chipping.

"With about 20 seconds to go, I was almost in tears — I was sad, I was happy, I didn't really know what to feel," David McKinney said.

"I looked over at my dad, he looked at me — he didn't smile, but I could read how proud he was.

"He was happy."

That whole, wonderful coach-and-son thing was blooming again.

"After the sectional, J.R. Holmes came up to me — I felt for him, but I was so happy for me," David McKinney said. Holmes is the Bloomington South coach who had his team so ready for the Cougars, his near-miss upset bid built around his own son, Jon — No. 1-ranked student in his class, hero of a sectional-championship effort the year before, as a freshman.

"Coach Holmes put an arm around me and told me how much it meant to him when his son won a sectional," McKinney said, "and how much that will mean to my father. I really appreciated that.

"I didn't hear from him for a few weeks after that. A couple of days after we won, I got a letter from him: 'I told you how much the sectional would mean to him. Words can't explain what it must mean to win the State.' "

'Wouldn't give it up for anything'

Way, way back, on that January night when the two Bloomington teams first had met, Tom McKinney tried to explain what those years of coaching his son had meant to him.

"Now that he's a senior, I do reflect on that," he said. "It has been a very, very great experience for me, and I think a pretty good experience for him.

"We have tried to stay very low-key. He's a very hard worker, and unselfish. J.R.'s situation is tougher, maybe — Jon's a sophomore and so much is expected of him offensively.

"But that part of it, coaching my son — I wouldn't give it up for anything.

"I have gone to four or five coaches about that. They all have said the same thing: Be sure you go ahead and coach another year after your son gets out, and then you will know for sure your true feeling.

"Danny Bush (who coached Bedford North Lawrence and Damon Bailey to the 1990 state championship and stayed on through son Alan's career) was one who left right away. He had his state championship. And wear and tear . . .

"I've had no wear and tear. It's probably tougher on the son than it is the coach. The Bloomington North people have been more than fair to me.

"It *is* tough sometimes. Martinsville played us a zone. The first half, David hits five 3s. As a dad, you want to pull for him, but you can't allow that to happen.

"I have been very, very lucky, to be able to coach my son. A lot of guys get fired before they have that opportunity."

When you look back on it, a friend said, you'll see it as something really good.

"I consider it one now," Tom McKinney said.

The Eagles' Lynch-pin

As much fun as it was for North, playing out those final minutes with the game decided, it had to be a long experience of proud despair for the game Delta team that had worked such cumulative wonders to get to that championship night.

For one Eagle, there was the extra pain of special familiarity. Delta guard Billy Lynch had played his first two high school years at Bloomington South. These Cougars were his rivals, and his boyhood buddies. He moved to Delta when his dad, Bill, was hired off Bill Mallory's Indiana staff to be the new head football coach at Ball State. Billy Lynch didn't go away from the biggest basketball game of his life trophyless. He was the 71st winner of the tournament's mental attitude award.

McKinney felt for Keller and his kids and made a point of mentioning their handicap. North, he noted, had been blessed by the draw all the way along, playing the first game in the regional, semistate and State. "In fairness to Delta, I don't think they had the same legs tonight that they had this morning," he said. "If we had both played at 10:30 today, it would have been a different game."

Keller was as gracious. "I'm very proud of my kids," he said. "They did a lot for me this year . . . and they played with a lot of heart. They may not be state champs on the scoreboard, but they are in my heart. I told them we've earned some respect around the state this year, and to hold their heads up like winners."

The Cougars, he said, "are very well coached. They do some very good things that hurt you from a defensive standpoint.

"Give them everything they deserve. They're the state champs. They've been No. 1. Everybody they played was trying to knock them off. We were underdogs. We could kind of sneak in the backdoor the whole way.

"They're a heck of a team."

"Important to me, but . . . '

"I think we *are* a pretty good team," McKinney said. "We're certainly not one of the best teams that ever won the State. You have to have some luck along the way. We had some.

"The sectional was tremendous pressure. Not the regional or the semistate, for me. Then last Sunday I woke up and saw that we were really in the Final Four, and I felt that great pressure again.

"We try to keep it from the kids. Even coming back here tonight, I was just talking about playing hard.

"I just feel fortunate. The last three years, these seniors have been 67-10."

There was, a postgame questioner noted, the matter of being the last champion of the tournament format Hoosiers have always known.

"I'm 49," he said. "It is special to me, but I brought three or four juniors and sophomores here — we've never talked about that being a special thing. I think it's very special to us older adults, but they're all going to play next year.

"We'll have a tough sectional next year, but we've had a tough sectional the last six years. It's not that significant with me. Where we are is significant.

"I've been against class basketball, but I also have an understanding about a lot of smaller schools wanting to have class basketball. It's important to me as an older coach, but I don't think it's important to the underclassmen at all."

A champion, a model

This is a champion unlike any Indiana ever had.

Start with the McKinneys — the first time a son started for a championship coach since . . . Murray Mendenhall and Murray Jr. for Fort Wayne Central in 1943? Some coaches had won the State championship with their son on the team — recent examples Dan and Alan Bush of Bedford North Lawrence in 1990, the Bill Smiths on Indianapolis Broad Ripple in 1980, Doug and Mike Adams of Michigan City in 1966. Some had come excruciatingly close with their sons in a starring role, none closer than Homer and Bryce Drew of Valparaiso in 1994 and Jim and Richie Hammel of Lafayette Jeff in 1992. Jack and Bill Butcher of Loogootee played in the championship game in 1975, Bill and Dave Shepherd of Carmel in 1970. Some of the most noted never got to the State: Sam and

Steve Alford (New Castle '83), Bill and Billy Shepherd (Carmel '68). Neither did Jack and Michael Edison (Plymouth '95), Alan Darner and Indiana All-Star sons Linc (Anderson Highland '90) and Tige ('94), Tim and Ryan Wolf (Martinsville '91), Tom and Jeff Oliphant (L&M '85). Jack Colescott had just moved out of coaching at Marion when son Dave came along on back-to-back state champions ('75 and '76), Dave ranking with Bobby Plump and Damon Bailey as the only players to score a triple: Mr. Basketball and Trester Award winners from a state champion. With all that, the McKinneys represented a 54-year first.

Go to the Reed twins — one of the rare sets of twins on a state championship team . . . the second, maybe, ever? There were the Heinemans, Chris and Mike, on Basil Mawbey's 1983 Connersville champions. And there were such great ones who came so very close, headed by maybe the best twins sports ever has seen: the Van Arsdales (Dick and Tom, on the '61 Indianapolis Manual team that lost in overtime to Kokomo). Great players, too, were Terre Haute Gerstmeyer's Andrews twins (Arley and Harley, who, along with uncle Harold, lost 42-41 in 1953 to South Bend Central). Jon and Don McGlocklin of Franklin twice reached the Final Four (1973 and '74). Jim and Jerry Heath played in the championship game for Lafayette Jeff in 1956.

And there was the United Nations makeup of the championship team and school.

The tag sometimes came across — sometimes seemed intended — as a pejorative when it should have been high praise. The Cougars were the basketball representatives of a student body that included, according to the school's proud count, 70 nationalities. All 70 weren't out there on the basketball court, but there were several: Duany, born in The Sudan but brought up from early childhood in Bloomington; Kante, born in Bloomington but a frequent back-and-forth resident of three African nations before settling in Bloomington prior to high school; Wuysang, born in Indonesia but an American citizen for about as long as he can remember, and junior Jay Robles, born in the Philippines. Their interests, their speech, their locker room chatter were Hoosier. Their accomplishments, their exceptional team tightness, said more than the U.N. Charter about how well this world can work when people are together in purpose, opportunity and melded skills — so very well that the whole never even seemed to notice, indeed as a group rather resented *your* noticing, whatever differences such inconsequentials as place of birth made in its parts.

A lesson about culture

There were differences. "We've got about 1,300 kids in our school — we're seven or eight blocks from Indiana University," McKinney had said in trying to give a group of sportswriters an introductory course in Anatomy of the Cougars opening State Tourney week.

"We're a really unique school, a lot of diversity. An awful lot of kids in our school have parents who are either going to IU or teach at IU. We have kids from three different African countries, the Philippines and Indonesia. One player on our reserve team is a Nigerian prince — his grandfather is the king, or premier, of Nigeria.

"It's a great place to teach and coach. I have coached kids from three or four different continents and probably eight or nine different countries.

"I have had to adjust myself to some of their cultures. One time I yelled at one of these players: 'When I talk to you, look me right in the eye.'

"In his culture, he's not allowed to."

Minor details, on the way to a major accomplishment.

A tough kid's bargain

One other detail: Matt Reed's teeth.

Early in this championship game, the older of the twins showed the 26,187 at the game and the millions in the statewide TV audience just how the Reeds go at basketball.

With about a minute left in the first quarter, Delta tried to slip a pass to Roosevelt Jackson, posted high on the left side of the court. Matt Reed punched the pass away and then dived to try to come up with it before it went out of bounds. "I got a hand on it and tried to throw it back," he said. "But my hands were down and my legs were up, so I was tilted forward and I went head-first into the floor."

Mouth-first, actually.

Two of his teeth "broke off halfway and stuck in the floor," Matt said. "Adam Hawley picked them up. They left two indention marks in the floor where they broke off, and there were scratches where the rough edges of the broken tooth scraped across the floor."

Matt got up, quietly went over to twin Ryan and said, "Man, my mouth's hurt." Ryan took one quick glance and advised his brother, "Don't look."

Ryan didn't even consider suggesting that Matt should sit down. "No. I've always been taught, if you can walk, you can play."

Matt wouldn't have listened anyway. He didn't listen when Tom McKinney suggested it might be better if he would come out. He didn't listen to an official who tried to talk him into leaving the game because of the pain that would be coming.

"In a game like that, your adrenaline is pumping. You don't really feel it."

Really?

"Really.

"You have a chance to win the State championship. You don't have time to think about teeth."

Ultimately, he had to have major work done on both teeth: one in front, one on the side. It hasn't done a thing to his smile.

"Just the name 'State Champ' is worth two teeth."

Summary

The Man
and the
Tombstone

A man close to him said of Bob Gardner, "He already knows what it's going to say on his tombstone."

Gardner heard of the comment and let it pass with a comfortable, easy laugh. Not arrogant, not dismissive, but easy, as opposed to uneasy. Late-spring and summer may be a calm between the storms in the life of the sixth commissioner of the Indiana High School Athletic Association, but he is understandably happy to be moving on toward whatever is to come after what he has just been through.

Yes, the obituaries if not the epitaph almost certainly will read: "Robert (Bob) Gardner, the commissioner when the IHSAA moved to class basketball . . . "

There is a chance, of course, that by that time way, way out in the future those will be words of high praise. High dudgeon is the more common context for them now, because sportswriters compose such obituary leads on sports figures and the media majority, in Indiana and even out, clearly opposed the change.

In his office in the IHSAA's 20-year-old headquarters building on the far north side of Indianapolis, closer to Carmel than to Monument Circle, Gardner seems comfortable about his own role in the change and unaffected by how others see it.

"I just don't concern myself with that," he said.

"You can't. People are on one side or the other. Some think I should get all the credit in the world. Others think I should get all the blame in the world.

"Neither is true. I know that in my own mind, so I just have to let it go."

He had heard a friend mention seeing him as he left the Basketball Hall of Fame induction ceremony in March, where a few shots had been fired at the change about to come. The friend saw Gardner as looking tired, drained, aged — "not the Bob Gardner I know."

Bob Gardner

The Gardner smile is back now, with one school year over and another out there on the horizon.

It has been a personal ordeal, Gardner acknowledged, "probably more than even I might know. My kids say, 'You've got a lot more gray hair this year, Dad.' And I think that's probably right.

"I've tried to take the philosophy that it's not an issue I can take personally. You have a job to do, you work for a board, you make recommendations to the board, and then you play with whatever hand you're dealt. You make the best of it."

Erosion of a role

That isn't acceptable to some of his critics. There was the comment earlier in this book, from Washington coach Dave Omer: "I can't visualize how we let this happen. If we still had Phil Eskew, we wouldn't have it. Phil Eskew would never have let 'em in the door." It is a widespread perception: Gardner could have stopped this if he had wanted; his predecessors would have.

Eskew was the third man to occupy the seat Gardner now has. He is gone now, and Gardner is among the many who miss him. "After his retirement, Phil used to stop by the office occasionally and just sit down and talk with the rest of us," said Gardner, who joined the IHSAA staff in 1985. "I can't tell you how I looked forward to those sessions. He had such great stories and great experiences."

Eskew almost certainly would have been more openly antagonistic toward the change than Gardner was. It's a difference in men but also a difference in times, Gardner feels.

"The role of the commissioner has changed," he said. "It's not the absolute authority that Mr. Trester (first commissioner Arthur L.) probably had in the beginning. There has certainly been an erosion of that over the course of time.

"I don't think that's the fault of any individual. It's just how times change.

"At one time, the commissioner made a ruling and that was it. There was no appeal. Then there became an appeal process. Now we go to court frequently after the appeal process. That's part of an evolution that was at work long ago."

'I'd do it again,' but differently

There's also a perception that Gardner is the commissioner because when the fifth commissioner, Gene Cato, retired in January 1995, assistant commissioner Gardner was seen as more harmonious with pro-class supporters than either Cato or another veteran assistant, Ray Craft — the leading scorer for Milan in that 1954 championship game that is this whole issue's landmark.

"One thing that I've gotten the blame for and people have lost sight of," Gardner said, "is the Study Committee was put in place before I ever took the job as commissioner." That's the committee, headed by Crawfordsville athletic director Bruce Whitehead, that wound up making the recommendation that the IHSAA's Board of Control, then principals throughout the state, ratified by vote.

"The forces that were coming together were already at work," Gardner said. "Who knows whether the outcome would have been the same (under another commissioner)?

"A lot of people have said: 'You've never really come out and said whether you were totally for it or against it.'

"Well, I grew up in Indiana, I played in Indiana, I love the underdog story as much as anybody else.

"But on the other hand, being a realist, I saw there weren't a lot of underdog stories that were happening anymore. I'm kind of torn; I can see good to both sides of it.

"That's one of the things that maybe makes me the right or the wrong guy for the job, because I can see both sides of it."

The bottom-line question: if you had known what this last year would be like, if you had known the uncertainties that would be lying ahead, if you had known the "tombstone" impact on your life — would you have taken the job?

"Yes. I don't hesitate to answer that. I feel very strongly about that.

"If the question were: Would you do things the exact same way, I'd answer rather quickly, 'No.'

"There were some things we could have done differently. I don't know if it would change the outcome. But I would go through it again, because I think the time had come to go through it and make a decision one way or the other."

Spell it out

The primary change Gardner now would make in what was done would be to lay out more precisely what the New World would look like — sectional assignments, tournament sites, details that weren't supplied when the vote was simplified to a choice between one-class or four-class play.

"As we went through the process, we tended to not communicate well from the committee level to the schools and on beyond that to the public," Gardner said.

"I know how that happened. The committee wanted people to make the decision based on I'm either for it philosophically or I'm not."

The concern implied was that too many would let personal interests override the full state's interests, the tournament's interests, somewhere in there — not always uppermost for either side — the interests of the players of today and tomorrow. In Gardner's view, the committee in holding back details wanted to minimize provincial peeves: "If we tell everybody where they're going to play, some are going to say, 'We can't beat these people. So I don't like it.'

"That was the philosophical approach. But the real world is: that *is* how we make our decisions. Is it better or is it worse for me and my school?

"I think we would have been better off from the very beginning if we had said: There's going to be 16 sectionals in each class, a one-game regional, a semistate, and so forth. And here's how we see the alignment."

The alignment was based on enrollments, which change. The picture as drawn at voting time was slightly different from the one at implementation time.

"But I still think, with hindsight, we would have gained more credibility doing that. People took an awful lot of potshots — maybe at me, maybe at this office, maybe at the executive committee and the study committee — thinking that someone was trying to hide something. That was never the intent. We knew the enrollments would go up and down and wouldn't be the exact ones we would use. Vincennes at one time was in the top (fourth) class and ended up in the third, and McCutcheon went the other way. But I think we should have done that."

'Kind of rejuvenated' now

Another criticism dealt with a matter that preceded the Gardner commissionership: formation of a Study Committee heavily weighted with small-school representation.

"When that committee was formed, there was a pretty strong feeling that there shouldn't be a stacked deck against the class sports people," Gardner said.

"It happened once before, and at that time people thought the class sports people really fought a deck stacked totally against them. This time, in order not to stack the deck, the committee makeup was primarily of the smaller schools.

"But when the committee was appointed, philosophically those people from the smaller schools were opposed to class sports. Bruce

Whitehead was one; Jim Babcock of Paoli was another. They were saying initially, and I think they were sincere: 'We're not for class sports.'

"What happened was over the course of time, as the people who were pro began to gather information and support, people on the committee who were opposed began to step back and say: 'This doesn't look as bad as we thought. Maybe we should give this a chance.' "

That's not far from where Gardner puts himself as the New World dawns.

In the immediate months after the final vote was announced in November, he said, "I traveled the state a good bit, meetings with principals and athletic directors and talking with coaches' groups, just getting out and talking with people.

"Now that everything has kinda been settled, there's a certain new excitement out there. I'm kind of rejuvenated by that. There's a feeling: 'Let's see how this turns out.'

"I'm looking forward to it."

And the group most affected, the kids who will be playing:

"Kids will adapt to whatever system you have, probably much quicker than adults."

Third-generation coach

It's not an issue that looks to be over. The atmosphere at the Final Four in March seemed so defensive that some people once resigned to a permanent switch to classes went away feeling a change back after a two-year trial was not out of the question.

Gardner acknowledged that a sense of rallying around a treasured institution was partly responsible for the big increase in Final Four attendance in 1997, compared to 1996.

"I think that's probably fairly accurate," he said. "That, and the fact that we had four new teams who hadn't been there for a while and had never played in the Dome. That didn't hurt, either."

Before being a commissioner, Bob Gardner was a third-generation coach. His grandfather, Bruce, coached basketball at

Owensville in Gibson County in the late '20s and early '30s. His father, Bob, was a 10-year basketball coach in southern Indiana before moving into school administration — principal at Lynnville for three years, superintendent of schools in Warrick County for more than 20.

He never played for his dad. He was a fourth-grader the last year his father coached. "Even when my dad was principal, he'd go to the school and work and I'd go to the gym and play basketball." He was a football quarterback and (under future Hall of Famer Ed Siegel) a basketball player at Boonville. He got his degree at Evansville, and his first coaching job was as assistant to another young fellow, Basil Mawbey, at West Washington High.

His first head coaching job came after he had reached a coaching fork and chosen to follow football, not basketball. "I was probably a better player in football than in basketball," he said. His dad's contribution to the decision was a wry reminder that "the season is over for the football coach in the fall and they've got all winter to forget about your record while the basketball coach is different," Gardner remembers. "There was a lot of truth in that then, before we had playoffs. I'm not sure it still is true today."

A taste of Milan

Gardner's first head coaching job was in football. In the fall of 1972, at Milan.

It's an ironic base for the man with the filled-out epitaph, and it was more than just a coaching stop. After three years as football coach there, he went to Scottsburg as coach, then returned as principal at Milan — the job he had when he was tapped from membership on the IHSAA's Board of Control to join the Indianapolis staff. That was in 1985, after assistant commissioner Charles Maas died.

"Milan is a special place — I wouldn't trade the years I was there for anything," Gardner said. "There's a lot of wonderful people there and a lot of community spirit and pride." The 1954 state championship, so much the source of that spirit, "is both a great source of pride and a little bit of an albatross," Gardner feels.

"During the time I was there there was a good bit of talk about consolidation. Sunman, directly to the north, went across the county line into East Central, with North Dearborn. Moores Hill, in Dearborn County but just two miles from Milan, went into South Dearborn. There were conversations between the Milan and Jac-Cen-Del school boards about consolidation.

"Milan was not opposed to consolidation, with one stipulation: the school had to be called Milan. They just did not want to give up the name.

"You can imagine what that did to archrivals. I believe Jac-Cen-Del would have gone with them if they had called it North Ripley. Moores Hill probably would have gone; Sunman may have. But Milan wouldn't give up the name Milan."

Letting heritage die

The idea of preservation of a golden name has been dealt with differently in other points of the state.

No longer is there a South Bend Central, a Fort Wayne Central, an Indianapolis Washington, or an Indianapolis Crispus Attucks — to mention major urban schools that once won state basketball championships, nine among the four mentioned, to which a non-winner with its own special heritage, Indianapolis Shortridge, should be added. School boards closed those high schools for various reasons that usually dealt with a city's changed racial makeup. Closed with them were the very thing Milan stubbornly protected: a link to past greatness, a sense of heritage.

Physical buildings do deteriorate, but other avenues are available. Anderson is taking one this year, in going from one aging building to another more modern and taking all the lore that a proud city attaches to the name Anderson High School with it to the new location. Evansville Central faced the same situation as the other Centrals but the city reacted differently. Today's Evansville Central High School is north of Evansville North High School, but its alumni — *e.g.*, Congressman Lee Hamilton, Indiana University athletic director Clarence Doninger — still have a name to follow, on the score lists and in other ways.

Bob Gardner's mother graduated from Evansville Central. He knows what has been preserved. "I think Evansville retained some-

No longer in existence, Indianapolis Washington had a rich athletic tradition. The Continentals won the 1969 State Championship with this team, which included, front row (from left), Alan Glaze, George McGinnis, Wayne Pack, Steve Downing, Louis Day, James Riley; back row, assistant coach Basil Sfreddo, Steve Stanfield, Abner Nibbs, Kenneth Carter, James Arnold, Kenneth Parks, Harvey Galbreath and coach Bill Green. (Photo courtesy Indiana High School Athletic Association)

thing that Indianapolis lost when they let some of these names die," he said. "Fort Wayne let Central die and went out and named one of its new schools Wayne.

"Surely they could have retained some of those things and preserved their heritage, and maybe in turn helped athletics, and school pride and spirit. It may be an illustration of why things are as they are in some communities. Evansville is still a great high school sports town. Maybe that's part of the reason."

This is not a non-traditionalist talking.

No mood for compromise

Gardner said the IHSAA's study committee did look at Kentucky's unofficial small-school tournament. That, indeed, was the germination for a plan presented in 1995 as an alternative to class basketball: separate tournaments in all four classes starting over the Christmas holidays, bringing everybody back together in March.

Purists — make that personal, *we* purists — opposed to any change at all saw it as an insincere plan front-loaded for failure, to permit saying "Well, we tried" before an all-out switch to classes. There was, it seemed, no real push for separation in anything but the smallest classes — certainly no desire among the 4A schools for a big state tournament preview. And, absolutely, administrators weren't going to vote for anything that committed them and some faculty members to duty that tied up the holidays.

"I'll be honest," Gardner said, "I was the one who threw out that idea to the committee: 'If this is where we're headed, let's try this. It would do a couple of things for us: we can see what the financial impact will be before we jump off the cliff to try it, and we can see what the impact of travel is.' "

It was an example of how perceptions and intentions separated so dramatically as the issue escalated into its decisive hours.

Purists weren't listening to any alternatives. Period.

"I think a lot of people felt through the whole process that any real change just wasn't going to happen," Gardner said. "It was like: 'We've been down this road; even though it looks like they have support on the board, when the push comes to shove and the final vote comes, they're not going to vote for it.'

"Even when it went to the referendum of the principals, I think people on that side still felt it wasn't going to happen. 'No, we don't want any part of a compromise.' They just kinda dug in their heels.

"Some people now say they could accept classes in the sectional and regional, bringing everybody back together at the semistate. They weren't supporting that at all when that was discussed.

"If they could do it over, they might be far more receptive to a compromise."

What about the fire trucks?

And there was the matter of not the Final Final Four but the penultimate one, the next-to-last one in 1996 with Ben Davis, New Albany, Lafayette Jeff and Warsaw — all from big enrollments, with the vote about to come up.

"I think that played some part in it," Gardner said. "I don't mean to put anything on Ben Davis. They are fine people, and they have an excellent program. But the fact that it was Ben Davis again, and Ben Davis again — they were the largest high school in the state and people were beginning to say, 'When is this dynasty going to be broken? Here we are out here with 250 kids. We aren't going to be able to do it.' "

If the vote was a response to the 1996 Final Four, the sudden switch from a straight four-class tournament to a season-ending Tournament of Champions may have had something to do with 1997 and its Final Final Four theme. Now, there will be a Final Four of a different sort, a single champion of champions.

And it certainly won't be the same as before. Now four teams will win "state championships," and there will be community celebrations of that, but fire trucks? Streets lined with people? Or, something more like the late-night full gyms that greeted LaPorte and Delta after semistate championships this year — joy, restrained by a job still to be done?

Gardner favored a playoff of champions even before pressure from the state legislature seemed to force the IHSAA's hands on doing something to bring back a one-champion tournament.

"I have always been intrigued with the idea of a playoff among the multiple classes," Gardner said. "It allows us to keep alive the Hoosier tradition that the small school has an opportunity.

"If I'm at a big school, I certainly understand I don't like that very well. By the same token, what I have said to the big school people who have been very critical of it, and certainly there have been some: 'It's OK if you play that little school at the sectional level, but it's not OK to risk your title?' "

End of an error?

Meanwhile, the playoff formats are set.

The girls' Tournament of Champions will be played on the boys' semistate weekend. "Our plan is to play the two semifinal games on Friday night for the girls, and play our championship game probably at 4 p.m. Saturday. We're going to continue that same philosophy with the boys.

"The boys and girls semistates will be the only times where teams will play two games in one day. If we can make it work with our Tournament of Champions, then we make a strong case for going to Friday and Saturday with the semistates, too.

"It's not that playing two games in any way harms kids, but going to two days would give them an opportunity to have better performances."

It's the one change I would have been for all along — even back in the purist days, when Gardner is right: neither I nor those like me wanted any kind of alterations. Just that little one for me: no two-game days, to give the short-rostered small schools a better chance — to give all kids, even the Rick Mounts from high-profile programs, a better chance. It was wrong when it cut down Mount in the '60s and it was wrong right to the end of the one-class era. Now, with great irony in timing, that wrong may be getting fixed.

Maybe that won't be the last change.

Maybe, in some future year, after alterations and new votes and experiments, after some revising and pitching out and even a little bit of getting-used-to, Indiana once again will have a state tournament the rest of the nation respects and envies.

We had one once, kiddies. *Let me tell you about the time back in '97 . . .*

And maybe, before very long, we'll have one a whole lot like that again.

Appendix

Final Four Records

Total Points, Final Game

Year	Player	School	Points
1970	Dave Shepherd	Carmel	40
1956	**Oscar Robertson**	**Indianapolis Attucks**	**39**
1982	**Scott Skiles**	**Plymouth**	**39**
1949	Dee Monroe	Madison	36
1969	**George McGinnis**	**Indianapolis Washington**	**35**
1987	**Jay Edwards**	**Marion**	**35**
1994	Tim Bishop	Valparaiso	35
1973	Jimmy Webb	South Bend Adams	34
1983	Troy Lewis	Anderson	34
1994	Bryce Drew	Valparaiso	34
1955	Wilson Eison	Gary Roosevelt	31
1946	**Johnny Wilson**	**Anderson**	**30**
1955	**Oscar Robertson**	**Indianapolis Attucks**	**30**
1962	Bobby Miles	East Chicago Washington	30
1980	Dave Bennett	New Albany	30
1990	**Damon Bailey**	**Bedford North Lawrence**	**30**
1994	**Jaraan Cornell**	**South Bend Clay**	**30**

Boldface: team won game

Total Points, Semifinal Game

Year	Player	School	Points
1983	James Blackmon	Marion	52
1983	**Troy Lewis**	**Anderson**	**42**
1960	**Ron Bonham**	**Muncie Central**	**40**
1981	**Pete Trgovich**	**East Chicago Washington**	**40**
1977	**Drake Morris**	**East Chicago Washington**	**37**
1989	Pat Graham	Floyd Central	37
1973	**Bill Finley**	**New Albany**	**36**
1967	**Bob Ford**	**Evansville North**	**35**
1978	**Jack Moore**	**Muncie Central**	**34**
1957	Howard Dardeen	Terre Haute Gerstmeyer	33
1981	Rob Brandenburg	Warsaw	33
1962	**Bobby Miles**	**East Chicago Washington**	**32**
1980	Dan Dakich	Andrean	32
1988	**Chandler Thompson**	**Muncie Central**	**32**
1973	**Steve Austin**	**South Bend Adams**	**31**
1973	**Jimmy Webb**	**South Bend Adams**	**31**
1983	Brad Fichter	Princeton	31
1996	Kevin Ault	Warsaw	31
1946	**Bobby Milton**	**Fort Wayne Central**	**30**
1981	**Doug Crook**	**Vincennes**	**30**
1982	**Scott Skiles**	**Plymouth**	**30**
1986	Anthony Kelley	Anderson	30

Boldface: team won game

Total Points, Both Games

Year	Player	School	Points
1983	Troy Lewis	Anderson	76
1960	Ron Bonham	Muncie Central	69
1982	**Scott Skiles**	**Plymouth**	**69**
1970	Dave Shepherd	Carmel	68
1971	**Pete Trgovich**	**E. Chicago Washington**	**68**
1973	Jimmy Webb	South Bend Adams	65
1977	Drake Morris	East Chicago Washington	64
1962	Bobby Miles	East Chicago Washington	62
1967	**Bob Ford**	**Evansville North**	**62**
1969	**George McGinnis**	**Indianapolis Washington**	**62**
1978	**Jack Moore**	**Muncie Central**	**61**
1994	Tim Bishop	Valparaiso	60

Boldface: team won game

Career
(Number of games in parentheses)

Year(s)	Player	School	Points
1985-86-87	Lyndon Jones	Marion	133 (6)
1985-86-87	Jay Edwards	Marion	131 (6)
1955-56	Oscar Robertson	Indpls. Attucks	107 (4)
1987-88-90	Damon Bailey	Bedford NL	100 (4)
1975-76	Dave Colescott	Marion	85 (4)
1976-77	Drake Morris	E.C. Washington	82 (3)
1993-94-95	Damon Frierson	Ben Davis	81 (5)
1958-60	Ron Bonham	Muncie Central	78 (3)
1983	Troy Lewis	Anderson	76 (2)
1920-21-22	Fuzzy Vandivier	Franklin	74 (6)
1961-62	Jim Ligon	Kokomo	73 (3)
1988-90	Jamar Johnson	Concord	72 (4)
1992-93	Brien Hanley	Jeffersonvile	72 (3)

Team Total Points

One Team, Final Game

Year	Schools	Points
1955	Indianapolis Attucks vs. Gary Roosevelt	97
1993	South Bend Clay vs. Valparaiso	93
1959	Indianapolis Attucks vs. Kokomo	92
1994	Valparaiso vs. South Bend Clay	88
1962	Evansville Bosse vs. East Chicago Washington	84
1973	New Albany vs. South Bend Adams	84

Both Teams, Final Game

Year	Schools	Points
1994	South Bend Clay/Valparaiso	181
1955	Indianapolis Attucks/Gary Roosevelt	171
1962	Evansville Bosse/East Chicago Washington	165
1973	New Albany/South Bend Adams	163
1976	Marion/Rushville	158

One Team, Semifinal Game

Year	Schools	Points
1960	Muncie Central vs. Bloomington	102
1971	East Chicago Washington vs. Floyd Central	102
1973	South Bend Adams vs. Anderson	99
1973	Anderson vs. South Bend Adams	95
1992	Richmond vs. Jeffersonville	94

Both Teams, Semifinal Game

Year	Schools	Points
1973	South Bend Adams/Anderson	194
1971	East Chicago Washington/Floyd Central	190
1992	Richmond/Jeffersonville	186
1983	Anderson/Marion	176
1978	Muncie Central/Elkhart Central	174

Winning Margin

Final Game

Year	Schools	Margin
1912	Lebanon over Franklin	40
1959	Indianapolis Attucks over Kokomo	38
1958	Fort Wayne South over Crawfordsville	29
1914	Wingate over Anderson	28
1936	Frankfort over Fort Wayne Central	26

Semifinal Game

Year	Schools	Margin
1960	Muncie Central over Bloomington	36
1991	Gary Roosevelt over Whitko	30
1963	South Bend Central over Terre Haute Garfield	27
1911	Crawfordsville over Bluffton	26
1959	Indianapolis Attucks over Logansport	26

Both Games

Year	School	Total Margin
1959	Indianapolis Attucks	64
1912	Lebanon	55
1991	Gary Roosevelt	49
1936	Frankfort	42
1958	Fort Wayne South	42

Final Four Appearances

	FINAL FOUR	FINAL TWO	CHAMPION
Anderson	1914,1918,1920,1921,1923, 1935,1936,1937,1944,1946, 1948,1973,1979,1981,1983, 1986,1990	1914,1918,1921,1935,1937, 1946,1979,1981,1983,1986	1935,1937,1946
Andrean	1980		
Argos	1979		
Auburn	1949		
Batesville	1943		
Bedford	1924,1926,1927,1928, 1938,1943		
Bedford N. Law.	1987,1988,1990	1990	1990
Ben Davis	1993,1994,1995,1996	1993,1995,1996	1995,1996
Bloomington	1918,1919,1922,1960	1919	1919
Bloomington N.	1997	1997	1997
Bluffton			1911
Brebeuf	1991		1991
Carmel	1970,1977,1993	1970,1977	1977
Cloverdale			1966
Columbus E.			1977
Columbus N.	1938,1964,1975		
Concord	1988,1990	1988,1990	
Connersville	1927,1930,1972,1983	1972,1983	1972,1983
Crawfordsville	1911,1913,1916,1919, 1923,1942,1958	1911,1916,1958	1911
Delta	1997	1997	
EC Roosevelt	1970	1970	1970
EC Washington	1947,1960,1962,1966, 1971,1976,1977,1985	1960,1962,1971,1977	1960,1971
Elkhart Cent	1954,1956,1971,1978,1995	1971	
Evansville Bosse	1932,1939,1944, 1945,1962,1982	1944,1945,1962	1944,1945,1962
Evansville Central	1926,1936,1946,1948	1948	
Evansville North	1967	1967	1967
Evansville Reitz	1951	1951	
Evansville RMi	1964		
Fairmount	1915		
Flora	1946		
Floyd Central	1971,1989		
FW Central	1936,1937,1943,1946,1960	1936,1943,1946	1943
FW North	1933,1955,1965	1965	
FW Northrop	1974	1974	1974
FW South	1938,1940,1958,1967	1938,1958	1938,1958
Frankfort	1924,1925,1928,1929, 1930,1936,1939,1942	1924,1925,1929,1936,1939	1925,1929, 1936,1939
Franklin	1912,1920,1921,1922, 1939,1973,1974	1912,1920,1921, 1922,1939	1920,1921,1922
Gary Emerson	1917	1917	
Gary Froebel	1941		
Gary Mann	1929		
Gary Roosevelt	1955,1965,1968, 1982,1987,1991	1955,1968, 1982,1991	1968,1991
Gary Tolleston	1969	1969	
Gary West	1972	1972	
Greencastle	1931,1932,1933	1931,1933	
Hammond	1938	1938	
Hammond Noll	1988		
Hammond Tech	1940	1940	1940

Hartford City	1920		
Huntingburg	1937	1937	
Huntington	1918,1945,1964	1964	
Ind. Attucks	1951,1955,1956,1957,1959	1955,1956,1957,1959	1955,1956,1959
Ind. Broad Ripple	1945,1980	1980	1980
Ind. Cathedral	1982		
Ind. Manual	1915,1961	1961	
Ind. Shortridge	1933,1968 .	1968	
Ind. Tech	1929,1934,1952,1966	1929,1934,1952,1966	
Ind. Washington	1965,1969	1965,1969	1965,1969
Jasper	1934,1949	1949	1949
Jeffersonville	1934,1935,1972,1974, 1976,1992,1993,1995	1935,1974,1993	1993
Kokomo	1925,1941,1944,1959, 1961,1962,1989,1997	1925,1944,1959, 1961,1989	1961
Lafayette Jeff	1913,1916,1919,1920,1921 1948,1950,1951,1952,1956 1957,1963,1964,1967,1974 1992,1996	1916,1919,1920,1948,1950 1956,1964,1967,1992	1916,1948,1964
Lake Central	1984		
Lapel	1940		
LaPorte	1944,1997		
Lawrence North	1989	1989	1989
Lebanon	1911,1912,1914,1917, 1918,1943,1975	1911,1912,1917,1918,1943	1912,1917,1918
Logansport	1931,1934,1959,1961	1934	1934
Loogootee	1970,1975	1975	
Madison	1941,1949,1950,1962	1941,1949,1950	1950
Madison Heights	1972		
Marion	1922,1926,1947,1950,1968 1969,1975,1976,1980,1983 1985,1986,1987	1926,1975,1976, 1986,1987 1987	1926,1975,1976, 1985,1986,1987
Martinsville	1916,1917,1924,1926, 1927,1928,1933	1924,1926,1927,1928,1933	1924,1927,1933
Merrillville	1978,1995	1995	
Mich. City Elston	1966	1966	1966
Milan	1953,1954	1954	1954
Mitchell	1940	1940	
Montmorenci	1915	1915	
Muncie Burris	1939,1942	1942	
Muncie Central	1921,1923,1927,1928,1930, 1931,1948,1951,1952,1954, 1958,1960,1963,1970,1978 1979,1988	1923,1927,1928,1930,1931, 1951,1952,1954,1960,1963, 1978,1979,1988	1928,1931,1951, 1952,1963,1978 1979,1988
New Albany	1911,1950,1952,1955,1959 1973,1980,1994,1996	1973,1980,1996	1973
New Castle	1932,1967,1971,1984	1932	1932
Orleans	1912		
Plymouth	1982	1982	1982
Princeton	1965,1983		
Richmond	1935,1953,1985,1987,1992	1985,1987,1992	1992
Rochester	1914,1917,1937		
Rushville	1976	1976	
Shelbyville	1935,1947,1986	1947	1947
Shenandoah	1981		
S. Bend Adams	1973	1973	
S. Bend Central	1913,1949,1953,1957,1963	1913,1953,1957,1963	1953,1957
S. Bend Clay	1994	1994	1994
S. Bend Riley	1945	1945	
S. Bend St. Joe	1989,1993		
Southport	1990		

Southridge	1985,1986	
Springs Valley	1958	
Tell City	1961	
TH Garfield	1922,1947,1963	1922,1947
TH Gerstmeyer	1953,1954,1956,1957	1953
TH South	1977,1978,1979,1991	1978
TH Wiley	1924,1931	
Thorntown	1915,1919	1915	1915
Valparaiso	1994	1994
Vincennes	1916,1923,1925,1968, 1969,1981,1984	1923,1981,1984	1923,1981
Warsaw	1981,1984,1992,1996	1984	1984
Washington	1925,1929,1930,1941,1942	1930,1941,1942	1930,1941,1942
Whiting	1912	
Whitko	1991	
Winamac	1932	1932
Wingate	1913,1914	1913,1914	1913,1914

Enrollments, Vote, History
(State rank based on IHSAA survey 1996)

	State Rank	Fr.-Jr. Enrllmt.	97-98 Class	Vote on Change	State Ch.	2nd	Final Four	Last Sect.
Adams Central	283	290	2A	Yes	0	0	0	1994
Alexandria	195	457	2A	No	0	0	0	1995
Anderson	43	1,313	4A	No	3	7	17	1997
Anderson Highland	36	1,384	4A	No	0	0	0	1991
Andrean	126	702	3A	Yes	0	0	1	1995
Angola	140	642	3A	Yes	0	0	0	1985
Argos	351	165	1A	Yes	0	0	1	1981
Attica	332	205	1A	Yes	0	0	0	1993
Austin	279	294	2A	Yes	0	0	0	1986
Avon	86	894	4A	No	0	0	0	1978
Barr-Reeve	360	138	1A	Yes	0	0	0	1997
Batesville	189	464	3A	No	0	0	1	1997
Bedford N. Lawrence	47	1,280	4A	No	1	0	3	1995
Beech Grove	163	529	3A	Yes	0	0	0	1992
Bellmont	125	716	3A	No	0	0	0	1997
Ben Davis	1	2,798	4A	No	2	1	4	1997
Benton Central	168	523	3A	No	0	0	0	1997
Bethany Christian	349	173	1A	Yes	0	0	0	None
Blackford	158	551	3A	Yes	0	0	0	1991
Bloomfield	288	284	1A	No	0	0	0	1995
Bloomington North	70	1,026	4A	No	1	0	1	1997
Bloomington South	28	1,471	4A	No	*1	0	4	1996
Blue River Valley	339	192	1A	Yes	0	0	0	None*
Bluffton	233	377	2A	Yes	0	0	1	1977
Boone Grove	234	376	2A	No	0	0	0	1997
Boonville	110	793	3A	No	0	0	0	1984
Borden	362	135	1A	Yes	0	0	0	None
Brebeuf	159	551	3A	No	0	1	1	1991
Bremen	242	357	2A	Yes	0	0	0	1993
Brown County	149	588	3A	Yes	0	0	0	1976
Brownsburg	69	1,045	4A	No	0	0	0	1997
Brownstown	196	444	2A	Yes	0	0	0	1994
Calumet	142	633	3A	Yes	0	0	0	1996
Cambridge City	266	307	2A	Yes	0	0	0	1961

	State Rank	Fr.-Jr. Enrllmt.	97-98 Class	Vote on Change	State Ch.	2nd	Final Four	Last Sect.
Cannelton	379	62	1A	Yes	0	0	0	1952
Carmel	4	2,264	4A	No	1	1	3	1995
Carroll (Flora)	290	279	1A	Yes	0	0	*1	None*
Carroll (Ft.Wayne)	99	842	3A	No	0	0	0	1985
Cascade	226	390	2A	Yes	0	0	0	1984
Cass	217	409	2A	Yes	0	0	0	1997
Castle	55	1,182	4A	No	0	0	0	1990
Caston	334	203	1A	Yes	0	0	0	1993
Center Grove	25	1,515	4A	No	0	0	0	1994
Centerville	197	442	2A	Yes	0	0	0	1944
Central Noble	249	338	2A		0	0	0	1977
Charlestown	185	478	3A	Yes	0	0	0	1997
Chesterton	34	1,405	4A	No	0	0	0	1987
Churubusco	258	320	2A	Yes	0	0	0	None
Clarksville	244	350	2A	Yes	0	0	0	1986
Clay City	328	217	1A	Yes	0	0	0	1976
Clinton Central	302	261	1A	Yes	0	0	0	1983
Clinton Prairie	292	277	1A	No	0	0	0	1982
Cloverdale	268	305	2A	Yes	0	0	1	1983
Columbia City	87	886	4A	No	0	0	0	1978
Columbus East	72	1,008	4A	No	0	0	1	1996
Columbus North	39	1,334	4A	No	0	0	*3	1997
Concord	85	896	4A	No	0	2	2	1997
Connersville	63	1,115	4A	No	2	0	4	1997
Corydon	152	579	3A		0	0	0	1994
Covington	310	250	1A	Yes	0	0	0	1988
Cowan	356	150	1A	Yes	0	0	0	1976
Crawford County	198	441	2A	No	0	0	0	1995
Crawfordsville	154	562	3A	Yes	1	2	7	1989
Crothersville	352	165	1A	No	0	0	0	None
Crown Point	35	1,395	4A	No	0	0	0	1986
Culver	291	278	1A	Yes	0	0	0	1985
Culver Military	177	500	3A	Yes	0	0	0	None
Daleville	354	163	1A	Yes	0	0	0	1985
Danville	178	497	3A	Yes	0	0	0	1964
Decatur Central	59	1,142	4A	Yes	0	0	0	1997
DeKalb	75	972	4A	No	0	0	*1	1997
Delphi	221	402	2A	Yes	0	0	0	1996
Delta	127	700	3A		0	1	1	1997
East Central	79	948	4A	No	0	0	0	1991
E. Chicago Cent.	33	1,435	4A	No	*3	2	9	1995
East Noble	82	926	4A	No	0	0	0	1997
Eastbrook	213	417	2A	No	0	0	0	None
Eastern (Greene)	272	302	2A	Yes	0	0	0	None*
Eastern (Howard)	252	335	2A	Yes	0	0	0	1956
Eastern Hancock	273	302	2A	Yes	0	0	0	1981
Eastside	250	338	2A	Yes	0	0	0	1993
Edgewood	138	654	3A	Yes	0	0	0	1993
Edinburgh	335	202	1A	Yes	0	0	0	1973
Elkhart Central	51	1,204	4A	No	0	*1	5	1995
Elkhart Memorial	64	1,109	4A	No	0	0	0	1989
Elwood	176	503	3A	Yes	0	0	0	1960
Eminence	363	120	1A	Yes	0	0	0	1978
Evansville Bosse	115	757	3A	No	3	0	6	1997
Evansville Central	57	1,151	4A	No	0	1	4	1996
Evansville Day	372	81	1A	Yes	0	0	0	None
Evansville Harrison	50	1,206	4A	No	0	0	0	1995
Evansville Mater Dei	193	458	2A	No	0	0	0	None

	State Rank	Fr.-Jr. Enrllmt.	97-98 Class	Vote on Change	State Ch.	2nd	Final Four	Last Sect.
Evansville Memorial	134	668	3A	No	0	0	0	1996
Evansville North	61	1,137	4A	No	1	0	1	1980
Evansville Reitz	46	1,289	4A	No	0	1	1	1997
Fairfield	253	333	2A	Yes	0	0	0	1994
Floyd Central	65	1,108	4A	No	0	0	2	1989
Forest Park	247	343	2A	Yes	0	0	0	1993
FW Blackhawk	370	89	1A	Yes	0	0	0	None
FW Canterbury	357	149	1A	Yes	0	0	0	None
FW Christian	381	55	1A	Yes	0	0	0	None
FW Concordia	118	739	3A	Yes	0	0	0	1989
FW Dwenger	117	740	3A	No	0	0	0	1997
FW Elmhurst	124	721	3A	Yes	0	0	0	1988
FW Luers	201	439	2A	Yes	0	0	0	None
FW North	48	1,271	4A	No	0	1	3	1995
FW Northrop	19	1,550	4A	No	1	0	1	1987
FW Snider	27	1,477	4A	No	0	0	0	1982
FW South	54	1,184	4A	No	2	0	4	1997
FW Wayne	89	875	4A	No	0	0	0	1994
Fountain Central	256	328	2A	No	0	0	0	1991
Frankfort	131	683	3A	No	4	1	8	1997
Franklin	100	838	3A	Yes	3	2	7	1997
Franklin Central	53	1,186	4A	No	0	0	0	1996
Franklin County	128	690	3A	No	0	0	0	None*
Frankton	259	319	2A	Yes	0	0	0	None
Fremont	304	260	1A	Yes	0	0	0	1973
Frontier	342	189	1A	Yes	0	0	0	1989
Garrett	238	367	2A	Yes	0	0	0	1992
Gary Mann	137	657	3A	Yes	0	0	1	1975
Gary Roosevelt	60	1,142	4A	No	2	2	6	1991
Gary Wallace	37	1,381	4A	Yes	0	0	0	1996
Gary West	56	1,158	4A	Yes	0	1	1	1997
Gary Wirt	90	875	4A	No	0	0	0	1989
Gibson Southern	181	490	3A	Yes	0	0	0	1975
Glenn	215	411	2A	Yes	0	0	0	1991
Goshen	73	1,003	4A	No	0	0	0	1992
Graceland Christian	378	71	1A	Yes	0	0	0	None
Greencastle	204	434	2A	Yes	0	2	3	1996
Greenfield	98	844	3A	No	0	0	0	1993
Greensburg	170	517	3A	No	0	0	0	1993
Greenwood	105	811	3A	No	0	0	0	1991
Griffith	107	803	3A	Yes	0	0	0	1973
Hagerstown	277	299	2A	Yes	0	0	0	1965
Hamilton	350	171	1A	Yes	0	0	0	1991
Hamilton Heights	169	521	3A	Yes	0	0	0	1975
Hamilton S'eastern	62	1,130	4A	No	0	0	0	None*
Hammond	58	1,148	4A	No	0	1	1	1997
Hammond Clark	113	766	3A	Yes	0	0	0	1972
Hammond Gavit	116	743	3A	Yes	0	0	0	1985
Hammond Morton	88	878	4A	No	0	0	0	1976
Hammond Noll	121	733	3A	Yes	0	0	1	1990
Hanover Central	240	361	2A	Yes	0	0	0	1986
Harding	160	551	3A	No	0	0	0	1985
Harrison	66	1,086	4A	No	0	0	0	1997
Hauser	326	222	1A	Yes	0	0	0	None*
Hebron	300	262	1A	Yes	0	0	0	1994
Henryville	340	190	1A	Yes	0	0	0	None

	State Rank	Fr.-Jr. Enrllmt.	97-98 Class	Vote on Change	State Ch.	2nd	Final Four	Last Sect.
Heritage	231	381	2A	Yes	0	0	0	None*
Heritage Hills	175	506	3A	No	0	0	0	1997
Highland	84	903	4A	No	0	0	0	1995
Hobart	94	854	4A	Yes	0	0	0	1992
Homestead	44	1,302	4A	No	0	0	0	1992
Howe Military	367	103	1A	Yes	0	0	0	1958
Huntington North	16	1,580	4A	No	0	*1	3	1996
Indian Creek	214	413	2A	Yes	0	0	0	1987
Indiana Blind			1A	Yes				
Indiana Deaf	376	74	1A	Yes	0	0	0	None
Indpls Arlington	23	1,520	4A	No	0	0	0	1984
Indpls Broad Ripple	11	1,724	4A	No	1	0	2	1986
Indpls Cathedral	109	796	3A	No	0	0	1	1997
Indpls Chatard	184	479	3A	Yes	0	0	0	1988
Indpls Lutheran	331	207	1A	Yes	0	0	0	None
Indpls Manual	29	1,453	4A		0	1	2	1992
Indpls Northwest	31	1,450	4A	No	0	0	0	1976
Indpls Ritter	284	289	2A	Yes	0	0	0	None
Indpls Scecina	191	462	3A	Yes	0	0	0	1978
Indpls Tech	5	2,196	4A	No	0	4	4	1978
Jac-Cen-Del	324	228	1A	Yes	0	0	0	1992
Jasper	122	723	3A	No	1	0	2	1996
Jay County	77	958	4A	No	0	0	0	1996
Jeffersonville	17	1,576	4A	No	1	2	8	1996
Jennings County	68	1,061	4A	No	0	0	0	1997
Jimtown	232	379	2A	Yes	0	0	0	None*
Kankakee Valley	112	780	3A	Yes	0	0	0	1992
Knightstown	260	316	2A	Yes	0	0	0	1987
Knox	206	432	2A	No	0	0	0	1973
Kokomo	22	1,527	4A	No	1	4	8	1997
Kouts	345	183	1A	Yes	0	0	0	1996
LaCrosse	373	81	1A	No	0	0	0	1991
Lafayette Cath	341	190	1A	Yes	0	0	0	1987
Lafayette Jeff	13	1,623	4A	No	3	6	17	1996
Lake Central	8	2,009	4A	Yes	0	0	1	1997
Lake Station	219	404	2A	Yes	0	0	0	1946
Lakeland	164	525	3A	No	0	0	0	1982
Lakeview Chrstn	377	72	1A	Yes	0	0	0	None
Lanesville	355	154	1A	Yes	0	0	0	None
Lapel	318	238	1A	Yes	0	0	1	1942
LaPorte	24	1,519	4A	No	0	0	2	1997
LaVille	263	314	2A	Yes	0	0	0	1986
Lawrence Cent	12	1,654	4A	No	0	0	0	1977
Lawrence No	20	1,547	4A	No	1	0	1	1996
Lawrenceburg	218	406	2A	No	0	0	0	1997
Lebanon	120	734	3A	No	3	2	7	1993
Leo	202	438	2A	No	0	0	0	1994
Linton	257	328	2A	Yes	0	0	0	1982
Logansport	80	932	4A	No	1	0	4	1996
Loogootee	313	246	1A	Yes	0	1	2	1996
Lowell	95	851	4A	No	0	0	0	1993
Maconaquah	205	433	2A	Yes	0	0	0	None*
Madison	102	831	3A	No	1	2	4	1994
Madison Heights				No	0	0	1	1988

	State Rank	Fr.-Jr. Enrllmt.	97-98 Class	Vote on Change	State Ch.	2nd	Final Four	Last Sect.
Madison Shawe	371	82	1A	Yes	0	0	0	None
Madison-Grant	229	383	2A	Yes	0	0	0	1996
Manchester	203	435	2A	No	0	0	0	1995
Marian Heights Acad. (girls)								
	351	172	1A	Yes				
Marion	41	1,323	4A	No	6	0	7	1997
Martinsville	42	1,322	4A	No	3	2	7	1995
McCutcheon	91	874	4A	Yes	0	0	0	1995
Medora	374	78	1A	No	0	0	0	1949
Merrillville	18	1,574	4A	Yes	0	1	2	1997
Michigan City	10	1,750	4A	No	*1	0	1	None*
Mich. City Marq	344	188	1A	Yes	0	0	0	None
Milan	299	266	1A	No	1	0	2	1985
Mishawaka	49	1,253	4A	Yes	0	0	0	1986
Mishawaka Marian	156	552	3A	Yes	0	0	0	1969
Mississinewa	174	507	3A	Yes	0	0	0	1954
Mitchell	199	441	2A	Yes	0	1	1	1997
Monroe Central	297	271	1A	No	0	0	0	1968
Monrovia	255	331	2A	Yes	0	0	0	1996
Mooresville	83	908	4A	No	0	0	0	1997
Morgan Twp.	359	148	1A	Yes	0	0	0	None
Morristown	311	248	1A	Yes	0	0	0	1967
Morton Memorial	375	77	1A	Yes	0	0	0	1953
Mt. Vernon (Fortville)	148	607	3A	Yes	0	0	0	1992
Mt. Vernon (Posey)	129	689	3A	No	0	0	0	1988
Muncie Burris	267	306	2A	No	0	1	2	1947
Muncie Central	67	1,080	4A	No	8	5	17	1994
Muncie South	101	837	3A	No	0	0	0	1997
Munster	78	956	4A	No	0	0	0	1989
New Albany	9	1,774	4A	No	1	2	9	1997
New Castle	93	872	4A	No	1	0	4	1997
New Harmony	380	56	1A	Yes	0	0	0	None
New Haven	151	584	3A	Yes	0	0	0	1996
New Palestine	147	608	3A	Yes	0	0	0	1997
New Prairie	157	552	3A	Yes	0	0	0	None*
New Washington	346	183	1A	Yes	0	0	0	1989
Noblesville	45	1,301	4A	No	0	0	0	1997
North Central (Farmersburg)								
	289	280	1A	Yes	0	0	0	1967
North Central (Indpls)	2	2,414	4A	Yes	0	0	0	1997
North Daviess	316	241	1A	No	0	0	0	None*
North Decatur	282	291	2A	Yes	0	0	0	1988
North Harrison	145	626	3A	No	0	0	0	1996
North Judson	235	376	2A	Yes	0	0	0	1996
North Knox	211	420	2A	Yes	0	0	0	1964
North Miami	264	312	2A	Yes	0	0	0	1968
North Montgomery	192	459	2A	Yes	*2	0	2	1984
North Newton	200	441	2A	Yes	0	0	0	1978
North Posey	208	427	2A	Yes	0	0	0	1966
North Putnam	224	395	2A	Yes	0	0	0	1990
North Vermillion	308	256	1A	Yes	0	0	0	1987
North White	305	260	1A	Yes	0	0	0	1984
Northeast Dubois	303	261	1A	No	0	0	0	1988
Northeastern	248	339	2A	Yes	0	0	0	None
Northfield	261	316	2A	Yes	0	0	0	1997
Northridge	133	671	3A	No	0	0	0	1997
Northview	92	874	4A	No	0	0	0	1988
Northwestern	210	424	2A	Yes	0	0	0	1982

	State Rank	Fr.-Jr. Enrllmt.	97-98 Class	Vote on Change	State Ch.	2nd	Final Four	Last Sect.
NorthWood	146	623	3A	Yes	0	0	0	1995
Norwell	132	672	3A		0	0	0	1995
Oak Hill	222	400	2A	Yes	0	0	0	1971
Oldenburg Academy (girls)			1A	Yes				
Oregon-Davis	337	197	1A	Yes	0	0	0	1988
Orleans	347	183	1A	No	0	0	0	1995
Owen Valley	119	737	3A	Yes	0	0	0	1985
Paoli	236	376	2A	Yes	0	0	0	1994
Park Tudor	295	273	1A	Yes	0	0	0	None
Pekin Eastern	239	365	2A	Yes	0	0	0	1991
Pendleton Heights	103	814	3A	No	0	0	0	1996
Penn	6	2,144	4A	Yes	0	0	0	1996
Perry Central	278	296	2A	Yes	0	0	0	1997
Perry Meridian	40	1,328	4A	No	0	0	0	1984
Peru	139	645	3A	Yes	0	0	0	1987
Pike	21	1,542	4A	No	0	0	0	1990
Pike Central	179	492	3A	No	0	0	0	1997
Pioneer	280	294	2A	Yes	0	0	0	1964
Plainfield	104	813	3A	No	0	0	0	1996
Plymouth	106	808	3A	No	1	0	1	1997
Portage	7	2,020	4A	No	0	0	0	1996
Prairie Hts	216	411	2A	Yes	0	0	0	None
Princeton	153	576	3A	No	0	0	2	1992
Providence	173	510	3A	Yes	0	0	0	1984
Randolph Southern	348	178	1A	Yes	0	0	0	1994
Rensselaer	190	464	3A	Yes	0	0	0	1995
Richmond	30	1,453	4A	No	1	2	5	1996
Rising Sun	309	252	1A	Yes	0	0	0	1989
River Forest	270	304	2A	Yes	0	0	0	None
Riverton Parke	323	230	1A	Yes	0	0	0	None*
Rochester	188	466	3A	Yes	0	0	3	1978
Rockville	336	201	1A	Yes	0	0	0	1997
Roncalli	130	685	3A	Yes	0	0	0	None
Rossville	327	221	1A	No	0	0	0	1992
Rushville	123	723	3A	No	0	1	1	1993
Salem	172	512	3A	No	0	0	0	1985
Scottsburg	143	633	3A	No	0	0	0	1996
Seeger	271	304	2A	Yes	0	0	0	1978
Seymour	76	961	4A	No	0	0	0	1992
Shakamak	322	231	1A	No	0	0	0	1990
Shelbyville	114	760	3A	No	1	0	3	1996
Shenandoah	286	285	2A	No	0	0	1	1987
Sheridan	301	262	1A	Yes	0	0	0	1983
Shoals	338	195	1A	Yes	0	0	0	None
Silver Creek	187	469	3A	Yes	0	0	0	1982
South Adams	251	336	2A	Yes	0	0	0	1993
S.Bend Adams	74	985	4A	Yes	0	1	1	1984
S.Bend Clay	71	1,014	4A	No	1	0	1	1996
S.Bend LaSalle	81	931	4A	Yes	0	0	0	1983
S.Bend Riley	52	1,201	4A	No	0	1	1	1995
S.Bend St. Joseph's	135	666	3A	Yes	0	0	2	1993
S.Bend Washington	97	850	3A	No	0	0	0	1997
S.Central (Elizabeth)	329	217	1A	Yes	0	0	0	1974
S.Central (Union Mills)	319	237	1A	Yes	0	0	0	1982
South Dearborn	111	781	3A	No	0	0	0	1995
South Decatur	285	289	2A	Yes	0	0	0	1991

	State Rank	Fr.-Jr. Enrllmt.	97-98 Class	Vote on Change	State Ch.	2nd	Final Four	Last Sect.
South Knox	265	311	2A	Yes	0	0	0	1993
South Newton	306	260	1A	Yes	0	0	0	1995
South Putnam	275	300	2A	Yes	0	0	0	1994
South Ripley	262	316	2A	No	0	0	0	1988
South Spencer	237	368	2A	Yes	0	0	0	1996
South Vermillion	162	531	3A		0	0	0	1986
Southern Wells	314	245	1A	Yes	0	0	0	1996
Southmont	209	427	2A	Yes	0	0	0	1994
Southport	38	1,370	4A	No	0	0	1	1994
Southridge	243	356	2A	No	0	*1	3	1994
Southwestern (Hanover)								
	254	332	2A	No	0	0	0	1997
Southwestern (Shelbyville)								
	344	186	1A	Yes	0	0	0	None
Southwood	276	300	2A	Yes	0	0	0	None*
Speedway	246	346	2A	Yes	0	0	0	1973
Springs Valley	320	236	1A	No	0	0	1	1986
Sullivan	171	516	3A	Yes	0	0	0	1991
Switzerland County	227	386	2A		0	0	0	1994
Taylor	230	383	2A	Yes	0	0	0	None
Tecumseh	312	248	1A	Yes	0	0	0	None*
Tell City	182	483	3A	No	0	0	1	1993
Terre Haute North	14	1,618	4A	No	0	0	0	1996
Terre Haute South	26	1,497	4A	No	0	1	4	1997
Tippecanoe Valley	165	525	3A	Yes	0	0	0	1997
Tipton	194	458	2A	Yes	0	0	0	1989
Tri	333	205	1A	Yes	0	0	0	1977
Tri-Central	293	277	1A	Yes	0	0	0	None*
Tri-County	325	228	1A	Yes	0	0	0	1993
Tri-West	274	301	2A	Yes	0	0	0	1991
Triton	287	285	2A	Yes	0	0	0	1965
Triton Central	223	396	2A	Yes	0	0	0	1997
Turkey Run	353	164	1A	No	0	0	0	1992
Twin Lakes	136	665	3A	Yes	0	0	0	1997
Union (Dugger)	366	106	1A	Yes	0	0	0	1997
Union (Modoc)	365	108	1A		0	0	0	1970
Union City	317	240	1A	Yes	0	0	0	1984
Union County	225	393	2A	Yes	0	0	0	1979
Valparaiso	15	1,591	4A	No	0	1	1	1997
Vincennes Lincoln	108	799	3A	No	2	1	8	1997
Vincennes Rivet	369	93	1A	Yes	0	0	0	None
Wabash	207	431	2A	Yes	0	0	0	1967
Waldron	294	275	1A	Yes	0	0	0	1960
Wapahani	296	273	1A	Yes	0	0	0	1990
Warren Central	3	2,279	4A	No	0	0	0	1991
Warsaw	32	1,439	4A	No	1	0	4	1997
Washington	144	627	3A	No	3	0	5	1983
Washington Cath	368	95	1A	No	0	0	0	1993
Washington Twp.	358	149	1A	Yes	0	0	0	None
Wawasee	96	851	3A	No	0	0	0	1995
Wes-Del	315	244	1A	Yes	0	0	0	1986
West Central	321	236	1A	Yes	0	0	0	1987
West Lafayette	180	491	3A	Yes	0	0	0	1989
West Noble	183	482	3A	Yes	0	0	0	None*
West Vigo	166	525	3A	No	0	0	0	1990

	State Rank	Fr.-Jr. Enrllmt.	97-98 Class	Vote on Change	State Ch.	2nd	Final Four	Last Sect.
West Washington	307	257	1A	Yes	0	0	0	1996
Western	155	562	3A	Yes	0	0	0	1990
Western Boone	220	403	2A	Yes	*1	0	2	1997
Westfield	186	473	3A	Yes	0	0	0	None
Westview	281	292	2A	Yes	0	0	0	1994
Westville	361	138	1A	Yes	0	0	0	None
Wheeler	245	348	2A	Yes	0	0	0	None
White River Valley	298	268	1A	No	0	0	0	1996
White's	364	111	1A	Yes	0	0	0	None
Whiteland	150	588	3A	Yes	0	0	0	1993
Whiting	330	216	1A	Yes	0	0	0	1981
Whitko	161	543	3A	No	0	0	1	1996
Winamac	241	361	2A	Yes	0	1	1	1997
Winchester	212	418	2A	Yes	0	0	0	1997
Wood Memorial	269	305	2A	Yes	0	0	0	1990
Woodlan	228	384	2A	Yes	0	0	0	1997
Yorktown	167	524	3A	No	0	0	0	1986
Zionsville	141	641	3A	Yes	0	0	0	1995

*School(s) in present corporation won sectional.

Sectional championships

First sectionals 1915

ADAMS CENTRAL (4): 1964-1966, 1994; **Kirkland Twp. (1),** 1928; **Pleasant Mills (2),** 1940, 1942; **Monroe (3),** 1921, 1943, 1947.

ALEXANDRIA (10): 1931-32, 1953-54, 1959, 1961, 1963, 1989, 1994-95.

ANDERSON (48): 1918-24, 1927-30, 1934-39, 1941, 1943-46, 1948, 1950-52, 1955-56, 1958, 1962, 1964-66, 1969, 1973-74, 1977-79, 1981, 1983-84, 1986, 1990, 1992-93, 1996-97.

ANDERSON HIGHLAND (3): 1976, 1980, 1991.

ANDREAN (9): 1977, 1980-81, 1986, 1989-91, 1994-95.

ANGOLA (14): 1920-22, 1924, 1926, 1928-29, 1934, 1959, 1962-63, 1978, 1982, 1985.

ARGOS (4): 1978-81.

ATTICA (21): 1927, 1929-30, 1940, 1942, 1946, 1948-49, 1953-55, 1958-59, 1961-62, 1968, 1976, 1980, 1983, 1986, 1993.

AUSTIN (3): 1928, 1985-86.

AVON (1): 1978.

BARR-REEVE (5): 1980, 1987, 1992, 1994, 1997; **Montgomery,** 1935, 1952.

BATESVILLE (23): 1927, 1933-34, 1940-41, 1943-45, 1949-52, 1963, 1971, 1974, 1976, 1979, 1983, 1989, 1994-97.

BEDFORD NORTH LAWRENCE (16): 1975-77, 1979-85, 1987-90, 1994-95; **Bedford (36),** 1920-24, 1926-30, 1932-33, 1936-38, 1941-49, 1951, 1957-58, 1961-63, 1966, 1969, 1971-74; **Shawswick (2),** 1952, 1959; **Needmore (1),** 1964; **Oolitic (3),** 1954, 1967-68.

BEECH GROVE (2): 1966, 1992.

BELLMONT (8): 1971, 1974, 1979, 1984-85, 1987, 1991, 1997; **Decatur (10),** 1922, 1927, 1932, 1941, 1944, 1949-52, 1959; **Decatur Catholic**
(1), 1966; **Monmouth (4),** 1953-56.

BEN DAVIS (14): 1935, 1965, 1974, 1978, 1984-86, 1988, 1992-97.

BENTON CENTRAL (12): 1971-72, 1977-79, 1982-83, 1987, 1992, 1994, 1996-97; **Ambia (2),** 1956, 1961; **Boswell (5),** 1925, 1927-28, 1931, 1946; **Earl Park (4),** 1933, 1935-36, 1952; **Fowler (13),** 1932, 1934, 1944, 1949, 1953-55, 1959-60, 1962-63, 1966-67; **Freeland Park (5),** 1929, 1940-41, 1948, 1950; **Montmorenci (3),** 1915, 1918, 1927; **Otterbein (9),** 1924, 1930, 1937, 1942, 1947, 1951, 1957-58, 1965; **Oxford (5),** 1926, 1938-39, 1943, 1945.

BLACKFORD (10): 1970-72, 1974-76, 1978, 1981, 1984, 1991; **Hartford City (14),** 1915, 1920, 1923, 1930-34, 1937, 1953-57; **Montpelier (5),** 1927, 1944, 1960, 1965, 1967; **Roll (1),** 1951.

BLOOMFIELD (26): 1928-29, 1932, 1937-40, 1959-65, 1970, 1972, 1978-81, 1983, 1986-87, 1989, 1994-95.

BLOOMINGTON NORTH (10): 1976, 1979-84, 1989, 1991, 1997; **University (2),** 1946, 1972; **Unionville (1),** 1966.

BLOOMINGTON SOUTH (8): 1973, 1978, 1985-88, 1992, 1996; **Bloomington (25),** 1915-23, 1939-41, 1945, 1948-49, 1951, 1953, 1955, 1958, 1960, 1965, 1967-68, 1970-71.

BLUE RIVER (0): Mooreland, 1923-24.

BLUFFTON (26): 1915, 1917, 1926, 1928-29, 1931-33, 1938, 1943, 1952, 1954-58, 1960-63, 1967-70, 1976-77.

BOONE GROVE (2): 1983, 1997.

BOONVILLE (23): 1933, 1942-48, 1951-53, 1956, 1960, 1963-67, 1976-78, 1983-84; **Tennyson (2),** 1930-32.

BREBEUF (3): 1983, 1988, 1991.

BREMEN (7): 1927, 1961, 1966, 1987-88, 1990, 1993.

BROWN COUNTY (2): 1972, 1976; Helmsburg (1), 1949; Nashville (1), 1959.

BROWNSBURG (16): 1927, 1938, 1942, 1951, 1959, 1968, 1971, 1972, 1981, 1988, 1990-92, 1994-95, 1997.

BROWNSTOWN (10): 1931, 1936, 1944-45, 1953, 1981, 1983-84, 1991, 1994; Freetown (1), 1925; Vallonia (1), 1950.

CALUMET (4): 1972, 1974, 1993, 1996.

CAMBRIDGE CITY (2): 1951, 1961; Milton (1), 1954.

CANNELTON (5): 1933, 1936, 1946, 1948, 1952.

CARMEL (20): 1925, 1966-1974, 1976-1980, 1987-88, 1992-93, 1995.

CARROLL (FLORA) (0): Burlington (2), 1927, 1943; Cutler (1), 1922; Flora (7), 1926, 1937, 1942, 1945-47, 1950.

CARROLL (FORT WAYNE) (2): 1984-85.

CASCADE (2): 1965, 1984; Amo (5), 1928, 1944, 1949, 1953, 1958; Clayton (3), 1924-25, 1947.

CASS (3): 1978, 1981, 1997; Walton (1), 1921; Washington Twp. (2), 1916, 1949; Young America (1), 1920.

CASTLE (4): 1961-62, 1987, 1990; Chandler (1), 1950; Newburgh (3), 1955, 1958-59.

CASTON (3): 1991-93; Fulton, 1934, 1942; Kewanna, 1927, 1954.

CENTER GROVE (11): 1943, 1960, 1972, 1975-76, 1979, 1985-86, 1988, 1992, 1994.

CENTERVILLE (1): 1944.

CENTRAL NOBLE (1): 1977; Albion (2), 1960, 1963; Wolf Lake (2), 1942, 1967.

CHARLESTOWN (6): 1962, 1975-76, 1981, 1990, 1997.

CHESTERTON (3): 1955, 1968, 1987.

CLARKSVILLE (3): 1978-79, 1986.

CLAY CITY (7): 1929, 1931, 1972-76; Cory (1), 1947.

CLINTON CENTRAL (5): 1960, 1966, 1979-80, 1983; Michigantown (1), 1933.

CLINTON PRAIRIE (2): 1964, 1982; Colfax (1), 1957; Jackson Twp. (2), 1941, 1956.

CLOVERDALE (9): 1965-66, 1968-69, 1972-73, 1981-83.

COLUMBIA CITY (22): 1926-27, 1929-30, 1932-39, 1950, 1959-61, 1963-64, 1972-73, 1975, 1978.

COLUMBUS EAST (8): 1977-80, 1985-86, 1990, 1996.

COLUMBUS NORTH (15): 1974-75, 1981-84, 1987-89, 1991-95, 1997; Columbus (34), 1917-25, 1928-29, 1931-33, 1937-38, 1940, 1942, 1946, 1948, 1951, 1954-57, 1961, 1963-66, 1968-71.

CONCORD (8: 1977, 1985-86, 1988, 1990-91, 1993, 1997; Concord Twp. (1), 1949.

CONNERSVILLE (57): 1922-37, 1939-41, 1944, 1948-49, 1951-57, 1960-63, 1968-74, 1978, 1980-87, 1989-92, 1994-97; Everton (1), 1947.

CORYDON (8): 1931, 1960-61, 1964, 1967, 1982, 1992, 1994.

COVINGTON (13): 1923, 1945, 1947, 1951, 1956, 1960, 1970-71, 1974, 1977, 1984-85, 1988.

COWAN (1): 1976.

CRAWFORD COUNTY (6): 1977, 1980-82, 1984, 1995; Leavenworth (1), 1967; Marengo (2), 1947, 1957; Milltown (2), 1970, 1976.

CRAWFORDSVILLE (41): 1915-16, 1919-20, 1922-24, 1926, 1928-30, 1932-33, 1936-38, 1940-43, 1946-48, 1955, 1957-60, 1963-65, 1968-69, 1971-73, 1976, 1978-79, 1985, 1989.

CROWN POINT (5): 1966, 1969, 1971, 1985-86.

CULVER (12): 1923, 1931, 1936, 1938, 1942, 1944-48, 1964, 1985; Monterey (1), 1961.

DALEVILLE (1): 1985.

DANVILLE (9): 1929, 1931-32, 1945-46, 1954, 1956, 1963-64; New Winchester (1), 1939.

DE KALB (17): 1968-70, 1974, 1977, 1979-1981, 1983, 1987-90, 1994-97; Ashley (2), 1946, 1964; Auburn (18), 1925, 1927-28, 1930-31, 1935-36, 1939, 1941, 1943, 1945, 1949-1955; Waterloo (1), 1960.

DECATUR CENTRAL (4): 1941, 1958, 1996-97.

DELPHI (20): 1924-25, 1928-33, 1936, 1938-41, 1944, 1948, 1951, 1957, 1967, 1978, 1996; Camden (3), 1934-35, 1949.

DELTA (5): 1980, 1985, 1989, 1993, 1997.

EAST CENTRAL (6): 1975, 1984, 1986-87, 1990-91; North Dearborn (4), 1962-64, 1968; Sunman (2), 1938, 1966.

EAST CHICAGO CENTRAL (7): 1987, 1989, 1991-95; East Chicago Washington (21), 1926, 1928, 1930, 1946-47, 1958-66, 1968, 1971, 1974-77, 1985; East Chicago Roosevelt (7), 1942, 1951, 1969-70, 1982-83, 1986; East Chicago (1), 1915.

EAST NOBLE (12): 1967, 1972, 1974-75, 1984-85, 1988, 1990, 1993, 1995-97; Avilla (3), 1941, 1955-56; Kendallville (27), 1917-21, 1923-24, 1926-28, 1930-33, 1937-40, 1943, 1946-47, 1950-53, 1957, 1961.

EASTERN (GREENE) (0): Solsberry (3), 1948, 1953, 1957.

EASTERN (HOWARD) (1): 1956; Greentown (3), 1923, 1942, 1950.

EASTERN HANCOCK (3): 1968, 1974, 1981; Charlottesville (2), 1953, 1958; Westland (1), 1932; Wilkinson (2), 1931, 1955.

EASTSIDE (2): 1966, 1993; Butler (1), 1942; Spencerville (1), 1947.

EDGEWOOD (1): 1993; Ellettsville (4), 1947, 1950, 1952, 1961.

EDINBURGH (3): 1951, 1959, 1973.

ELKHART CENTRAL (5): 1976, 1978-79, 1994-95; Elkhart (28), 1916, 1924-25, 1931, 1937-39, 1943-44, 1946-48, 1950-54, 1956-62, 1964, 1966, 1970-71.

ELKHART MEMORIAL (5): 1974, 1980-82, 1989.

ELWOOD (2): 1957, 1960.

EMINENCE (2): 1962, 1978.

EVANSVILLE BOSSE (23): 1930, 1932, 1935, 1939, 1941, 1944, 1945, 1950, 1959, 1961-63, 1973-76, 1982-85, 1990, 1994, 1997.

EVANSVILLE CENTRAL (36): 1920-29, 1931, 1933, 1936-38, 1940, 1942-43, 1946-49, 1952-54, 1958, 1965, 1977, 1981, 1988, 1991-96; Evansville (1), 1915.

EVANSVILLE HARRISON (2): 1992, 1995.

*EVANSVILLE LINCOLN (3): 1956-57, 1960.

EVANSVILLE (REITZ) MEMORIAL (7): 1966, 1970, 1986-87, 1989, 1993, 1996.

EVANSVILLE NORTH (4): 1967, 1978-80.

EVANSVILLE REITZ (7): 1934, 1951, 1955, 1968, 1971-72, 1997.

*EVANSVILLE REX MUNDI (2): 1964, 1969.

FAIRFIELD (4): 1969, 1971, 1983, 1994; New Paris (2), 1927, 1941.

FLOYD CENTRAL (14): 1971, 1973, 1975, 1977-81, 1983-86, 1988-89.

FOREST PARK (2): 1990, 1993.

*FORT WAYNE CENTRAL (21): 1925-28, 1930, 1936-37, 1942-44, 1946, 1949-53, 1960, 1962, 1964, 1968, 1970.

*FORT WAYNE CENTRAL CATHOLIC (2): 1968-69.

FORT WAYNE CONCORDIA (3): 1963, 1981, 1989.

FORT WAYNE DWENGER (5): 1988-89, 1994, 1996-97.

FORT WAYNE ELMHURST (5): 1971, 1983-84, 1987-88.

FORT WAYNE NORTH (21): 1931, 1933, 1941, 1945, 1950, 1954-55, 1965-66, 1969-73, 1975-76, 1978, 1990, 1992-93, 1995.

FORT WAYNE NORTHROP (8): 1973-74, 1980, 1983-87.

FORT WAYNE SNIDER (3): 1967, 1972, 1982.

FORT WAYNE SOUTH (27): 1923-24, 1929, 1934-35, 1938-40, 1947, 1956-59, 1961, 1966-67, 1974-75, 1977-80, 1991, 1993, 1995-97.

FORT WAYNE WAYNE (4): 1976, 1977, 1981, 1994.

FOUNTAIN CENTRAL (7): 1973, 1979, 1981-82, 1989-91; Hillsboro (5), 1926, 1932-33, 1943-44; Kingman (1), 1936; Mellot (1), 1928; Richland Twp. (3), 1950, 1952, 1957; Veedersburg (3), 1920, 1924, 1931; Wallace (1), 1925.

FRANKFORT (46): 1921-32, 1934-36, 1938-40, 1942-45, 1949-50, 1952-55, 1961, 1963, 1965, 1972-74, 1976-78, 1984-85, 1987, 1991, 1993-97.

FRANKLIN (43): 1918-39, 1942, 1945-48, 1954-55, 1962, 1964, 1968-69, 1971, 1973-74, 1977, 1984, 1989-90, 1995-97; Bargersville (1), 1952; Hopewell (1), 1916.

FRANKLIN CENTRAL (9): 1971, 1975-76, 1979-80, 1989-90, 1993, 1996; Franklin Twp. (2), 1950-51.

FRANKLIN COUNTY (0): Brookville (11), 1916,

1923, 1946, 1950, 1958-59, 1964-66, 1975, 1988.

FREMONT (4): 1925, 1956, 1958, 1973.

FRONTIER (7): 1966, 1968-69, 1973, 1976, 1981, 1989; Brookston (14), 1925, 1930-31, 1934, 1940-42, 1948-51, 1960-62; Chalmers (1), 1933.

GARRETT (17): 1923, 1931, 1937-38, 1940, 1944, 1948, 1957, 1961, 1964-66, 1971-72, 1984, 1986, 1992.

GARY MANN (5): 1929, 1931, 1942, 1949, 1977; Gary Emerson (14), 1917-20, 1923, 1927, 1932, 1937-38, 1944-45, 1947-48, 1975.

GARY ROOSEVELT (21): 1954-55, 1957, 1959-61, 1963, 1965-68, 1970, 1978-79, 1981-82, 1985, 1987-88, 1990-91.

GARY WALLACE (7): 1943, 1953, 1973, 1980, 1983, 1986, 1996.

GARY WEST (8): 1971-72, 1974, 1976, 1984, 1992-93, 1997; Gary Froebel (10), 1925, 1936, 1940-41, 1950-51, 1956, 1958, 1962, 1964; Gary Tolleston (4), 1952, 1964, 1967, 1969.

GARY WIRT (1): 1989.

GIBSON SOUTHERN (1): 1975; Fort Branch (8), 1941-42, 1949, 1954, 1959-60, 1962-63; Haubstadt (1), 1961; Owensville (10), 1925-27, 1931-32, 1937-39, 1945, 1953.

GLENN (2): 1989, 1991.

GOSHEN (9): 1922, 1928-30, 1936, 1942, 1963, 1969, 1992.

GREENCASTLE (33): 1919-20, 1922, 1927-28, 1930-34, 1936-39, 1941-43, 1947-48, 1950, 1952-53, 1956-57, 1960-61, 1963-64, 1968-69, 1988, 1993, 1996.

GREENFIELD (19): 1925-27, 1933, 1936, 1939-40, 1942-44, 1948, 1952, 1968, 1973, 1977, 1982, 1984, 1988, 1993; Eden, 1945-46; Hancock Central, 1956; Maxwell, 1941.

GREENSBURG (33): 1927, 1929-33, 1936-38, 1942-45, 1948-50, 1953-55, 1960, 1962-63, 1966-67, 1977, 1980-82, 1984, 1986, 1989-90, 1993.

GREENWOOD (8): 1940-41, 1961, 1963, 1965-66, 1970, 1991.

GRIFFITH (2): 1967, 1973.

HAGERSTOWN (4): 1928-29, 1959, 1965; Greensfork (1), 1936.

HAMILTON (2): 1967, 1991.

HAMILTON HEIGHTS (8): 1975; Arcadia (2), 1921, 1924; Atlanta (1), 1937; Cicero (3), 1916, 1928, 1932; Jackson Center (2), 1932, 1945.

HAMILTON SOUTHEASTERN (0): Fishers (1), 1922.

HAMMOND (30): 1933-39, 1944-45, 1948-50, 1952-56, 1965-66, 1973-75, 1979, 1982-84, 1987-88, 1996-97.

HAMMOND CLARK (4): 1943, 1970-72.

HAMMOND GAVIT (2): 1978, 1985.

HAMMOND MORTON (1): 1976.

HAMMOND NOLL (8): 1957, 1973, 1978-80, 1984, 1988, 1990.

*HAMMOND TECH (4): 1940, 1957, 1967-68.
HANOVER CENTRAL (1): 1986.
HARDING (3): 1979, 1982, 1985.
HARRISON (3): 1981, 1983, 1997; **Monitor (1),** 1943.
HAUSER (0): Hope (1), 1945.
HEBRON (7): 1953-54, 1973-74, 1976, 1990, 1994.
HERITAGE (0): Monroeville (1), 1948.
HERITAGE HILLS (7): 1980, 1982, 1985-86, 1988-89, 1997; **Chrisney (2),** 1965, 1969; **Dale (11),** 1934, 1937-40, 1944, 1949, 1956-58, 1968.
HIGHLAND (3): 1981, 1992, 1995.
HOBART (3): 1972, 1977, 1992.
HOMESTEAD (4): 1980-81, 1988, 1992.
HOWE MILITARY (2): 1949, 1958.
HUNTINGTON NORTH (20): 1969-79, 1982-86, 1993-96; **Huntington (36),** 1918-26, 1928-34, 1938, 1940-42, 1945-48, 1950, 1952-54, 1957, 1960-66; **Andrews (1),** 1943; **Clear Creek (3),** 1927, 1937, 1956; **Huntington Catholic (2),** 1949, 1959; **Huntington Twp. (3),** 1944, 1955, 1958; **Roanoke (2),** 1935-36; **Union Twp. (2),** 1939, 1951.
INDIAN CREEK (6): 1978, 1980-83, 1987; **Morgantown (1),** 1956; **Trafalgar (1),** 1917.
INDIANAPOLIS ARLINGTON (2): 1974, 1984.
*INDIANAPOLIS ATTUCKS (13): 1951, 1953-59, 1961-62, 1970, 1972-73.
INDIANAPOLIS BROAD RIPPLE (6): 1928, 1945, 1963, 1980, 1983, 1986.
INDIANAPOLIS CATHEDRAL (7): 1971-72, 1982, 1992, 1994-95, 1997.
INDIANAPOLIS CHATARD (2): 1981, 1988.
*INDIANAPOLIS HOWE (7): 1944, 1964, 1966, 1979, 1981-82, 1986.
INDIANAPOLIS MANUAL (10): 1915, 1919, 1922-23, 1960-61, 1974, 1980, 1983, 1992.
*INDIANAPOLIS MARSHALL (3): 1977, 1981, 1983.
INDIANAPOLIS NORTHWEST (3): 1970-71, 1976.
INDIANAPOLIS SCECINA (1): 1978.
*INDIANAPOLIS SHORTRIDGE (10): 1925-26, 1931, 1933, 1936, 1938, 1940, 1967-69.
INDIANAPOLIS TECH (19): 1920-21, 1927, 1929-30, 1932, 1934, 1937, 1946, 1949-50, 1952, 1960, 1964, 1966-67, 1971-72, 1978.
*INDIANAPOLIS WASHINGTON (10): 1948, 1965, 1968-69, 1975, 1977, 1979-80, 1982, 1995.
*INDIANAPOLIS WOOD (2): 1975, 1978.
JAC-CEN-DEL (7): 1965, 1967-69, 1972, 1977, 1992; **Napoleon (2),** 1947-48; **Osgood (1),** 1939.
JASPER (28): 1922, 1933-34, 1936, 1938, 1942-49, 1952, 1956-57, 1960-62, 1971-75, 1981, 1989, 1995-96; **Ireland (1),** 1963.
JAY COUNTY (12): 1976-79, 1981-83, 1987, 1992, 1994-96; **Bryant (2),** 1958, 1963; **Dunkirk (6),** 1925, 1928, 1943, 1945, 1959, 1961; **Pennville (4),** 1924, 1935, 1942, 1962; **Portland (12),** 1926, 1929, 1940-41, 1946-48, 1950, 1964,

1968-69, 1973; **Redkey (2),** 1939, 1952.
JEFFERSONVILLE (32): 1924, 1927, 1933-35, 1941-45, 1947, 1949, 1952-54, 1958, 1963, 1968, 1970, 1972, 1974, 1976-77, 1982, 1987-88, 1991-96.
JENNINGS COUNTY (8): 1972, 1976, 1980, 1986, 1993, 1995-97; **Butlerville (1),** 1926; **North Vernon (13),** 1926, 1934-35, 1937, 1939-40, 1947, 1952, 1958-59, 1961, 1965-66; **Scipio (1),** 1928.
JIMTOWN (0): Baugo Twp. (1), 1945.
KANKAKEE VALLEY (11): 1971, 1975, 1977, 1979-82, 1984-85, 1988, 1992; **DeMotte (2),** 1964, 1970; **Wheatfield (3),** 1950, 1965, 1967.
KNIGHTSTOWN (2): 1958, 1987.
KNOX (12): 1939, 1952-53, 1960, 1962-63, 1966, 1968-69, 1971-73.
KOKOMO (66): 1916-20, 1924-27, 1929-31, 1933-41, 1943-49, 1951-54, 1958-69, 1971, 1973-80, 1984-89, 1991-97; **Kokomo Haworth (2),** 1970, 1972.
KOUTS (3): 1987, 1995-96.
LA CROSSE (3): 1977, 1989, 1991.
LA PORTE (22): 1925-31, 1933, 1936-40, 1944, 1946, 1949, 1976, 1988, 1990-91, 1996-97.
LA VILLE (3): 1968, 1985-86; **Lakeville (1),** 1924; **Lapaz (5),** 1951, 1954-56, 1958.
LAFAYETTE CENTRAL CATHOLIC (2): 1973, 1987.
LAFAYETTE JEFFERSON (63): 1916-17, 1919-23, 1928, 1930-33, 1935, 1937-42, 1944-72, 1974-77, 1980, 1982, 1984-86, 1988, 1990-93, 1996.
LAKE CENTRAL (8): 1970, 1979-80, 1984, 1988, 1991, 1994, 1997.
LAKE STATION EDISON (2): 1941, 1946.
LAKELAND (8): 1965, 1968, 1970, 1977-78, 1980-82; **Brighton (1),** 1959; **LaGrange (6),** 1926-29, 1933, 1954; **Lima (3),** 1930-32.
LAPEL (3): 1925, 1940, 1942.
LAWRENCE CENTRAL (4): 1942-43, 1976-77.
LAWRENCE NORTH (8): 1985, 1987, 1989-90, 1992-94, 1996.
LAWRENCEBURG (26): 1927-28, 1931-32, 1938, 1940, 1945-50, 1960, 1967, 1970-74, 1979, 1981-82, 1991-92, 1996-97.
LEBANON (47): 1916-18, 1920, 1923-24, 1929, 1931-43, 1948, 1951-52, 1954, 1961, 1964, 1966, 1968-71, 1973-79, 1983-85, 1987-90, 1992-93; **Whitestown (1),** 1946.
LEO (4): 1975-76, 1993-94.
LINTON (20): 1926-27, 1930, 1934, 1936, 1942-43, 1945-47, 1951, 1954, 1958, 1966-67, 1971, 1974-76, 1982.
LOGANSPORT (56): 1919, 1923-37, 1939-48, 1950-54, 1956-57, 1959-62, 1965-67, 1969, 1971, 1974, 1976-77, 1979-80, 1983-84, 1986, 1988-90, 1994-96.
LOOGOOTEE (22): 1939, 1948-51, 1961-62, 1964, 1970-75, 1981-82, 1984, 1986, 1988, 1990, 1995-96.

LOWELL (5): 1968, 1972, 1976, 1989, 1993.
MACONAQUAH (0): Bunker Hill (2), 1924, 1960; Clay Twp. (2), 1925, 1962.
MADISON (34): 1933-35, 1937-38, 1940-43, 1945-52, 1957-67, 1971-72, 1983-84, 1991, 1994; Central (1), 1936; Deputy (1), 1925.
MADISON-GRANT (3): 1973, 1988, 1996; Fairmount (5), 1915, 1929, 1942, 1945, 1955; Summittville (2), 1926, 1949.
*MADISON HEIGHTS (9): 1967-68, 1970-72, 1975, 1982, 1987-88.
MANCHESTER (12): 1960, 1964-66, 1968, 1971, 1980, 1982, 1988, 1992, 1994-95; Chester Twp. (2), 1944, 1948; Laketon (1), 1926; North Manchester (8), 1924-25, 1927-28, 1930, 1940, 1942, 1947.
MARION (61): 1921-28, 1930-41, 1943, 1947-52, 1956-59, 1963, 1965-70, 1972, 1974-87, 1989-95, 1997.
MARTINSVILLE (33): 1916-21, 1923-31, 1933-38, 1943, 1954, 1957, 1959, 1963-64, 1969, 1974-75, 1977, 1990, 1995.
McCUTCHEON (9): 1981-82, 1986-88, 1990-91, 1994-95; Wainwright (1), 1968; West Point (3), 1925-26, 1929.
MEDORA (1): 1949.
MERRILLVILLE (11): 1975, 1978, 1982-83, 1987, 1990, 1993-97.
MICHIGAN CITY (0): Michigan City Elston (40): 1923-24, 1932, 1934-35, 1942-43, 1945, 1947-48, 1952-75, 1978, 1982, 1992-95. Michigan City Rogers (10): 1977, 1979-81, 1983-87, 1989.
MILAN (12): 1932, 1935-36, 1946, 1953-56, 1960, 1973, 1980, 1985.
MISHAWAKA (9): 1925, 1927-28, 1935, 1937, 1939, 1955, 1975, 1986.
MISHAWAKA MARIAN (1): 1969.
MISSISSINEWA (2): 1953-54; Gas City (2), 1944, 1946.
MITCHELL (12): 1931, 1934-35, 1939-40, 1950, 1956, 1960, 1970, 1987-88, 1997.
MONROE CENTRAL (2): 1965, 1968; Farmland (3), 1935, 1946, 1955; Parker (12), 1938-41, 1944-45, 1948, 1953, 1958-60, 1963, Stoney Creek (3), 1922, 1924-25.
MONROVIA (3): 1932, 1942, 1996.
MOORESVILLE (9): 1944, 1966, 1977, 1979, 1989, 1992-94, 1997.
MORRISTOWN (6): 1943, 1957, 1961-63, 1967.
MORTON MEMORIAL (1): 1953.
*MOUNT ST. FRANCIS (2): 1948, 1951.
MOUNT VERNON (FORTVILLE) (9): 1966, 1975, 1982, 1985-87, 1990-92; Fortville (6), 1935, 1937-38, 1947, 1949, 1954; Mount Comfort (6), 1923-24, 1928-30, 1934.
MOUNT VERNON (POSEY) (6): 1968, 1972, 1978, 1981-82, 1988.
MUNCIE BURRIS (7): 1939-44, 1947.
MUNCIE CENTRAL (50): 1917-18, 1921, 1923-38, 1945-46, 1948-63, 1968, 1970-71, 1977-80,

1982, 1988, 1990, 1992-94.
*MUNCIE NORTH (3): 1974-75, 1984.
MUNCIE SOUTH (14): 1964-67, 1969, 1981, 1983, 1985, 1987, 1989, 1991, 1995-97.
MUNSTER (4): 1969, 1976-77, 1989.
NEW ALBANY (41): 1925-26, 1929-30, 1932, 1936-40, 1946, 1948, 1950-56, 1958-60, 1966-67, 1969, 1973, 1975, 1980-81, 1983, 1985, 1987, 1989-97.
NEW CASTLE (52): 1915, 1922, 1925-28, 1930-37, 1939-41, 1943-44, 1946, 1948-50, 1952-53, 1955, 1957, 1959, 1963-65, 1967, 1969, 1971-73, 1978-79, 1983-86, 1988-97.
NEW HAVEN (4): 1991-92, 1995-96.
NEW PALESTINE (4): 1957, 1980, 1989, 1997.
NEW PRAIRIE (0): Rolling Prairie (2), 1941, 1951.
NEW WASHINGTON (2): 1988-89.
NOBLESVILLE (22): 1926-29, 1957-59, 1961-64, 1981-82, 1984-86, 1989-91, 1994, 1996-97.
NORTH CENTRAL (FARMERSBURG) (2): 1961, 1967; Farmersburg (1), 1954; Hymera (1), 1956; Shelburn (4), 1941, 1947-49.
NORTH CENTRAL (INDIANAPOLIS) (6): 1973, 1975, 1979, 1991, 1995, 1997.
NORTH DAVIESS (0): Plainville (2), 1938, 1956; Odon (1), 1959.
NORTH DECATUR (2): 1970, 1988; Clarksburg (1), 1964; Sandusky (1), 1921; St. Paul (2), 1941, 1956.
NORTH HARRISON (9): 1970, 1976, 1985-90, 1996; Morgan Twp. (2), 1962, 1965; North Central (1), 1966.
NORTH JUDSON (18): 1934-35, 1949, 1957-59, 1964, 1974-76, 1978, 1986, 1990, 1992-96.
NORTH KNOX (1): 1964; Bicknell (2), 1942, 1945; Freelandville (1), 1941; Sandborn (1), 1957.
NORTH MIAMI (1): 1968; Deedsville (1), 1926.
NORTH MONTGOMERY (6): 1974-75, 1977, 1980, 1983-84; Bowers (1), 1927; Coal Creek Central (1), 1966; New Richmond (1), 1934; Waynetown (3), 1944-45, 1970; Wingate (5), 1917-18, 1921, 1925, 1931.
NORTH NEWTON (1): 1978; Morocco (2), 1934, 1956; Mount Ayr (1), 1944.
NORTH POSEY (1): 1966; Poseyville (1), 1925.
NORTH PUTNAM (5): 1970-71, 1975-76, 1990; Bainbridge (12), 1923-26, 1940, 1944-45, 1958-59, 1962, 1966-67; Roachdale (2), 1929, 1935; Russellville (1), 1921.
NORTH VERMILLION (3): 1965, 1969, 1987; Cayuga (2), 1929, 1951; Perrysville (1), 1923.
NORTH WHITE (3): 1964, 1974, 1984; Monon (6), 1926, 1928, 1936-37, 1947, 1952.
NORTHEAST DUBOIS (3): 1977, 1984, 1988.
NORTHEASTERN (0): Fountain City (1), 1949; Whitewater (1), 1927.
NORTHFIELD (8): 1968, 1970, 1987, 1989-92, 1997; Roann (1), 1950.
NORTHRIDGE (4): 1975, 1993, 1996-97.
NORTHVIEW (1): 1988; Brazil (37), 1919, 1923-26, 1928, 1930, 1932-35, 1937, 1942-44, 1948-

50, 1952-56, 1959-61, 1967-71, 1973-74, 1976, 1980-81, 1983; **Posey Twp. (1)**, 1951; **Staunton (4)**, 1957-58, 1975, 1977; **Van Buren (3)**, 1978-80.

NORTHWESTERN (3): 1955, 1981-82.

NORTHWOOD (1): 1995; **Nappanee (7)**, 1926, 1932, 1934-35, 1940, 1955, 1967; **Wakarusa**, 1933 (1).

NORWELL (9): 1972-73, 1975, 1978, 1980-81, 1983, 1988, 1995; **Lancaster Central (4)**, 1925, 1949-51; **Ossian (6)**, 1934, 1939, 1941, 1953, 1959, 1965; **Rockcreek Center (1)**, 1927; **Union Center (1)**, 1936.

OAK HILL (4): 1960-62, 1971; **Amboy (1)**, 1940; **Converse (3)**, 1944, 1950, 1959; **Swayzee**, 1964 (1).

OREGON-DAVIS (6): 1967, 1979-81, 1983, 1988.

ORLEANS (5): 1953, 1965, 1972-73, 1995.

OWEN VALLEY (2): 1971, 1985; **Gosport (2)**, 1940-41; **Freedom (1)**, 1963; **Spencer (10)**, 1927, 1936, 1938-39, 1945-46, 1962, 1964-65, 1970.

PAOLI (19): 1931, 1934, 1936-38, 1944-45, 1949-50, 1955, 1965, 1968-69, 1978, 1989, 1991-94.

PEKIN EASTERN (2): 1972, 1991.

PENDLETON HEIGHTS (3): 1994-96; **Pendleton (2)**, 1917, 1947; **Markleville (1)**, 1933.

PENN (9): 1965, 1968, 1972-73, 1983-84, 1987, 1992, 1996.

PERRY CENTRAL (2): 1978, 1997; **Bristow (4)**, 1926, 1928, 1930, 1934.

PERRY MERIDIAN (2): 1976, 1984.

PERU (37): 1927-39, 1941-43, 1945-49, 1951-55, 1957-58, 1961, 1963, 1970, 1972-73, 1975, 1982, 1985, 1987.

PIKE (4): 1972, 1981, 1987, 1990.

PIKE CENTRAL (1): 1997; **Otwell (1)**, 1969; **Spurgeon (2)**, 1928-29; **Stendal (3)**, 1931-32, 1939; **Winslow (6)**, 1923-24, 1941, 1950-51, 1954.

PIONEER (1): 1964; **Royal Center (4)**, 1938, 1955, 1958, 1963.

PLAINFIELD (21): 1918, 1934-37, 1943, 1961-62, 1967, 1969-70, 1973, 1976, 1980, 1982-83, 1985-87, 1993, 1996.

PLYMOUTH (26): 1926-27, 1932, 1937, 1940-41, 1957, 1959-60, 1963, 1967, 1970-71, 1973-77, 1982-84, 1992, 1994-97.

PORTAGE (9): 1956, 1971-73, 1988, 1991-92, 1995-96.

PRINCETON (31): 1928, 1930, 1934-36, 1943-44, 1947-48, 1950-52, 1956-58, 1964-65, 1969, 1971, 1973-74, 1976-77, 1979-80, 1983-85, 1989, 1991-92; **Hazelton (1)**, 1933; **Mount Olympus (1)**, 1929; **Patoka (1)**, 1955.

PROVIDENCE (4): 1956-57, 1965, 1984.

RANDOLPH SOUTHERN (1): 1994; **Lynn (1)**, 1950; **Spartanburg (1)**, 1947.

RENSSELAER (17): 1936, 1938-39, 1941, 1946-47, 1949, 1951, 1957-59, 1961-63, 1969, 1991, 1995.

RICHMOND (62): 1917-19, 1921, 1923-26, 1930-35, 1937-43, 1945-48, 1950, 1952-53, 1955-58, 1960, 1962-64, 1966-80, 1985-93, 1995-96.

RISING SUN (5): 1930, 1983-84, 1987, 1989.

RIVERTON PARKE (0): Rosedale (3), 1926, 1952, 1984; **Montezuma (4)**, 1927, 1953-54, 1982; **Bridgeton (1)**, 1944.

ROCHESTER (28): 1915, 1917-26, 1928, 1930, 1932-33, 1935, 1937-38, 1940-41, 1943-45, 1949, 1971-72, 1975, 1978; **Richland Center (3)**, 1948, 1950, 1953.

ROCKVILLE (12): 1917-18, 1940, 1958-60, 1962-63, 1972, 1987, 1995, 1997.

ROSSVILLE (15): 1937, 1946-48, 1951, 1958-59, 1962, 1969-71, 1975, 1981, 1990, 1992.

RUSHVILLE (44): 1922, 1925-41, 1945, 1948-51, 1954-56, 1958-60, 1964-66, 1969, 1971-76, 1978-79, 1985, 1987, 1993; **Arlington (2)**, 1942, 1947; **Milroy (2)**, 1920, 1946; **New Salem (3)**, 1943-44, 1952.

SALEM (10): 1928, 1930, 1933, 1939-41, 1959, 1963, 1971, 1985.

SCOTTSBURG (19): 1921-22, 1930, 1932, 1939, 1944, 1953-56, 1968-69, 1978-79, 1990, 1992-93, 1995-96.

SEEGER (2): 1967, 1978; **Pine Village (6)**, 1921-22, 1934, 1939, 1941, 1972; **Williamsport (6)**, 1935, 1937-38, 1963-65.

SEYMOUR (44): 1916, 1923-24, 1926, 1928-30, 1932-35, 1937-43, 1946-48, 1951-52, 1954-65, 1967, 1970-71, 1973-75, 1977, 1982, 1992; **Cortland (1)**, 1927.

SHAKAMAK (4): 1964, 1966, 1988, 1990; **Jasonville (2)**, 1941, 1952; **Midland (1)**, 1924.

SHELBYVILLE (36): 1923-26, 1930, 1934-36, 1941, 1944, 1947, 1952-53, 1958, 1962, 1967-70, 1972, 1974, 1978-82, 1984-86, 1988, 1990-91, 1993-96.

SHENANDOAH (4): 1970, 1981-82, 1987; **Middletown (7)**, 1929, 1938, 1951, 1954, 1956, 1960, 1962.

SHERIDAN (13): 1926, 1938, 1940, 1943, 1949-55, 1960, 1983.

SILVER CREEK (10): 1955, 1961, 1964, 1968-70, 1978-80, 1982.

SOUTH ADAMS (5): 1986, 1989-90, 1992-93; **Berne (11)**, 1926, 1929, 1935, 1937, 1945-46, 1958, 1960-63; **Hartford Center (2)**, 1948, 1957.

SOUTH BEND ADAMS (8): 1944, 1958, 1967, 1971, 1973-74, 1979, 1984.

*SOUTH BEND CENTRAL (28): 1917-1921, 1923, 1926, 1929-31, 1941-43, 1946-50, 1953-54, 1956-57, 1959, 1961-64, 1966.

SOUTH BEND CLAY (3): 1985, 1994, 1996; **Washington-Clay (1)**, 1951.

SOUTH BEND LA SALLE (6): 1970, 1977-78, 1980, 1982-83.

SOUTH BEND RILEY (11): 1933-34, 1936, 1940, 1945, 1952, 1981, 1987, 1990-91, 1995; **South Bend Jackson (1)**, 1972.

SOUTH BEND ST. JOSEPH'S (9): 1960, 1968-69, 1972, 1976, 1988-89, 1992-93.

SOUTH BEND WASHINGTON (3): 1938, 1965, 1997.

SOUTH CENTRAL (ELIZABETH) (1): 1974.

SOUTH CENTRAL (UNION MILLS) (1): 1982; Union Mills (1), 1950.

SOUTH DEARBORN (6): 1980, 1985-86, 1990, 1993, 1995; Aurora (23), 1925-26, 1929, 1933, 1935-36, 1939, 1941-44, 1951-54, 1958-59, 1965-1966, 1969, 1976-78; Dillsboro (1), 1961

SOUTH DECATUR (2): 1983, 1991; Jackson Twp. (2), 1951, 1957; Sand Creek (1), 1946; Westport (1), 1915.

SOUTH KNOX (4): 1970, 1976-77, 1993; Decker (2), 1943-44; Monroe City (3), 1949, 1953, 1961.

SOUTH NEWTON (5): 1968, 1970, 1985, 1990, 1995; Brook (12), 1923, 1925-26, 1929-33, 1940, 1942, 1948, 1953; Goodland (4), 1928, 1937, 1955, 1960; Kentland (6), 1927, 1935, 1952, 1954, 1964-65.

SOUTH PUTNAM (7): 1974, 1977, 1984, 1986, 1989, 1991, 1994; Fillmore (4), 1949, 1951, 1954-55; Reelsville (1), 1946.

SOUTH RIPLEY (5): 1970, 1978, 1981-82, 1988; Cross Plains (1), 1942; Holton (3), 1929, 1962, 1964; New Marion (1), 1961; Versailles (5), 1924, 1928, 1957-59.

SOUTH SPENCER (7): 1979, 1981, 1991, 1993-96; Rockport (2), 1954-55.

SOUTH VERMILLION (1): 1986; Clinton (23) 1916, 1923, 1925, 1928, 1930-35, 1938-39, 1942-43, 1945-47, 1949-50, 1955-56, 1961, 1968; Dana (4), 1936-37, 1941, 1948.

SOUTHERN WELLS (2): 1982, 1996; Chester Center (4), 1940, 1945, 1947-48; Liberty Center (8), 1916, 1923-25, 1930, 1942, 1944, 1964; Petroleum (1), 1946.

SOUTHMONT (1): 1994; New Market (2), 1950, 1967; New Ross (4), 1954, 1956, 1961-62; Waveland (8), 1935, 1939, 1944-45, 1949, 1951-53.

SOUTHPORT (20): 1924, 1939, 1947, 1956-57, 1959, 1962-63, 1967-68, 1970, 1977, 1985, 1987-91, 1993-94.

SOUTHRIDGE (11): 1976, 1979-80, 1982-83, 1985-87, 1991-92, 1994; Huntingburg (10), 1925-27, 1930, 1935, 1937, 1940, 1955, 1959, 1970; Holland (3), 1953, 1967-68.

SOUTHWESTERN (HANOVER) (5): 1973-74, 1977, 1987, 1997; Hanover (1), 1923.

SOUTHWOOD (0): Noble Twp. (1), 1962; Somerset (2), 1932, 1941.

SPEEDWAY (7): 1948, 1950, 1952, 1955, 1965, 1967, 1973.

SPRINGS VALLEY (11): 1958, 1964-66, 1969, 1971, 1974-75, 1979, 1983, 1986; French Lick (4), 1932, 1942-43, 1946; West Baden (1), 1935.

SULLIVAN (19): 1921, 1924-25, 1933, 1935, 1939, 1942-46, 1950, 1953, 1957, 1959, 1963, 1965, 1987, 1991; Carlisle (7), 1927-28, 1934, 1951-52, 1960, 1962; Gill Twp. (1), 1955; Graysville (1), 1929.

SWITZERLAND COUNTY (3): 1975, 1988, 1994; Patriot (1), 1926; Vevay (8), 1927-29, 1931, 1937, 1955-57.

TECUMSEH (0): Lynnville (8), 1935-36, 1939-41, 1949, 1954, 1957.

TELL CITY (33): 1924-25, 1927, 1929, 1931-32, 1935, 1937-38, 1941-43, 1945, 1947, 1950-51, 1953, 1959-64, 1966, 1968-69, 1970-75, 1993.

TERRE HAUTE NORTH (12): 1972, 1974-75, 1978-79, 1986-87, 1990, 1993-96; Fontanet (1), 1933; Glenn (1), 1951; Terre Haute Garfield (16), 1921-22, 1925-26, 1928, 1939-40, 1947, 1952, 1955, 1960, 1962-64, 1966-67; Terre Haute Gerstmeyer (11), 1941, 1945, 1950, 1953-54, 1956-59, 1961, 1971.

TERRE HAUTE SOUTH (16): 1973, 1976-85, 1988-89, 1991-92, 1997; Honey Creek (1), 1946; Terre Haute Normal (1), 1920; Terre Haute State (3), 1944, 1949, 1965; Terre Haute Wiley (16), 1924, 1927, 1929-32, 1934-38, 1942-43, 1948, 1969-70.

TIPPECANOE VALLEY (4): 1979, 1987-88, 1997; Akron (4), 1929, 1956, 1968, 1974; Beaver Dam (3), 1932-34; Mentone (6), 1931, 1935, 1939-40, 1954, 1962.

TIPTON (17): 1928, 1930-31, 1933-36, 1939, 1941-42, 1944, 1946-47, 1965, 1986, 1988-89; Jefferson Twp. (1), 1956.

TRI (2): 1976-77; Lewisville (2), 1945, 1961; Spiceland (3), 1919-20, 1947; Straughn (1), 1942.

TRI-CENTRAL (0): Sharpsville (3), 1927-28, 1948.

TRI-COUNTY (3): 1975, 1988, 1993; Remington (2), 1943, 1945; Wolcott (4), 1923, 1953-54, 1959.

TRI-WEST (1): 1991; Lizton (1), 1917; North Salem (3), 1930, 1957, 1960; Pittsboro (7), 1922, 1926, 1933, 1940-41, 1974-75.

TRITON (1): 1965; Bourbon (3), 1943, 1950, 1962; Etna Green (1), 1958.

TRITON CENTRAL (3): 1983, 1989, 1997; Fairland (2), 1949-50.

TURKEY RUN (4): 1964, 1966, 1975, 1992; Bloomingdale (1), 1915; Tangier (1), 1957.

TWIN LAKES (6): 1980, 1986, 1991-92, 1994, 1997; Monticello (16), 1924, 1927, 1929, 1932, 1935, 1938-39, 1943-46, 1955-58, 1963.

UNION (DUGGER) (11): 1926, 1930-32, 1936-38, 1940, 1958, 1985, 1989, 1997.

UNION (MODOC) (1): 1970; Losantville (1), 1923.

UNION CITY (13): 1927, 1930-31, 1933-34, 1954, 1962, 1966, 1969, 1972-73, 1976, 1984; Ward-Jackson (1), 1961; Wayne Twp. (1), 1937.

UNION COUNTY (2): 1977, 1979; Kitchell (2), 1942-43; Liberty (3), 1938, 1945, 1967.

VALPARAISO (44): 1916, 1925-35, 1939, 1952,

1957-67, 1969-70, 1974-76, 1978-86, 1989-90, 1993-94, 1997.

VINCENNES LINCOLN (67): 1916-19, 1921-40, 1946-48, 1950-52, 1954-56, 1958-60, 1962-63, 1965-69, 1971-75, 1978-92, 1994-97.

WABASH (25): 1923, 1929, 1931, 1933-39, 1943, 1945-46, 1949, 1951-59, 1961, 1967.

WALDRON (3): 1927, 1939, 1960.

WAPAHANI (3): 1983, 1988, 1990; **Selma (1),** 1967.

WARREN CENTRAL (8): 1969, 1982, 1984-88, 1991.

WARSAW (33): 1923-24, 1936-38, 1942-44, 1951-52, 1955-56, 1965-67, 1969-70, 1973, 1976, 1980-81, 1983-86, 1989-94, 1996-97; **Atwood (1),** 1922; **Silver Lake (1),** 1947.

WASHINGTON (39): 1917-20, 1925-34, 1936-37, 1940-46, 1953-55, 1957-58, 1960, 1963, 1965-68, 1976-79, 1983.

WASHINGTON CATHOLIC (5): 1947, 1985, 1989, 1991, 1993.

WAWASEE (3): 1977, 1982, 1995; **Milford (5),** 1925, 1929-30, 1946, 1948; **North Webster (1),** 1953; **Syracuse (5),** 1921, 1926-27, 1945, 1949.

WES-DEL (3): 1977, 1982, 1986.

WEST CENTRAL (1): 1987; **Francesville (1),** 1955.

WEST LAFAYETTE (5): 1924, 1934, 1936, 1979, 1989.

WEST NOBLE (0): Cromwell (1), 1945; **Wawaka (3),** 1925, 1929, 1948; **Ligonier (4),** 1934-36, 1962.

WEST VIGO (1): 1990.

WEST WASHINGTON (2): 1990, 1996.

WESTERN (2): 1983, 1990.

WESTERN BOONE (4): 1981-82, 1996-97; **Thorntown (5),** 1915, 1919, 1944, 1957, 1960; **Pinnell (1),** 1962; **Advance (2),** 1925, 1930; **Wells (1),** 1963.

WESTVIEW (9): 1973, 1976, 1979, 1986-87, 1989, 1991-92, 1994; **Shipshewana (1),** 1944.

WHITE RIVER VALLEY (4): 1991-93, 1996; **L&M (4),** 1968-69, 1984-85; **Lyons (4),** 1923, 1925, 1933, 1935; **Marco (1),** 1950; **Switz City (5),** 1931, 1944, 1955-56, 1973; **Worthington (2),** 1949, 1977.

WHITELAND (4): 1944, 1950, 1967, 1993; **Clark Twp. (1),** 1953.

WHITING (4): 1921-22, 1924, 1981.

WHITKO (12): 1974, 1976, 1979, 1981, 1983, 1986-87, 1989-91, 1993, 1996; **Larwill (1),** 1969; **Pierceton (3),** 1928, 1941, 1957; **South Whitley (3),** 1922, 1925, 1963.

WINAMAC (17): 1928-33, 1936, 1939, 1946-47, 1951-52, 1956, 1965, 1970, 1984, 1997.

WINCHESTER (17): 1928-29, 1932, 1936, 1942-43, 1949, 1951-52, 1956-57, 1964, 1971, 1974-75, 1980, 1997; **Jefferson Twp. (1),** 1949. **Ridgeville (5),** 1920-21, 1926, 1936, 1938.

WOOD MEMORIAL (5): 1967, 1970, 1986-87, 1990; **Mackey (1),** 1946; **Oakland City (1),** 1940.

WOODLAN (3): 1986, 1990, 1997.

YORKTOWN (3): 1972-73, 1986.

ZIONSVILLE (12): 1945, 1947, 1949-50, 1953, 1955-56, 1958-59, 1980, 1986, 1995.

*Discontinued schools.

Regional championships

First regionals 1921

ALEXANDRIA (1): 1995.

ANDERSON (29): 1921-24, 1928, 1935-39, 1941, 1944, 1946, 1948, 1958, 1962, 1966, 1973-74, 1978-79, 1981, 1983-84, 1986, 1990, 1992-93, 1996.

ANDERSON HIGHLAND (2): 1976, 1991.

*ANDERSON MADISON HEIGHTS (4): 1971-72, 1975, 1982.

ANDREAN (2): 1980-81.

ARGOS (1): 1979.

ATTICA (4): 1929, 1949, 1953, 1968.

AUSTIN (1): 1985.

BARR-REEVE (0): Montgomery (1), 1935.

BATESVILLE (6): 1934, 1943, 1951-52, 1971, 1994.

BEDFORD NORTH LAWRENCE (6): 1976, 1982, 1987-88, 1990, 1995; **Bedford (20),** 1922-24, 1926-29, 1933, 1937-38, 1941-47, 1949, 1969, 1974.

BELLMONT (0): Decatur (1), 1944.

BEN DAVIS (6): 1988, 1992-96.

BENTON CENTRAL (2): 1978, 1983; **Otterbein (1),** 1924; **Oxford (1),** 1945.

BLACKFORD (0): Hartford City (3), 1934, 1953, 1955.

BLOOMFIELD (4): 1961, 1965, 1986, 1994.

BLOOMINGTON NORTH (2): 1982, 1997.

BLOOMINGTON SOUTH (3): 1985, 1987-88.

*BLOOMINGTON (10): 1921-22, 1940-41, 1948-49, 1960, 1965-66, 1971.

BLUFFTON (4): 1931-32, 1958, 1960.

BOONVILLE (2): 1976, 1978.

BREBEUF (1): 1991.

BROWN COUNTY (1): 1976.

BROWNSBURG (6): 1981, 1988, 1991-92, 1994-95.

BROWNSTOWN (1): 1931.

CARMEL (6): 1925, 1970, 1977, 1980, 1987, 1993.

CARROLL (FLORA) (0): Cutler (1), 1922; **Flora (1),** 1946.

CASS (0): Walton (1), 1921.

CENTER GROVE (1): 1972.

CENTRAL NOBLE (0): Wolf Lake (1), 1942.

CLAY CITY (1): 1974.

CLINTON CENTRAL (1): 1980; **Michigantown**

(1), 1933.

CLOVERDALE (3): 1965-66, 1983.

COLUMBIA CITY (3): 1929, 1932, 1975.

COLUMBUS EAST (2): 1977-78.

COLUMBUS NORTH (4): 1975, 1981, 1984, 1993; Columbus (13), 1923, 1928-29, 1932, 1938, 1954-55, 1961, 1963-65, 1968, 1970.

CONCORD (4): 1986, 1988, 1990-91.

CONNERSVILLE (20): 1924-25, 1927, 1930, 1932-33, 1936, 1956-57, 1961-63, 1972, 1974, 1978, 1980, 1982-83, 1986, 1989.

CORYDON (1): 1961.

COVINGTON (3): 1945, 1951, 1960.

CRAWFORD COUNTY (2): 1980, 1995; Milltown (1), 1970.

CRAWFORDSVILLE (11): 1923, 1936-37, 1940-42, 1946, 1948, 1955, 1958, 1979.

CULVER (2): 1944, 1946.

DE KALB (2): 1983, 1997; Auburn (6), 1938, 1945, 1949-52.

DELPHI (4): 1928, 1930, 1932, 1938.

DELTA (1): 1997.

EDINBURGH (1): 1951.

EAST CHICAGO CENTRAL (3): 1989, 1992, 1994; East Chicago Roosevelt (1), 1970; East Chicago Washington (13), 1928, 1946-47, 1958-60, 1962-63, 1966, 1971, 1976-77, 1985.

EAST NOBLE (2): 1996-97. Kendallville (5), 1927-28, 1930-31, 1938.

EDGEWOOD (0): Ellettsville (1), 1950.

ELKHART CENTRAL (2): 1978, 1995; Elkhart (13), 1925, 1931, 1939, 1951-52, 1954, 1956, 1958, 1960-62, 1964, 1971.

ELKHART MEMORIAL (2): 1974, 1989.

EMINENCE (1): 1962.

EVANSVILLE BOSSE (12): 1932, 1939, 1941, 1944-45, 1950, 1962-63, 1974, 1982, 1985, 1990.

EVANSVILLE CENTRAL (21): 1922, 1925-28, 1931, 1936-38, 1942-43, 1946-49, 1952-54, 1977, 1988, 1992.

*EVANSVILLE LINCOLN (1): 1957.

EVANSVILLE (REITZ) MEMORIAL (5): 1966, 1970, 1986-87, 1989.

EVANSVILLE NORTH (2): 1967, 1980.

*EVANSVILLE REX MUNDI (2): 1964, 1969.

EVANSVILLE REITZ (3): 1951, 1955, 1968.

FLOYD CENTRAL (6): 1971, 1981, 1983-84, 1986, 1989.

*FORT WAYNE CENTRAL (12): 1926-28, 1930, 1936-37, 1943-44, 1946, 1953, 1960, 1962.

*FORT WAYNE CENTRAL CATHOLIC (1): 1968.

FORT WAYNE CONCORDIA (1): 1989.

FORT WAYNE DWENGER (3): 1988, 1994, 1996.

FORT WAYNE ELMHURST (1): 1984.

FORT WAYNE NORTH (12): 1933, 1941, 1954-55, 1965, 1969-70, 1975-76, 1978, 1992, 1995.

FORT WAYNE NORTHROP (5): 1973-74, 1985-87.

FORT WAYNE SOUTH (14): 1924, 1929, 1938, 1940, 1947, 1956-59, 1966-67, 1977, 1980, 1993.

FORT WAYNE WAYNE (1): 1981.

FOUNTAIN CENTRAL (0): Hillsboro (1), 1926.

FRANKFORT (20): 1921-31, 1935-36, 1938-39, 1942, 1944, 1949, 1978, 1985.

FRANKLIN (12): 1921-24, 1926, 1930, 1933, 1939, 1946, 1973-74, 1997.

FRANKLIN COUNTY (0): Brookville (1), 1965.

FRONTIER (2): Brookston (2), 1949, 1951.

GARRETT (4): 1940, 1964, 1971-72.

GARY MANN (3): 1929, 1931, 1942; Gary Emerson (2), 1927, 1975.

GARY ROOSEVELT (11): 1955, 1957, 1961, 1965, 1967-68, 1979, 1982, 1987, 1990-91.

GARY WALLACE (4): 1943, 1953, 1986, 1996.

GARY WEST (3): 1972, 1974, 1997; Gary Froebel (5), 1925, 1936, 1941, 1951, 1956; Gary Tolleston (2), 1964, 1969.

GIBSON SOUTHERN (1): 1975.

GOSHEN (3): 1922, 1930, 1969.

GREENCASTLE (14): 1927, 1930-34, 1938-39, 1952, 1957, 1963-64, 1968, 1988.

GREENFIELD CENTRAL (0): Greenfield (1), 1943.

GREENSBURG (5): 1931, 1937, 1966-67, 1984.

HAMILTON HEIGHTS (0): Cicero (1), 1932.

HAMILTON SOUTHEASTERN (0): Fishers (1), 1922.

HAMMOND (9): 1934, 1937-38, 1945, 1948-50, 1952, 1954.

HAMMOND NOLL (2): 1973, 1988.

*HAMMOND TECH (1): 1940.

HARDING (2): 1979, 1982.

HARRISON (1): 1997.

HAUSER (0): Hope (1), 1945.

HERITAGE (0): Monroeville (1), 1948.

HUNTINGTON NORTH (1): 1969; Huntington (10), 1921, 1923, 1941-42, 1945, 1947, 1961-64.

INDIAN CREEK (1): 1983.

INDIANAPOLIS ARLINGTON (1): 1974.

*INDIANAPOLIS ATTUCKS (8): 1951, 1953-57, 1959, 1970.

INDIANAPOLIS BROAD RIPPLE (3): 1945, 1963, 1980.

INDIANAPOLIS CATHEDRAL (3): 1972, 1982, 1997.

*INDIANAPOLIS HOWE (2): 1964, 1981.

INDIANAPOLIS MANUAL (2): 1922, 1961.

*INDIANAPOLIS SHORTRIDGE (3): 1931, 1933, 1968.

INDIANAPOLIS TECH (10): 1929, 1932, 1934, 1950, 1952, 1960, 1966-67, 1971, 1978.

*INDIANAPOLIS WASHINGTON (3): 1965, 1969, 1975.

JAC-CEN-DEL (2): 1968-69.

JASPER (13): 1934, 1943, 1945-46, 1948-49, 1956-57, 1961-62, 1972-73, 1996; Ireland (1), 1963.

JAY COUNTY (0): Portland (2), 1946, 1948.

JEFFERSONVILLE (14): 1934-35, 1953-54, 1958, 1972, 1974, 1976-77, 1982, 1991-93, 1995.
JENNINGS COUNTY (0): North Vernon (5), 1926, 1934, 1937, 1940, 1966.
KANKAKEE VALLEY (1): 1981.
KNOX (1): 1962.
KOKOMO (33): 1925, 1927, 1929-30, 1933, 1936, 1939-41, 1944-45, 1949, 1951-54, 1958-62, 1964-68, 1985, 1988-89, 1992, 1995-97; **Kokomo Haworth (1),** 1970.
LAFAYETTE CENTRAL CATHOLIC (2): 1973, 1987.
LAFAYETTE JEFF (38): 1921, 1937, 1940-41, 1946, 1948, 1950-52, 1954-60, 1962-65, 1967, 1970-72, 1974-77, 1980, 1982, 1984-86, 1988, 1990, 1992-93, 1996.
LAKE CENTRAL (1): 1984.
LAPEL (1): 1940.
LA PORTE (7): 1925-26, 1930, 1939, 1944, 1991, 1997.
LAWRENCE CENTRAL (2): 1942, 1977.
LAWRENCE NORTH (2): 1985, 1989.
LAWRENCEBURG (5): 1946-49, 1992.
LEBANON (12): 1932, 1934, 1943, 1961, 1966, 1973-76, 1983-84, 1990.
LINTON (1): 1946.
LOGANSPORT (27): 1924, 1926-29, 1931, 1933-37, 1939-42, 1945, 1947, 1952-54, 1956, 1959-61, 1966-67, 1974.
LOOGOOTEE (6): 1970-71, 1975, 1981, 1988, 1990.
MCCUTCHEON (3): 1987, 1994-95; **West Point (1),** 1925.
MADISON (10): 1941-43, 1948-50, 1958-60, 1962.
MADISON-GRANT (0): Summittville (2), 1926, 1949.
MANCHESTER (1): 1994; **Chester Twp. (1),** 1948; **North Manchester (1),** 1924.
MARION (33): 1922, 1925-26, 1931, 1943, 1947, 1950-52, 1956-57, 1959, 1965, 1967-69, 1972, 1975-87, 1989, 1991, 1994.
MARTINSVILLE (16): 1921, 1923-30, 1933, 1936-38, 1943, 1964, 1990.
MERRILLVILLE (3): 1978, 1993, 1995.
MICHIGAN CITY (0): Michigan City Elston (12), 1924, 1932, 1935, 1966-68, 1970-72, 1975, 1992-93; **Michigan City Rogers (5),** 1979, 1984-87.
MILAN (3): 1953-54, 1973.
MISHAWAKA (2): 1927, 1955.
MISSISSINEWA (0): Gas City (1), 1946.
MITCHELL (1): 1940.
MONROE CENTRAL (0): Monroe (1), 1943.
MOORESVILLE (2): 1944, 1977.
MOUNT VERNON (FORTVILLE) (2): 1987, 1991.
MUNCIE BURRIS (5): 1939, 1941-42, 1944, 1947.
MUNCIE CENTRAL (32): 1921, 1923, 1925, 1927-31, 1933, 1937-38, 1945, 1948, 1951-52, 1954-63, 1970, 1978-79, 1980, 1982, 1988, 1994.
*MUNCIE NORTH (1): 1975.
MUNCIE SOUTH (4): 1964-65, 1985, 1989.

NEW ALBANY (15): 1936, 1948, 1950-52, 1955-56, 1959-60, 1967, 1973, 1980, 1994, 1996-97.
NEW CASTLE (16): 1926, 1932, 1936, 1940, 1949-50, 1967, 1971, 1983-84, 1986, 1990, 1993, 1995-97.
NOBLESVILLE (3): 1957, 1963, 1997.
NORTH CENTRAL (INDIANAPOLIS) (1): 1979.
NORTH CENTRAL (FARMERSBURG) (0): Shelburn (1), 1947.
NORTH DAVIESS (0): Odon (1), 1959; **Plainville (1),** 1938.
NORTH DECATUR (0): Sandusky (1), 1921.
NORTH HARRISON (2): 1987, 1995.
NORTH JUDSON (3): 1934, 1958, 1995.
NORTH MIAMI (1): 1968.
NORTH MONTGOMERY (0): Waynetown (1), 1944.
NORTH PUTNAM (0): Bainbridge (3), 1959, 1966-67; **Roachdale (1),** 1935; **Russellville (1),** 1921.
NORTH VERMILLION (1): 1969; **Perrysville (1),** 1923.
NORTHEAST DUBOIS (2): 1977, 1984.
NORTHFIELD (1): 1990.
NORTHVIEW (0): Brazil (4), 1934-35, 1959, 1981.
NORTHWOOD (0): Nappanee (2), 1926, 1935; **Wakarusa (1),** 1933.
NORWELL (2): 1973, 1988; **Ossian (1),** 1939.
OAK HILL (1): 1971; **Converse (1),** 1944.
PAOLI (4): 1989, 1992-94.
PENDLETON HEIGHTS (0): Pendleton (1), 1947.
PENN (2): 1972, 1987.
PERRY MERIDIAN (2): 1976, 1984.
PERU (2): 1943, 1948.
PIKE (2): 1972, 1987.
PIKE CENTRAL (1) 1997: **Winslow (3),** 1950-51, 1954.
PIONEER (0): Royal Center (1), 1963.
PLAINFIELD (2): 1986, 1996.
PLYMOUTH (7): 1970, 1973, 1977, 1982-83, 1995, 1997.
PORTAGE (2): 1988, 1996.
PRINCETON (6): 1934-35, 1956, 1958, 1965, 1983; **Hazleton (1),** 1933.
RENSSELAER (1): 1991.
RICHMOND (21): 1923-24, 1934-35, 1943, 1946, 1953, 1966, 1968-69, 1972-74, 1976-77, 1985, 1987-88, 1990-92.
RIVERTON PARKE (0): Montezuma (1), 1954.
ROCHESTER (6): 1921, 1924, 1928, 1937-38, 1943; **Richland Center (1),** 1950.
ROSSVILLE (4): 1947, 1969-71.
RUSHVILLE (19): 1922, 1925, 1928-29, 1931, 1935, 1938, 1940-41, 1945, 1950, 1945, 1958-60, 1964, 1975-76, 1979.
SALEM (3): 1930, 1939, 1971.
SCOTTSBURG (4): 1956, 1969, 1978-79.
SEYMOUR (8): 1932, 1957, 1962-65, 1970, 1975.
SHELBYVILLE (13): 1924, 1935-36, 1947, 1952-53, 1979-80, 1986, 1991, 1994-96.
SHENANDOAH (1): 1981.

SHERIDAN (3): 1938, 1950, 1955.
SILVER CREEK (1): 1969.
SOUTH ADAMS (1): 1993; Berne (3), 1935, 1961, 1963.
SOUTH BEND ADAMS (1): 1973.
*SOUTH BEND CENTRAL (10): 1941-42, 1947-50, 1953, 1957, 1959, 1963; South Bend (2), 1921, 1923.
SOUTH BEND CLAY (1): 1994.
SOUTH BEND LA SALLE (3): 1977-78, 1982.
SOUTH BEND RILEY (4): 1936, 1940, 1945, 1990.
SOUTH BEND ST. JOSEPH'S (4): 1969, 1989, 1992-93.
SOUTH BEND WASHINGTON (1): 1965.
SOUTH DEARBORN (0): Aurora (4), 1926, 1942, 1966, 1977.
SOUTH RIPLEY (2): 1970, 1981.
SOUTH SPENCER (3): 1979, 1993-94.
SOUTH VERMILLION (0): Clinton (4), 1928, 1943, 1947, 1950.
SOUTHERN WELLS (0): Liberty Center (1), 1924.
SOUTHMONT (0): New Ross (3), 1956, 1961-62.
SOUTHPORT (1): 1990.
SOUTHRIDGE (2): 1985-86; Holland (1), 1968; Huntingburg (1), 1937.
SPEEDWAY (1): 1973.
SPRINGS VALLEY (2): 1958, 1964.
SULLIVAN (1): 1923; Carlisle (1), 1960.
TECUMSEH (0): Lynnville (1), 1940.
TELL CITY (3): 1959-61, 1973.
TERRE HAUTE NORTH (5): 1972, 1975, 1987, 1990, 1996; Glenn (1), 1951; Terre Haute Garfield (6), 1922, 1939, 1947, 1952, 1963, 1967; Terre Haute Gerstmeyer (6), 1945, 1953-54, 1956-58.
TERRE HAUTE SOUTH (9): 1973, 1976-80, 1982, 1984, 1989, 1991; Terre Haute Wiley (4), 1924,

1931-32, 1942.
TIPPECANOE VALLEY (0): Beaver Dam (2), 1933-34; Mentone (1), 1935.
TIPTON (3): 1935, 1942, 1989.
TRI-CENTRAL (0): Sharpsville (1), 1927.
TRITON (1): 1965.
TRITON CENTRAL (1): 1989.
TWIN LAKES (0): Monticello (2), 1955, 1957.
UNION (DUGGER) (1): 1930.
UNION COUNTY (0): Liberty (1), 1967.
VALPARAISO (8): 1933, 1964, 1974, 1976, 1980-81, 1983, 1994.
VINCENNES LINCOLN (18): 1921-23, 1925, 1929, 1932-33, 1939, 1952, 1955, 1966, 1968-69, 1981, 1984, 1991, 1996-97.
WABASH (3): 1934, 1937, 1956.
WALDRON (1): 1927.
WARREN CENTRAL (1): 1986.
WARSAW (11): 1923, 1936-37, 1976, 1980-81, 1984-85, 1992-93, 1996; Atwood (1), 1922.
WASHINGTON (17): 1925, 1927-31, 1936-37, 1940-42, 1944, 1953, 1967, 1978-79, 1983.
WASHINGTON CATHOLIC (1): 1991.
WAWASEE (0): Milford (1), 1925; Syracuse (2), 1921, 1926.
WEST LAFAYETTE (2): 1979, 1989.
WESTERN BOONE (1): 1982.
WHITE RIVER VALLEY (2): 1992-93; L&M (1), 1985; Lyons (1), 1923; Switz City Central (1), 1955.
WHITELAND (1): 1944.
WHITING (1): 1922.
WHITKO (2): 1990-91.
WINAMAC (2): 1929, 1932.
WINCHESTER (0): Jefferson Twp. (1), 1949. Ridgeville (1), 1921.
ZIONSVILLE (1): 1953
*Discontinued schools.

Semistate championships

First semistates 1936
ANDERSON (11): 1936-37, 1944, 1946, 1948, 1973, 1979, 1981, 1983, 1986, 1990.
ANDREAN (1): 1980.
ARGOS (1): 1979.
BATESVILLE (1): 1943,
BEDFORD NORTH LAWRENCE (3): 1987-88, 1990. Bedford (2): 1938, 1943.
BEN DAVIS (4): 1993-96.
BLOOMINGTON NORTH (1): 1997. Bloomington (1): 1960.
BREBEUF (1): 1991.
CARMEL (3): 1970, 1977, 1993.
CARROLL (FLORA) (0): Flora (1): 1946.
CLOVERDALE (1): 1966.
COLUMBUS EAST (1): 1977.
COLUMBUS NORTH (1): 1975. Columbus (2): 1938, 1964.
CONCORD (2): 1988, 1990.
CONNERSVILLE (2): 1972, 1983.
CRAWFORDSVILLE (2): 1942, 1958.

DEKALB (0): Auburn (1): 1949.
DELTA (1): 1997.
EAST CHICAGO CENTRAL (0). East Chicago Washington (8): 1947, 1960, 1962, 1966, 1971, 1976-77, 1985. East Chicago Roosevelt (1): 1970.
ELKHART CENTRAL (2): 1978, 1995. Elkhart (3): 1954, 1956, 1971.
EVANSVILLE BOSSE (5): 1939, 1944-45, 1962, 1982.
EVANSVILLE CENTRAL (3): 1936, 1946, 1948.
EVANSVILLE NORTH (1): 1967.
EVANSVILLE REITZ (1): 1951.
*EVANSVILLE REX MUNDI (1): 1964.
FLOYD CENTRAL (2): 1971, 1989.
*FORT WAYNE CENTRAL (5): 1936-37, 1943, 1946, 1960.
FORT WAYNE NORTH (2): 1955, 1965.
FORT WAYNE NORTHROP (1): 1974.
FORT WAYNE SOUTH (4): 1938, 1940, 1958, 1967.

FRANKFORT (3): 1936, 1939, 1942.
FRANKLIN (3): 1939, 1973-74.
*GARY FROEBEL (1): 1941.
GARY ROOSEVELT(6): 1955, 1965, 1968, 1982, 1987, 1991.
*GARY TOLLESTON (1): **1969.**
GARY WEST (1): 1972.
HAMMOND (1): 1938.
HAMMOND NOLL (1): 1988.
*HAMMOND TECH (1): 1940.
HUNTINGTON NORTH (0): Huntington (2): 1945, 1964.
*INDIANAPOLIS ATTUCKS (5): 1951, 1955-57, 1959.
INDIANAPOLIS BROAD RIPPLE (2): 1945, 1980.
INDIANAPOLIS CATHEDRAL (1): 1982.
INDIANAPOLIS MANUAL (1): 1961.
*INDIANAPOLIS SHORTRIDGE (1): 1968.
INDIANAPOLIS TECH (2): 1952, 1966.
*INDIANAPOLIS WASHINGTON (2): 1965, 1969.
JASPER (1): 1949.
JEFFERSONVILLE (6): 1972, 1974, 1976, 1992-93, 1995.
KOKOMO (7): 1941, 1944, 1959, 1961-62, 1989, 1997.
LAFAYETTE JEFFERSON (12): 1948, 1950-52, 1956-57, 1963-64, 1967, 1974, 1992, 1996.
LAKE CENTRAL (1): 1984.
LAPEL (1): 1940.
LAPORTE (2): 1944, 1997.
LAWRENCE NORTH (1): 1989.
LEBANON (2): 1943, 1975.
LOGANSPORT (2): 1959, 1961.
LOOGOOTEE (2): 1970, 1975.
MADISON (4): 1941, 1949-50, 1962.
*MADISON HEIGHTS (1): 1972.
MARION (11): 1947, 1950, 1968-69, 1975-76, 1980, 1983, 1985-87.

MERRILLVILLE (2): 1978, 1995.
MICHIGAN CITY (0): Michigan City Elston (1): 1966.
MILAN (2): 1953-54.
MITCHELL (1): 1940.
MUNCIE BURRIS (2): 1939, 1942.
MUNCIE CENTRAL (11): 1948, 1951-52, 1954, 1958, 1960, 1963, 1970, 1978-79, 1988.
NEW ALBANY (8): 1950, 1952, 1955, 1959, 1973, 1980, 1994, 1996.
NEW CASTLE (3): 1967, 1971, 1984.
PLYMOUTH (1): 1982.
PRINCETON (2): 1965, 1983.
RICHMOND (4): 1953, 1985, 1987, 1992.
ROCHESTER (1): 1937.
RUSHVILLE (1): 1976.
SHELBYVILLE (2): 1947, 1986.
SHENANDOAH (1): 1981
SOUTH BEND ADAMS (1): **1973.**
*SOUTH BEND CENTRAL (4): 1949, 1953, 1957, 1963.
SOUTH BEND CLAY (1): 1994.
SOUTH BEND RILEY (1): 1945.
SOUTH BEND ST. JOSEPH'S (2): 1989, 1993.
SOUTHPORT (1): 1990.
SOUTHRIDGE (2): 1985-86. Huntingburg (1): 1937.
SPRINGS VALLEY (1): 1958.
TELL CITY (1): 1961.
TERRE HAUTE SOUTH (4): 1977-79, 1991. Terre Haute Garfield (2): 1947, 1963. Terre Haute Gerstmeyer (4): 1953-54, 1956-57.
VALPARAISO (1): 1994.
VINCENNES LINCOLN (4): 1968-69, 1981, 1984.
WARSAW (4): 1981, 1984, 1992, 1996.
WASHINGTON (2): 1941-42.
WHITKO (1): 1991.
*Discontinued schools.

State Scoring Leaders
Top 50

(1997 graduates in bold face)

Player	School	Total Points
1. Damon Bailey	Bedford North Lawrence, 1990	3,134
2. Marion Pierce	Lewisville, 1961	3,019
3. Arley Andrews	Terre Haute Gerstmeyer, 1954	2,772
4. Rick Mount	Lebanon, 1966	2,595
5. Billy Shepherd	Carmel, 1968	2,465
6. Alan Henderson	Brebeuf, 1991	2,419
7. Mike Edwards	Greenfield, 1969	2,343
8. Delray Brooks	Michigan City Rogers, 1984	2,324
9. Brady Adkins	Morristown, 1992	2,319
10. Dave Shepherd	Carmel, 1970	2,226
11. Charlie McKenzie	Claypool/Warsaw, 1967	2,145
12. Kenny Rowan	Northview, 1989	2,138
13. Michael Lewis	Jasper, 1996	2,138
14. Kyle Macy	Peru, 1975	2,137
15. Shawn Kemp	Concord, 1988	2,134
16. Richie Mount	Lebanon, 1989	2,130
17. Doug Linville	New Salem, 1965	2,120

Now Indiana's second-leading scorer of all time, Marion Pierce rides through the streets of Lewisville during a parade on Marion Pierce Day in 1961. (Photo courtesy Indiana High School Athletic Association, ©Richmond Palladium-Item)

Player	School	Total Points
18. Steve Alford	New Castle, 1983	2,116
19. Dan Palombizio	M.C. Rogers, 1981	2,092
20. Daryl Warren	Linden, 1971	2,083
21. Lloyd Bateman	Plainville, 1958	2,078
22. George McGinnis	Indianapolis Washington, 1969	2,070
23. Kojak Fuller	Anderson, 1993	2,060
24. Caleb Springer	**Logansport, 1997**	**2,042**
25. Ron Bonham	Muncie Central, 1960	2,028
26. Kevin Ault	Warsaw, 1996	2,028
27. Steve Collier	Southwestern (Jeff.), 1974	2,023
28. Jeff Perlich	Churubusco, 1988	2,019
29. Pat Manahan	Delphi, 1973	2,003
30. Steve Anspaugh	West Noble, 1969	1,992
31. Woody Austin	Richmond, 1988	1,990
32. Buster Briley	Madison, 1960	1,985
33. Steve Baugh	Jackson Twp. (Decatur), 1965	1,982
34. Rusty Miller	Switz City, 1975	1,978
35. Troy Lewis	Anderson, 1984	1,966
36. Keith Gailes	Michigan City Rogers, 1987	1,964
37. Kirk Manns	North Judson, 1986	1,962
38. Danny Brown	Jennings County, 1973	1,960
39. Scott Combs	Lebanon/Paoli, 1984	1,958
40. Pete Pritchert	Oolitic, 1952	1,952
41. Shannon Arthur	New Washington, 1990	1,935
42. Kent Ayer	South Spencer, 1995	1,929
43. Ken Montgomery	Perry Meridian, 1977	1,928
44. Charley Hall	Terre Haute Gerstmeyer, 1958	1,920
45. Rick Hoskins	Brown County, 1988	1,913
46. Tony Patterson	L&M, 1985	1,909
47. Bruce Dayhuff	John Glenn, 1973	1,903
48. Jim Ligon	Kokomo, 1962	1,900
49. James Blackmon	Marion, 1983	1,897
50. Kent Carson	Hamilton Heights, 1968	1,894

Others of note

Player	School	Total Points
54. Pat Graham	Floyd Central, 1989	1,886
57. Eric Montross	Lawrence North, 1990	1,873
58. Larry Humes	Madison, 1962	1,864
60. Jay Edwards	Marion, 1987	1,860
65. Jared Chambers	**Union (Dugger), 1997**	**1,835**
67. Oscar Robertson	Indpls. Attucks, 1956	1,825
70. Harley Andrews	T.H. Gerstmeyer, 1953	1,815
Bob Ford	Evansville North, 1968	1,815
77. Matt Carter	**Perry Central, 1997**	**1,797**
81. Scott Skiles	Plymouth, 1982	1,787
93. Jeff Grose	Warsaw, 1985	1,754
94. Michael Fosnaugh	**Southern Wells, 1997**	**1,752**
95. Bruce Parkinson	Yorktown, 1972	1,751
97. John Garrett	Peru, 1971	1,746
99. Benji Boyd	Union (Dugger), 1974	1,744
100. Frank Radovich	Hammond, 1956	1,739
109. Sam Drummer	Muncie North, 1975	1,712
111. Lyndon Jones	Marion, 1987	1,711
113. Glenn Robinson	Gary Roosevelt, 1991	1,710
116. Jaraan Cornell	South Bend Clay, 1996	1,700
Michael Menser	**Batesville, 1997**	**1,700**
121. Jeff Oliphant	L&M, 1985	1,695
126. Jack Moore	Muncie Central, 1978	1,677
Matt Waddell	Tipton, 1990	1,677
132. Stew Robinson	Madison Heights, 1982	1,656
134. Jerry Memering	Vincennes, 1969	1,654
139. Larry Steele	Bainbridge, 1967	1,648
149. Jimmy Rayl	Kokomo, 1959	1,632
150. Kip Jones	Bellmont, 1985	1,628
154. Brian Walker	Lebanon, 1976	1,623
155. Nick Wise	Plymouth, 1997	1,617
158. Andy Foster	Frankfort, 1997	1,612
161. Cedric Moodie	**South Bend Washington, 1997**	**1,607**
163. Willie Long	Fort Wayne South, 1967	1,606
168. Ted Kitchel	Cass, 1978	1,602
Charlie Wills	**Angola, 1997**	**1,602**
175. Jim Master	Fort Wayne Harding, 1980	1,592
176. Roger Harden	Valparaiso, 1982	1,590
178. John Adams	Rising Sun, 1961	1,586
184. Steve Walker	Lebanon, 1975	1,580
187. Kyle Runyan	**Madison-Grant, 1997**	**1,579**
191. Bryce Drew	Valparaiso, 1994	1,577
199. Don Schlundt	Washington Clay, 1951	1,569
202. Larry Weatherford	Evansville Bosse, 1967	1,559
203. Drake Morris	E.C. Washington, 1977	1,556
205. Leroy Johnson	Mishawaka, 1957	1,554
209. Roger Kaiser	Dale, 1957 (Georgia Tech)	1,549
210. Mike Flynn	Jeffersonville, 1971	1,545
214. Fuzzy Vandivier	Franklin, 1922	1,540
217. Drake Roberts	**Brown County, 1997**	**1,538**
220. Duany Duany	Bloomington North, 1994	1,531
223. Dave Colescott	Marion, 1976	1,529
226. Jim Krivacs	Southport, 1974	1,528
228. John Ritter	Goshen, 1969	1,523
238. Greg Graham	Warren Central, 1989	1,509
246. Eugene Parker	F.W. Concordia, 1974	1,503
252. Kent Benson	New Castle, 1972	1,498
287. Levron Williams	**Evansville Bosse, 1997**	**1,469**
289. Danny Bush	Oolitic, 1968	1,467

Player	School	Total Points
293. Chuck Bavis	Garrett, 1966	1,463
294. Chad Hunter	**New Albany, 1997**	**1,463**
295. Travis Best	**Frankfort, 1997**	**1,463**
296. Bob Wilkinson	LaPorte	1,462
303. Terry Dischinger	T.H. Garfield, 1958	1,455
310. Damon Frierson	Ben Davis, 1995	1,452
319. Richie Hammel	Lafayette Jeff, 1992	1,447
324. Craig Neal	Washington, 1983	1,440
344. Tom Bolyard	Fort Wayne South, 1958	1,420
366. Ron Brooks	Jennings County, 1997	1,408
367. Cory Brunson	**Evansville Reitz, 1997**	**1,408**
368. Bob Leonard	T.H. Gerstmeyer, 1950	1,407
375. Steve Green	Silver Creek, 1971	1,404
387. Wayne Radford	Indpls. Arlington, 1974	1,397
412. Jim Bradley	E.C. Roosevelt, 1970	1,381
425. Jamaal Davis	**Merrillville, 1997**	**1,375**
470. Harold Andrews	T.H. Gerstmeyer, 1955	1,350
498. Scott Hicks	Indpls. Cathedral, 1983	1,336
510. Andy Berger	**Portage, 1997**	**1,327**
557. Dave Schellhase	Evansville North, 1962	1,310
595. Mel Garland	Indianapolis Tech, 1960	1,295
606. Ben Meyer	**New Haven, 1997**	**1,291**
612. Mike Warren	South Bend Central, 1963	1,289
625. Sylvester Coalmon	S.B. Central, 1959	1,285
672. Steve Platt	Union (Huntington), 1965	1,270
750. Jerry Sichting	Martinsville, 1975	1,242
753. Ruben Kercheval	**Sheridan, 1997**	**1,241**
776. Mike Price	Indianapolis Tech, 1966	1,234
782. Zach Henson	**Whitko, 1997**	**1,231**
798. Dick Van Arsdale	Indpls. Manual, 1960	1,227
843. Todd Borgmann	**Greensburg, 1997**	**1,210**
847. Jon McGlocklin	Franklin, 1960	1,209
849. Corey Yost	**Twin Lakes, 1997**	**1,208**
878. Mike Cogill	**Elwood, 1997**	**1,198**
879. Tom Van Arsdale	Indpls. Manual, 1960	1,197
905. Brian Sturgeon	**Lawrenceburg, 1997**	**1,194**
914. Ray Pavy	New Castle, 1959	1,190
959. Chad Dickson	**Oregon-Davis, 1997**	**1,176**
976. Antwan Freeman	Indianapolis Tech, 1997	1,168
Jayme Mathews	**Fairfield, 1997**	**1,168**
979. Doug Mitchell	Hamilton Heights, 1975	1,167
982. Doug Pardue	**Triton Central, 1997**	**1,166**
And Some Others		
Randy Wittman	Ben Davis, 1978	1,160
Matt Renn	Silver Creek, 1997	1,150
Matt McKim	**Washington Twp., 1997**	**1,149**
Clyde Lovellette	Terre Haute Garfield, 1948	1,144
Josh Whitman	**Harrison, 1997**	**1,142**
Bonzi Wells	Muncie Central, 1984	1,139
Pete Mount	Lebanon, 1944	1,133
Jack Edison	Green Twp. (St. Joseph), 1963	1,132
John Mengelt	Elwood, 1967	1,130
Larry Bird	Springs Valley, 1974	1,125
Scott Rolen	Jasper, 1993	1,123
Phil Summers	**Bellmont, 1997**	**1,113**
Joe Otis (Hill)	Valparaiso, 1970	1,111
Bobby Wilkerson	Madison Heights, 1972	1,071
Calbert Cheaney	Evan. Harrison, 1989	1,064
Mike Woodson	Ind. Broad Ripple, 1976	1,063
Chad Ashcraft	**Muncie Burris, 1997**	**1,044**

Player	School	Total Points
Bob Griese	Evan. Rex Mundi, 1963	1,041
Louie Dampier	Southport, 1963	1,025
Tim Majors	**Martinsville, 1997**	**1,024**
Mike Broughton	Hebron, 1973	1,018
Jeff George	Warren Central, 1986	1,002
Travis Hays	**Cambridge City, 1997**	**1,001**

Source: Indiana High School Basketball Record Book (Gene Milner)

Damon Bailey's career totals

Won 99, Lost 11

	3FG	Pct.	FG	Pct.	FT	Pct.	Reb.	Av.	Ast.	Av.	Pts.	Avg.
Fr. (23-4)			228-382	.596	181-250	.724	227	8.4	102	3.8	637	23.6
So.(26-2)	11-40	.275	329-537	.613	203-264	.769	255	9.1	117	4.2	872	27.4
Jr.(21-3)	26-74	.351	256-450	.569	115-154	.747	198	8.3	120	5.0	653	27.2
Sr.(29-2)	59-136	.434	363-580	.626	187-237	.789	292	9.4	211	6.8	972	31.4
Career	**96-250**	**.384**	**1176-1949**	**.603**	**686-905**	**.758**	**972**	**8.8**	**550**	**5.0**	**3134**	**28.5**

The Bailey Log
1986-87: WON 23, LOST 4

	FG	FT	R	A	Pts.	Career
Scottsburg, a, W 82-70	5-6	10-12	4	2	20	20
Salem, h, W 63-48	6-9	4-8	9	4	16	36
Bloomington North, a, W 45-38	4-8	2-4	6	4	10	46
Indianapolis Cathedral, a, L 41-44	9-12	5-7	5	2	23	69
Edgewood, a, W 52-46	4-12	5-9	10	4	13	82
Bloomington South, a, W 73-62	15-18	7-10	11	3	37	119
New Albany, h, W 77-62	7-11	11-14	10	8	25	144
Madison, h, W 52-51	8-16	7-8	8	2	23	167
Jennings County, h, W 58-48	9-18	8-12	12	2	26	193
Mitchell, h, W 65-48	8-13	12-13	8	2	28	221
Bloomfield, h, W 52-45	9-13	4-7	10	2	22	243
Seymour, a, W 65-45	8-16	4-4	10	2	20	263
Brownstown, h, W 93-40	10-13	1-1	5	5	21	284
Jeffersonville, h, W 103-92	12-20	16-24	13	3	40	324
Terre Haute South, a, L 63-74	13-21	3-4	6	3	29	353
Floyd Central, a, W 68-53	8-15	2-5	12	7	18	371
Vincennes, a, L 48-50	3-9	8-10	6	2	14	385
Martinsville, h, W 84-52	14-18	4-7	9	5	32	417
Evansville Central, h, W 68-45	9-16	6-10	8	3	24	441
Columbus East, a, W 72-56	11-18	6-7	14	4	28	469
Seymour sectional						
Seymour, W 63-60	9-13	8-10	5	1	26	495
Jennings County, W 61-55	3-6	6-9	4	6	12	507
Seymour regional						
New Albany, W 76-66	10-14	5-5	9	7	25	532
Jeffersonville, W 89-64	8-13	19-22	10	6	35	567
Evansville semistate						
North Harrison, W 70-53	6-17	6-8	10	6	18	585
Evansville Memorial, W 59-51	12-22	8-12	6	4	32	617
State						
Marion, L 61-70	8-15	4-8	7	3	20	637
Totals	**228-382**	**181-251**	**227**	**103**		**637**

1987-88: WON 26, LOST 2

	3FG	FG	FT	R	A	Pts.	Career
Scottsburg, h, W 68-60	1-2	12-21	3-4	9	2	28	665
Salem, a, W 80-63	0-2	16-24	5-6	10	6	37	702
Bloomington North, h, W 81-59	0-2	5-22	0-2	8	2	30	732
Indianapolis Cathedral, h, W 82-76	0-0	12-20	14-16	11	5	38	770
Edgewood, h, 78-51	0-1	12-15	4-6	5	6	28	798
Bloomington South, h,W 66-54	1-3	9-20	7-8	9	3	26	824
New Albany, a, W70-65	1-1	18-22	6-8	10	3	43	867
Perry Meridian, h, W 75-51	0-2	5-14	8-12	17	7	18	885
Madison, a, W59-49	0-1	12-19	10-15	9	2	34	919
Jennings County, a, W 65-43	0-0	6-9	0-1	5	2	12	931
T.H. South, h, W 77-74ot	1-2	13-25	15-20	9	2	42	973
Mitchell, a, W 60-43	1-3	11-18	3-4	13	5	26	999
Bloomfield, a L 64-66	0-2	9-17	6-11	5	5	24	1023
Seymour, h, W 66-57	0-0	9-19	4-6	10	3	22	1045
Brownstown, a, W 80-48	0-2	14-20	4-4	10	6	32	1077
Jeffersonville, a, W 81-77	0-0	15-23	8-12	9	4	38	1115
Floyd Central, h, W 69-67	1-2	15-29	11-12	11	2	42	1157
Martinsville, a, W 80-54	0-1	14-17	8-11	8	3	36	1193
Evan. Central, a, W 62-48	0-0	7-15	9-13	10	1	23	1216
Columbus East, h, W 100-69	1-3	13-21	5-5	12	8	32	1248
Seymour sectional							
Jennings County, W 72-59	1-2	13-17	6-7	4	5	33	1281
Brownstown, W 90-60	0-0	5-10	7-8	2	8	17	1298
Seymour, W 85-74	0-1	14-22	19-24	8	3	47	1345
Seymour regional							
New Washington, W 73-62	1-1	13-20	3-6	10	2	30	1375
Jeffersonville, W 91-68	0-1	18-24	15-17	11	7	51	1426
Terre Haute semistate							
Loogootee, W 72-63	1-2	13-22	3-5	10	4	30	1456
Greencastle, W 62-47	1-2	8-12	11-11	11	7	28	1484
State							
Muncie Central, L 53-60	0-2	8-20	9-11	9	4	25	1509
Totals	11-40	329-537	203-264	255	117	872	

1988-89: WON 21, LOST 3

	3FG	FG	FT	R	A	Pts.	Career
Salem, h, W 80-55	2-4	17-19	14-16	7	2	50	1559
Bloomington North, MSA, W 41-37	0-3	6-21	7-13	11	2	19	1578
Washington, a, W 56-53	1-5	9-22	2-3	11	6	21	1599
Bloomington South, a, W 59-52	0-1	5-12	4-6	8	4	14	1613
Madison, h, W 88-59	0-1	8-19	4-4	6	7	20	1633
Perry Meridian, a, W 81-49	1-3	10-19	7-8	8	8	28	1661
Edgewood, a, W 75-72	2-4	18-24	3-4	6	5	41	1702
Carmel, a, W 78-47	2-5	12-17	8-10	13	5	34	1736
Jennings County, h, W 73-45	1-3	9-17	3-3	7	4	22	1758
T.H. South, Hulman, L 48-52	1-1	9-19	5-9	10	4	24	1782
Mitchell, h, W 94-65	4-5	11-19	9-11	9	7	35	1817
Bloomfield, h, W 85-48	1-3	12-19	0-2	13	8	25	1842
Seymour, a, W 60-55	0-2	8-15	0-0	6	7	16	1858
Brownstown, h, W 65-40	0-5	8-19	2-2	13	4	18	1876
Jeffersonville, h, W 97-69	0-1	9-17	5-6	9	10	23	1899
Floyd Central, a, L 65-67	1-3	8-17	4-5	10	3	21	1920
New Albany, h, W 63-53	0-3	14-20	7-9	4	3	35	1955
Martinsville, h, W 89-51	1-3	15-18	6-10	9	5	37	1992
Evansville Central, h, W 71-48	1-4	10-13	2-2	4	8	23	2015
Columbus East, a, W 90-50	3-5	16-26	5-6	11	3	40	2055
Seymour sectional							
Crothersville, W 64-30	1-2	11-17	1-1	4	2	24	2079
Seymour, W 77-58	1-1	12-17	8-11	9	5	33	2112
Jennings County, W 92-64	1-2	5-10	2-4	3	5	13	2125

	FG	FT	R	A	Pts.	Career
Seymour regional						
Floyd Central, L 72-76 ot	2-5	14-24	7-9	7	3	37	2162
Totals	**26-74**	**256-450**	**115-154**	**195**	**120**	**653**	

1989-90: WON 29, LOST 2 - STATE CHAMPIONS

	3FG	FG	FT	R	A	Pts.	C'rer
Salem, Seymour, W 92-36	3-3	14-21	4-6	11	6	35	2197
Bloomington North, h, W 64-55	2-4	14-20	7-8	4	2	37	2234
Washington, h, W 93-55	1-5	11-19	0-0	11	14	23	2257
Bloomington South, h, W 88-82	1-4	16-26	4-7	6	12	37	2294
Perry Meridian, h, W 92-45	2-6	15-25	7-7	8	9	39	2333
Edgewood, h, W 105-75	6-8	13-17	4-4	8	9	36	2369
Hall of Fame Classic, Assembly Hall							
Pike, W 65-60	2-4	11-17	7-8	13	7	31	2400
Lawrence North, L 50-51	4-6	8-21	6-7	7	3	26	2426
Carmel, Hinkle, W 88-73	3-3	17-19	5-8	10	6	42	2468
Jennings County, a, W 62-40	2-5	10-18	1-2	13	6	23	2491
Terre Haute South, h, W 68-55	1-3	17-27	3-9	10	3	38	2529
Mitchell, a, W 84-46	0-2	11-18	2-2	13	12	24	2553
Bloomfield, a, W 70-33	2-4	10-12	3-4	11	7	25	2578
Seymour, h, W 89-67	2-5	12-18	4-5	5	11	30	2608
Brownstown, a, W 66-60, dot	1-8	15-29	6-8	12	2	37	2645
Jeffersonville, a, W 85-81	4-5	13-19	6-9	10	7	36	2681
Floyd Central, h, W 85-61	2-4	10-16	4-5	10	7	26	2707
Madison, a, W 71-51	1-2	18-24	4-6	8	5	41	2748
New Albany, a, L 59-60	1-3	10-19	9-12	10	4	30	2778
Martinsville, a W 82-69	3-5	9-13	11-12	10	7	32	2810
Evansville Central, a, W 77-47	3-5	13-19	3-4	13	15	32	2842
Columbus East, h, W 81-75	1-7	16-28	7-9	14	6	40	2882
Seymour sectional							
Brownstown, W 77-55	4-8	10-17	2-3	6	6	26	2908
Jennings County, W 82-48	1-5	9-16	8-9	10	9	27	2935
Seymour, W 69-64	1-1	10-15	11-12	8	4	32	2967
Seymour regional							
Charlestown, W, 65-51	1-2	7-9	13-15	10	4	28	2995
Scottsburg, W, 78-58	2-5	11-16	7-9	6	7	31	3026
Terre Haute semistate							
TerreHaute North, W 56-54	1-4	4-10	10-12	8	5	19	3045
Evansville Bosse, W 72-67	1-5	10-18	13-14	9	4	34	3079
State							
Southport, Dome, W 58-55	0-3	8-18	9-12	10	7	25	3104
Concord, Dome, W 63-60	1-2	11-16	7-9	8	5	30	3134
Totals	**59-136**	**363-580**	**187-237**	**292**	**211**	**972**	

Bailey vs. Opponents

	3FG	FG	FT	R	Pts.	Avg.	High
Bloomfield (3-1)	3-9	40-61	13-24	39	96	24.0	25
Bloomington No. (4-0)	2-9	39-71	16-27	29	96	24.0	37
Bloomington So. (4-0)	2-8	45-76	22-31	34	114	28.5	37
Brownstown (6-0)	5-23	62-108	22-26	48	151	25.2	37
Carmel (2-0)	5-8	29-36	13-18	23	76	38.0	42
Charlestown (1-0)	1-2	70-90	13-15	10	28	28.0	28
Columbus East (4-0)	5-15	56-93	23-27	51	140	35.0	40
Concord (1-0)	1-2	11-16	7-9	8	30	30.0	30
Crothersville (1-0)	1-2	11-17	1-1	14	24	24.0	24
Edgewood (4-0)	8-13	47-68	16-23	29	118	29.5	41
Evansville Bosse (1-0)	1-5	10-18	13-14	9	34	34.0	34
Evansville Central (4-0)	4-9	39-63	20-29	35	102	25.5	32
Evansville Memorial (1-0)		12-22	8-12	6	32	32.0	32
Floyd Central (3-2)	6-14	55-101	28-36	50	144	28.8	42

Damon Bailey (with trophy) celebrates with his teammates after Bedford-North Lawrence won the 1990 State Championship. (Photo courtesy Indiana High School Athletic Association, ©Mark Wick)

	3FG	FG	FT	R	Pts.	Avg.	High
Greencastle (1-0)	1-2	8-12	11-11	11	28	28.0	28
Indpls. Cathedral (1-1)	0-0	21-32	19-23	16	61	30.5	38
Jeffersonville (6-0)	4-7	75-116	69-90	62	223	37.2	51
Jennings County (8-0)	6-17	64-111	34-47	58	168	21.0	33
Lawrence North (0-1)	4-6	8-21	6-7	7	26	26.0	26
Loogootee (1-0)	0-1	13-22	3-5	10	30	30.0	30
Madison (4-0)	1-4	46-78	25-33	31	118	29.5	41
Marion (0-1)		8-15	4-8	7	20	20.0	20
Martinsville (4-0)	4-9	52-66	29-40	36	137	34.3	37
Mitchell (4-0)	5-10	40-68	26-30	43	113	28.3	35
Muncie Central (0-1)	0-2	8-20	9-11	9	25	25.0	25
New Albany (4-1)	2-7	59-86	38-48	43	158	31.6	43
New Washington (1-0)	1-1	13-20	3-6	10	30	30.0	30
North Harrison (1-0)		6-17	6-8	10	18	18.0	18
Perry Meridian (3-0)	3-11	30-58	22-27	33	85	28.3	39
Pike (1-0)	2-4	11-17	7-8	13	31	31.0	31
Salem (4-0)	5-9	53-73	27-36	37	138	34.5	50
Scottsburg (3-0)	3-7	28-43	20-25	19	79	26.3	31
Seymour (8-0)	4-10	82-135	58-72	61	226	28.3	47
Southport (1-0)	0-3	8-18	9-12	7	25	25.0	25
Terre Haute North (1-0)	1-4	4-10	10-12	8	19	19.0	19
Terre Haute South (2-2)	3-6	52-92	26-42	35	133	33.3	42
Vincennes (0-1)		3-9	8-10	6	14	14.0	14
Washington (2-0)	2-10	20-41	2-3	22	44	22.0	23

Hoosiers in NBA, ABA, NBL

	Yrs.	Points
Oscar Robertson, Indianapolis Attucks/Cincinnati	14	26,710
Larry Bird, Springs Valley/Indiana State	13	21,791
George McGinnis, Indpls. Washington/Indiana	11	17,009
Dick Barnett, Gary Roosevelt/Tennessee State	14	15,358
Louie Dampier, Southport/Kentucky	12	15,279
Dick Van Arsdale, Indianapolis Manual/Indiana	12	15,079
Tom Van Arsdale, Indianapolis Manual/Indiana	12	14,232
Clyde Lovellette, T.H. Garfield/Kansas	11	11,947
Junior Bridgeman, E.C. Washington/Louisville	12	11,517
Mike Woodson, Indpls. Broad Ripple/Indiana	11	10,981
Shawn Kemp, Concord/no college	8	10,148
Jon McGlocklin, Franklin/Indiana	11	9,169
Terry Dischinger, T.H. Garfield/Purdue	9	9,012
Don Buse, Holland/Evansville	13	6,890
Allen Leavell, Muncie Central/Oklahoma City	10	6,684
Scott Skiles, Plymouth/Michigan State	10	6,652
Billy Keller, Indianapolis Washington/Purdue	7	6,588
Kent Benson, New Castle/Indiana	11	6,168
Jim Ligon, Kokomo/no college	7	5,560
Bobby Wilkerson, Madison Heights/Indiana	7	5,424
Kyle Macy, Peru/Purdue-Kentucky	7	5,259
Glenn Robinson, Gary Roosevelt/Purdue	3	5,104
Jim Price, Indianapolis Tech/Louisville	7	5,088
Larry Steele, Bainbridge/Kentucky	9	5,009
Rick Fox, Warsaw/North Carolina	6	4,759
Winston Garland, Gary Roosevelt/Southwest Mo.	6	4,351
Bobby Leonard, T.H. Gerstmeyer/Indiana	7	4,204
Jerry Sichting, Martinsville/Purdue	10	4,141
Randy Wittman, Ben Davis/Indiana	9	4,034
Jim Davis, Muncie Central/Colorado	8	3,997
Calbert Cheaney, Evansville Harrison/Indiana	4	3,964
John Barnhill, Evansville Lincoln/Tennessee State	10	3,648
Rick Mount, Lebanon/Purdue	5	3,330
Paul Hoffman, Jasper/Purdue	6	3,234
Leo Barnhorst, Indpls. Cathedral/Notre Dame	5	3,232
Johnny Logan, Richmond/Indiana	5	3,196
Vince Boryla, E.C. Washington/Notre Dame-Denver	5	3,187
Boag Johnson, Union (Huntington)/Huntington	6	2,425
Willie Long, Fort Wayne South/New Mexico	3	2,418
Charley Shipp, Indpls. Cathedral/Catholic	13	2,042
Enoch "Bud" Olsen, Vincennes/Louisville	8	1,935
Herm Schaefer, F.W. Central/Indiana	7	1,903
Leo Klier, Washington/Notre Dame	4	1,825
George Sobek, Hammond/Notre Dame	5	1,780
Tom Abernethy, South Bend St. Joseph's/Indiana	5	1,779
Tellis Frank, Gary Wallace/Western Kentucky	5	1,710
Milo Komenich, Gary Wallace/Wyoming	4	1,665
Eric Montross, Lawrence North/North Carolina	4	1,562

Dick Farley, Winslow/Indiana 3 1,378
Tom Kron, Tell City/Kentucky 4 1,351
Mike Flynn, Jeffersonville/Kentucky 3 1,317
Henry James, F.W. North/St. Mary's (Tex.) 6 1,212
Gene Tormohlen, Holland/Tennessee 6 1,191
Steve Green, Silver Creek/Indiana 4 1,179
Jimmy Rayl, Kokomo/Indiana 2 1,125
Willie McCarter, Gary Roosevelt/Drake 3 1,090
Paul "Curly" Armstrong, Fort Wayne Central/Indiana 8 1,040

Career Points

900: 974, Bill Dinwiddie, Muncie Central/New Mexico Highlands; 968, Billy Shepherd, Carmel/Butler; 964, Erv Inniger, Berne/Indiana; 951, Ron Reed, LaPorte/Notre Dame; 928, Ray Tolbert, Madison Heights/Indiana; 924, Duane Klueh, Terre Haute State/Indiana State; 922, Greg Graham, Warren Central/Indiana.

800: 886, Dale Hamilton, Fort Wayne South/Franklin; 877, Davage Minor, Gary Froebel/UCLA; 848, Ralph "Buckshot" O'Brien, Indianapolis Washington/Butler; 832, John Laskowski, South Bend St. Joseph's/Indiana; 800, Eddie Ehlers, South Bend Central/Purdue.

700: 744, Steve Alford, New Castle/Indiana; 723, Ron Bonham, Muncie Central/Cincinnati; 702, Alan Henderson, Brebeuf, Indiana.

600: 687, Jim Bradley, East Chicago Roosevelt/Northern Illinois; 676, Ralph Hamilton, Fort Wayne South/Indiana; 649, Jay Miller, Goshen/Notre Dame; 643, DeWitt Menyard, South Bend Central/Houston; 601, Darrell Elston, Tipton/North Carolina.

500: 595, Mel Payton, Martinsville/Tulane; 580, Bobby Joe Edmonds, Indianapolis Attucks/Tennessee State; 567, Cliff Barker, Yorktown/Kentucky.

100-499: 450, Cotton Nash, Jeffersonville/Kentucky; 438, Dan Sparks, Bloomington/Weber State; 397, Mike Price, Indianapolis Tech/Illinois; 369, Charles Jordan, Indianapolis Shortridge/Canisius; 323, Wallace Bryant, Gary Emerson/San Francisco; 319, Monte Towe, Oak Hill/North Carolina State; 296, Bob Dille, Chesterton, Valparaiso; 236, Nick Mantis, East Chicago Washington/Northwestern; 232, Bob Lochmueller, Elberfield/Louisville; 215, Ward Williams, Colfax/Indiana; 213, Scott Haffner, Noblesville/Illinois-Evansville; 208, Dave Schellhase, Evansville North/Purdue; 202, Wayne Radford, Indianapolis Arlington/Indiana; 196, Ted Luckenbill, Elkhart/Houston; 158, Craig Neal, Washington/Georgia Tech; 150, Jim Riffey, Washington/Tulane; 137, Richie Atha, Otterbein/Indiana State; 131, Herschel Turner, Indianapolis Shortridge/Nebraska; 106, Rod Freeman, Anderson/Vanderbilt.